The Hysteric's Revenge

The Hysteric's Revenge

FRENCH WOMEN WRITERS AT THE FIN DE SIÈCLE

Rachel Mesch

Vanderbilt University Press
NASHVILLE

10 09 08 07 06 1 2 3 4 5
Printed on acid-free paper.
Manufactured in the United States of America

Designed by Wendy McAnally

Library of Congress Cataloging-in-Publication Data

Mesch, Rachel.
The hysteric's revenge : French women writers at the fin de siècle / Rachel Mesch.
p. cm.
Includes bibliographical references and index.
ISBN-13: 978-0-8265-1530-8 (cloth : alk. paper)
ISBN-13: 978-0-8265-1531-5 (pbk. : alk. paper)
1. French literature—Women authors—History and criticism.
2. French literature—19th century—History and criticism.
3. Women and literature—France—History—19th century.
4. Women in literature. I. Title.
PQ149.M46 2006
840.9'928709049—dc22
2005035344

Portions of Chapter 3 appeared in "The Sex of Science: Medicine, Naturalism, and Feminism in Lucie Delarue-Mardrus' Marie, fille-mère," Nineteenth Century French Studies (Spring–Summer 2003): 324–40.

For Eric

Contents

Illustrations

Acknowledgments

This project grew out of my work as a doctoral candidate at the University of Pennsylvania, under the direction of Gerald Prince. Thanks to his encyclopedic knowledge of literature beyond the conventional parameters of the French canon, a world of women writers was revealed to me that I might never otherwise have discovered. His support and friendship throughout the years since, and his help with drafts of this project along the way, have been deeply appreciated. I am also grateful to Philippe Met, Jean-Marie Roulin, and Michèle Richman for their insights in the beginning stages of this project. I was fortunate to have worked closely at Penn with the late Charles Bernheimer. As an enthusiastic teacher and mentor until weeks before his death, he helped shape my understanding of nineteenth-century naturalist and decadent literature. My thinking on these topics continues to be influenced by what I learned from him in such a short time; his unique enthusiasm and energetic engagement were sorely missed throughout the completion of this work.

Travel grants from the University of Pennsylvania and Barnard College allowed me to complete the research in Paris necessary for this book. I am also grateful to the staffs of the Bibliothèque Nationale de France, the New York Public Library, and the Columbia University Library Office of Interlibrary Loan. This project would not have been the same without the invaluable comments of my anonymous readers at Vanderbilt University Press, both of whom offered perceptive, detailed advice about how to sharpen my ideas. My editor, Betsy Phillips, guided me through each step of the publication process with patience, kindness, and wisdom. I feel very fortunate to have had the opportunity to work with her. I am also grateful to Dariel Mayer, Debby Smith and Wendy McAnally for their diligent work in the production of this book.

Peter Connor generously offered helpful insights and suggestions, and Serge Gavronsky never ran out of wisdom or enthusiasm. Additional thanks to my colleagues and former colleagues at Barnard for their support and friendship: Anne Boyman, Terri Gordon, Isabelle Jouanneau-Fertig, Brian O'Keeffe, Laurie Postlewate, Sarah Sasson, and Caroline Weber. I am also grateful to the students in my comparative literature and first-year seminars at Barnard, from whom I learned a great deal about sexuality, storytelling, women writers, and fictions of hysteria. Lisa Gordis and Maurice Samuels wisely provided answers to my numerous "quick questions" at various stages of the publication process. Laura Spagnoli and Claire Goldstein have been cherished friends and interlocutors since our days together as graduate students. Both read and reread drafts at different stages. Their insightful comments, tireless encouragement, and camaraderie have made all the difference. I also owe a debt of gratitude to my friend and fellow *dix-neuvièmiste* Masha Belenky, who generously read several chapters in the final phases, and whose shrewd criticism was crucial to the editing of this book. Special thanks to Judith Rosenbaum, who talked me through various critical and psychological impasses as this project became a book and who offered heaping doses of friendship and encouragement along the way, and to Tova Mirvis, who listened attentively to my discoveries from our shared "office" at Starbucks, where we worked through our very different projects, and from whom I have learned so much about being a woman and a writer. As wonderful friends and neighbors, Rachel Rosenfield and Jessica Hirsch made my home a much less solitary work space than it might have been as I finished my revisions.

I would like to thank my family, on both the Mesch and Fisher sides, for their support as well, offered up at times in the most prized currencies for the working mother: home-cooked meals and child care for my two daughters, Abigail and Eliza. Reflecting on the countless pleasant hours I have spent studying the authors in these pages, I realize the tremendous debt I owe to my father, Barry Mesch, who taught me by example the simple, pure pleasures of the life of the mind. Still in the category of family, special thanks go to Charmaine Banton Murray; without her competence and care this book would not have been possible. My sister, Elana Mesch, has offered love, friendship, and much-needed humor throughout. Finally, I would like to thank my husband, Eric Fisher, who read every page of this book (and will probably be the only corporate lawyer to claim that honor). His belief in this project has been unflinching; his counsel invariably wise; his patience beyond measure. I dedicate this book to him.

Introduction

In the 1889 preface to the French edition of Rachilde's *Monsieur Vénus,* Maurice Barrès introduces the author as a young woman suffering from "la maladie du siècle" (the disease of the century).[1] He describes the novel as a symptom of its author's disease, claiming that the book will be of interest to doctors and psychologists. Barrès thus likens his friend Rachilde (with her permission, of course) to a hysteric herself. In Renée Vivien's 1904 autobiographical novel *Une Femme m'apparut,* the female protagonist objects to a letter addressed to "Mademoiselle Willoughby, femme de lettres." She demands: "Mettrait-on à la poste une enveloppe libellée de la sorte: *Mademoiselle Maximilienne de Chateau-Fleuri, Prostituée?*" (Would you mail an envelope labeled *Mademoiselle Maximilienne de Chateau-Fleuri, Prostitute*?), since the public has for both professions "le même indulgent mépris" (the same indulgent scorn).[2] Finally, in Marcelle Tinayre's 1912 *Madeleine au miroir, journal d'une femme*—published at the peak of Tinayre's lucrative literary career—a male character advises women not to become writers. "Même avec du talent, vous pourrez connaître la gêne," (even with talent, you can encounter financial trouble) he warns. "Si le talent vous manque, vous ne serez pas une artiste pauvre; vous serez une déclassée pitoyable et quasi ridicule" (If you do not have talent, you will not be a starving artist; you will be a déclassé woman, pitiful and basically ridiculous).[3]

What do these examples over a space of two decades have in common? All three writers received favorable reviews and enjoyed literary success. Yet all three recognized—and Rachilde even exploited—the association of female authorship with moral decay and mental instability. In what follows I consider how fin-de-siècle French women writers confronted a culture very much threatened by their intellectual and creative potential.

The woman writer's reputation had suffered throughout the nineteenth century. As women's roles were reimagined following the French Revolution, medical literature stressed the inherent biological differences between men and women and linked female mental exertion to venereal disease and infertility.[4] The woman writer surfaced in turn as a favored symbol of the transgression of woman's traditional domestic role. The emergence of a mass print culture contributed to the sullied image of the *femme de lettres,* allowing images and stereotypes to infiltrate the public imagination increasingly quickly and effectively. In 1844, for example, Henri Daumier published a series of forty images of women writers called the "Bas-bleus" in the satirical paper *Le Charivari.* These images made direct reference to Germaine de Staël and George Sand, while also depicting everyday women abandoning the home front for intellectual pursuits.[5] The drawings also echo the link between women writing and libertinism found in Balzac's novels, particularly *La Muse du department* from 1843. In 1878, Jules Barbey d'Aurevilly published his own *Bas-bleus,* in which women writers are held responsible for social disintegration. Barbey views women writers as products of the moral depravity of the era and compares their effect on French society to that of prostitution in other civilizations.[6] By the late nineteenth century, women writers were associated with the much feared New Women, who were often caricatured as "whores, bluestockings or desiccated old maids."[7]

The history of French women writers is thus not a simple tale of progressive advancement and acceptance. Beginning in the Middle Ages with Marie de France and Christine de Pisan, French women writers offered major literary contributions alongside their male counterparts. With Louise Labé and Marguerite de Navarre during the Renaissance, Madeleine de Scudéry and Marie-Madeleine de Lafayette in the seventeenth century, and Françoise de Graffigny, Isabelle de Charrière, and Germaine de Staël through the eighteenth century, France established early on a tradition of female authorship.[8] In particular, the salon culture of the seventeenth and eighteenth centuries fostered female literary sensibilities, while the political climate surrounding the Fronde brought women into more visible public roles than had previously been acceptable. These circumstances made it possible for women to offer significant literary contributions earlier than in other European cultures.[9]

The other side of this illustrious history of women writers, however, is the enigmatic erasure that followed the promising tradition of female authorship: the nineteenth century. During this period the novel established itself as the most prestigious literary form and became recognized as an authoritative vehicle of social and cultural commentary. Yet if we look back on this time through the annals of literary history, the female voices that had originally shaped the genre appear to be largely absent from its production. A closer examination reveals that women novelists were not absent in the nineteenth century, although they did go through periods of lessened production. Instead, their writing experienced what Margaret Cohen has described as a decline in stature. According to Cohen, the French sentimental novel that had earned women authors great esteem in the early nineteenth century was progressively delegitimized as a literary genre following the July Revolution. During this time, male writers transformed the novel into a "struggle of principles" reflecting the social concerns of the era, while women continued to write love stories, which were no longer considered intellectually legitimate.[10] No female authors, for example, are linked canonically to the realist literary practices that defined this period. George Sand, the most renowned nineteenth-century woman writer, is set apart in literary history and best remembered for her sentimental idealism.[11]

Examining the continuation of this decline in stature at the fin de siècle is an essential step toward making sense of the virtual absence of female authors in the French canon between George Sand and Colette. The denigration of women writers at the end of the nineteenth century was largely a reaction to their increased visibility, a fact that is often overlooked. Because of an auspicious confluence of factors, including educational reforms allowing girls access to secondary schools, relaxation of censorship laws, technical innovations in book printing, and the rapid expansion of the mass press and women's periodicals in particular, the widely recognized increase in female readers in the nineteenth century culminated in an outpouring of women's writing at the fin de siècle.[12] In an era when female professionalism was widely discouraged, writing was accessible to increasing numbers of women, who embraced this form of expression without having to leave home. Thus, despite the prevailing association of women's writing with decay and instability, and the law that forbade married women to publish without their husband's permission, French women at the fin de siècle began to produce novels in record numbers. According to the literary and social critic Octave Uzanne, by 1894, 1,211 women were members of the Société des gens de lettres, and this number was to rise steadily throughout the next decade; in 1907, a writer in the popular journal *Je sais tout* claimed that there were 5,000 professional women writers in France, making up 20 percent of the total number.[13] Although the statistics are not reliable, what is certain is that by 1900, the French woman writer (most often described as a *bas-bleu* or *femme de lettres,* although her preferred term was *femme auteur*) had become a force to be reckoned with.[14] Whatever the actual numbers, critics did not fail to take note of her increased presence, which was perceived as a challenge to the men in the field. Numerous books and essays were devoted to the topic, including Charles Maurras's *Le Romantisme féminin* (1905), Jean de Gourmont's *Les Muses d'aujourd'hui* (1910), Jean de Bonnefon's *La*

Corbeille des roses ou les dames de lettres (1909), Jules Bertaut's *La Littérature féminine d'aujourd'hui* (1909), Paul Flat's *Nos femmes de lettres* (1909), and Ernest Tissot's *Nouvelles princesses des lettres* (1909). Critics described the "concurrence épouvantable" (horrible competition) of this "foule de femmes" (crowd of women) in the stark terms of an imminent crisis.[15] With the growing numbers of women novelists, male critics recognized the novel as an increasingly female domain, where female readers could find "leur propre image, comme au fond d'un miroir fidèle" (their own image, as in a faithful mirror) and which, according to some, was unworthy of men, "que son intelligence réserve à d'autres travaux" (whose intelligence keeps him to other work).[16] This increased feminization of the novel may have contributed to the diminishment of its intellectual status, as well as to the exclusion of almost all the women novelists of this period from long-term literary memory.[17]

In the light of these circumstances, this book reconstructs a crucial moment in the history of French women's writing during the years that overlap between the fin de siècle and the Belle Epoque, extending from Zola's *Nana* (1880) to Colette's *La Vagabonde* (1910), her first independent success. This period is understood as both an ending and a beginning. As the ending of what is known as "the long nineteenth-century," the fin de siècle is often described through images of decay that convey cultural anxieties surrounding depopulation, fears of loosening sexual mores, and political strife. Yet it is also the beginning of a new era of vibrant urbanism insured through Haussmanized boulevards, a burgeoning mass press, and educational reforms. The critical reception of the fin-de-siècle woman writer very much encapsulates the tensions of this periodization between the momentum of a new century's innovations and the lingering anxieties of a complex past.[18]

How did it happen that in fin-de-siècle France—decades after the success of Germaine de Staël and George Sand, centuries after Pisan, Lafayette, and Scudéry, and on the cusp of the twentieth century—the woman writer was as reviled and as intimidating a figure as the prostitute and the hysteric? Did women writers figure in dominant literary movements between the canonical bookends of George Sand and Colette?[19] What role did medicine and science play in linking women writers to depravity, and how did women confront and negotiate these associations in their own writings? And finally, at a time when the woman writer was sister to the hysteric and the prostitute, while female sexuality was a subject of critical fascination across disciplines, under what epistemological circumstances was it possible for women to write about sexuality and their own bodies?

In addressing these questions, this book offers a new lens through which to view the history of sexuality and sexual difference in France at the fin de siècle. The fascination with female sexuality and the obsession with hysteria in the second half of the nineteenth century have been well documented by contemporary scholars of French literature. Critics such as Janet Beizer, Charles Bernheimer, Bram Dijkstra, and Jann Matlock have explored extensively the anxieties creatively projected onto nineteenth-century female bodies in medicine, art, and literature, and the social factors that precipitated this phenomenon.[20] Historians, including Vernon Rosario, Robert Nye, Alain Corbin, and Michelle Perrot, have further contextualized this cultural trend.[21] In contrast to previous scholarship, my contention here is that the widespread interest in female sexuality among doctors, writers, and scientists during this period has obscured an equally dangerous perceived threat to the nineteenth-century social body—that of the female mind.[22] The anxiety that women might actually have the potential to produce literature (and science, medicine, and law) as well as men reveals itself consistently in nineteenth- and early twentieth-century sociological, literary, and medical theories that argue the necessity of keeping women in the private sphere. I propose, however, that what has been described by Michel Foucault as the hysterícization of the female body in the nineteenth century—the suffusion of the body with its sexuality—was a way of expunging the powers of the female mind that threatened to reveal themselves with the implementation of the Napoleonic code, when women's roles were actively redefined.

The conception of a fluid relationship between the female mind and body, developed in France during the nineteenth century, created fundamental discursive obstacles for fin-de-siècle French women writers. The collapsing of the Cartesian distinction between mind and body amplified and medicalized the risks of female professionalism and intellectual engagement and thus contributed to the marginalization of women throughout nineteenth-century French social structures. The writers I consider are significant because in writing about female sexuality, they unsettle the entrenched relationship between *esprit* and *sexe* that couched the threat of female intellect. Each of the texts I examine attempts to reformulate the mind/body problem; in doing so, they release the female mind from its imprisonment in the feminized soul and from its role as sublimator of the body's threats, suggesting instead a variety of other possibilities. In these novels, the critical engagement with the discourse of sexuality is a way to insure women's authority and subjectivity.

SEXUAL DISCOURSE

According to Foucault, modern sexual discourse, or what he calls the *scientia sexualis,* perceived the female body as a privileged object of analysis because of its inherent sexuality, and this epistemological framework shaped the way that sexuality could be spoken about—determining its contexts, its speakers, and its subject matter.[23] Foucault's historical sketch of sexual discourse points to a pinnacle reached in the second half of the nineteenth century, when the central strategies of the deployment of the *scientia sexualis* are fully developed. With the widespread dissemination of the discourses of psychiatry and medicine, the epistemology of sex had become a cultural fascination. The inclusive transdisciplinary term *scientia sexualis* enables us to consider the shared trajectory of medical and literary discourse during this time as part of the same phenomenon; this joint quest to determine the truth of sexuality can also be described under the term *sexology.*[24] Scientific and literary discourses had devoted an increasing attention to female sexuality throughout the century. As much as writers were inspired by medical discourse, gleaning vivid descriptions from its anatomical details, doctors turned to literature to undergird their own arguments, with the result that standardized notions of acceptable sexual expression were promoted in both medical and literary texts through the voice of male authority.[25]

Because naturalism and decadence, the two most prominent literary discourses of the late nineteenth century, grew out of the discursive fusion of medicine and fiction, these movements were destined for a primarily male audience, more than their realist predecessors. Naturalism in particular, popularized by Zola, Huysmans, Edmond and Jules Goncourt, Alphonse Daudet, and Henry Céard, among others, openly boasted its positivistic ideals and drew inspiration from Hippolyte Taine, Auguste Comte, and Claude Bernard. Although never fully accepted by critics, naturalist novels enjoyed a popular success throughout the 1870s and 1880s. In many naturalist novels, from Zola's *Nana* to the Goncourt brothers' *Madame Gervaisais* to Huysmans's *Marthe,* female sexuality was a primary theme and was represented as a source of danger, or the locus of social degeneration. The medical lens through which the female body was presented in clinical detail buttressed the positivistic pretense of naturalism's voyeuristic narrator. The prostitute was a favored figure, symbol of contagion, through which disease, social and physiological, transgressed class lines.

Decadence eschewed naturalism's pretensions to positivism by glorifying the mystical and the occult.[26] Yet decadent fiction is equally marked by the medicalization of contemporary discourse, and particularly the fascination with psychiatry. This influence can be felt in the depictions of perversion, hysteria, fetishism, and nymphomania found in the pages of Maupassant, Barbey d'Aurevilly, Mirbeau, Mendès, and others. Although the decadent writers saw themselves as rivals to naturalism, their discourses were propelled by many of the same phantasmatic associations, particularly in regard to sexuality.[27] In decadent fiction, however, a distinction was made between the feminine, which was valorized for its link to artifice, and the female, which was linked to base corporeality.[28]

Scholars are long accustomed to recognizing the misogynistic depictions of women that fill the pages of fin-de-siècle French literature. However, we have not adequately considered the intellectual consequences of a literature authorized at least in part by a collective project to determine the truth of sexuality through analysis of the female subject. These consequences for the female speaking and writing subject are further amplified once we recognize the extent to which dominant representations of female sexual depravity and pathology obscured anxieties about female intellect. To highlight the way such a discursive structure (amid other social obstacles) obstructed female expression, I turn to the history of hysteria and look to the iconography of Jean-Martin Charcot as a model for late nineteenth-century gender relations. By the 1880s, Charcot's lessons at the Salpêtrière had become cultural fodder, and he himself a notorious celebrity with access to the highest echelons of political power.[29] Inscribing his research with positivistic certainty, Charcot classified the hysterical attack into four periods, the visual drama of which was chronicled assiduously through sketches that later gave way to photographic records published annually in the *Iconographie photographique de la Salpêtrière.*

In many ways, Charcot's legacy provides a vivid image for the nineteenth century's contribution to the history of the body: with Charcot decoding the expressions and gestures of his largely female patients, he demonstrates how the body had become a sign, a producer of knowledge and meaning—and in particular how the female body had become the prime text to be studied by male intellectual authorities. While it is easy to imagine how Charcot and the male audience surrounding him in André Brouillet's painting *Une Leçon clinique à la Salpêtrière* (Fig. 1)—on display for all of Paris to see at the Salon of 1887—could produce volumes of medical treatises and fictional tales, it is just as difficult to imagine Charcot's patient becoming similarly productive from where she lay, motionless, in his assistant's arms.[30] Women at the fin de siècle were not, discursively speaking, in an ideal position to write, interpret, and produce texts that engaged in the scientific questions of the day.

Using the discourse of homosexuality as an example, Foucault has argued that the production of counterdiscourses is always paradoxically dependent on the mechanisms of the dominant discourse. Thus, through its extensive attention to homosexuality as a sexual perversion, the *scientia sexualis* "also made possible the formation of a 'reverse' discourse: homosexuality began to speak in its own behalf, to demand that its legitimacy or 'naturality' be acknowledged, often in the same vocabulary, using the same categories by which it was medically disqualified."[31] In this sense, what Foucault indirectly seems to identify as a kind of early gay-rights movement employed the mechanisms that once insured its oppression. A similar phenomenon is recognizable, I believe, in the female counterdiscourses present in the

Figure 1. André Pierre Brouillet, *Une Lecon clinique à la Salpêtrière*, 1887.

novels I analyze. The study of sexuality through the objectification of the female body, at the same time as it perpetuated female subjugation, made possible the critique of the body that would eventually empower modern feminism. The discursive production of sexuality exposed the mechanisms of patriarchal power over the female body, opening them up to challenge and subversion as women writers began to speak on their own behalf. It also supplied a wide-ranging vocabulary, as it brought questions of sexuality into everyday conversation and popular literature.

What Foucault belittles, however, in his brief and idealized description of the reverse-discourse of homosexuality are the limits that a factor like gender imposes on groups or individuals who in other circumstances might have offered discursive resistance. Women writers constituted such a group, and their counterdiscourses of sexuality could not be easily expressed through the same authoritative avenues of science, medicine, and literature used by their male counterparts.[32] This point brings out another major shortcoming of Foucault's thinking: his failure to recognize the existence of different kinds of relationships between bodies and discourse stemming from the extent of their access to power.[33] Foucault's history of the body in *Surveiller et punir* has been a central text for modern criticism and seems particularly relevant to our study.[34] In it, he outlines the ways in which the modern state transformed individuals into "docile bodies," marked and manipulated by forces of power, and thus a locus for political and economic struggles. Yet Foucault's bodies have no apparent self-consciousness. His theory is therefore unable to account for the process by which women produced meaning from their own bodies, deriving knowledge from their own physical experience. In fact, this process was a major source of discursive power for women writers and helped them overcome the gender hierarchy of the *scientia sexualis,* through which men produced meaning from female bodies.

Hundreds of women were writing novels at the fin de siècle, and many of the authors I examine wrote dozens of novels each. But this study is not meant to be a comprehensive examination of women's novels from this period. Instead, the texts that I highlight here are significant because of the very reason they are rare: they represent instances where women found the means to develop a counterdiscourse of sexuality from their seemingly inauspicious social and cultural positions as objects of the *scientia sexualis.* In fact, one of the most interesting aspects of the novels I have selected is the marginalized positions from which their female protagonists speak—be they that of a prostitute (Liane de Pougy), a medical patient (Lucie Delarue-Mardrus), a music-hall dancer (Colette), a young woman diagnosed with hysteria (Rachilde), or a woman writer herself (Renée Vivien). In his groundbreaking book *Making Sex,* Thomas Laqueur laments the absence of what he calls his "most obvious and persistent omission . . . : a sustained account of experience in the body."[35] The novels presented here compensate for such an omission, offering their own stories of experience in the female body. Without access to the clinical and intellectual authority supplied by medical and literary domains, women writers often resorted to the personal, pitting female experience—from first-hand tales of sexual solicitation to explicit descriptions of sexual pleasure to details of labor pains—against the observations of a removed scientific gaze. This capacity to interpret women's own physical experiences offered women writers both an intellectual authority and a power over their bodies that were otherwise inaccessible.

THE CRISIS OF WOMEN'S WRITING

My reading of fin-de-siècle women's novels is governed by an interdisciplinary approach that recognizes the imbrication of nineteenth-century social, literary, and medical discourses, particularly with respect to the question of female sexuality. In order to contextualize the woman writer's attempt to assert her intellectual authority, I map out in the rest of this introduction some of the ways in which anxieties surrounding the threat of female intellect presented themselves in these interlocking discourses.

In the early 1900s, women's writing proliferated to the point that prominent male critics deemed it a "crisis" and an "epidemic." According to the literary and social critic André Billy, Huysmans remarked in 1905 that "les femmes [écrivains] ont plus de talent que les hommes" (women writers have more talent than men). Looking back on this period from 1951, Billy commented: "La tâche des historiens sera de rechercher pourquoi 1900 a vu . . . le triomphe de la femme" (The task of historians will be to discover why 1900 saw . . . the triumph of woman).[36] This task is at best incomplete more than half a century later, but it was already being engaged in 1909 when the essayist and literary critic Jules Bertaut wrote *La Littérature féminine d'aujourd'hui.* In this three-hundred-page volume, Bertaut announces: "Ayons le courage et la sincérité de l'avouer dès la première page de ce livre: le succès de la littérature féminine actuelle a été foudroyant, il nous a tous surpris, il nous a tous mortifiés, il nous a tous un peu humiliés" (Let's have the courage and sincerity to admit it from the first page of this book: the success of current women's literature has been striking; it has surprised us all, it has shamed us all, and it has humbled us all a little)—the "us" implicitly joining him with his male readers.[37] In a similar venture from the same year entitled *Nos femmes de lettres,* Paul Flat, another prominent literary critic, asks: "Est-il besoin d'observer que l'élite de celles qui possèdent un don est infiniment supérieure à la moyenne de ceux qui, tenant une plume, n'ont pour écrire d'autres motifs valables que l'obligation de gagner leur vie ou la satisfaction légèrement puérile de la vanité?" (Is it necessary to note that the most gifted women writers are infinitely superior to the average of those male writers who have no other valid motive in writing than the obligation to make a living or the satisfaction of a slightly puerile vanity?)[38] Both critics thus propose an objective reading of the new women's literature to determine its true merits.[39] Yet despite their forays into genuine literary analysis, an underlying anxiety consistently unveils itself, demonstrating a clear obstacle to an unbiased critique.

Bertaut betrays this tension from the beginning when he asks, "S'agit-il d'une crise ou de la première étape d'une évolution?" (Is it a crisis at hand or the first stage in an evolution?).[40] The crisis he refers to is that of women writers outnumbering men, and thus overtaking the literary profession.[41] Marcelle Tinayre points to the economic implications of this crisis in *Madeleine au miroir* when she recounts a conversation between male and female writers at a dinner party. Discussing the poor performance of male-authored texts, one guest exclaims: "Si les livres ne se vendaient plus, il fallait chercher la cause principale de cette mévente dans l'épouvantable concurrence que les femmes de lettres font aux hommes de lettres" (If books are not selling anymore, we should look for the principal cause of this problem in the horrible competition that women writers represent for male writers).[42] At this point another male guest jumps in: "Quand il y en avait quatre ou cinq seulement, bien douées ou favorisées par la chance, on ne disait rien. On les supportait. . . . Maintenant, elles sont trois cents, cinq cents; demain elles seront mille . . . si on ne les décourage pas" (When there were only four or five of them, talented or lucky, nothing was said. They were tolerated. . . . Now, there are three hundred, five hundred; tomorrow there will be a thousand . . . if they are not discouraged).[43] This demographic shift is the ostensible problem that motivates Bertaut's critical work. In his twenty-page preface, he delineates a variety of reasons why women have recently come to writing in such numbers, addressing the confluence of social change and women's propensity to read in a tone of thinly veiled hostility. Admitting that women constitute "le vrai public littéraire" (the true literary public), those who determine a book's success or failure, he adds: "Que voulez-vous? Pour lire, il faut des loisirs" (What do you expect? To read, you must have spare time).[44] Through the sociological analysis that follows, he seeks to explain the disproportionate presence of women writers in the field.

The ideological underpinnings of Bertaut's inquiry surface vividly in his conclusion, where he declares his hopes that the newly acquired "vertige de la liberté" (vertigo of freedom) felt by women writers will not last: "Le tempérament français, qui est un tempérament d'harmonie, ne peut s'accommoder de telles extravagances, qui sont à la mode aujourd'hui, mais qui passeront vite demain" (The French temperament, which seeks harmony, cannot accommodate such fashionable extravagances that will quickly vanish tomorrow).[45] This somewhat weak assurance points up the anxiety underlying Bertaut's analysis, and his sense of loss of control over the population of women writers. Flat, for his part, is explicit in articulating the moral implications of women's writing in his own final pages. Women's writing is described as a "ferment" that signifies "la dissolution des idées morales" (the dissolution of moral ideas) which he hopes can be recuperated at some future date.[46] As suggested by Tinayre's text, these critics were not alone in their sense of dread. In his study of female romanticism published in 1905, the influential right-wing critic Charles Maurras warns of a secret city of women where "l'homme ne paraît qu'en forme d'intrus ou de monstre, de jouet lubrique et bouffon, où c'est un désastre, un scandale qu'une jeune fille parvienne à l'état de fiançée, où l'on annonce un mariage comme un enterrement" (man appears only as an intruder or a monster, a lecherous plaything or a buffoon, where it's a disaster, a scandal that a young woman becomes engaged, where a marriage is announced like a funeral).[47]

Despite the economic threat suggested by Tinayre, the most widely articulated reasons for discouraging women's writing had not changed much since the beginning of the nineteenth century. As Maurras makes clear, the threat of the woman writer was that she had diverted her attention from her divinely determined role as wife and mother. This, rather than writing, was the task for which her body had prepared her since birth, as numerous nineteenth-century medical and literary texts made clear. In this vein, in 1842, a commentator in the *Revue des deux mondes* struggled for a linguistic term with which to label the woman writer, asking how to describe a creature "dont toutes les facultés et tous les organes ont pris une destination contraire à celle qui leur était assignée" (whose every faculty and organ has taken a route contrary to the one [nature] intended).[48] Similarly, the doctor and popular medical writer Alexandre Mayer followed his supplication, "Que Dieu nous garde d'une épidémie de bas-bleus!" (May God protect us from an epidemic of bas-bleus!) with the explanation that "la femme est créée et mise au monde pour perpétuer l'espèce d'abord" (woman is created and put on this earth first of all for perpetuating the species) and only after that should be allowed to make her limited social contribution.[49]

The fear of women's choosing writing over procreative and domestic duties was undoubtedly a factor for twentieth-century literary critics like Bertaut, Flat, and Maurras, and we can easily identify this anxiety in their criticism. But this issue was a stale one, with a long history in nineteenth-century discourse, and thus does not adequately explain the ferocity of men's reactions to women's writing in the early 1900s. Instead, I suggest that the Belle Epoque "crisis" of women's literature hit a nerve with these critics because it brought to the fore a different, long-diverted issue, made fresh by the realization of educational reforms expanding girls' education: the possibility of female intellectual prowess.[50]

For both Flat and Bertaut, the task at hand is to separate the talented women from the mediocre to demonstrate that women were not rivaling men on any grand scale. Thus, Flat declares his project as selecting "un critérium pour faire sortir du rang l'élite de ces bataillons serrés" (a competition to separate the elite from those crowded battalions), which will allow him to distinguish between those with economic motives and "celles qui marquent un réel souci d'art littéraire" (those who have a real concern for literary art).[51] The need for this distinction is echoed by Bertaut, who is troubled by the multitude of women writing, in contrast to the isolated numbers of women participating in other professions:

> Mais quel triomphe vaudra jamais celui des femmes de lettres! Cette doctoresse, cette avocate, ce professeur féminin sont des unités, brillantes sans doute, mais elles ne sont encore que cela: des unités,—les railleurs diraient: des exceptions. Au lieu que le bataillon des femmes de lettres, c'est une sorte de masse qui marche d'un seul élan à la victoire.[52]

> [But what triumph will ever equal that of women writers! The female doctor, the female lawyer, the female professor are unique individuals,

brilliant no doubt, but they are still only that: individuals—naysayers would say, exceptions. Whereas the battalion of women writers, they're a sort of mass marching in one unified spirit toward victory.]

In addition to the demoralizing threat these "battalions" of female authors seemed to pose for the male population, Bertaut is concerned that the naïve public will conclude that all women writers are stellar based on the merits of a few great works. In this light, the "crisis" of women's literature disguises the intellectual threat as demographic—the possibility that there could be as many talented female writers as male ones (or more). This threat to male intellectual authority—more than the threat to family stability—elicits the painstaking critical work comprising both volumes. Bertaut arrives at the following conclusion:

> Parcourez une des rares anthologies féminines. . . . Vous discernerez tout de suite cette "féminité," cette disposition particulière de l'esprit qui se traduit par une disposition particulière du style et de l'affabulation littéraire, et nous fait deviner aussitôt le sexe de l'auteur. . . . Est-ce une infériorité? Est-ce une supériorité? J'ai plusieurs fois été amené à étudier la question au cours de ce livre, et j'ai toujours conclu à un caractère d'infériorité.[53]
>
> [Skim one of these rare female anthologies. . . . You will notice right away this "femininity," this particular disposition that translates into a particular literary and creative style, and makes us instantly guess the sex of the author. . . . Is it an inferiority? Is it a superiority? I have been led to study this question several times in this book, and I have always concluded that it was an inferiority.]

Perhaps even more than the occasional abandonment of motherhood, the possibility of female intellectual parity (or superiority) is significant—and terrifying—to these male critics because it threatens to destabilize French patriarchal social structures at nearly every level. Indeed, one could argue that the marginalization of women in nineteenth-century France was based on the perceived public health dangers of exercising the female mind. Nineteenth-century notions of femininity, and particularly theories of the relationship between the female mind and body, assiduously denied women intellectual strength. If some of these notions were attenuated in principle with the passing of educational reforms, the long-held belief in the dangers of female intellect would remain deeply entrenched in French society for years to come.

THE MIND/BODY PROBLEM

The fragile relationship between the female mind and body underlying fin-de-siècle views of female intellect finds its modern origins in the construction of the French social body following the Revolution. In the egalitarian spirit of this period, women were granted an *esprit* for the first time, and their equality with men was recognized within certain limits. As Sylvain Maréchal, author of an 1801 treatise that semi-seriously proposes that women be forbidden to read, puts it: "Les deux sexes sont parfaitement égaux, c'est-à-dire aussi parfaits l'un que l'autre dans ce qui les constitue. Rien dans la nature n'est comparable à un bel homme qu'une belle femme" (The two sexes are perfectly equal, that is, equally perfect in what constitutes them. Nothing in nature is more like a beautiful man than a beautiful woman).[54] The recognition of the female *esprit* flows from the abandonment of the Cartesian mind/body split that had previously dominated French thought. Up to that time, the *esprit* had been genderless, a point celebrated, for example, in Poulain de La Barre's *Egalité des deux sexes* in 1673, where the mind is described as having no sex ("L'esprit n'ayant point de sexe"). However, as the boundary between body and soul was effaced, in tandem with a straying from the Church doctrine under which the soul was a spiritual entity, the *esprit* became saturated with gender. Thus, Maréchal notes, "L'esprit et le coeur ont un sexe comme le corps" (The mind and the heart have a sex like the body).[55]

This interdependence of mind and body is problematized as male and female social roles are revisited in the wake of the Revolution. For although female intellectual capacity was recognized, its use was thought to disrupt the delicate balance of the female constitution. Women's most crucial role as subject of the state was, after all, procreation. Maréchal's arguments are consistent with the trends of biological theories promoted in the early 1800s by influential doctors such as Pierre Cabanis, Julien-Joseph Virey, and Pierre Roussel, who emphasized the biological basis of sexual difference and argued that women were unable to reason because their sexuality permeated their entire bodies.[56] The physical weakness that once excluded women from power thus translated directly into intellectual inferiority. The linguistic conflation of the mind/body dichotomy with the soul/body one may have worked further against female intellect: the general term *esprit,* which could include mind and soul—the realms of thoughts and feelings—helped to camouflage the repression of the female mind within a more spiritual, feminized domain.[57]

The social implications of procreation and motherhood were magnified by nineteenth-century demographics, furthering the discouragement of female intellect. Toward the beginning of the century, a decline in the birth rate alarmed the political establishment and fueled the promotion of motherhood in political discourse. Any other female role was seen as harmful, dangerous, and infectious to women and the social structure at large. The well-known socialist theorist Pierre-Joseph Proudhon's infamous 1846 formulation encapsulates the dominant thinking: a woman was either "courtisane ou ménagère," housewife or harlot.[58] Historian Geneviève Fraisse comments: "Parce que leur esprit est sexué . . . l'activité de leur raison les entraîne dans la vie sexuelle, et par conséquent les pousse à la corruption. Les femmes qui étudient sont virtuellement ce que sont les femmes de lettres, des courtisanes" (Because their *esprit* is sexed . . . , the activity of their mind leads them into sexual activity and thus leads to corruption. Women who study are virtually what women of letters are: courtesans).[59] In fact, throughout the nineteenth century, it was commonly feared that the exertion of the female mind would have deleterious effects on the body and the sexuality to which it was physiologically linked, or that it would lead to sexual impropriety. In both cases, the danger stems from the lack of controls shielding the body from the workings of the mind. In the ideal nineteenth-century woman, the soul was to supplant the mind, offering a feminized realm of feelings that was to work in concert with the female body in fulfilling its domestic agenda.[60]

Nineteenth-century arguments against female education or professionalism almost always pointed to the danger of female intellectual exertion. For Maréchal, it was a question of a slippery slope through which girls reading would lead to women writing, a logic that predicts that of Bertaut: "Combien la lecture est contagieuse: sitôt qu'une femme ouvre un livre, elle se croit en état d'en faire" (Reading is so contagious: as soon as a woman opens a book, she thinks she is writing one).[61] The vocabulary of contagion here already anticipates the language of degeneration that will dominate later in the century, blurring the intellectual question into one of epidemiology. There are numerous reasons why Maréchal found writing to be abhorrent behavior for women, all of which emphasize the importance of women remaining in the private sphere, and, in particular, their maternal obligation, for, as he writes: "Il est prouvé que les *Femmes-Auteurs* sont moins fécondes que les autres" (It is proven that women writers are less fertile than other women).[62] In hinging his arguments on a nascent science, he demonstrates a powerful new trend. In the post-Revolutionary period, biology was only beginning to be invoked as a justification for excluding women from the professional arena. French feminists of the period protested what Carla Hesse calls "scientific chauvinism"—hostility rather than truth. Prominent women from the late eighteenth to the early nineteenth century, from Germaine de Staël to Isabelle de Charrière to Madame Stéphanie de Genlis, who wrote the 1811 treatise *De l'influence des femmes sur la littérature française,* responded to the new biology by staunchly disputing the intellectual inferiority of women. By the late nineteenth century, however, volumes upon volumes of scientific research, especially the research on hysteria, had examined the question of sexual difference. Some of these texts purported to demonstrate female mental incapacity through empirical evidence, such as cranial comparisons showing women's smaller brains, and the rapidly developing genre of the case study.[63] This kind of evidence, predicated on a new scientific method, was much more difficult for women to refute than the blanket generalizations of earlier in the century.[64] Thanks to decades of this new science, by the late nineteenth century Maréchal's assertion seems commonplace. In 1877, the doctor and popular medical writer J. P. Dartigues echoed the conventional wisdom: "La grande fécondité de l'esprit chez les femmes produit presque toujours la stérilité corporelle, ou du moins des dérangements vicieux dans les fonctions de l'utérus" (Great fertility of the mind in women almost always produces physical sterility, or at least serious troubles in the functioning of the uterus).[65]

HYSTERIA AND THE FEMALE BRAIN

As the century aged, post-Revolutionary rationalizations for separate gender roles became increasingly medicalized, following the prevailing interests of French culture. By mid-century, fiction reading was discouraged in girls not because it led to writing but because it led directly to hysteria, a disease that had been the object of intense scrutiny long before Charcot made it part of the cultural landscape. In 1847 the prominent physiologist Jean-Louis Brachet described the perils of reading in his treatise on the disease, warning parents: "Ne lui souffrez d'autre lecture que celle des ouvrages utiles et intéressants. Malheur à la jeune fille qui dévore les romans avant de connaître le monde! Son imagination exaltée la trompe et l'égare, et elle s'en fait un qui lui causera bien des désappointements" (Don't allow her any other reading but works that are useful and interesting. Woe to the young woman who devours novels before knowing the world! Her exalted imagination fools her and leads her astray, and she creates a world that will cause her a lot of disappointment).[66] The medical reasoning behind this admonition remains unchanged, stemming from that lack of boundary between mind, or *esprit,* and body: reading provides the young girl with a curiosity that might unsafely stimulate other physical drives. Yet whereas in 1801 reading led to writing, which might in turn create a physical imbalance, by the 1840s the middle step had been notably elided, excising the place of female intellect in the process by refusing to acknowledge the possibility of the woman writer. This change is partially explained by the fact that by the mid-nineteenth century, there was no longer simply a fluidity between mind and body; instead, doctors saw the female body as thoroughly saturated with her sexuality, making the dangers of reading even more pronounced. Any stimulation of the mind put the body immediately at risk. This anatomical coalescence comes to define femininity and provides a simple explanation for the female disposition to neurosis. Hysteria, often described in the nineteenth century as an exaggerated display of femininity, became shorthand for this dangerously fluid female anatomy, and for female sexual difference in a more general sense.[67]

The hysteria diagnosis is at the heart of my study because it encapsulates the positivistic project to understand the female body pursued throughout the nineteenth century. More specifically, it constitutes an attempt to determine the enigmatic relationship between the female mind and body that can be seen as an effort to locate the site of female sexual difference. Throughout the first half of the century, scientists focused the hysteria debate on the origins of the disease. Was it situated in the female reproductive organs, following the uterine theory that had prevailed for centuries (the term *hysteria* itself coming from the Greek word for uterus)? Or was hysteria located elsewhere, in the brain? Inscribed in this debate was another central question: what, biologically speaking, makes women so susceptible to this condition? After all, according to the epigraph to Brachet's *Traité de l'hystérie,* most women become hysterical eventually.[68] Similarly, later in the century, Augustin Fabre, a doctor and professor of clinical medicine, wrote: "As a general rule, all women are hysterical. . . . Every woman carries within her the seeds of hysteria."[69]

Until the mid-nineteenth century, the influential doctors J.-B. Louyer-Villermay, Frédéric Dubois d'Amiens, A. L. Foville, and Hector Landouzy held to hysteria's location in the female reproductive organs.[70] The tides turned, however, with Brachet's treatise and that of Pierre Briquet in 1859, both of whom posited the roots of hysteria in the encephalon. Charcot, himself a neurologist, followed this line of thought, as did his contemporary Legrand du Saulle; hysteria became a disease of the brain. This notion was critical to recognizing hysteria in men, but doctors continued to emphasize women's predisposition to the disease.[71] Furthermore, because of their simultaneous insistence on the homogeneity and fluidity of the female body, these doctors seemed to undermine the significance of their new line of thinking. In addressing the origins of hysteria, Brachet writes: "Ce n'est pas seulement par l'utérus que la femme est ce qu'elle est; elle est telle par sa constitution entière. Depuis la tête jusqu'aux pieds, à l'extérieur comme à l'intérieur quelles que soient les parties de son corps que vous examiniez, vous la trouvez partout la même. Partout vous trouvez ses tissus et ses organes différents des mêmes tissus et des mêmes organes de l'homme" (It is not only through the uterus that the woman is what she is; she is such in her entire constitution. From head to toe, on the outside as on the inside, whatever parts of the body you examine, you will find her the same all over. You will find all her tissue and her organs different from the same tissues and same organs in man).[72] Similarly essentializing statements can be found in Briquet and Legrand du Saulle.[73] In this context, the site of the disease seems insignificant; there is no etiological difference between the female encephalon and the uterus. More than thirty years after Brachet, Dartigues confirms this principle at his text's opening when he asserts that the female constitution derives directly from "la faiblesse innée de ses organes" (the innate weakness of her organs). He continues: "tout est subordonné à ce principe par lequel la nature a voulu la rendre inférieure à l'homme. Elle n'est pas femme seulement par les attributs de son sexe, elle l'est en toute chose" (everything is subordinate to the principle through which nature wanted to make her inferior to man. She is female not only through the attributes of her sexual organs, but in everything).[74] All boundaries between intellect and physicality, mind and body, have been collapsed, making it impossible to speak of one without the other.

Despite scientific studies situating hysteria in the brain, the belief in hysteria's gynecological roots persisted in popular medical texts and in the public imagination through the end of the nineteenth century and beyond.[75] Hysteria was associated with femininity, and this association unavoidably factored into consideration of women's proper societal role. It is perhaps not surprising, then, that Brachet's and Dartigues's logic surfaces in a text on female intellect, underlying Bertaut's analysis of women writers: not only is femininity pervasive in the female body but for this reason all women (and all women's writings) are the same: "La femme de lettres est avant tout la Femme, c'est-à-dire un être d'une certaine sensiblité, d'une certaine intelligence, d'un certain goût et d'un certain tempérament, caractères qui varient fort peu selon les individus et qu'on est toujours assuré de retrouver en chacun d'eux" (The woman of letters is above all a Woman, that is, a creature of a certain sensitivity, a certain intelligence, a certain taste and temperament, traits that vary little among individuals and that one is guaranteed to find in each one of them).[76] Perhaps Bertaut is also saying: the woman writer—the one who dares to exercise her mind—is *avant tout* a hysteric.

In *The History of Sexuality,* Foucault describes what he calls "the hystericization of the female body," which became a central strategic mechanism for the production of sexuality as a discourse in the nineteenth century. He explains that it was "a threefold process whereby the feminine body was analyzed—qualified and disqualified—as being thoroughly saturated with sexuality; whereby it was integrated into the sphere of medical practices, by reason of a pathology intrinsic to it; whereby, finally, it was placed in organic communication with the social body."[77] We can contrast this hystericized female body with the frail social body described by Carolyn Dean in her history of modern French pornography. As she explains, the bodily metaphor for the state developed alongside the rapidly growing interest in medicine in the eighteenth and nineteenth centuries and drew on the conclusions of the medical profession. After the Revolution, the sacred body politic of the ancien régime—where the monarch was "a metaphorical head and the other 'parts' symbolic extensions of that body"—had been replaced with a body whose members had equality before the law. By the mid-nineteenth century, a medical model had been adopted, such that "cultural critics conceived of the nation's life in organic terms to be regulated by experts in a struggle against contamination and infection," in the light of escalating demographic, military, and medical threats to the social body's health.[78] The female body figured as part of this social body only to the extent that it produced children; thus, women's contribution to the social sphere took place safely in the private sphere. Building on Dean's analysis, we can understand the increased policing of female sexuality in the nineteenth century as a means of protecting the frail male social body from the debilitating influence of any female behavior that did not remain contained by maternal obligations. The deviant female body was frequently figured as a source of contagion (as Maréchal anticipated with his description of the female reader), the animus of degeneration threatening the population and requiring regulation.

In addition to understanding the policing of female sexuality as a means of protecting healthy male bodies from a contaminating femininity and ensuring the virility necessary for military might, we can also recognize it as a way to protect the patriarchal mind, equally critical to the social body, from female intellectual opposition. This threat, and its implications for the male social body—even at the birth of the twentieth century—come into relief through the military analogies of Bertaut and Flat, who repeatedly imagine battalions of women writers arriving en masse. Bertaut refers to "la poussée de tout un clan" (the thrust of a whole clan) and "la clameur de toute une classe" (the clamor of a whole class), and Flat fears the "groupement pressé de celles qui tiennent une plume" (the crowded grouping of those pen-wielding women).[79] These phallic women, armed with pens, are described as amazons, but their physical threat comes purely from intellectual muscle.

Throughout the nineteenth century, the female body was an object of widespread fascination in medicine. Yet the question of female intelligence always seemed to find its place in physiological studies, revealing the extent to which it was intimately bound up with—if often also obscured by—the study of female pathology in general and hysteria in particular. If hysteria was indeed a nervous illness, located in the encephalon, and not in the reproductive organs, there was all the more reason to consider the dangers of women using their brains. For Pierre Briquet, a doctor, professionalism was a root cause of hysteria in susceptible females. He writes: "La stimulation que certaines occupations exercent sur l'ensemble du système nerveux, en provoquant son activité, a généralement été considérée comme une prédisposition aux maladies nerveuses. Aussi regarde-t-on la culture exclusive des lettres et des beaux-arts comme une prédisposition à l'hystérie" (The stimulation that certain occupations induce in the nervous system as a whole by provoking its activity has generally been considered a predisposition to nervous illness. Thus, we can consider the exclusive cultivation of arts and letters as a predisposition to hysteria).[80] In his study of hysteria, Brachet addresses the question of female intelligence in a chapter entitled "Etudes du physique et du moral de la femme" (Studies of women's physiology and mentality). He explains that women's judgment is hampered by women's naturally excessive emotion because of the way that the two are linked in the female mind. In women, "l'intelligence semble se modeler sur la sensibilité" (intellect seems to be shaped by feelings) such that acts of comprehension seem to translate into emotional response; according to Brachet, feeling and judgment are essentially one process ("Sentir et juger en font, pour ainsi dire, qu'un"). As a result of this interdependence, however, female creativity becomes impossible: "Malgré ce goût et cette exaltation, son imagination ne crée rien: elle ressemble au miroir qui réfléchit vivement les impressions qu'il reçoit. Presque toutes les femmes écrivains sont convenues de cette disposition intellectuelle" (Despite her capacity for taste and her excitement, her imagination creates nothing; it resembles a mirror that actively reflects the impressions it receives. Almost all women writers admit to this intellectual disposition). Taking his argument one step further out of scientific bounds, Brachet adds: "Rien au monde n'est ridicule comme un bas-bleu" (Nothing in the world is as ridiculous as a *bas-bleu*).[81] Twenty years later, in 1874, Mayer offers ostensibly scientific reasons why women cannot be scientists, in his *Des Rapports conjugaux considérés sous le triple point de vue de la population, de la santé, et de la morale publique,* in its sixth edition after twenty-five years.[82] Mayer's book is written for a popular audience and demonstrates the trickle-down effect of nineteenth-century medicine. The writings of well-established doctors like Briquet and Brachet were frequently quoted and paraphrased in more popular medical writing, bringing clinical treatises to increasingly wider audiences.[83] Weighing in on women's intellectual potential, Mayer does admit that women might have some advantages in fiction writing. But he offers the following antidote to that conclusion, vividly demonstrating the ideological underpinnings of much of nineteenth-century medicine:

> Eh bien! Nonobstant de si glorieux succès, celle dont le front sera orné d'une auréole de gloire, excitera sans doute une admiration enthousiaste, mais rarement elle inspirera un véritable amour; parce qu'en voyant s'allumer en elle la flamme du génie, elle a senti s'éteindre en même temps le foyer du coeur. Ce n'est plus une femme, puisque c'est *un* poète, *un* romancier, ou *un* peintre.[84]

> [Well! Notwithstanding such glorious successes, she whose head is crowned with a halo of glory will probably arouse enthusiastic admiration but rarely inspire true love; because in seeing the flame of genius ignite in her, she felt the hearth of the heart extinguish at the same time. This is no longer a woman, because she is *a* (with masculine article) poet, *a* novelist, *a* painter.]

In French, these professions are grammatically gendered as masculine, which Mayer emphasizes through his use of italics. In other words, women cannot be artists because such a role is by definition masculine; the argument has become tautological and its biological basis has been abandoned.

WRITING AGAINST HYSTERIA

In its classic form, nineteenth-century hysteria revealed itself through spasms and convulsions over which the suffering woman had no control. In a 1905 play by the psychiatrist Joseph Grasset, an alienist counsels his female patient as follows: "You will be cured as soon as you resolve to abdicate all personal control. . . . Do not get discouraged, put yourself in the hands of your doctor, obey him blindly."[85] In an article published in 1983, Gladys Swain cites the birth-control pill as the end of hysteria. With the ability to regulate their menstrual cycles, she argues, women finally gained the mastery over their bodies that hysteria denied them ("elle est devenue maîtresse de son corps").[86] But this conclusion is unsatisfying: it leaves the hysteric voiceless, her centuries of distress abruptly quieted by the invention of a male doctor. Furthermore, by the end of the nineteenth century, hysteria was more than a medical diagnosis; it was a cultural phenomenon, linked to notions of femininity pervasive in nearly all aspects of French society. As an alternative to Swain's clinical history of the disease, then, I suggest that the novels presented here represent an important step toward women's gaining control over their own bodies, in response to the hegemonic determinations of nineteenth-century medicine and culture. They constitute the hysteric's revenge, as my title suggests, because, by virtue of their own writing, these authors refuse fin-de-siècle scientific and literary discourses their power over women's bodies. Through their novels, they present the relationship between the female mind and body as a productive and edifying aspect of female identity, rather than a dangerous and potentially debilitating one. The result is a group of texts that very much confirm the threat of female intellect as a challenge to the symbolic structures of patriarchal authority.

In the chapters that follow, I begin with an examination of Zola's *Nana* as an example par excellence of the imbrication of literary, scientific, and sociological discourses at the fin de siècle. I demonstrate how even in this novel, where the dangers of female sexuality are explicit, there is an underlying anxiety about female intellect that helps us understand the widespread comparison between the woman writer and the prostitute. In Chapter 2, I turn the tables to ask how the narration of the story by the prostitute herself alters both the story that is told and the way it must be read. I consider three autobiographical novels of the *fille publique,* a term I adopt to demonstrate the association of women who were public figures with promiscuity. The *filles publiques* of this chapter are the courtesan in Liane de Pougy's 1901 *Idylle saphique,* the music hall dancer in Colette's 1910 *La Vagabonde,* and the woman writer in Renée Vivien's 1904 version of *Une Femme m'apparut.* I explore how these figures make themselves into writing subjects as a way of transcending their denigrated public personae, and I demonstrate the unexpected role of lesbian sexuality in this process.

In Chapters 3 and 4, I examine how women's efforts to carve out a place for themselves in the context of the late nineteenth century's dominant literary movements were obstructed by the intimate link between intellect and virility. I first consider two women's adaptations of naturalist tropes: Marcelle Tinayre's *La Maison du péché,* which conducts a Zolian experiment through an ill-fated love story, and Lucie Delarue-Mardrus's *Marie, fille-mère,* the story of a young peasant girl's brutal rape and subsequent pregnancy. I demonstrate the way these women challenged fundamental aspects of the naturalist optic by giving prominence to women's experiences. I then examine how the decadent writer Rachilde displaced the female body from its traditional role in nineteenth-century narratives of hysteria and made the male body the battleground for intellectual and sexual power. I suggest that Rachilde's success was tied to a series of ambiguous collaborations with the structures of male authority.

Finally, I examine the discourse of female pleasure in sentimental novels by women: Anna de Noailles's *Le Visage émerveillé,* Gyp's *Autour du mariage,* Colette's *L'Ingénue libertine,* and Odette Dulac's *Le Droit au plaisir.* I analyze the explicit discussions of female orgasm in these novels and demonstrate how the pursuit of pleasure was a path to female self-knowledge. The countersexology offered in these novels forges a connection between women's minds and bodies that poses a stark challenge to fin-de-siècle views of female sexuality.

The novels I present have not been previously considered together, perhaps because of their wide variety of styles and genres.[87] As Sandra Gilbert and Susan Gubar have noted with respect to British literature, female authors who did not conform to conventional literary categories were often cast aside as oddities by literary history. By emphasizing the ways in which fin-de-siècle women writers struggled to overcome a shared discursive obstacle, I hope to avoid the generalizing tendencies of canon formation and offer a new literary-historical framework. Recognizing their relationship to the dominant discourses against which they wrote allows us to read Colette with Rachilde and to appreciate the discursive kinship between these relatively familiar writers and lesser-known writers such as Anna de Noailles, Lucie Delarue-Mardrus, Marcelle Tinayre, and Odette Dulac.

When I use the term *feminist* to describe fin-de-siècle women writers, I am recognizing the multiple and sometimes contradictory ways in which they express resistance to gender norms. But in the oppositional era of Dreyfusard versus anti-Dreyfusard of the Belle Epoque, feminism was a polarizing issue that discouraged shades of gray. Women identified as either feminist or antifeminist, and for a number of complex reasons, the majority of writers in this study preferred the anti- side of this label. At the same time, their writings supported values that seem undoubtedly feminist in spirit to a modern reader for whom feminism can be recognized in a plurality of forms.[88] At the fin de siècle, the French feminist movement was on the rise. Yet the term *feminist* was always a loaded one, associated with the militant positions of its nineteenth-century pioneers. Stephen Hause estimates that in 1900, twenty to twenty-five thousand women were involved in women's organizations that had ties to the moderate feminist movement, whose principal causes were access to the workforce, coeducation, women's wages, and the right to file paternity suits. (Suffrage was associated with the militant end of the movement.) Of these participants, he also estimates, however, that not more than five hundred were active feminists.[89] One of the most important developments in fin-de-siècle feminism was Marguerite Durand's creation of the newspaper *La Fronde* in 1897, an entirely female-run daily. Yet, while Durand supported feminism, she did not want her paper to be limited by this label.[90] *La Fronde* published a variety of opinions and featured writing by many of the women in this study, regardless of the way they labeled themselves. I believe the resistance to the feminist label among the women writers in this study can best be understood in the light of the essentializing tendencies of their critics. From the perspective of the fin-de-siècle press, women writers were a homogenous group—a class or clan of pen-wielding amazons—all writing in the same transparently feminine way. The subjects of this study devoted themselves in large measure to proving their individuality. They did not want to be among the *bas-bleus* or *femmes de lettres* who wrote en masse; they saw themselves as women but also as individuals and were perhaps for that reason reluctant to identify with each other through feminism, or any other group label.

In acknowledging the feminist import of all of these writers' representations of sexuality, I am also recognizing a kind of feminist expression that was at the time largely unrecognizable as such: the questioning of sexual relationships, the subversion of heterosexual norms, and the embrace of sexual pleasure were not associated with the politics of fin-de-siècle feminism. Issues of birth control and sexual emancipation were present in this early feminist movement but were marginal, associated with the militant Maria Deraismes in the 1880s and 90s and with the neo-Malthusians Nelly Roussel and Madeleine Pelletier in the 1900s. In general terms, the strategies of resistance expressed in the sexual counterdiscourses of women's writings could not yet be theoretically articulated in terms of a feminist sexual politics. At the same time, I propose that in these texts, many of which are not explicitly polemical, the representation of sexuality is the site of a nascent feminist consciousness, in which the linking of the discourse of sexuality to personal power struggles demonstrates the beginnings of a modern feminist sensibility.[91] More explicitly and extensively than in previous generations, these women identified sexuality (in addition to previously identified targets such as politics, the institution of marriage, and religion) as the site of gender hierarchies and constructed a critique of sexual relations. Indeed, these women authors forge a connection between sexual self-knowledge and intellectual authority in their novels that anticipates the theoretical tenets to be propounded by twentieth-century French feminists ranging from Simone de Beauvoir to Hélène Cixous, Luce Irigaray, and Monique Wittig.

In *Only Paradoxes to Offer,* Joan Scott describes the theoretical challenges to nineteenth-century feminism: to make demands for women as a group, feminist activists were forced to reject the universalism associated with French liberal ideology.[92] As a result, the notion of "woman" was reconceived repeatedly throughout the century in efforts to articulate a consistent point of view. The stories told by the writers in this study demonstrate a shared attempt to reimagine the relationship between the female mind and body through fiction that implicitly engages the paradoxes of nineteenth-century femininity. The books I present suggest that the novel may have offered a freer space for protest than feminist activism, because it required neither the theoretical rigor nor the consistency associated with other types of discourse. Yet these novels have far-reaching critical implications in their challenges to prevailing notions of gender difference. Further, by writing about sexuality, these fin-de-siècle women authors took an important step in self-determination, claiming for the first time intellectual and discursive sovereignty over their own bodily experiences and challenging a century of male-authorized medical expertise. Although not recognized as such in their time, this exploration of sexuality through writing would become an essential aspect of modern French feminism. This study thus demonstrates the relationship of fin-de-siècle French women writers to both the male-authorized literary trends they wrote against and the feminist criticism they pointed toward.

1

Literary Science and the Female Subject

THE BRAINS BEHIND EMILE ZOLA'S *NANA*

Throughout the second half of the nineteenth century, French male authors repeatedly imagined the dangers of uncontained female sexuality, creating characters whose unbridled sexual energy reached pathological proportions as they fueled the fictions that framed them. From Flaubert's *Madame Bovary* (1856) and later *Salâmmbo* (1862) to Edmond de Goncourt and Jules de Goncourt's *Germinie Lacerteux* (1864) and *Fille Elisa* (1887) to the woman in question in this chapter, Zola's Nana—perhaps the quintessential *femme fatale*—the women of these male-authored fictions have something beyond their threatening sexuality in common: they all die by their text's end. Janet Beizer describes this necessary expulsion of subversive female sexuality in fin-de-siècle fiction as "the process whereby the disabling of the hystericized body paradoxically becomes an enabling force for the discourse that produces it."[1] The literary paradox to which Beizer alludes is that of the writer's desire to portray female sexuality as a demonic force threatening society at the same time that he needs to reassure himself of the limits of this power by bringing the female protagonist to her end. In this chapter, I show how the tension between male author and female protagonist in Zola's *Nana* brings into relief a male mind/body problem that sets the stage for the fin-de-siècle woman writer.

Ostensibly, the hystericized female body within the nineteenth-century text is a threat to the physical well-being of the male population. For Zola's infamous courtesan Nana, her prostitution threatens to emasculate Parisian men en masse, and to physically destroy their virility. The literary expulsion of subversive female sexuality, however, aims to save not only these fictional male bodies but also the male mind that has imagined them; it is a defense mechanism that protects the author himself, affirming and enabling his authority. The incapacitation of the hysteric thus rescues not only virility but also intellectual prowess; indeed, these things cannot be separated. In *Nana* in particular, Zola seems caught by this hysterical paradox, as it were: he constructs a horrific female character who in her theoretical extreme threatens his own authority as a writer and scientist. For his narrative to succeed as a step toward scientific mastery, he must rid it of this threat and bring his heroine to her unequivocal end to re-empower the discourse that her existence had challenged.

Viewed in this light, *Nana* can be read as a discursive struggle between a male writer and the fantasmatic demon he is attempting to master. Zola considered his novel a scientific enterprise, the theory of which he documented in his essay "Le Roman expérimental." Yet I propose that in *Nana,* a different kind of science experiment is taking place—of which Zola himself was most likely unaware—because the author has his protagonist engage in activities that seem to threaten his own authority over such a being, if she were truly to exist. In this sense, Zola's novel offers a fascinating example of the nineteenth-century tension between the male mind and the female body. In this novel, the strength of Zola's literary science is posed against the mystery of the female subject. His novel reveals what is at stake for the *scientia sexualis,* the sexual discourse developing at the fin de siècle through the confluence of science and literature, as Nana herself threatens the success of Zola's naturalist project. But what is also worth considering is why a fictional prostitute should pose a challenge to the male mind, if not for the conventional conflation of the female mind and body. Thus, I begin with *Nana* to demonstrate that even in a novel where the consuming dangers of female sexuality are explicitly thematized, the threat of the female mind is not as irrelevant as one might suppose. Indeed, I would like to ask whether the possibility of an independent, free-thinking, uncontainable subjectivity—that is, a mind—is not also suggested by the uncontainable body Zola so vividly describes in Nana. To what extent does a subjective or "intellectual" (although it is hard to use that word to describe her) threat—as opposed to the bodily one—surface in *Nana,* and what does this reveal about both the stakes of Zola's novel and the discursive place of the French woman writer at the turn of the century?

In "Le Roman expérimental," which was originally published in the same issue of *Le Voltaire* as *Nana,* Zola describes his vision for a scientific literature modeled on the experimental methods of the physiologist Claude Bernard. Just as the scientist conducts experiments to arrive at physiological conclusions, the naturalist writer conducts textual experiments, by observing the reactions of characters in various contexts and relationships, to arrive at a fuller understanding of human behavior. The workings of the mind and the passions, Zola argues, must result from causes that can be determined by the same mechanisms that control the body's organs.[2] Zola's interdisciplinary foray in this essay is consistent with his literary criticism. He saw the modern naturalist novel as serving society's basic needs. "Il est la poésie et il est la science" (It is poetry and it is science), he writes in "Les Romanciers naturalistes." No longer simply an "amusement," Zola continues, his enthusiasm gushing onto the page, the naturalist novel is "tout ce qu'on veut, un poème, un traité de pathologie, un traité d'anatomie, une arme politique, un essai moral" (everything one desires, a poem, a treatise in pathology, a treatise in anatomy, a political weapon, a moral essay).[3]

In confirming the indebtedness of the naturalist novel to the scientific method, Zola also reveals the dependence of his science on the female subject, and the gender specificity of his scientific process. By conflating the role of writer with that of the doctor and scientist, Zola determines the gender of this position as masculine. Whereas there were women writers throughout the nineteenth century, a woman doctor or scientist was a rare exception. (The young widow Madeleine Bres, for example, was given special permission in 1866 to enroll in the faculté de médicine de Paris.)[4] Indeed, Zola's contemporaries were very familiar with the notion of the male doctor/scientist investigating links between anatomy and psychological effects: this was the fundamental premise of the newly burgeoning field of psychiatry and the underlying principle of its favored diagnosis, hysteria. Under the auspices of Jean-Martin Charcot, the Salpêtrière became the center of hysteria studies in the 1870s.[5] Over the next two decades, more inaugural theses on the topic would be written than in the previous seventy years.[6] During this time, Charcot became something of a celebrity and made his largely female patients' symptoms recognizable through sketches and photographs published annually in the *Iconographie photographique de la Salpêtrière.* Through their research on hysteria, Charcot and his peers were steadily confirming the interrelationship between female anatomy and neurosis, and many writers visited the Salpêtrière to gain medical authority for their fictional renderings.[7] The female body was thus the perfect specimen for the kinds of experiments Zola wanted to conduct (and already had) in his writing, and this relationship of male scientist to female object of study was already a well-established scientific paradigm in medicine and literature.

Zola's weaving of literary and scientific theory becomes problematic with the notion of the *circulus,* a term borrowed from Claude Bernard to define "une solidarité qui lie les différents membres, les différents organes entre eux, de telle sorte que, si un organe se pourrit, beaucoup d'autres sont atteints, et qu'une maladie très complexe se déclare" (a unity that links different body parts, different organs, together, such that if one organ rots, many others are infected, and a very complex illness presents itself). Applying this notion to the novel, Zola announces: "Dès lors, dans nos romans, lorsque nous expérimentons sur une plaie grave qui empoisonne la société, nous procédons comme le médecin expérimentateur" (Consequently, in our novels when we experiment on a serious wound that is poisoning society, we proceed as does the experimental doctor) seeking to identify the "initial determinant" of the complex illness before him.[8] Zola thus imagines himself as continuing Bernard's research in the social domain, searching through his literary experiments for the root cause of social deterioration, the originary wound or *plaie grave* poisoning society.[9] But Zola never quite releases himself from Bernard's physiological basis. While Zola substitutes *circulus social* for Bernard's *circulus vital,* Zola's adaptations of Bernard's images are not purely metaphorical: social determinism has its origins in the physical. Indeed, Zola was greatly influenced by the research of the criminologist Cesare Lombroso, who established links between physical traits and criminal behavior.[10]

This conflation of the social and the physical is realized in the character of Nana and illuminates the underlying gendered presuppositions of Zola's deterministic theory as well as his view of the female body's particular relationship to the social sphere. At the end of *Nana,* after the title character's death has been narrated in gory scientific detail, the narrator concludes: "Il semblait que le virus pris par elle dans les ruisseaux, . . . ce ferment dont elle avait empoisonné un peuple, venait de lui remonter au visage et l'avait pourri" (It seemed that the virus she caught in the gutters . . . this ferment with which she poisoned a people, had just risen to her face and destroyed it), reprising in this sentence the theme of contagion through the female body that is woven throughout the text.[11] On one hand, this virus seems to be an independent agent poisoning Parisian society—a social disease, the *circulus social,* that Nana happens to pick up. On the other hand, the virus cannot be separated from its conductor—Nana's sexual organs, which house and incubate the disease before passing it on through her many contacts. It is not a virus passed from one person to the next, with each progressive step dissimulating its origin. Instead, the dynamic *circulus* conflates with the single rotting organ that alone wreaks havoc ("si un organe se pourrit").

Typically in Zola's writing the female body takes on this role as the force of contagion, depicted alternately as leaking, gushing, and bleeding. Zola's transposition of this lesion onto the female body bears an interesting correlation to the theories of Charcot, who was influenced by many of the same medical theories. Mark Micale summarizes Charcot's version of degeneration theory as follows: "Following Morel, Moreau, and later Magnan, Charcot believed that hysterical patients possessed from birth a latent flaw or lesion of the nervous system. This *tare nerveuse,* he claimed, was inherited directly or indirectly from defective parental stock and stood ready at all times to be activated by appropriate environmental circumstances."[12] Zola's *plaie grave,* figured on the female body and passed on through heredity, returns the *tare nerveuse* of hysteria to its gynecological origins, making the female reproductive organs once again the originating site of this disease.[13]

If it is the virus that constitutes the initial determinism, then Nana's sex is the serious wound poisoning society. As Nana brings the filth of the underworld to infect the bourgeoisie, the female sex is implicated as the organism that disrupts social equilibrium by transgressing class boundaries and thus facilitating the virus's path of ruin. The figuration of Nana's sex as the *plaie grave* hearkens back to the notorious *fêlure* (crack) that winds through Zola's epic Rougon-Macquart series taking on alternate forms. In *Nana* the *fêlure* explicitly conflates with Nana's genitals, as it snakes through Nana's house, announcing "l'effondrement prochain" (the imminent crumbling) of society, while Nana, swinging her hips, "décomposait ce monde, le pénétrait du ferment de son odeur flottant dans l'air chaud" (penetrated and corrupted this world with the ferment of her odor floating in the warm air) (380).[14] Although the *fêlure* is tied to forms of degeneracy in both male and female characters in the *Rougon-Macquart,* it is physically inscribed on the female body. In addition to its relationship to Nana's sex, the *fêlure* is linked to the menstruation of the matriarch of the Rougon-Macquart clan, Tante Dide—whose mental illness is described by Zola as hysteria—and to what Beizer calls "the leak in Clotilde's head," Clotilde being the family's progeny.[15] Thus, while according to Zola's theory Nana's sex should constitute the *plaie grave* only in this instance, a larger perspective on his literary imagery reveals that the *plaie grave* referred to in the "Roman expérimental" intersects with the *fêlure* of the Rougon-Macquart, and it is no accident that both terms evoke the female anatomy. Both play on traditional mythological constructs of the female sex as unrepresentable, an absent presence, the thing that both science and literature struggle to understand and contain. In his theory and in his novels Zola inscribes this wound on the female body, whose effects will manifest themselves in various forms of social degeneration.

Zola is explicit in articulating the goal of experimental science as creating an "all-powerful man" (*l'homme tout-puissant*) who can spread justice and liberty throughout the world. Our goal as human beings, he explains, is to "pénétrer le pourquoi des choses, pour devenir supérieur aux choses" (penetrate the why of things, in order to rule over them).[16] In *Le Docteur Pascal* (1893), the last novel of the Rougon-Macquart, in which the eponymous character develops his scientific theories of heredity, Zola is even more succinct in describing his utopic fantasy of mastery: "tout dire pour tout connaître pour tout guérir" (say everything in order to know everything in order to cure everything).[17] It follows quite simply that if female sexuality is the originary wound, then female sexuality must be mastered, dominated, and controlled, a task not unfamiliar to the late nineteenth-century writer and scientist. It is possible to read *Nana* as the accomplishment of this task: the description of sexuality as a disease that the author ultimately vanquishes through Nana's terrible death, seen as her destructive sexual force ultimately turned against her own body. The situation of this disease in the body of a prostitute echoes a trend that began earlier in the century and would continue in both realist and popular literature, in which the prostitute was depicted as social scourge.[18]

Through much of the novel, however, Nana's threat comes not only from her unbridled sexuality but also from the possibility that science, or any male-authorized framework, will not be able to determine her. She first appears in the text playing the role of Venus in the theater producer Bordenave's production of *La Blonde Vénus.* From the moment of her *entrée en scène* she is a subversive presence, not just through her overwhelming sexuality but through her rejection of the carefully chosen frameworks meant to showcase her. In the first paragraphs of the novel, the journalist Fauchery proclaims: "Nana est une invention de Bordenave" (Nana is Bordenave's invention) (32). The dubiousness of this statement, uttered by the character who most represents the novel's authorial voice, is proven almost immediately and quickly points out a central tension of the novel: who controls the terms of Nana's performance? In fact, Bordenave has been preparing *le tout Paris* for Nana's arrival, with large yellow posters "avec le nom de Nana en grosses lettres noires" (with Nana's name in bold black letters) around the city (33). His role in what is fundamentally Nana's prostitution is stated outright as he insists that the theater be called his *bordel,* and as Fauchery refers to "votre Nana" (your Nana). Yet as Nana appears on stage, laughing at the audience with her entrance, it becomes clear that she is an invention of none other than herself. "Est-ce une plaisanterie, quelque gageure de Bordenave?" (Is it a joke, some gag of Bordenave's?) the narrator asks (42). But it is Nana's own joke; she gazes out to her audience, "ayant l'air de dire elle-même d'un clignement d'yeux qu'elle n'avait pas de talent pour deux liards, mais que ça ne faisait rien" (looking as if she herself [were] saying with a wink that she didn't have two cents' worth of talent, but that it didn't matter) (43).

This innocuous laughter is soon subsumed by something terrifying in a different way: the performance reaches its climax in the final act, when Nana appears to be completely nude, "n'ayant pour voile que ses cheveux" (with no veil except her hair) (54). At this point the relationship between spectators and performer is completely transformed, bringing the laughter to a halt.[19] Indeed, Nana's physical presence effectively dissolves the psychological barrier separating the spectators from the spectacle, or the viewers from the object of their gaze. Her body implicates the male viewers by eliciting their untamed desires; they are transformed from individuals into a joint male victim, their faces grave and tense, "la bouche irritée et sans salive" (their mouths dry and irritated) (53).[20] Bordenave's insistence that his theater be a bordello becomes literalized as the spectators are implicated in a sexual encounter with the actress on stage. As the narrative continues, the male spectators, captured in their desire, become the spectacle, framed by their own act of looking. Fauchery, who as a critic supplies an authorial voice within the text that mimics Zola's own voice, is supposed to be reviewing Nana's performance but instead turns his gaze on his fellow audience members. His attention to the consuming pleasure of the men around him, from the very pale Count of Vandeuvres to "l'échappé de collège que la passion soulevait de son fauteuil" (the truant school boy who was drawn out of his seat by passion) and "Daguenet dont les oreilles saignaient et remuaient de jouissance" (Daguenet whose ears flushed and shook with pleasure) (54) seems to be the only thing preventing him from becoming consumed as well. This is one of our first indexes to Nana's power over discursive frames, as Fauchery is driven to turn away from the female object of his analysis to record the effects of her behavior on men who come into contact with her.

Nana's effect on her spectators reveals her defiance of the boundaries constructed for her performance. As she laughs at the audience, it is almost as if she is laughing at their watching her and thus eerily participating in the spectacle while remaining also outside of it, viewing the men as a spectacle as well. This is the same position that she occupies within the mechanics of male desire. By appearing as Venus, goddess of love, she at once typifies male desire and asserts her liberty from its functioning. Even as she controls the men's reactions with every swing of her hips, Nana remains free from the imprints of the desire she evokes. As the scene closes, she is described as "victorieuse avec sa chair de marbre, son sexe assez fort pour détruire tout ce monde et n'en être pas entâmé" (victorious with her marble flesh, her sex strong enough to destroy all these people and not be affected by it) (7).[21]

Throughout the novel, Nana's clients—Steiner, Muffat, Georges, Fontan—attempt to assert their power over her sexual freedom through various means, ranging from financial promises to a series of marriage proposals. The futility of these efforts marks not only the failure of male control but Nana's refutation of the practice of male sexuality. Instead, Nana satisfies herself through various forms of self-love, through which she escapes any dependency on men and sidesteps their efforts to view her through a patriarchal framework. In the most explicit scene of autoseduction, Nana admires herself in the mirror while one of her lovers, the Count Muffat, reads an article by Fauchery describing Nana's debilitating effects on the entire city of Paris. The mirror that enables Nana's pleasure dramatically reinforces the exclusion of masculine desire from Nana's sexuality.[22] There is no room to imagine any mechanism of her arousal other than her own reflection. Furthermore, by examining herself in the mirror while Muffat looks on, Nana reveals her control over the scope of the male gaze. The mirror cuts off the man's view, allowing Nana to frame herself.[23] Autoeroticism for Nana means not only satisfying herself but also delighting in her plurality, in the various reflections of her grandeur. She is thrilled by her doubling before the mirror, taking pleasure not so much in seeing her image as in dancing with another version of herself. She kisses herself, "en riant à l'autre Nana, qui, elle aussi, se baisait dans la glace" (laughing with the other Nana, who was also kissing herself in the mirror) (217). This self-adoration cannot be separated from her various experiments with new identities—from the attempts to be a "femme chic" to the titillating exploration of Satin's lesbian underworld to her insistence on playing the "femme honnête" in Fauchery's new play. In this latter instance, Nana refuses to play the role Fauchery has written for her, thus once again stepping out of a male-authorized narrative framework. In reinventing herself, Nana does not forgo her previous existences. Rather than seeking to change her identity, she seems concerned with accumulating and increasing her identities and experiences a subversive pleasure in her magnitude. When Vandeuvres tells her he has renamed his horse for her, she is not upset in the least. Instead, she delights in this multiplication of herself and refers to the horse in the first person, asking, "A combien suis-je?" (How much do I go for?) (320) to find out the horse's betting rate.

Nana's unflinching preoccupation with her grandeur is vividly displayed in her reaction to Fauchery's brutal account of her destructive effects on Parisian society. When Daguenet admits to shielding the article from Nana to avoid upsetting her, she is bewildered. "Pourquoi?" she asks, "Il est très long, son article" (His article is very long) (214), flattered to have been mentioned in *Le Figaro.* She thus ignores Fauchery's fierce critique, instead reveling in the attention given to her. Here again, Nana slips from inside to outside of the discourse, commenting on a text about her while disturbingly ignoring its message; this position is highlighted once more when Nana hands the article to Muffat. Fauchery's journalistic signature visibly signals Zola's authorial presence, his article a *mise en abyme* of the novel, with passages lifted from Zola's own notes. The article is rich with naturalism's scientific moralism, telling the story of "une fille, née de quatre ou cinq générations d'ivrognes, le sang gâté par une longue hérédité de misère et de boisson, qui se transformait chez elle en un détraquement nerveux de son sexe de femme" (a prostitute, born of four or five generations of drunkards, her blood spoiled by a long heritage of misery and alcohol that was transformed in her into a nervous disorder of the female genitals) (215). Through Fauchery's article Nana's sex is most explicitly inculpated as a force of social destruction, in one of Zola's most brazenly misogynist moments: "Elle devenait une force de la nature, un ferment de destruction, sans le vouloir elle-même, corrompant et désorganisant Paris entre ses cuisses de neige, le faisant tourner comme des femmes, chaque mois, font tourner le lait" (She became a force of nature, a ferment of destruction, without meaning to, corrupting and disorganizing Paris between her snowy thighs, making it turn just as women make milk curdle each month) (215). And yet, despite the presence of this incisive commentary on female morbidity, Nana remains unscathed, only blithely amused by her power.

As Muffat reads the article, however, he watches his subject before him and for the first time clearly recognizes her danger, seeing himself "empoisonné," his family destroyed, and social structures crumbling to the ground (216). Yet rather than being empowered by his newfound epistemological advantage, following Zola's logic that *connaître* (knowing) will lead to *maîtriser* (mastering), Muffat is ultimately crippled by the disjunction between what he has understood and what he sees before him: the innocent young girl. Staring at Nana, Muffat moves from the reality of her body to his own thoughts—"son ancienne horreur de la femme" (his old horror of woman)—relying on Fauchery's terms to assimilate the creature before him: "C'était la bête d'or, inconsciente comme une force, et dont l'odeur seule gâtait le monde" (It was the golden beast, unconscious like a natural force, and whose odor alone spoiled the world) (217). Finally closing his eyes to escape the image of what he sees, he cannot, because what is traumatizing is not his vision but what he believes he is seeing. Even with the lioness imprinted on Muffat's eyelids, Nana slides back into the young girl before him, still prancing unsuspectingly with herself.

This, it seems, is what Nana symbolizes for the male imagination: that which exceeds his imagination. Ultimately the naturalist discourse of Fauchery's article fails to determine Nana, or to explain her essential plurality, and she slips past its analytical grip, refusing to be mastered or understood. Zola seems willing here, midpoint in the novel, to acknowledge the limits of science to contain the threat of female sexuality. For his novel to reach its climax of social destruction caused by Nana, he must represent the horrific triumph of female sexuality—at least temporarily—over discourse: even with Fauchery's accurate critique, men still flock to the *mouche d'or*, and even when they recognize her destructive power they cannot escape its effects.

This is not the only instance where Nana challenges Zola's own project. Later she comments on the very possibility for *Nana* the novel to exist.

> Elle avait lu dans la journée un roman qui faisait grand bruit, l'histoire d'une fille; et elle se révoltait, elle disait que tout cela était faux, témoignant d'ailleurs une répugnance indignée contre cette littérature immonde, dont la prétention était de rendre la nature; comme si l'on pouvait tout montrer! (318)[24]

> [She had read during the day a novel that was causing quite a stir, the story of a prostitute; and she was outraged, she said that it was all false, and she showed moreover an indignant repugnance toward this lowly literature whose pretension was to render nature; as if one could show all!]

Although unfazed by Fauchery's article, Nana is outraged by the idea of a novel about a prostitute; it is as if fiction is more threatening than reality. It is especially interesting that Zola articulates the challenge to his naturalism in the voice of his protagonist. On one hand, any critique suggested by Nana must be disregarded as facile and unsophisticated. In this vein, Zola underlines her literary naiveté in the passage, noting that she had "des opinions très arrêtées" (very fixed opinions) and a typically feminine reading sensibility: "elle voulait des oeuvres tendres et nobles, des choses pour la faire rêver et lui grandir l'âme" (she wanted tender and noble works, things to make her dream and elevate her soul) (318). Her general lack of subtlety is further underlined as she continues to speak, affirming the strength of the emperor—whose coming ruin will coincide with her own.

Nana's affront to Zola's naturalist project can be seen differently, however, when considered in the larger context of the novel and the chapter in which it is situated. In this wider view, her comment seems out of character, a singular refusal to recognize herself in the midst of a particularly solipsistic chapter. In addition to describing her narcissistic romps with Satin, the surrounding passages introduce the horse named for her; they then culminate with a moment of grandiose self-fetishization in which Nana's entire living room becomes an uncanny condensation of her, which she herself recognizes when she stands frozen before it, "comme si elle avait oublié et qu'elle fût rentrée dans un endroit inconnu" (as if she had forgotten and had come back to an unfamiliar place) (324). The description of her salon, its furniture, its odor, and the sensation it evokes concludes: "C'était un élargissement d'elle-même, de ses besoins de domination et de jouissance, de son envie de tout avoir pour tout détruire. Jamais elle n'avait senti si profondément la force de son sexe" (It was an enlargement of herself, of her need for domination and pleasure, of her desire to have everything in order to destroy everything. Never had she felt as profoundly the power of her sex) (324). Nana, in this description, seems potently and accurately aware of her sexual power, and willing to recognize its presence. Her desires—"tout avoir pour tout détruire"—are in symmetric opposition to Zola's own as summed up in *Le Docteur Pascal*—"tout dire pour tout connaître pour tout guérir" (say everything in order to know everything in order to cure everything) (147). Yet the insistence on the "tout" also showcases the similarity between Zola and his protagonist in their totalitarian ambitions. She is the dystopia to his utopia.

In this context, Zola's playful inscription of Nana as literary critic and her unique unwillingness to recognize her own reflection in the realist novel stand out. They reinforce the possibility that Nana herself is the greatest obstacle to Zola's naturalist project and point to the disturbing tension between author and female subject. If the realist novel relating the *histoire d'une fille* refers to *Nana* itself, Nana the woman is placed once again both inside and outside the discourse Zola has authorized, thus betraying Zola's anxiety about being able to represent completely (read: master) his protagonist in her fantasmatic implications.

Indeed, Nana's disdain for the idea that one could *tout montrer* in a book about her can be seen as a direct challenge to Zola's literary ideal and allows her a rare glimpse of subjectivity that dramatically restages the relationship of male author to female subject. When Nana says "comme si l'on pouvait tout montrer" (as if one could show all) the *on* she calls up is the voice of male discursive authority—he who writes naturalist novels—and she poses this voice against the knowledge of the *fille* herself—the only one qualified to judge the authenticity of his novels. For a fleeting moment Zola allows to rise to the surface something more frightening than Nana's destructive sex: the possibility that a woman like her could have a critical voice, a voice that could know something about female sexuality much different from (and more authentic than?) his own determinations.

As I demonstrate in the Introduction, the nineteenth-century fascination with female sexuality and its volatility stems from a concern over the fragile relationship between the female mind and body. Evelyne Ender has argued that nineteenth-century medical literature on hysteria betrays a profound anxiety about female sexual knowledge, revealing a concern that "the privilege of knowing, and especially of knowing about the sexual, the erotic . . . , must remain within the male province."[25] According to Ender, the hysterical female (i.e., she who has read too many novels) can be defined as one who knows too much about sex. Hysteria thus becomes a bodily translation of, and reaction to, a cognitive state. This lack of sexual innocence is indeed part of the hysteric's titillating literary and cultural appeal and is all the more apt for the characterization of the prostitute, who surpasses the hysteric as a woman with too much sexual knowledge.[26] But this implied knowledge remains inaccessible and unrepresentable in *Nana* and through its inaccessibility fuels the narrative dynamic even more so than the hidden genitals that critics have pursued.[27] Indeed, this factor contributes to the novel's underlying dramatic tension: Zola wants to show and tell all—*tout montrer*—yet only a prostitute herself would have access to this information. For this reason, Nana's repudiation of the *histoire d'une fille* might be as unsettling for its author as any aspect of her devouring femininity. In fact, Zola was well aware of the relevance of the prostitute's experience. In preparing his novel, he researched and interviewed several famous courtesans. Yet the one detail he most blatantly ignores about these women is their intelligence, the sharpness necessary to succeed in this competitive domain. Thus the critic Paul de Saint-Victor, a contemporary of Zola, complained that Zola did not "understand the richness, complexity, and originality of the courtesan and her world."[28]

The extent of Nana's subjective awareness of her actions and of the power of her sexuality is one of the most enigmatic aspects of the novel. Is she a *femme fatale,* as she appears in her salon, conscious of the "power of her sex"? Or is she an innocent *bonne fille,* childlike and ignorant of her power? Zola, reassuringly perhaps, insists on her naïveté as the novel closes. At the end of the penultimate chapter, she is described as maintaining "son inconscience de bête superbe, ignorante de sa besogne, bonne fille toujours" (the unconsciousness of a great beast, ignorant of her work, still the good girl) (422). Yet this description seems to contradict much of what has just preceded. Nana's manipulations and subversions of male authorized frameworks undermine the effects of her naïve innocence. Through his inability to determine Nana's subjectivity, to exact the relationship between the *bonne fille* and the *femme fatale,* Zola leaves open the possibility that she has a subjectivity that exists outside of the male economy, which cannot be interpreted or controlled through male authorized discourse.[29] Within Zola's writing, then, is this subtle acknowledgment that female sexuality, and female subjectivity, also exist outside of Zola's imagination, and that there are aspects of female sexuality that man cannot penetrate. Nana's continued reinvention and pleasure in her plurality, in seeing herself in many discursive frames, points to an extradiagetic threat more chilling than her social destructiveness: she is a threat to the male imagination, a threat to the possibility for men to determine female sexuality through discourse.

This particular threat puts into perspective the incapacitation of the sexually deviant female body as an enabling force for the discourse that produces it. In this novel, Nana's annihilation is a necessary violence that hides the fact that the naturalist scientist cannot *tout dire* or *tout montrer,* except by disabling the object of his gaze. As the novel closes, Nana's threat quietly dissipates; she disappears, swallowed by competing legends of her whereabouts. Ultimately the only way for Nana to be discursively determined is through her death, which saves Paris from further decay but also saves Zola from the threat of Nana's subjectivity. At this point scientific discourse finally prevails, and Zola is able to use his medical research to offer a terrifying clinical description of Nana's decomposing corpse.[30] In her death, Nana cannot refute the narrator's description or undermine it through her giggles. The author can safely confirm Fauchery's theory of Nana as social scourge, concluding that the virus she picked up in the gutters had come back to poison her as well. Nana's death also confirms Zola's experiment:

he has discovered the *plaie grave* and demonstrated its destructive force. Although Nana has clearly infected others with her genitals—as Fauchery had communicated in his description of the golden fly—it is striking that her face alone bares the disease's disastrous effects. In particular, Nana's eyes are destroyed, one literally becoming a rotting black hole—"un trou noir et gâté" (438). Readers have traditionally interpreted this loss as a Freudian "displacement upward."[31] I would suggest a more literal reading. Perhaps equally important to the empowerment of Zola's discourse as the expunging of his protagonist's subversive bodily threat was the elimination of her ability to see, and thus to know.

PROSTITUTION AND THE WOMAN WRITER

When women wrote novels at the end of the nineteenth century, they radically altered a primary aspect of dominant literary discourses: the relationship between the male author and the female subject. From Balzac's physiological narrator earlier in the century, voyeuristically noting women's mysterious qualities, to the Goncourts' scientific documentation of Germinie Lacerteux to Barbey d'Aurevilly's old-boys club communal storytelling about diabolical women, this relationship was a critical narrative device woven into the thematics of much nineteenth-century fiction. Furthermore, the very act of a woman writing challenged the presuppositions about femininity that subtended fin-de-siècle realist fiction and pervaded its intellectual culture. According to popular distinctions, discursive authority was necessarily male, while female language was irrational, veering toward the hysterical. This dichotomy repeats the fundamental gender hierarchy of fin-de-siècle scientific discourse, which relied in part on the empowerment of the male voice through the study of women's bodies. While male discourse contributed to science and knowledge, women's voices were inscrutable on their own; they could be filtered only through the voice of male authority.[32] Medical doctrine consistently affirmed this intellectual hierarchy, contrasting women's emotional instincts to man's capacity for reason. Thus, Alexandre Mayer writes, in a typical example: "La femme accomplit par instinct, avec facilité, une multitude de choses auxquelles nous n'arrivons pas aussi sûrement par la réflexion; mais nous lui sommes incontestablement supérieurs dans tout ce qui demande de l'application et du raisonnement, comme dans l'interprétation des lois de la nature, dans la philosophie et les sciences mathématiques" (Woman accomplishes by instinct, with ease, a multitude of things that we would not arrive at as surely by reflection; but we are incontestably superior to her in all that requires application and reasoning, such as in the interpretation of the laws of nature, philosophy or mathematical science).[33]

In this context, it is understandable that women's writing would be fundamentally alien to nineteenth-century science as well as to the literary movements it so influenced. When women did write, not only could their writings not be assimilated into patriarchal discursive categories but they were often perceived as a threat in much the same way as female sexuality was. Hence, as more women became writers in the last decades of the nineteenth century, a corpus of novels and plays was dedicated to ridiculing and scandalizing their type, including Albert Cim's *Emancipées* (1889) and *Bas-bleus* (1891), Paul Hervieu's *Les Tenailles* (1896), Maurice Donnay's *L'Affranchie* (1898), and Marcel Prévost's *Les Vierges fortes* (1908). In Barbey D'Aurevilly's *Les Bas-bleus,* published in 1878 as part of his series Les Oeuvres et les hommes, the author describes women writers through images of social disintegration leading to the downfall of civilization. He views women writers as a vice, a product of the moral depravity of the era, and compares their effect on French society to that of prostitution in other civilizations, announcing a breakdown of the family structure and traditional patriarchal power hierarchies: "Beaucoup de peuples sont morts pourris par des courtisanes, mais les courtisanes sont dans la nature et les Bas-bleus n'y sont pas! Ils sont dans une civilisation dépravée, dégradée, qui meurt de l'être, et telle que, dans l'histoire, on n'en avait pas vu encore" (A lot of peoples have died out, extinguished by courtesans, but courtesans are in nature and the *bas-bleus* are not! They are part of a depraved, degraded civilization that is dying from being this way, such that has never before been seen in history).[34] From this perspective, not only does the character of Nana represent the male writer's view of deviant female sexual behavior as a threat to male authority but she becomes a metaphor for the woman writer as a threat to the social order and patriarchal institutions.

The political ideology linking the woman writer to the breakdown of the family is not hard to identify. Humiliated by the loss of the Franco-Prussian War, France was concerned with producing healthy boys and reversing the downward population trend.[35] The moral implications of sexual behavior were often tied to this social and political aspect of public health, as explicitly expressed in the introduction to Mayer's text on conjugal relations, where he protests contraceptive behavior (*l'onanisme conjugal*) as acts that "altèrent la santé, dépravent les moeurs, et, en fin de compte, diminuent la *natalité*" (alter health, contribute to moral depravity, and finally, diminish the *birth rate*).[36] Women writers, it was believed, were refusing their moral imperatives as wives and mothers and contributing to social degeneration. Barbey's comments are thus perfectly consistent with the representation of femininity in Zola's novel. As the text closes, the destruction of Paris between Nana's thighs announces the disgrace of the Franco-Prussian War, just as in Barbey's view the depravity of women writers augurs the downfall of French familial structures buttressing society.

Again and again, this reference to the bodily danger of the woman writer—the danger, that is, of the prostitute—masked the underlying question of her intellectual potential, leaving it safely unanswered while calling up the ghost of Parent-Duchatelet.[37] Jules Bertaut invokes this fear toward the end of *La Littérature féminine d'aujourd'hui,* one of a series of books addressing the perceived crisis of women's authorship, in which he addresses the quality of recent women's fiction. He describes the choice of women as being between "la mission de femme et de mère" (the mission of wife and mother) and "l'émancipation totale qu'elle mène depuis plusieurs années" (the total emancipation she has been pursuing for several years).[38] In Bertaut's terms, this emancipatory movement is neither political nor intellectual but sexual: a quest for "une jouissance plus immédiate" (a more immediate pleasure). Describing a women's movement determined by "le droit au bonheur" (the right to happiness), he writes:

> Ce que l'on veut, c'est la somme la plus grande de liberté qui se puisse accorder, précisément pour en user et en abuser au mieux de l'assouvissement de tous les instincts. Ce que l'on veut, c'est qu'aucune entrave ne vienne plus gêner les inclinations, les passions, toute la gamme des désirs malsains et des penchants troubles—sous prétexte d'un affranchissement glorieux![39]
>
> [What they want is the greatest amount of freedom that could be allotted, precisely in the interest of using and abusing it to best satisfy all their impulses. What they want is for no obstacle to get in the way of their inclinations, their passions, the whole spectrum of unhealthy desires and troubling penchants—under the pretext of a glorious liberation!]

The woman writer whose intellectual merit the critic had initially set out to determine has now been transformed into a full-fledged *femme fatale* seeking only her own sensual satisfaction. Barbey embraces this same principle when he invites the reader to sample any piece of female art and discover for himself its poor quality: "Etudiez leurs oeuvres et ouvrez-les au hasard! A la dixième ligne, et sans savoir de qui elles sont, vous êtes prévenu; vous sentez la femme! *Odor di femina*" (Study their works and open them at random! On the tenth line, and without knowing who they are, you are warned, you smell woman! *Odor di femina*).[40] Barbey summons his readers to study women's works, but this seems impossible according to his own terms: the male reader is instantly overcome by his own senses. He smells femininity (an odor that, like that of the prostitute, invokes morbidity): the female body manifests itself before he can analyze the female mind. In yet another similar example, in Cim's *Bas-bleus* inspired by Barbey, women writers are arrested for prostitution.

This link between female authorship and prostitution in the nineteenth-century imagination invites us to read both the prostitute and the woman writer differently. On one hand, Nana's uncontainable sexuality becomes a metaphor for the female mind and its ideas spreading their contagion through books. On the other hand, the anxiety surrounding female sexuality in Zola's *Nana* is the force against which the fin-de-siècle fiction woman was obligated to write. In this sense her novel was as unreadable as Nana's inscrutable body: just as glimpsing the Medusa's head turned the male viewer to stone and according to Freud threatened castration, approaching the female body or the woman's text, determining one or the other, threatened both virility and male intellectual prowess. Indeed, alongside the extensive exploration of the horrors of prostitution in fin-de-siècle fiction, women's intellectual transgression (through the assertion of intellect or subjectivity) represented an equally unspeakable truth, that which—like the woman's body—had to be covered over, refuted, or criminalized through the language of illicit sexuality. By comparing the woman writer to the prostitute and by linking them in the fin-de-siècle imagination, male critics and writers exploited this well-documented social scourge while avoiding addressing the seemingly pivotal question of female intellect. This slippage suggests that just as Nana's subjectivity ultimately proves as frightening to Zola as her oversexed body, the uncharted threat of the woman writer seems to have been as daunting—if not more so—to the fin-de-siècle man as that of the prostitute.

2

Memoirs of the *Fille Publique*

A la mémoire des deux grands écrivains Pierre-Joseph Proudhon et Jules Barbey d'Aurevilly . . . qui, tous les deux, ont si éloquemment célébré les femmes d'intérieur, et si vigoureusement fouaillé
Toutes celles qui—femme de plume, de club, ou de rue,
N'aspirent qu'à devenir "publiques."

[In memory of the two great writers Pierre-Joseph Proudhon and Jules Barbey d'Aurevilly . . . who both so eloquently celebrated women who stay home, and so vigorously lashed out at
Those women—of the pen, the club, or the street
Who only aspire to become "public."]

—Albert Cim, dedication to the novel *Bas-bleus,* 1891

In the middle of *Nana,* when the eponymous character comments on a novel she has just read, "the story of a prostitute," she scoffs at the attempt at realism. The irony in this episode is that Zola has his character comment on the very book she is starring in, so to speak; it is as if Nana had read *Nana* and disapproved.[1] We can safely assume that the realist novel Nana had read was written by a man. But what if this book had been written by a woman? Would Nana have had the same reaction? Did she believe it impossible to portray reality in fiction, or did she simply find it impossible to conceive of a man's faithfully conveying the details of the prostitute's existence? Or, more to the point, how does the narration of the story by the prostitute herself alter the story that is told, as well as the way it must be read?

In this chapter, I answer that question by considering three autobiographical novels by women whose identities were determined by their public role: Liane de Pougy's *Idylle saphique* (1901), Renée Vivien's *Une Femme m'apparut* (1904), and Colette's *La Vagabonde* (1910).[2] All of these novels can be described as memoirs of the *fille publique,* one of the figurative terms used for the prostitute in the nineteenth century.[3] I adopt this term here to call attention to the way public female roles were associated with sexual promiscuity in fin-de-siècle discourse, such that in the public imagination little distinction in social status was made among the performer (dancer or actress), the courtesan, and the woman writer.[4] A *fille publique* is thus a woman whose identity is determined entirely by the fantasmatic relationship to her sex. Against this backdrop, autobiographical writing was a means for Pougy, Colette, and Vivien to construct alternative selves that acted against the associations of their public personae. These memoirs of the *fille publique* actively promote female intellect, even as they unapologetically enter the dubious domains of the courtesan (Liane de Pougy), the music hall dancer (Colette), and the lesbian writer (Renée Vivien).

Pougy, Vivien, and Colette were all in their own ways manifestations of the New Woman, that illustrious female rebel who consumed the French imagination in the 1890s and early 1900s. The New Woman constructed an identity beyond her traditional domestic destiny while rejecting the feminist movement. According to Mary Louise Roberts, the reason for this rejection may have been that many Belle Epoque feminists hinged their demands for equal rights on their contributions as wives and mothers. The New Woman instead expressed her resistance to patriarchal structures by performing a variety of "disruptive acts," often in journalism, theater, and dance, through which she gained financial independence and invented new female roles beyond the private sphere.[5] I read the memoirs of the *fille publique* as another form of disruptive act for their authors, whose lives were filled with the kinds of behavior associated with the New Woman. At the same time, their performances of alternative femininities constantly left these women open to ridicule and denigration by the new urban mass culture that fed their celebrity and from which they profited financially. A large element of this culture was the mass press, which in Vanessa Schwartz's terms "acted as a printed digest of the flâneur's roving eye."[6] The women's autobiographical novels that I examine here attempt to control their authors' public images. In each novel the process of becoming a writer is bound up with the search for an ideal reader who will appreciate the female protagonist for her mind rather than view her through the fantasmatic associations of the *fille publique.*

According to Roberts, the New Woman was largely an Anglo-American import. For Pougy, Colette, and Vivien (who was herself a British import) this influence was enacted largely through the same woman: the self-described Amazon poet Natalie Clifford Barney. A young American heiress from the Midwest, Barney arrived in Paris in 1899 and almost immediately became smitten with the famous courtesan Pougy, whom she spotted walking through the promenades of the Bois de Boulogne.[7] Their affair lasted, in varying degrees of intensity, over several years and inspired Pougy's *Idylle saphiqe,* which appeared in 1901, where Barney appears as Flossie. During Pougy's absence with one of her male protectors, Barney met Renée Vivien, whose real name was Pauline Tarn. Barney became Renée's on-again-off-again lover, as well as the "N" to whom Vivien's first collection of poetry, *Etudes et préludes,* also from 1901, was dedicated. Around the same time, Barney met Colette and her husband, Willy, in the Comtesse de Chabanne's Parisian salon. Colette and Barney had their own brief affair, with Willy's tacit approval, although Barney considered her a "half" conquest rather than a "full" one.[8] She later made an appearance as the character Flossie in Colette's *Claudine* series, and Barney and Colette remained close friends throughout their lives.[9]

These women's relationships reflect the incestuous dynamics and amicable rivalry of the "Tout Lesbos," the lesbian subculture of the "Tout Paris" that flourished in the early 1900s and inspired a sizable corpus of women's writing.[10] For all three writers, the Tout Lesbos was an escape from domestic expectations of society and family, a virtual safe haven for their disruptive acts. Consequently, their social, personal, and artistic lives constantly overlapped and intertwined. To give just a few brief examples: Colette's theatrical debut took place in Barney's garden with Evalina Palmer, one of Vivien's beloved muses, with whom she studied Greek in an effort to emulate Sappho; shortly thereafter, Colette stayed with Vivien on a visit to Nice and attended a party with Liane de Pougy; Pougy was a former mistress of Auguste Hériot, who later became Colette's lover and an inspiration for Max Dufferein-Chautel in *La Vagabonde;* Colette was Vivien's neighbor and wrote a portrait of her in *Le Pur et l'impur* (1932); Colette and Willy, though no longer married, attended Liane de Pougy's wedding to the Romanian prince Georges Ghika in 1910, days before *La Vagabonde* was published.[11] Lucie Delarue-Mardrus, whose novel *Marie, fille-mère* I consider in Chapter 3, mingled in this world as well. Delarue-Mardrus also had an affair with Natalie Barney and wrote a novel about it (*L'Ange et les pervers,* 1930) and may have had an affair with Renée Vivien too. She and her husband, Joseph-Charles Mardrus, appear as Mr. and Mrs. Petrus in Vivien's *Une Femme m'apparut,* where Vivien laments her friend's submission to heterosexuality. Traditionally, Colette alone has been credited with what Jacob Stockinger describes as having "wrested the lesbian tradition from male authors," just as she alone succeeded in entering the French literary canon.[12] In their lifetimes, however, Pougy, Vivien, and Colette were peers, sometimes friends and sometimes rivals; they experienced comparable levels of fame, fortune, and critical attention. Together, their novels reveal an entirely new role for the lesbian in fin-de-siècle fiction.[13]

In analyzing these texts I use the category of autobiographical novel in the broadest sense to mean fictional novels based at least in part on the lives of their authors, although names and details may be substantially altered.[14] *Une Femme m'apparut* and *La Vagabonde* are told in the first person, *Idylle saphique* in the third person. Despite this formal difference, Pougy's novel, written close to the time of the actual events recounted, may even have been a kind of diary. The autobiographical element in women's writing has often been overemphasized, reinforcing assumptions like that of the early twentieth-century literary critic Jean Larnac, who in 1929 published one of the first histories of French women writers. He comments: "Au centre de tout roman féminin, on découvre l'auteur. . . . Incapables d'abstraire ainsi un fragment d'elles-mêmes pour en constituer un tout, il leur faut se mettre tout entières dans leur oeuvre" (In the center of every women's novel, one discovers the author. . . . Incapable of abstracting a fragment of themselves in order to constitute a whole, they must put themselves entirely in their work").[15] My intention in offering biographical details like the ones above is certainly not to reduce these women's work to autobiographical distillations of their lives. Instead, I present this information here and in later chapters as a form of what Jo Burr Margadant has described as "the new biography," which considers identities as "mobile, contested, multiple constructions of the self and others that depend as much on context as any defining traits of character."[16] Taken together with their writings, these biographical details display the challenges and contradictions inherent in their subjects' confrontations with fin-de-siècle notions of femininity and authorship. For Pougy, Vivien, and Colette, the overlapping circumstances of their lives suggest that their works were in dialogue with each other, while also revealing that these women were significant not only as writers but also as the kind of readers—ideal or otherwise—that each sought out through her fiction.

ZOLA'S WORST NIGHTMARE: THE COURTESAN WRITES A NOVEL

At the time *Idylle saphique* was published in 1901, Liane de Pougy was the sweetheart of Paris's demi-monde, on her way to becoming known in the popular press as a national treasure, "notre Liane nationale."[17] More than a decade earlier, Pougy had abandoned her bourgeois existence as Anne-Marie Pourpe, dissatisfied wife and unprepared mother, after her husband caught her having an affair with a marine lieutenant.[18] Leaving her two-year-old son behind, she quickly and skillfully reinvented herself as one of Paris's most sought-after courtesans and one of an elite few known as a "horizontale de grande marque."[19] Pougy became a celebrity whose image circulated in the press, on posters—some advertising her performances in the Folies-Bergères—and on international postcards and cigarette boxes. Her romantic peregrinations were adoringly documented in journals such as the *Gil Blas,* where some of her novels would appear in *feuilleton* and for which she was later a columnist.[20] Like that of many of her female peers, Pougy's entry into the literary world was facilitated by her link to a man with literary capital, the decadent writer and her close friend Jean Lorrain.[21] But Pougy's subject matter—the somber inner life of a famous courtesan, coupled with recognizable descriptions of her former lovers—virtually insured success: her first novel *L'Insaisissable* (1898) went through over twenty editions and sold over eighteen thousand copies in two years.[22]

Despite her impressive record (*Myrhille,* another bestseller, appeared in 1899), Pougy had some difficulty publishing *Idylle saphique* because of its content. In it, the famous courtesan represents herself as the character Annhine, or Nhine, to tell the story of her well-known romantic relationship with Natalie Clifford Barney, here as the character Flossie.[23] While lesbians had already populated male-authored fictions of the fin-de-siècle in large numbers and salacious detail, the presence of this theme in an autobiographical novel by a woman struck a hidden taboo. Fearing legal repercussions, the *Gil Blas* refused to print it; Pougy's secretary, Henry Albert, finally persuaded Karl Boès, editor of the *Librairie de la Plume* to take on the novel.[24] Although contemporary critics generally dismiss *Idylle saphique* as lacking in literary merit, at the time of the novel's publication, Pougy's personal style was recognized, within limits, for its own charm. An article in the *Gil Blas* (though the editors refused to publish the novel, they were happy to comment on it) complimented Pougy's style and described the novel as containing "la si originale tournure de phrase et d'esprit dont on parle beaucoup et que l'on connaît vraiment si peu" (That very original phrasing and spirit that is talked so much about but so little known).[25]

Pougy's story of the courtesan's encounter with lesbianism, only minimally titillating, is moving and full of pathos as it relates a complex emotional struggle that is not fully resolved even as the text closes. Yet more important to our concerns here, *Idylle saphique* stands against a French tradition of literary representations of the prostitute as a degraded figure, whose body wears the signs of society's own degeneration. Balzac, Maupassant, Barbey, the Goncourts, Zola, and Huysmans all offered portraits of this *fille publique,* whose demise is often clinically recorded in their texts. As in these authors' works, Pougy's text ends with the courtesan's death (disrupting the autobiographical trajectory), and decadent themes layer the novel. Recent criticism has focused on the presence of fin-de-siècle associations between femininity and morbidity in the text.[26] I believe, however, that rather than read Pougy's novel through the lens of late nineteenth-century decadent fiction and its concomitant anxieties about the female body, we must read it as an incisive commentary on them. Indeed, the overlooked significance

Figure 2. Postcard of Liane de Pougy, 1905. (Courtesy of Mary Evans Picture Library.)

of this novel is two-fold: first, it lies in the efforts of the protagonist to sever her mind and soul from her body—through the aid of the lesbian relationship—in order to carve out an identity untainted by her profession. These efforts challenge widely held assumptions about femininity and the female body in fin-de-siècle medical and social discourse. Second, the protagonist's efforts are significant in that they are ultimately realized through the recourse to writing itself—an intellectual assertion that speaks directly against this male-authorized discourse. When these aspects of the novel are considered more closely, Pougy's critical voice comes into sharper relief. Her novel can be recognized as far more than just the *histoire d'une fille;* instead, it is a glimpse of the extent to which fin-de-siècle views of femininity obstructed the expression of female intellect and provides proof of one woman's unexpected struggle to think beyond these notions.

Pougy's novel follows Nhine's homoerotic friendship with Flossie (Natalie Clifford Barney). While the extent of their physical contact remains vague, Flossie seduces Nhine and they become, at least temporarily, inseparable, frequenting parties and spending long evenings together. When Flossie's former lover Jane kills herself after spotting the new couple, Nhine falls ill and is sent away to rest. During this time, Nhine and Flossie begin an epistolary correspondence that rekindles their unresolved romantic tension. But their brief reunion is followed by the return of Nhine's illness, which disrupts Flossie's plan to adopt Nhine into her planned marriage to Will, her fiancé, and ultimately leads to Nhine's death.[27]

Nhine's fundamental obstacle at the novel's opening can be described as a problem of seeing herself. Just as Nana does not recognize herself in the fictional work before her, Nhine's fundamental unhappiness at the start of *Idylle saphique* stems from the disjunction between her self-image and the one offered to her by contemporary society. Such an image is embraced by her confidante Tesse (a character based on Valtesse de la Bigne, one of the models for Zola's novel).[28] The novel opens with Nhine confiding her feelings of boredom to Tesse, echoing the feelings of her nineteenth-century romantic predecessors: "Ah! Tesse, Tesse, que je suis lasse de vivre!" (Ah! Tesse, Tesse, how weary I am of living!), she exclaims. "Que je m'ennuie!" (How bored I am!).[29] Tesse attempts to cheer her sorrowful friend by sharing her own philosophy. Rather than suffering weariness with the world, Tesse sees herself in a privileged position:

> Je suis heureuse parce que je le veux, parce que le jour où je me suis faite courtisane j'ai rayé de ma vie tout souvenir, toute attache, la moindre obligation, j'ai abdiqué ce qu'on appelle de la sensibilité d'âme. Pour moi il n'existe plus de devoirs ni aucune responsibilité qu'envers moi-même et mon désir! Quelle indépendance, quelle enivrante liberté! . . . Une cour-

> tisane peut tout faire sans voiles . . . sans craindre le moindre reproche ou blâme, car rien ne la touche! . . . Rebelle victorieuse! (17–18).
>
> [I am happy because I want to be, because the day that I made myself a courtesan I erased from my life all memory, all attachment, the least obligation; I abdicated what they call sensitivity of the soul. I no longer have any duty or any responsibility except to myself and my desires! What independence, what intoxicating freedom! . . . A courtesan can do everything without hiding . . . without fearing the slightest reproach or blame, for nothing can touch her! . . . Victorious rebel!]

This glorification of the life of the courtesan reads like the voice of fin-de-siècle fiction; this is the description we might expect Nana to offer of her lifestyle. Tesse, whom the narrator later describes using verses from a Baudelaire poem, represents the fin-de-siècle stereotype of the courtesan, and—to Nhine's consternation—she consistently responds to Nhine's angst with prejudices that conform to such a perspective.[30]

Tesse's initial comment signals the fundamental issue at the heart of Nhine's identity crisis: the conflict between her mind and her body. Tesse admits to having sacrificed subjectivity, interiority, and emotional depth in favor of her existence as a courtesan and tries to cheer Nhine by pointing her back to outside appearances. Ignoring the internal strife, she reminds Nhine of her external beauty and essentially holds up a mirror to her through her response: "N'as-tu pas de l'or dans tes cheveux? . . . N'as-tu pas du ciel dans tes yeux? Des perles à ton cou et dans ta bouche rose? . . . Ne philosophons plus, jouons!" (Don't you have gold in your hair? . . . Don't you have the sky in your eyes? Pearls at your neck and in your rosy mouth? . . . Let's not philosophize any more, let's play!) (16). But Nhine's unwillingness to abdicate her interiority in the interest of her identity, her need, in fact, to philosophize, lands her in trouble: "Annhine avait une petite âme qui n'allait pas avec son corps! Elle pensait, elle analysait, elle avait une imagination vive, un esprit droit, une justesse d'observation très remarquable" (Annhine had a little soul that did not go with her body! She thought, she analyzed, she had a vivid imagination, an honest mind, a quite remarkable power of observation) (24). Unfortunately, these qualities are considered useless in the luxurious and hedonistic world of the Parisian courtesan. Indeed, the narrator suggests that none of Nhine's intellectual talents can be assimilated by her Parisian public, and, thus, her imagination and analytic capacity are interpreted as sickness, causing her friends to call her "déséquilibrée" (unstable). The conflict Nhine experiences is not wholly unlike that of the "prostitute with the heart of gold" found in the novels of Eugène Sue and Balzac. Upon renouncing their professions, both Sue's Fleur de Marie and Balzac's Esther struggle to overcome the degradation associated with their bodies, at odds with their newly purified spirits. Yet Nhine's challenge is distinct for at least two reasons. Nhine is not interested in renouncing her profession, or sexual desire generally; instead, she would like to maintain the integrity of her *âme* while still enjoying the pleasures of her body. Also, Nhine's particular conflict develops several decades after Sue and Balzac constructed their heroines, and as such reckons with the more pathologized notion of femininity by this point pervasive in social and medical discourse.[31]

Nhine's conflict between mind and body is brought into focus later in the novel, when Nhine, traumatized after witnessing the suicide of Jane, Flossie's former lover, sees a doctor. Without mentioning the word *hysteria,* the doctor blandly echoes in his conclusions the voice of fin-de-siècle medical authority over the female body: "Repos, calme, hygiène, un peu de distraction. Le moins possible de lecture ou de correspondance, de la marche, repos de tête et exercices de corps. . . . Vous n'avez rien, mon enfant, et cependant c'est pis que tout" (Rest, calm, hygiene, a little distraction. As little reading and letter-writing as possible. Walk, rest the mind and exercise the body. . . . There's nothing wrong with you [literally, *you have nothing*], my child, however that is worse than anything) (152).[32] In its paternalistic tone, this diagnosis epitomizes, and perhaps even ironizes, patriarchal readings of femininity at the turn of the century. By telling Nhine that she has "rien," the doctor essentially underlines the equivalence between femininity and illness; despite evolving clinical considerations of the origins and nature of hysteria, in popular parlance, the condition was seen less as a disease than as a kind of pronounced form of womanhood. In turn, femininity itself became a kind of illness.

The hysteria diagnosis is significant as an unspoken undercurrent here because it underlines the doctor's necessary blindness to Nhine's internal conflict. Hysteria is the prime example of how nineteenth-century medical discourse blurred all distinctions between the female mind and body. The hysteria diagnosis broke down the separation between physiology and subjectivity in women, who in the nineteenth century were already seen as saturated with their sexuality. In his treatise on hysteria, Jean-Louis Brachet, for example, insists on the anatomical pervasiveness of femininity, reflective of the disease as well: "Ce n'est pas seulement par l'utérus que la femme est ce qu'elle est; elle est telle par sa constitution entière. Depuis la tête jusqu'aux pieds, à l'extérieur comme à l'intérieur, quelles que soient les parties de son corps que vous examiniez, vous la trouvez partout la même" (It is not only in the uterus that the woman is what she is; she is such through her entire constitution. From head to toe, outside as inside, whatever part of her body that you examine, you will find her everywhere to be the same).[33] This pathological link between mind and body is readily apparent in Nhine's doctor's counsel, which prohibits mental labor (the link between hysteria and reading was well documented) as a way of restoring health. In fact, it is precisely this inability to separate the mind from the body that sickens Nhine. One could say, then, that rather than being sick with hysteria, she is sick because of hysteria, or she is sick of hysteria: sick from that blurring of mind and body that prevents her from thriving on her intellect as well as on her sensuality.

Nhine's fixed public identity as an eroticized body that ought not to have any emotional depth is fundamentally challenged when she meets Flossie, who has admired Nhine from afar and shows up at her residence, hoping to gain entrance to her chambers. Their first encounter announces the radical shifting of perspectives Flossie's presence will cause as it both reenacts and rejects the fin-de-siècle trope of voyeurism, one of the primary ways through which female sexuality was fantasmatically assimilated in fin-de-siècle fiction.[34] It thereby underlines the specular aspect of Nhine's conflict, which is tied up in the way her body (and thus her mind as well) is seen. When Nhine's servant announces Flossie's presence, Nhine decides to hide behind the window while Tesse, pretending to be her, meets the female suitor. This is a variation of the voyeuristic *mise en abyme,* defined by Emily Apter as the "viewer-gazing-at-viewer-gazing-at-object-of-desire." Apter's chief example is from none other than *Nana:* when the Comte Muffat watches Nana fetishizing herself in the mirror. According to Apter, Zola uses voyeurism "to enhance his literary rendering of visual fixation and to underscore the variety-show aspect of his presentation of prostitutional sensations."[35] Pougy, however, seeks to dismantle these very same strategies. From her corner, Nhine will watch Flossie meet Tesse, who is pretending to be Nhine; in other words, Nhine will watch Flossie watch her. The scene's titillation is prepared by its lesbian undertones and its location in the courtesan's boudoir, the same setting as Nana's self-admiration before the Count Muffat. With Flossie's entrance, however, the scene undermines rather than fulfills its scopophilic promise. The encounter between Flossie and Tesse is a dialogue rather than an erotic tableau, and Nhine derives no fetishistic pleasure from watching her double; nor is the visitor's body put on display. Furthermore, in a final disruption of the voyeuristic scene, just as Flossie realizes that she is speaking to the wrong woman and bursts into tears, Nhine reveals herself, unmasking herself as voyeur.

Flossie and Nhine's friendship begins from this moment of disruption and revelation, as Flossie proposes an alternative way of seeing and being seen. Through the voyeuristic *mise en abyme,* Nhine has looked at herself in the mirror—that is, Tesse—through Flossie's eyes. Flossie's realization that Tesse is not Nhine, despite their superficial resemblance, and her refusal to accept one as a substitute for the other signals the rejection of Tesse as a double for Nhine, and thus the rejection of Tesse's image of the courtesan. As the narrative continues, Flossie's displacement of Tesse announces the possibility for the establishment of a new libidinal relationship that will enable Nhine, finally, to see herself differently.

In several instances, Flossie's scopic fix on Nhine allows her to escape from her identity as *fille publique* and see herself through a new gaze. The transition from being an object of public consumption to becoming part of a feminocentric, if not explicitly lesbian, viewing economy is enacted most explicitly when the two go to the theater together. In their private loge, Flossie positions herself at Nhine's feet so that she can watch her watch the play: significantly, Sarah Bernhardt in *Hamlet.* As a kind of "disruptive act," Bernhardt's performance functions not so differently from Pougy's: it might be seen conservatively by male critics while at the same time inspiring certain women.[36] In the scene, Flossie's gaze on Nhine is set in opposition to the competing glances from the theater-goers whose "yeux inquisiteurs" (inquiring eyes) keep a voyeuristic watch on "ce coin d'ombre où, derrière le léger mystère des écrans à demi levés, surgissait la touffe blonde et rosée de la provocante beauté d'Annhine" (that shadowy corner, where, behind the slight mystery of half opened screens, the blond, rosy tuft of Annhine's provocative beauty protruded) (50). Pougy's narration here purposely mimics the fin-de-siècle discourse that renders the prostitute's presence automatically titillating: from the point of view of the public, she is described suggestively behind half-raised curtains, her fetishized hair peeking out. But unlike the others that admire her for her beauty and her physical appearance, which effaces any interior life according to the conventions of the patriarchal desiring gaze, Flossie is able to perceive the relationship between the two. She valorizes the outside for its transparence to a complex inside and never puts her friend's body on display for its own sake: "Voyant qu'Annhine s'attentionnait à la pièce, Flossie se mit à étudier les traits de sa bien-aimée, curieuse d'y lire l'impression de ses sensations intérieures" (Seeing that Annhine was concentrating on the play, Flossie began to study the features of her beloved, curious to read on them the impression of her inner feelings) (53).

Because of her public persona, Nhine struggles to define the boundaries between her public and private life. Initially she seems unhappily resigned to being a figure of public consumption: "Rien à faire, Flossie, que de mettre de la poudre sur le nez, de m'onduler et de m'exhiber au public ainsi qu'une poupée" (Nothing to do, Flossie, but powder my nose, sway about, and show myself in public like a doll) (66). The theater scene temporarily repositions Nhine with respect to her public persona, however, by inscribing a barrier between her private experience with Flossie and the domain of performance. The theater itself becomes an entanglement of mirrors where spectators and spectacle are blurred. Yet Flossie and Nhine are able to escape from the spectacle because they recognize the difference between performance and reality, which is underlined by the fact that Sarah Bernhardt is playing Hamlet. They discuss the implications of the play they are watching, and the ways in which as women they identify with Hamlet. This discussion, within the private loge, reinforces the boundary between spectacle and spectator, fiction and reality. It again undermines the expectations brought on by the courtesan's provocative presence, demonstrating her presence of mind over that of her body.

Finally, the shift in perspectives announced by this scene is inscribed in the genesis of the text itself; in reality, Pougy had Natalie Barney transcribe part of this scene for her, and she incorporated it into her novel with only minimal editing. According to Jean Chalon's analysis of the original manuscript, Pougy's narration takes over at the point where they enter the loge.[37] Literally, then, this scene enacts the transition from the position of the courtesan, product of patriarchal culture, to the lesbian's perspective, and, at the same time, highlights their tenuous relationship: Nhine will not wholly escape from her identity as *fille publique.*

Flossie, for her part, seems to strategically avoid self-definition through patriarchal constructs. When Tesse is on the verge of calling her a lesbian, Flossie interrupts her: "Oh! de grace, ne flétris d'aucun nom le sentiment qui m'a toujours possédée depuis que je me suis sentie sentir" (Oh heavens! Don't ruin with a label the feeling that has always overwhelmed me ever since I first felt myself feel) (29). She seems wary of describing her natural feelings through the available vocabulary. It is Tesse who insists on this word, telling Nhine, "Lesbienne, ce serait la moindre de ses défauts!" (Lesbian, that would be the least of her faults!) (36). Again, Tesse is the voice of fin-de-siècle cultural norms, as she worries to her friend that "la contagion de ce vice ne t'atteigne en plein coeur" (the contagion of this vice may attack you right in the heart) (36). While underplaying the dangers of "ce plaisir pervers" (this perverse pleasure), Tesse hinges her concern on Nhine's profound sensitivity and her "imaginations ardentes et cérébrales" (ardent, cerebral thoughts), suggesting again that it is the fragile relationship between mind and body that puts the thinking woman at risk.

Through Flossie, Nhine begins to explore the possibility of an alternative perspective. Initially, Flossie is the voice of Nhine's desire; through her friend Nhine's feelings are interpreted and translated. When Nhine says, "Partir, mourir . . . au moins dormir profondément" (Leave, die, . . . or at least go into a deep sleep) (74), Flossie translates this fatigue into the need for a new way of seeing and experiencing the world: "allons vagabonder dans la vie, devenons plus impressionnables à ce qui nous entoure. C'est quelquefois ce qui est le plus près qui est le moins connu et le plus étrange" (let's go wander through life, let's become more sensitive to what is around us. Sometimes it is what is the closest that is the least known and the strangest) (74). This desire to *vagabonder*, interestingly anticipating Colette's 1910 text, is a quest for a fresh perspective, a desire for a defamiliarization with one's own world. Flossie's solution contrasts with Tesse's reaction to Nhine's ennui: whereas Tesse tried to remind her of how she was seen, Flossie directs her to a new way of seeing.

Nhine's initial resistance to Flossie comes in large part from her own inability to see herself beyond social constructions of the courtesan's sexuality: like Fleur de Marie and Esther, she sees her body as tainted, "souillé," contaminated and contaminating by her history of "contacts dégradants" (degrading contacts) (128).[38] In response to this obstacle, Nhine separates out a part of her identity that she considers unscathed: "Ah!! prends donc de moi ce que j'ai de meilleur, ce que nul n'a atteint: mon âme . . . , je te la donne" (Ah!! Take from me the best part then, what no one has touched: my soul . . . , I give it to you) (128). But what exactly is this *âme?* It is certainly not the spiritual soul of religious doctrine meant to govern libidinal drives. Instead, what the narrator earlier referred to as her "petite âme" is her mind, the place of thinking, analyzing, observing, and philosophizing. Yet through Nhine's renunciation of her body in the context of her relationship with Flossie, her *âme* also becomes the landscape of desire.

To insure her recovery from the trauma of Jane's suicide, Nhine does not follow the doctor's advice but instead follows Flossie's and travels to Italy with Tesse. This distance enables the shift in perspectives that leads Nhine to the realization of her desire and forces her into an active position: she is no longer simply an object of desire but a desiring subject in her own right. The awakening of this desire is expressed through a new fantasy that bypasses scopophilia—through which the visual relationship to the *fille publique* is eroticized in the service of a sexualized gaze—in favor of an alternative mode of desire. Scopophilia has traditionally worked in tandem with epistemophilia, or the quest for knowledge through bodily desire. In such cases, the act of seeing satisfies the epistemophilic desire to know.[39] Pougy's narrative, however, replaces scopophilia with a different form of desire, what I call transcriptophilia, where epistemophilic drives are satisfied through writing rather than through the workings of an eroticized gaze.[40] Through this new mode Nhine's desire is further severed from her body, and the workings of the mind—or of the *âme*—are fully eroticized. The workings of transcriptophilia are first suggested in Nhine's initial longing for the now absent Flossie:

> Elle se disait qu'en ce cadre de soleil et de vie et de multiples décors on vivrait, nus, un délicieux roman d'amour et de voluptés étranges, inconnues, désirées! . . . Elle *voulait* connaître, elle brûlait de savoir, désirant achever ce livre dont elle avait feuilleté les pages sans aller plus loin que

> le premier chapitre cruellement exquis qui l'avait si violemment attirée en dehors de la banalité coutumière. (157)
>
> [She told herself that in this sunny setting, full of life and varied scenery, they would live out, naked, a delicious novel of love and strange pleasures, pleasures unknown and longed for! . . . She *wanted* to know, she was burning to know, with a desire to finish this book whose pages she had leafed through without going further than the tantalizing first chapter, which had so violently attracted her to something beyond the usual banality.]

Nhine's transcription of her sexual desire for Flossie into a desire for knowledge figured through the book brings together lesbian desire and the desire to write and thus signals an important moment in the staging of Pougy's own path to authorship. The *délicieux roman d'amour* represents Nhine's quest for self-understanding through the exploration of an unknown sexuality. This epistemophilic drive for knowledge transforms the object of desire into a text. From the desire to complete this *délicieux roman d'amour,* Nhine will move to the process of writing to Flossie: epistemophilia becomes transcriptophilia, reminding us that the book that she desires may indeed be the one we are reading. Indeed, Nhine's transcriptophilia is symbolic of the author's own coming to autobiographical writing for which the events narrated in this text prepare her. One could say, then, that rather than reading the book, Nhine ends up, in this sense, writing it.

The book metaphor is also a means of unhinging desire from corporeality; the book stands in for what Nhine desires in Flossie. As the text continues, writing for Nhine becomes the expression of a private part of herself, in opposition to the public persona that she shares with all of Paris; it reproduces the split between her external, physical self and her spiritual, intellectual, and sensual self brought on by a society intolerant of any form of female sexuality outside of marriage. It is primarily the latter part of Nhine's identity that she would like to share with Flossie: "Tes cheveux, Floss, et le charme de ton esprit, le choix ensorcelant de tes mots, l'émerveillement de tes pensées, oui, mais plus jamais tes lèvres, plus le moindre contact de nos corps" (Your hair, Flossie, and the charm of your mind, your bewitching choice of words, the marvel of your thoughts, but never again your lips, never again the least contact of our bodies) (217). Writing allows her to express her desire through her interior world, while at the same time fulfilling a need to externalize these feelings. Writing to Flossie maintains this privacy, because Flossie is able to assimilate thoughts that remain inaccessible to the outside world. As she rereads the letter, she assures herself that Flossie will understand her, for "elle est la seule au monde qui soit en accord parfait d'idées avec moi" (she is the only one in the world who is in perfect accord with my ideas) (176).

As Nhine gives in to the epistolary pull, her writing substitutes for sexual contact, an alternative way to satisfy her desire for Flossie. Even a quick note betrays her powerful feelings: "C'est cela, elle allait écrire: une petite image, un paysage de givre, puis derrière, une ligne, un souhait: *Je te désire mille joies d'âme et de nerfs*" (That's it, she was going to write: a small image, a frosty landscape, and then after, a line, a wish: *I want for you a thousand joys of soul and sensation*) (158). Despite her engagement in several heterosexual trysts during her separation from Flossie, Nhine finds herself pulled to their correspondence, until ultimately the desire to write overpowers her. The tempo of her writing follows a pattern of sexual tension leading up to crescendoed fulfillment. She succumbs to temptation, initially promising herself "un mot, un mot seulement" (one word, just one word) but finds it impossible to restrain herself, writing more than she intended. And once she is finished, she finds herself spent, "à demi-ébranlée" (somewhat shaken up) and resigned to "une amitié très pure, lointaine, qu'on sentirait à soi à travers toute la vie, ce serait doux, gentil, consolant" (a pure friendship, from afar, that you would always sense throughout life, that would be sweet, kind, consoling) (218).

According to Theresa De Lauretis's theories of lesbian sexuality, "it takes two women, not one, to make a lesbian," a formulation that she repeats throughout her discussion of lesbian desire. "Lesbian desire is not the identification with another woman's desire," she argues, "but rather the desire for her desire."[41] This doubling aptly describes Nhine's feelings for Flossie. Her first letters to Flossie begin from the desire to "fixer un peu cela qui m'est passé dans l'esprit en ces heures d'union à travers les espaces pour te l'envoyer et . . . peut-être? causer quelque plaisir. . à qui? à Toi? à Moi? à Nous!" (to concretize somewhat what has gone through my mind during these hours of union across separate spaces, in order to send it to you and—perhaps?—cause a little pleasure . . . for whom? for You? for Me? for Us!) (175). This "Nous" is the union of "Toi" and "Moi," two independent subjects, now "inhabiting the subject position together," to borrow Sue-Ellen Case's formulation.[42] In a discussion of performances of the gaze in *Corinne,* Nancy K. Miller observes, "Corinne wants, I think, not so much a match in marriage as the perfect *destinataire:* the addressee basic to the transactions of narrative communication; a privileged interlocutor and reader in the form of a friend and lover." Corinne's vulnerability stems from the fact that Oswald can never fulfill this desire; his is ultimately a patriarchal gaze "which surveys, judges and regulates."[43] The relationship between Nhine and Flossie, in contrast, provides a model for this ideal *destinataire,* which, like De Lauretis's lesbian, requires not one but two women. It is above all a relationship of symmetry: "[Nhine] songeait sans cesse, absente, en recherche . . . ; sa pensée se portait vers une autre nudité, soeur de la sienne" (Nhine was always dreaming, absent, searching . . . , her thoughts carried her toward another nudity, sister of her own) (157). Through the relationship of symmetrical *destinataires,* the lesbian is cast as the figure for female authority; the lesbian discursive relationship represents the possibility of a feminocentric discourse uncorrupted by patriarchal reading strategies.

The fetishization of writing and its link to epistemophilia through their shared sexualization of the quest for knowledge enables the fulfillment of lesbian desire beyond physical contact. It should be noted, however, that the limiting of sexual contact between women in favor of an intellectualized lesbian eros in this novel and the others I consider cannot be entirely separated from the rampant homophobia of the fin-de-siècle that associated such sexuality with perversion, disease, and contagion. This homophobia was part of the same outlook that reduced a woman to her sexuality once she stepped out of the private sphere. As a result, the promotion of intellect in these novels challenges the patriarchal view of public women as purely erotic objects, yet it also ends up sanitizing lesbian sexuality in a way that might be seen as succumbing to certain elements of fin-de-siècle homophobia, even as the lesbian becomes a symbol of authority.

As Nhine's correspondence with Flossie continues, writing—or lesbian transcriptophilia—is identified as an escape from corporeality: the solution to the body/soul conflict plaguing Nhine. In a postscript to one of her letters, Nhine tells of a daydream where she sees herself as a naked body exposed on the road, subject to the humiliation of passers-by:

> Ce corps ressemblait au mien, à celui que tu désires . . . , et les passants l'injuriaient, le violaient, le salissaient ainsi que la route, d'ordures, de crachats, de baisers, de morsures, de taches, de coups, de baves et de meurtrissures. . . . Qui me voulait m'avait. Nul ne voyait mes flétrissures, car la lune boudait, invisible, et je pourrissais dans ma fange, sans force pour me relever, pour fuir! (175)
>
> [This body resembled mine, the one that you desire . . . , and the passers-by insulted it, violated it, soiled it as they did the road, with garbage, spittle, kisses, bites, stains, kicks, drool, and bruises. . . . Whoever wanted me had me. No one saw the marks on my body, for the moon was hiding, invisible, and I rotted in my mud, without the strength to pick myself up and flee!]

Loaded with naturalist detail, this description calls up the decomposing female bodies of fin-de-siècle fiction that wore the signs of society's own degradation, and with which Nhine identifies.[44] One remembers Zola's Nana in particular. This image of rotting flesh is the end-point of the specular mode, the drastic consequences of being the eroticized (and hystericized) object of the patriarchal gaze; like Nana's, Nhine's sexual objectification leads to physical disintegration. In her dream, Nhine sees herself as a naturalist antiheroine and is unable to help herself until Flossie comes along and covers her with flowers, shielding her vision so that Nhine may conclude: "Mes regards ne verront plus l'obscène, l'inique; comme eux, mon front restera pur, parfumé de la senteur des feuilles pâles que ta main a versées sur moi" (My gaze will no longer see the obscene, the iniquitous; like it, my forehead will remain pure, perfumed with the fragrance of pale leaves that your hand laid upon me) (175). Flossie's gesture is Nhine's salvation, freeing her from self-loathing and granting her a sense of security. Flossie's desire for Nhine's body enables Nhine to shift her entire visual paradigm, blocking her from the self-image imposed on her by fin-de-siècle discursive and social structures. Nhine proclaims her desire to reciprocate Flossie's feelings and forge a new self-image, "au fil de la plume et de la pensée, pour Toi, pour Moi . . . pour ce qui fut Nous!" (with the flow of the pen and the mind, for You, for Me . . . for what was Us!) (176). The lesbian relationship is thus the vehicle to Nhine's empowerment through intellect and writing, enabling her to reject her bodily degradation and announce her literary rebirth.

This passage reflects in microcosm the fundamental problematic of the novel. Nhine recognizes that her way out of "la convoitise des hommes"—her sense of oppression by patriarchal notions of female corporeality—is through the act of writing itself, through which she will represent herself differently. Yet Nhine's writing, though infused with desire, seems to elide the physical relationship of the lovers. This abstinence continues even after the couple's reunion, when Nhine is still unwilling to give herself physically. Even when they do have physical—even sexual—contact, the body is written out of the encounter. It is unclear to what extent their physical contact takes place; their union is described through a mirroring, doubling, and mingling of self and other made possible by the lack of sexual difference: "Elles se réfugièrent dans le coin le plus obscur du boudoir et y restèrent longtemps . . . mêlant leurs larmes, leurs souffles, leurs frissons, échangeant leurs âmes. . . . Elles se séparèrent, sans se quitter, trop près l'une de l'autre spirituellement pour qu'un effet physique pût agir directement contre leur impression d'union" (They took refuge in the darkest corner of the bedroom and stayed there a long time . . . mingling their tears, their breaths, their shudders, exchanging their souls. . . . They separated, without leaving each other, too emotionally close to one another for a physical change to affect their feeling of togetherness) (222). Here what might have been read simply as a return to a romanticized spiritual union of souls can be recognized in the light of Nhine's and Flossie's epistolary exchange as a far more subtle designation of desiring space beyond the bounds of patriarchal structures.

Nhine's story, however, does not have a "happy ending." Shortly after she seems to have given in to her overpowering desire, she falls into depression. Unlike Nana, whose mirror games mysteriously excluded the male viewer, Nhine used to assume the perspective of the male gaze when admiring herself naked before the mirror, imagining herself as a prototypical object of patriarchal desire, straight out of a Renoir painting: "tantôt elle éloignait les bras aussi loin que possible devant elle, réunissant les paumes de ses mains en un allongement de toute sa personne, et semblait s'élancer en criant joyeusement: "La Baigneuse!" (she would hold out her arms as far as possible in front of her, bringing together her palms while stretching out her whole body, and seeming to throw herself forward while crying out joyously: "The Bather!") (233). This day, however, she is consumed with anxiety, suddenly realizing the possibility that she may be pregnant. Nhine's shift of perspectives has destabilized her self-image; she is now uncertain about how to see herself. Standing before the mirror, Nhine is caught between the possibility of pregnancy, and thus, in this context, entrapment within the patriarchal paradigm, and her comfort, finally, with her lesbian relationship. Perhaps before the mirror she sees this irreconcilability between her public, physical self—the female body she must live with—and her private, internal self—the intellectual side she has devoted to Flossie. The last part of the novel spins out of this confusion of inside and outside, physical and emotional health. Nhine is not pregnant, but she is ill and ends up in the hospital as a result of a hemorrhaging condition. Her female protectors shield Nhine from Flossie, but Flossie eventually makes her way to Nhine's side by disguising herself. Nhine is thrilled and plans to enter as a third party into Flossie and her fiancé, Will's marriage.[45] But before this can happen, Nhine dies.

One way of reading Pougy's ending is that she succumbed to fin-de-siècle notions of lesbian morbidity as well as fin-de-siècle narrative structures that traditionally expunged deviant female sexuality by the text's end. Following Gilbert and Gubar's reading of nineteenth-century English women's writing, one might add that Pougy finally identifies with the reflection she finds in the mirror of patriarchally imposed femininity and kills the evil demon that she recognizes in herself. (In fact, Pougy had flirted with the idea of suicide and made more than one half-hearted attempt to take her own life.)[46] Yet Nhine's death is also metonymically related to her pregnancy; it can thus be read as a pathological manifestation of patriarchal pressures on the female body. She dies not because of her internal condition but from her original disease, the incompatibility of the outside and the inside, of mind and body. One could then ask whether any progress has been made by the narrative at all. Does she not die from the same condition with which her story began? The answer to this comes from Pougy's own particular narrative position, which alters the sense of her protagonist's death. Nhine's death is Pougy's fictional suicide, allowing her a more active role. This suicide enacts the authorial fantasy she described to Flossie in the postscript to her letter: death as literary rebirth. For, indeed, Pougy does not die, just the character she has created of herself, or, in other words, her self-image. With Nhine's death, Pougy kills the prostitute and the tainted body that limited her possibilities, perhaps to recover her mind and to let triumph the writer generated by the lesbian relationship. Thus, Pougy's dénouement is not simply the succumbing to fin-de-siècle literary models of female death as narrative closure; it is also a poignant commentary on the limits of these models for female self-expression. Furthermore, her novel identifies its major source of empowerment in writing itself, making the text's very existence an antidote to its sad conclusion. Finally, *Idylle saphique* is also a commentary on the limits of writing about lesbian sexuality in fin-de-siècle culture. Pougy acknowledged these limits in her journals *Mes cahiers bleus,* which she kept between 1919 and 1941. In them she admits that for the book to be published, she could not portray the lesbian relationship in a positive light.[47] This may also explain her need to downplay the physical aspect of lesbian sexuality. In reality, Pougy continued to oscillate between erotic female friendship and the stability of heterosexual relationships throughout her life. Her marriage in 1910 to the Romanian prince Georges Ghika lasted until his death in 1945, yet, as she documents in her journals, she continued to privilege above all her sensual attachment to women.[48]

TOWARD A SAPPHIC DISCOURSE: RENÉE VIVIEN'S *UNE FEMME M'APPARUT*

By the time of her death in 1909 at the age of thirty-two, Renée Vivien had published over thirty volumes of poetry, short stories, a novel, and translations of Sappho's fragments into French. To the extent that she has been remembered in French literary history, it is in large part for her mysterious lesbian identity, which was memorialized in Colette's *Le Pur et l'impur.* In 1906 Colette had moved next door to Vivien after leaving her husband, Willy; she had also been her guest in Nice with both Willy and her lover, the Marquise de Belboeuf, better known as Missy. Colette described Vivien as childlike and eccentric, living in a dark, suffocating, incense-filled apartment whose windows were nailed shut, operating according to the demands of a domineering lover (at the time, the baroness Hélène van Zuylen), and speaking indiscreetly of her sexual preferences. Firmly ensconced in the Tout Lesbos of the Belle Epoque, Vivien later inspired the literary critic André Billy's expression "Sappho 1900, Sappho cent pour cent" (Sappho 1900, Sappho one hundred percent). Once she was rediscovered in the 1970s by scholars of gay and lesbian history, Vivien was hailed as a member of "the early homosexual movement" in France.[49] As Elaine Marks has argued, however, such readings of Vivien are anachronistic; they are based on a desire to identify a transcendent, authentic lesbian experience that aligns Vivien with contemporary political and ideological objectives.[50]

Furthermore, such readings belie the complex history of Vivien's careful attention to her literary identity and her attempts to separate it from her personal life. Born Pauline Mary Tarn in 1877, Vivien continued to be addressed as Pauline by her friends, even as she gained notice under her pseudonym. The daughter of an American mother and British father, Vivien took her sizable inheritance and left a troubled family life in London behind to become a permanent resident of Paris at the end of 1898.[51] She was quickly introduced to Natalie Clifford Barney, a childhood friend of her own childhood friend, Violette Shiletto, whose death is described in *Une Femme m'apparut.* Her first collection of poetry, *Etudes et préludes,* was published in 1901 by the small yet prestigious publisher Alphonse Lemerre under the name R. Vivien; it was distributed to the press with a card that read "René Vivien" and gained some limited notice with the help of her friend, the literary critic and founder of the Fédération Régionaliste Française, Jean Charles-Brun. Her second collection, *Cendres et poussières,* received warm reviews in several prominent journals.[52] By 1903, Pauline was signing her third book as Renée Vivien, and the fact that it was a pseudonym was officially exposed by the influential literary critic and right-wing politician Charles Maurras.[53]

Maurras's article on Vivien's romanticism is typical of many of Vivien's critics: he lauded Vivien's unusual talent, while expressing disdain for what was deemed the perversity of her subject matter.[54] Indeed, Vivien's writing unabashedly embraces sapphic love. Unlike Pougy, who admitted to censoring herself in the interest of her book's reception, or Colette, who continued to foreground heterosexual relationships in her writing, Vivien never hid her idealization of lesbianism, nor, as I show, her contempt for heterosexuality. This fact, in addition to her fierce sense of privacy (unlike many of her female peers, she refused to be photographed for publicity), contributed to what was often an adversarial relationship with the press. By 1904, the critic F. Viallet of *La Brise* openly refused to read her latest publications, which he described as the literature of hysterics and neurotics.[55] As Virginie Sanders documents, Vivien was extremely sensitive about her work; she continually revised already published texts and was known to write back to critics whose readings of her poetry she disagreed with or whose comments offended her.[56] In 1907, Vivien took a more drastic means of control over her literary reputation: she removed her works from circulation.[57] She went on to distribute her new collection of poetry, *Flambeaux éteints,* only to her closest friends, a fact that garnered further attention from the press.[58] In 1909, Vivien died, probably because of a fatal mix of alcohol and anorexia that was widely acknowledged (by Colette and Barney among others) to have been a suicide.[59]

Vivien's autobiographical novel *Une Femme m'apparut* is better understood in the context of her attempts to control her readership. In fact, Vivien published two versions of the novel, in 1904 and 1905. Rather than rework stylistic or literary flaws, in the second version she replaces Vally, the character based on Natalie Barney in the first version, with Lorély, who also represents Barney. Lorély, however, is at the romantic center rather than Eva, who was based on Hélène van Zuylen. This second version was Vivien's attempt to reimagine her romantic past and thus elides some of the polemic surrounding the profession of the woman writer that flavors the first. The object of my study here is the first version, which at least one critic linked to pathology rather than literature.[60] In this text, Vivien's forthright representation of her lesbian identity is tempered by a pronounced anxiety and sense of vulnerability about subjecting herself to public scrutiny. The lesbian discursive community presented in *Une Femme m'apparut* addresses this anxiety by enabling the construction of a protected female authority, precluding patriarchal reading strategies and eliminating male readers. Lesbianism thus becomes once more a metaphor for a female textual ideal that insures the privacy of the woman writer and dismantles her identity as a *fille publique.* The critic Bonnefon claimed that Vivien wanted only female readers.[61] Indeed, Vivien addressed many of her poems to women directly and saw her writing as a means of reclaiming a lost female literary tradition.[62] Thus, the major aspect of Vivien's subversiveness may not have been the social ramifications of her sexual identity for the future homosexual movement but the textual ramifications of this identity for the woman writer.

Vivien's autobiographical novel tells the story of her relationship with Natalie Clifford Barney through a creative mixing of genres by which poetry, music, letters, and philosophic dialogue are integrated into the narration. I consider this short text as an experiment in what Vivien might have called sapphic discourse, an alternative literary mode that attempts to inscribe within the text itself a female way of reading to prevent the female subject from being apprehended according to traditional patriarchal fantasms. The novel is a roman à clef that provides a thinly disguised history of Vivien's social life. Vivien is represented in the text through two distinct voices: the unnamed narrator—whom I refer to as Renée—who is engaged in a struggle for romantic satisfaction, and San Giovanni, the female poet who is the spiritual and intellectual leader of the women in the novel.

The ostensible plot of the novel follows Renée's faltering relationship with Vally and draws on Vivien's own life experiences. Renée's quest for lesbian love is tied to an equally important "plot," or perhaps more aptly, conversation, about the possibility of female authority, which takes place through salonlike meetings. Lesbian identity in the novel is developed through a female community, the followers of San Giovanni of Mytilène. San Giovanni, however, is described as "l'Androgyne" and speaks in favor of chastity. As Karla Jay argues, Vivien's androgyne is sexless but identifies with women, making her a gynandromorph.[63] As San Giovanni turns to Sappho for precedent, her poetic philosophy maps onto a theory of sapphic chastity, bringing writing and sexuality together in their elimination of heterosexual structures. Vivien explains that the historic dearth of women writers is due to female alienation from the male body, which symbolizes "l'inesthétique par excellence" (the Unaesthetic par excellence); Sappho's triumph was in her ability to ignore masculine existence: "son oeuvre n'en porte ni la trace ni la souillure" (her work doesn't carry its trace or its tarnish).[64] She pities a male visitor to her salon for not recognizing the beauty of sapphic love, explaining: "Cet amour, évocateur de la Beauté dans ce qu'elle a de plus suave et de plus délicat . . . n'est-il pas mille fois plus chaste que cette cohabitation fondée sur l'intérêt qu'est devenu le mariage chrétien?" (This love, evoking beauty at its most suave and delicate . . . is it not a thousand times more chaste than the self-serving cohabitation that Christian marriage has become?) (37). Incidentally, this kind of attack on marriage demonstrates the critique of bourgeois structures and heterosexual relationships that led critics to label Vivien perverse.

In conjunction with the glorification of Sappho, the essentialization and delegitimization of the male perspective is rather crudely developed throughout the text in speeches given by many of the characters. The male point of view is seen as aesthetically suspect, and men are criminalized for their past abuse of women. The narrator, for example, describes her basic philosophy to San Giovanni as "une pensée hermaphrodite" (a hermaphroditic thought) separating men from women whereby all that is "laid, injuste, féroce et lâche" (ugly, unjust, ferocious and cowardly) comes from the Male Principle and all that is "douloureusement beau et désirable" (painfully beautiful and desirable) comes from the Female Principle (37). San Giovanni's goal is defined as the triumph of the female over the male, or beauty over cruelty. This is in essence the battle that takes place in Vivien's text, which can be seen as the enactment of the female principle rising up against the pre-existing hegemony of the male.

San Giovanni's experiences as a writer underline the sexual tensions that arise when a woman becomes a subject for public consumption. She is constantly confronted with evidence that a woman's textual presence, whether as an author or as a character, can be assimilated by male readers only through their fantasmatic relationship with female sexuality. The best evidence appears in a letter that San Giovanni receives from a male reader, addressed to the "Déesse," whom he refers to as "Madame et chère fée" (Madam and dear enchantress) (101). In the letter he requests a portrait of the author, a boldness he excuses by pointing out that he has not actually sexually solicited her. San Giovanni is outraged that because of her female signature, her reader conflates the author of erotic poetry with its subject.

Vivien's commentary is amplified by the fact that this letter was a rewriting of an exchange with the critic Pierre Borel, who had asked for Vivien's photograph.[65] With this transposition, Vivien reduces the literary status of the critic to simply a reader among others. In ignoring the poetic merits of her work and reading it through his sexual fantasies, the critic falls into the same category as his peers Jules Bertaut and Paul Flat, whose comments I consider in the Introduction. Like Barbey d'Aurevilly, who was interrupted by the "odor di femina," these critics were unable to judge women's literature because of their anxieties about its authors. In turn, the woman writer, by virtue of the spectacle of her signature and thus the publicness of her femininity, becomes a kind of *fille publique,* determined entirely by the fantasmatic relationship to her sex. San Giovanni's reader wants to have her portrait to satisfy a voyeuristic pleasure—he explicitly requests the portrait as a substitute for sex. San Giovanni is forced to point out his misreading of the female signature in her response to him: "Parce qu'on a le malheur d'écrire en vers et en prose, même lorsqu'on vit célébrant la caresse, suivant votre élégant expression, il ne s'ensuit pas de toute nécessité qu'on doive être une femme facile" (Because one is unfortunate enough to write verse and prose, even when one does live celebrating the caress, following your elegant expression, it does not necessarily follow that one is a loose woman) (102). By reminding him of her authority and sending him a letter rather than a portrait, she demonstrates the potential role of discourse in displacing the spectacle of the *fille publique;* she literally substitutes her text for her body as a means of affirming female intellect and separating it from sexuality. This gesture mirrors Pougy's embrace of "la plume et la pensée" to undermine her bodily degradation.

Even so, bitterly aware of the circumstances of her reception, San Giovanni equates her public identity with shame. When she receives a letter addressed to her as "Femme de lettres" she asks indignantly whether one would address a letter to "Mademoiselle Maximilienne de Chateau-Fleuri, Prostituée," since both professions share the same social status (99). Despite the pride that San Giovanni clearly displays for her actual art, then, she has disdain for her public role, "ce douloureux métier de femme de lettres" (this painful profession of woman writer) (104), which strips her of authority. "San Giovanni était poète" (San Giovanni was a poet) is the phrase with which she is introduced to us in the text; this gender-neutral designation elides the complex connotations of the "femme de lettres." San Giovanni explains to the narrator: "le châtiment de mon ignorance est dans ces soi-disant admirations qui s'adressent à la femme plus qu'à l'artiste" (the curse of my ignorance is in these so-called compliments addressed to the woman rather than the artist) (104). Once her texts enter the public domain, her relationship to them is based no longer on her art but on her sex.

Perhaps to counteract this dynamic, in Vivien's novel the female reader is a role inscribed and interpreted within the text itself. Much of the novel records conversations between San Giovanni, Renée, and Vally, during which poems or stories are read aloud and then explained, thus making misreading by an outside reader impossible. Reading is never an isolated act but an ongoing conversation, through which the reader's interpretations can be guided. The feminocentric circumscription of the reading process implicitly sets itself in opposition to the invasiveness of the male readers whose ignorant comments and assumptions San Giovanni decries. Indeed, even the letters cited above are not simply quoted in the text but read aloud by San Giovanni and framed with her commentary. This female discussion as an element of literary production and interpretation recalls the salon culture so essential to the French tradition of women's writing. Within the context of the salon, women maintained a kind of control over their texts that was no longer available to them once a text was published.[66] The fin-de-siècle lesbian community was just beginning to recreate this culture in its own mode. As Colette describes them, Vivien's salons were limited to women, with few exceptions.[67] Vivien seems to inscribe this private domain into the text itself, placing the salon and its voices of authority in the novel. San Giovanni's limited literary success is associated with this kind of enclosed world: "Sa renommée ne s'étendait point au delà d'un cercle très restreint de lettrés et d'artistes" (her renown did not extend beyond a very small circle of writers and artists) (36)—a success that closely predicts Vivien's own.[68]

Through the conversations between San Giovanni and her followers, many of Vivien's own writings are contextualized as part of a larger feminocentric project that enables San Giovanni to express her feelings about men. She links her early hatred for men to the poor quality of men's writing. This realization in her youth led her to compose the poem "Vashti" as a celebration of women's rebellion. San Giovanni's mention of the poem exemplifies the complex dynamics of reading with which Vivien is concerned. The poem "Vashti" appears as the story "Le Voile de Vashti" in Vivien's 1904 collection *La Dame à la louve*. Vivien's text is a re-interpretation of a story from the Hebrew biblical tradition, a feminist reclaiming of a minor yet critical character. This gesture follows the glorification of Sappho throughout the novel, a character described as "la grande Méconnue et la grande Calomniée" (the Great Misunderstood and Maligned One) (38), whose relationship to Phaon has historically been misconstrued. Much of Vivien's project is involved in reclaiming and recontextualizing forgotten heroines like Sappho and Vashti, as well as the biblical characters Naomi and Ruth, whom she embraces in the story "L'Amitié féminine" from the same collection. Furthermore, by glossing her own texts within her autobiographical novel, Vivien points to the link between her texts and her identity—between reading her stories and reading her story. At one point, for example, San Giovanni tells of how she fell in love with a young female companion and longed to disguise herself as a man so she might marry her. This same plot figures in Vivien's "Prince Charming" from *La Dame à la louve,* leading us to reread that tale as an autobiographic fantasy. This relay between texts and identity transforms the fin-de-siècle dynamics of reading femininity: the body is elided entirely, as female identity is situated in the texts that make up the individual woman.

Although both protagonists are projections of Vivien's writing persona, San Giovanni and Renée describe themselves through conflicting desires and fears and often disagree in the novel. Renée's story is being told; her love affairs and sorrows make up what little intrigue exists. Yet San Giovanni's voice is essential to the female autobiographical project, providing the stable identity against which Renée measures herself, and maintaining a narrative frame that protects the protagonist from the potential violence of the outside reader. The difference between these characters enacts the woman writer's conflict between a desire for authority and a desire for privacy. When San Giovanni complains of receiving mail addressed to her as "Femme de lettres" and compares this to being a courtesan, Renée responds: "C'est que la femme de lettres a infiniment moins de modestie que la courtisane. . . . L'une ne vend que son corps à un nombre en somme restreint d'individus, l'autre vend son âme, tirée à des milliers d'exemplaires" (The woman writer has infinitely less modesty than the courtesan. . . . One sells only her body to a relatively small number of individuals; the other sells her soul in a million copies) (99). San Giovanni reacts with hostility to this explanation; what troubles her is not the fact that her feelings are public but that she has become a public object, a projection of fantasies. Privacy in this context is the opposite of public in the sense of the *fille publique:* it means being spared the projections inspired by patriarchal culture. Because of the way women have traditionally been associated with the content of the novel rather than its authorship (even when they were in fact the authors, as Joan DeJean has shown in "Lafayette's Ellipses"), the female signature has meant forsaking privacy for authority; readers have been unable to separate the *femme de lettres* from the plot of her novels. San Giovanni is the poet, willing to bare her soul and abandon the privacy of her thoughts in search of authority. The poet fears death, as she insists repeatedly, even as she seeks immortality through her writing.

Renée, in contrast, describes herself as "l'être du silence et de la solitude" (the being of silence and solitude) (63) and has a passion for death, evoking decadent literary themes. Yet despite her desire for privacy and solitude, Renée is the voice of the "je" in the novel, the one who is telling her story; she describes to the reader her deeply emotional reactions to the romantic tumult she experiences. Ultimately, then, sapphic autobiography is the expression of the one who fears baring her soul and embraces death. The narrator seems to have found a way of protecting her voice in this layered autobiography where the act of reading is inscribed within the text. Indeed, as suggested by Vivien's real-life protectiveness of her writing, what both Renée and San Giovanni ultimately desire is authority and privacy, that is, the possibility of self-expression without being exposed to misreadings, without becoming the projection of the patriarchal sexual imagination.

In 1907, Vivien explained her decision to withhold her latest book from the market in a letter to Natalie Barney: "un de mes livres, celui que j'aime le plus peut-être, pourrait tomber entre des mains sales" (one of my books, the one I like the best perhaps, could fall into dirty hands).[69] In *Une Femme m'apparut,* Vivien's feminocentric discourse offers another possible solution to this same problem, by fulfilling the need for privacy with the inscription of the addressee within the text through the presence of compassionate female readers and readings, creating a kind of hermetic discursive universe that renders an outside reader obsolete. As a conversation between two versions of herself, Vivien's novel contains a certain reflexivity that makes it in some sense self-sufficient. Autobiography thus translates as discursive autonomy.

Furthermore, the feminocentric relationship between reader and writer in Vivien's novel mirrors the dynamics of the lesbian relationships that she represents. As in Pougy's novel, the symmetry of female companions determines the figure of the perfect reader, the female *destinataire.* San Giovanni expresses this longing to Renée: "Oh! rencontrer une compréhension fraternelle, sans étonnements, sans éloges, une compréhension muette et féminine qui consolerait de toutes les paroles lues et entendues!" (Oh! To meet someone who would understand me as a sister, without surprises, without praise, a silent feminine understanding that would heal all the spoken and written words!) (104). At the same time, at the end of the novel the quest for lesbian love is redefined as a quest for a perfect interlocutor, the possibility of which is imagined through a progression of female figures. When Renée is wandering in a depressed state, she finds the young woman Dagmar, who agrees to listen to her story: "J'écouterai le récit de vos peines, fût-il interminable" (I will listen to the story of your troubles, even if it is endless) (122).[70] This conversation prepares her for a romantic relationship, made possible through the figure of Eva, who represents Renée's *destinataire* because of their unspoken complementarity: "N'es-tu pas mon silence, Eva? N'es-tu pas ma solitude? Tu vois ma pensée plus clairement que moi-même" (Are you not my silence, Eva? Are you not my solitude? You see my thoughts more clearly than I do) (150). As Flossie was for Nhine, the lesbian lover is the metaphor for this ideal symmetrical understanding, the consoling *compréhension muette et féminine* that is the *destinataire.*

Ultimately, there is no resolution to either struggle represented in the novel. In the final chapters, her former lover Vally returns, and Renée must choose between her and Eva. The text closes on the act of choosing, without letting the reader in on the results: "Lorsque la parole finale fut prononcée, un soupir monta de la pénombre: 'Adieu . . . et au revoir' " (Once the final word was pronounced, a sigh arose in the dim light: Adieu . . . and goodbye) (163). By eliding Renée's ultimate choice, Vivien constructs a final frame with which to preserve Renée's privacy and to exclude the outsider from the hermetic text. This absence of resolution also underlines the dynamism of Vivien's sapphic text, emphasizing process over result. In *Fictions of Sappho,* Joan DeJean argues that Vivien's "obsessively repetitive fictions of Sappho are not about becoming Sappho but about a double redefinition: of sapphism as the poetic infinite, an (always impossible) union with Sappho, and of Sapphism as the desire, incessantly emitted by Sappho across the ages, for the ideal beloved girl."[71] Like Pougy's *Idylle saphique, Une Femme m'apparut* suggests that lesbian desire is not just for a female partner but for a female reader. For Vivien it is a desire that is expressed through a never-ending search. Female authority is strived for across this process of desiring, through a relationship rather than a product, and through which the "Principe Mâle" is progressively annihilated.

REINVENTING THE FLÂNEUR: COLETTE'S *LA VAGABONDE*

Signed "Colette Willy," *La Vagabonde* (1910) was written three years after Colette's break-up with her notorious first husband.[72] The novel received publicity (which she often sought out through her provocative behavior) in well-respected literary journals such as *Le Temps* and had immediate success, including a nomination for the Prix Goncourt.[73] *La Vagabonde* gives voice to Colette's ambivalence about the independent life she had invented for herself as her relationship with her husband faltered. Even before their divorce, Colette was determined to support herself without Willy, who had managed to burn through the record-breaking revenues of the *Claudine* series through gambling and lavish spending. In 1905, Colette dove into the world of Parisian theater, mime, and dance, with the help of Natalie Barney, in whose garden she had her amateur debut. The critics were not always kind to Colette, but she pursued this career, while squeezing in her writing on the side.[74]

La Vagabonde is thus told through the voice of Renée Néré, a music-hall dancer, who provides us with another image of the *fille publique.* Self-described as "une femme de lettres qui a mal tourné" (a woman of letters who went bad), Renée shares many qualities with her author, and the text has been widely acknowledged as autobiographical since its publication.[75] Like Colette, Renée enjoyed some success as a writer during her troubled marriage with a famous artist; here, Willy is Taillandy, whose celebrity ("Mon ex-mari? Vous le connaissez tous" [My ex-husband? You all know him]) adds spice to Renée's bitter accusations.[76] In addition, Renée turns to the theater after her divorce to support herself, despite a passion for literature ("d'autres soucis me réclament à présent, et surtout celui de gagner ma vie" [other worries claim me right now, and especially that of earning a living] [31]). The story *La Vagabonde* tells, in part, is the story of how the woman writer is reborn (Renée/renaît) during this transition to professional life that highlights the tension between Renée's intellectual sense of self and the sensual body she is reduced to by her paying audience. Like both Pougy's and Vivien's texts, the novel traces a moment of the author's recent history. Essential to the story being told is the process of writing itself, symbolic of the author's own literary realization as she breaks free from her domineering ex-husband.[77]

One autobiographical distinction worth noting is that at the time of writing, Colette's romantic affiliations were slightly more complex than those of her protagonist. Although like Renée she was dating a man who was also a backstage groupie (the twenty-four-year-old Auguste Hériot, heir to a department store fortune), she was more seriously engaged in an ongoing relationship with a woman, the Marquise de Belboeuf, or Missy, who was her unofficial guide in the world of Paris-Lesbos. In 1907, the couple had caused an uproar when they mimed a lesbian love scene in a performance at the Moulin Rouge; following the ensuing brawl, the police arrived to escort the performers home. (Although Willy had orchestrated the performance, having written the pantomime himself, he sued for divorce five days later in an effort to save his reputation. Colette responded by countersuing.)[78] Renée does not take part in a homosexual relationship in *La Vagabonde,* but neither is lesbianism absent. The brief discussion of lesbianism through the character Amalia Barally is critical to understanding Renée's rejection of her lover Max in the context of her creative choices.

In many ways, Renée's story is the same as that of Pougy's Nhine: as a *fille publique* who must exploit her appearance for her livelihood and who thrives on the romantic attention of men, Renée is dependent on the male gaze; she functions according to her "to-be-looked-at-ness," to borrow the term Laura Mulvey uses to describe the role of female film stars as objects of a voyeuristic male gaze.[79] At the same time, Renée feels limited by the pressures of this identity and longs for a fulfillment that she cannot seem to imagine within the structures of patriarchy and the confines of heterosexual bonds.[80] Yet whereas Pougy's drama was concerned chiefly with the way her protagonist was seen—Flossie symbolizing the possibility of freeing her mind and soul from the confines of the patriarchal gaze—Colette demonstrates how the possibility of the woman seeing for herself is essential to her intellectual expression. Renée's position as narrator thus unsettles

Figure 3. Photograph of Colette. (Print Collection, Miriam and Ira D. Wallach Division of Art, Prints and Photographs, The New York Public Library, Astor, Lenox and Tilden Foundations.)

the traditional relationship between active male viewer and passive female object of his gaze as Renée subverts her to-be-looked-at-ness with her own autonomous gaze. But this gaze is as unstable as her text itself, which moves from diary to dialogue to letters without settling into a familiar genre. In the discussion that follows, I consider Renée's unique point of view in the context of the evolving visual culture of the Belle Epoque, which Vanessa Schwartz has described as an arena of flânerie for the masses. Schwartz analyzes the Paris morgue, wax museums, and panoramas as sites for the "new, mobilized gaze of the precinematic spectator"—the fin-de-siècle flâneur.[81] Energized by a nascent celebrity culture, the worlds of the theater and music hall can also be considered sites for flânerie. As with the images in the other domains, spectacle and reality were blurred on the stage by spectators familiar with performers who regularly paraded through the Haussmanized promenades and arcades of Paris, whose images proliferated on posters and postcards, and whose lives were documented by the new mass press.

The modern urban pleasure of the flâneur was first described by Baudelaire in his 1863 essay "The Painter of Modern Life" as the immense joy of being "hors de chez soi, et pourtant se sentir partout chez soi; voir le monde, être au centre du monde et rester caché au monde" (away from home, and yet feeling at home; to see the world, to be in the midst of the world, and yet to remain hidden from everyone).[82] Baudelaire's flâneur, described as a prince who was undeniably male, enjoys the joint freedoms of mobility and privacy as he observes city life. As Parisian visual culture evolved through the proliferation of dioramas, panoramas, photography, a developing cityscape, and the advent of the department store, so did the possibilities for flânerie, opening up new ways of looking that were available to women for the first time and creating a new role for them outside the previously restricted categories of *fille publique* and *femme honnête*.[83] Yet the female position of "flâneuse" was limited—circumscribed by her role as consumer in the few public spaces where it was acceptable for women to roam freely.[84] In this light, I propose *La Vagabonde* as a commentary on the *fille publique*'s relationship to the modern urban spectacle she helped define. Renée's journey in this wandering text can be seen as the shift from to-be-looked-at-ness to vagabondage, a term in itself suggestive of the mobilized gaze of the flâneur.[85] The discovery of visual freedom allows Renée to construct an intellectual identity beyond the patriarchal structures of femininity imposed on her by her profession; her flânerie follows Schwartz's definition of the term: as a positionality of power through which the spectator is able to be part of the spectacle and yet command it at the same time.[86]

The tension between looking and being looked at is represented in several ways in the context of Renée's work as a music-hall dancer. The novel contains the letters of Renée's male admirers, only to undermine their declarations of desire with her own narrative rereadings. Renée receives such a letter in the first chapter: " 'Madame, j'étais au premier rang de l'orchestre; votre talent de mime m'invite à croire que vous en possédez d'autres, plus spéciaux et plus captivants encore; faites-moi le plaisir de souper ce soir avec moi ' " (Madam, I was in the first row of the orchestra; your talent as a mime leads me to believe that you have others, even more special and captivating; give me the pleasure of your dining with me tonight) (9). Like Vivien's readers, Renée's fans expect the woman and the public performer to be one and the same; the dancer, like the writer, is but a variation of the prostitute in the eyes of these desiring men. By virtue of her public role, her sexuality is also assumed to be public, an assumption that in fact had historical accuracy. Many dancers, including Liane de Pougy, who appeared many times at the Folies-Bergères, were also for hire. Renée describes her naïve suitors as vacuous brutes, thinking with their erotic desires rather than with their minds: "Leurs lettres pressées, brutales et gauches, traduisent leur envie, non leurs pensées" (Their hurried letters are awkward and aggressive, communicating their desire and not their thoughts) (26). Like Vivien, the juxtaposition of her scathing commentary alongside the presumptive missives and admissions of her male admirers showcases the way in which the woman writer's critical voice is constructed against a specular image of femininity that fuels and authorizes patriarchal male desire. Renée's critical acumen as both a reader and writer protects her autonomous identity as it instantly transforms her spectators into objects of her own critical gaze.

The novel opens with Renée hesitating between written text and specular image as she wavers between immersing herself in an old magazine or facing her own reflection, personnified as "cette conseillère maquillée qui me regarde, de l'autre côté de la glace, avec de profonds yeux aux paupières frottées d'une pâte grasse et violâtre" (that counselor covered in make-up, gazing at me from the other side of the mirror, with dark eyes and eyelids covered with a purplish greasepaint) (5). Inscribed symbolically in Renée's name, which is itself a kind of mirror image, the mirror captures the complex specular dynamics at the heart of the protagonist's identity. It frames Renée's relationship to the image of herself that is projected to the outside—the image of the *fille publique*'s to-be-looked-at-ness. The theatrical setting of this opening scene underscores the performative aspect of Renée's identity; dressing room, make-up, and costume call attention to the way her identity is assumed. In addition to her *conseillère maquillée,* the constant spy who forces Renée to recognize herself as the image in the mirror, other figures of this specular mode are found in her eventual lover Maxime Dufferein-Chautel, in her dog, Fossette, and in the numerous admirers at her music-hall performances, all of whom provide affirmation of her physical presence with little if any attention to her internal conflicts.

The trauma of Renée's engagement with the mirror is in the simultaneous recognition of and alienation from the image reflected back. Catching sight of herself, Renée remarks: "Moi . . . en pensant ce mot-là, j'ai regardé involontairement le miroir. C'est pourtant moi qui suis là, masquée de rouge mauve, les yeux cernés d'un halo de bleu gras qui commence à fondre" (Me . . . in thinking this word, I automatically looked in the mirror. Yet it is me who is there, masked in mauve rouge, with eyes ringed by a greasy blue halo that's beginning to melt) (7). "Moi" is at once present and hidden; the linguistic referent, like her caked-on make-up, symbolizes the layers of construction that make it difficult to reconcile image and reality. The response "c'est pourtant moi" codifies the joint process of recognition and negation inspired by the mirror that is repeated in other aspects of her specular existence in which she does and does not recognize herself. It is seen, for example, in her reaction to the way she is publicly acknowledged as a performer: "On me reconnaît . . . une 'mimique précise,' une 'diction nette', et une 'plastique impeccable'. C'est très gentil. . . . Mais . . . où cela mène-t-il?" (They acknowledge that my mimicry is "exact," my diction "clear," and my figure "impeccable." It's all very nice. . . . But . . . where does it lead?) (22).

Renée's relationship with the mirror takes the form of a dialogue that bypasses literary conventions. In the opening scene, the mirror famously interrogates Renée: "Est-ce toi qui es là? . . . Là, toute seule, dans cette cage aux murs blancs que des mains oisives, impatientes, prisonnières, ont écorchés d'initiales entrelacées, brodés de figures indécentes et naïves? (Is that you there? . . . Over there, all alone in this white-walled cage that impatient, idle, imprisoned hands have scraped with intertwined initials, emblazoned with indecent, foolish figures?) (6). That the mirror has its own voice points to the source of Renée's to-be-looked-at-ness in a process outside of the self. The images of imprisonment in this first comment reveal the oppressiveness of that process for Renée's self-determination and its opposition to the freedom of flânerie. Most significant, however, is Renée's ability to speak back, to respond to its accusations from an alternative perspective. Renée's responses are not stated in quotation marks; they are seamlessly integrated into the narrative. In other words, the text we are reading is a response to the mirror; this writing is the challenge to the spectacle of the *fille publique*—the alternative that will be realized through the mobilized gaze of the vagabond.[87]

As suggested by the novel's opening image in which Renée hesitates between reading and looking in the mirror, Renée's specular identity is constantly in tension with an alternative identification, symbolized through intellect, language, and text, or what she calls "l'habitude du soliloque" (the habit of soliloquy), the practice of talking to herself and her dog. Renée explains this habit as a "besoin littéraire de rythmer, de rédiger ma pensée" (a literary need to have a rhythm, to compose my thoughts) (15). The entire enigmatic text, which escapes simple generic categories (Is it a journal? a letter? to whom?), can be considered an expression of this *besoin littéraire,* a literary need that takes the form of a conversation bridging the gap between *fille publique* and woman writer.[88] Like Baudelaire's prose poems where the flâneur first found his voice, the novel is a fluid mix of observation and reverie, marking the transition from vision to writing. The need to bridge this gap is all the more urgent for Renée, because as a woman her flânerie depends on her overcoming her to-be-looked-at-ness. Renée's narrative voice, what she describes as "l'habitude du soliloque," is the expression of this desire to write—regardless of the fact that there is no reference in the novel to the generic nature of the text we are reading. This literary need expresses the desire for what Paul Ricoeur calls narrative identity, an identity that uses narrative to reconstruct itself.[89] Indeed, the possibility of writing is for Renée the possibility of writing the self; written expression is coextensive with self-expression: "Ecrire! verser avec rage toute la sincérité de soi sur le papier tentateur" (To write! To pour out angrily my whole self onto the tempting paper) (16). Writing may even precede speech for Renée: "Je l'ai lue écrite dans ma pensée" (I read it inscribed in my thoughts) (226), such that the narrative in its orality becomes the product of a written mode.

The shift of narrative positions that stages the process of moving away from the mirror and to-be-looked-at-ness toward an autonomous literary sensibility is most dramatically enacted in the scene of Renée's performance: a unique description of spectacle focalized through the eyes of the performer. The subversiveness of this perspective is underlined by the spectacle. Dressed in a wig and extensive veil, Renée will perform the dance of Salomé at a private soirée. Salomé was a favorite subject of fin-de-siècle male writers, inspiring Flaubert's *Salammbô* and *Hérodias,* Mallarmé's *Hérodiade,* Huysmans's *A Rebours,* and Wilde's *Salomé* (which was originally written in French with the help of Pierre Louÿs) and figured in many of Gustave Moreau's paintings as well.[90] In assuming this role, then, Renée will incarnate the symbol of mysterious and dangerous female sexuality, object par excellence of the fin-de-siècle voyeuristic and fetishistic male gaze. Yet within the text this gaze is represented only through Renée's own eyes. Wrapped in the long veil that is her costume, Renée peers out at her audience:

> Je ne distingue rien, d'abord, à travers le fin treillis de ma cage de gaze. Mes pieds nus, conscients, tâtent la laine courte et dure d'un beau tapis de Perse . . . Peu à peu le voile se desserre, s'enfle, vole et retombe, me révélant aux yeux de ceux qui sont là, qui ont tu, pour me regarder, leur enragé bavardage. . . . Je les vois. Malgré moi, je les vois. En dansant, en rampant, en tournant, je les vois, et je les reconnais! (51)

> [I cannot distinguish anything at first through the thin trellis of my gauzy cage. My nude feet, conscious, feel the short, hard wool of a beautiful Persian rug. . . . Slowly the veil loosens, rises, flies and falls again, revealing me to the eyes of those who are there, who have silenced their rowdy chatter in order to look at me. . . . I see them. Despite myself, I see them. While dancing, creeping, turning, I see them, and I recognize them!]

Unlike the panoply of male-authored female performers whose image she evokes, Colette's *fille publique* is both spectacle and spectator, meeting the eyes of her audience with her own discerning gaze. And unlike Nana, whose veil was the symbol of both her nudity and the mysterious sexuality that it covered, and—according to several critics—a fetish marking the disavowal of her castration by the male spectators, Renée's veil and her unveiling mark the possibility of her own ability to see, despite her specular status.[91] From this perspective, she gains power over her observers—among whom are some friends of her ex-husband—and reclaims the pleasure of her performance: "Ces gens là existent-ils? . . . Non, non, il n'y a de réel que la danse, la lumière, la liberté, la musique" (Do these people exist? . . . No, no, the only real things are the dance, the lights, the freedom, the music) (53). The textual power of the voyeur is further undermined when he is caught in the act of looking:

> Sur les côtés et au fond, il y a une ligne sombre d'hommes, debout. Ils se pressent et se penchent, avec cette curiosité, cette courtoisie rossarde de l'homme du monde pour la femme dite "déclassée," pour celle à qui l'on baisa le bout des doigts dans son salon et qui danse maintenant, demi-nue, sur une estrade. (53)

> [On the sides and in back, there is a dark line of men standing. They squeeze together and lean forward with that nasty curiosity well-to-do men have for a déclassé woman, for the one whose fingers were kissed in the salon and who dances now, half-naked, on a platform.]

In Degas's ballerina paintings, the sexualization of the dancers' profession is suggested through the representation of men waiting in the wings.[92] This same scene is represented here by Colette, but transformed by virtue of Renée's focalization. Renée's very ability to describe this scene from the position of the "femme dite 'déclassée' " reveals how the woman's linguistic authority—stemming from her critical gaze—transforms the hierarchy of the spectacle and the nature of the reader's identification. The image of herself—"qui danse demi-nue"—described *en abyme* through these men's eyes, seems to belong to another narrative, focalized through the male gaze; but here, by virtue of her own vision, the men's voyeuristic power over her is negated. Like the flâneur, then, she is part of the spectacle yet in command of it.[93]

On another level, Renée's need to translate her thoughts into narrative saves her from slipping into to-be-looked-at-ness, and this is a critical element of her flânerie. As for Baudelaire, this literary sensibility allows her to forge a relationship between observation and text. For Renée however, dance also becomes a form of self-expression, a bodily translation of her thoughts and an expression of her *besoin littéraire,* through which she is able to "rythmer sa pensée, la traduire en beaux gestes" (give rhythm to her thoughts, translate them into beautiful gestures) (53). Renée's realization that she can see while she dances is thus a crucial step toward her ultimate recognition that she can be a dancer and a writer.

In Colette's novel, writing is symbolic of an idealized refuge from the world that sets itself in opposition to the harshness of the mirror. Renée begins writing when her husband begins cheating on her. Described as a "balzacien génie du mensonge" (Balzacian genius of lying), his betrayals are lodged in discursive deception, reflecting an altogether different relationship to writing than her own. Wounded by Taillandy's betrayals, Renée turns to writing, "pour le seul plaisir de me réfugier dans un passé tout proche" (for the sole pleasure of finding refuge in a very recent past) (30). Her *besoin littéraire* is thus also an expression of resistance to the bonds of an oppressive marriage. But writing does not always provide this kind of refuge, Renée discovers. Her first book's success reaffirms her link to her husband, casting them both in a public light, as they become " 'le couple le plus intéressant de Paris' " ("the most interesting couple in Paris") (31). Refuge is finally accorded to Renée through her third book, which failed publicly but provides her with private pleasures. She describes it as "mon 'chef-d'oeuvre inconnu' à moi" (my own "unknown masterpiece"). Whereas others found it "diffus et confus, et imcompréhensible, et long" (diffuse and muddled, and incomprehensible, and long), when she opens it, she finds a positive affirmation of herself: "je l'aime, je m'y aime de tout mon coeur" (I love it, I love myself in it with all my heart) (31). Remarking on her personal relationship with her book as her own privileged reader, she writes: "Incompréhensible? pour vous, peut-être. Mais pour moi, sa chaude obscurité s'éclaire; pour moi, tel mot suffit à recréer l'odeur, la couleur des heures vécues, il est sonore et plein et mystérieux comme une coquille où chante la mer" (Incomprehensible? For you, perhaps. But for me, its warm obscurity is clear; for me, a single word is enough to recreate the odor, the color of hours past; it is as sonorous and full and mysterious as a shell in which the sea sings) (31).

Recalling Nhine's transcriptophilia in its evocation of the pleasures of written communication, this literary ideal precludes the scopic violence of the patriarchal gaze; its enjoyment is dependent on the outside (male) reader's not having access to it. Indeed, Renée confesses, "je l'aimerais moins, je crois, si vous l'aimiez aussi" (I would love it less, I think, if you loved it as well) (31). In this unique form of transcriptophilia, Renée's ideal addressee is herself rather than a lover, affirming the reflexivity inscribed in her own name.[94] The positive, nonalienating recognition of self affirmed in her narcissistic love for her third novel recalls Vivien's decision to hide her *Flambeaux éteints* because she loved it so dearly. Renée's third book represents a female literary ideal of perfect communication—like Flossie and Nhine's mutual understanding, and Vivien's feminocentric reading community. This ideal is the opposite of Renée's relationship with Max, which will impede communication and force her to choose silence. On one hand we can note the angst with which Renée laments the absence of writing in her current life, unfavorably comparing herself to Balzac, symbol of literary success. But Balzac is also linked discursively to duplicity, as in Taillandy's Balzacian "génie du mensonge." Renée's satisfaction with her third novel suggests that the Balzacian model is not necessarily her ideal and implicitly situates the novel we are reading in an alternative discursive category: this is not Balzac either, this writing. This text functions differently, dictated by Renée's literary affirmation of self through the construction of a liberated female gaze.[95]

The key to Renée's success will be the ability to sustain the link between her literary voice and the mobilized and liberated gaze that fueled her dance of Salomé. Maxime Dufferein-Chautel, known affectionately as "Le Grand Serin" (the Big Noodle) or Max, is the central obstacle in this process. Like her other male admirers, he sees her first on stage and never seems to overcome his initial status as a spectator, a fact that is underlined throughout the text, suggesting an implicit link between heterosexual relations dictated by male authority and women's to-be-looked-at-ness. After succumbing to Max's wishes, Renée admits to her overriding desire to have "un avide *spectateur* de ma vie et de ma personne" (an avid *spectator* of my life and my person) (125), rather than have a lover or a friend. The attention of this "spectateur passionné" (passionate spectator) is pleasing to Renée. But this pleasure, like that of her performance, depends on her ability to look back, and only from this critical position, when, as she puts it, "c'est lui qui devient pour moi le spectacle" (he is the one who is becoming my spectacle) (106) does Renée tolerate Max's gaze. Her need to balance her pleasure in being watched with her own visual vigilance and pleasure in watching is made clear in one of their first moments of intimacy when Renée refuses to close her eyes, observing instead the slow approach of "cette sérieuse figure étrangère, cet homme que je connais si peu" (that serious foreign face, that man whom I don't know at all) (142). As her lover leans in to kiss her, Renée's open eyes are a mode of self-defense, for Max seems to pose a threat to the autonomy of her gaze: "Je n'ai pas fermé les yeux. Je fronce les sourcils, pour menacer au-dessus de moi ces prunelles qui cherchent à réduire, à éteindre les miennes" (I did not close my eyes. I knit my brows, to threaten those dark eyes overhead that sought to reduce mine, to extinguish them) (142). The kiss that eventually takes place is described with complex choreography over several paragraphs. As in her performance, Renée's pleasure is contingent on visual control.

Ultimately Max cannot be for Renée what Flossie was for Nhine, the possibility of an alternative specularity that will not impinge on her subjectivity. Indeed, Max's perspective is for Renée no different from that of the mirror; being with him means confronting the way that she is seen from the outside, and he never seems to allow her to move beyond this view. His company is compared to the way in which "quelque miroir inattendu, au détour d'une rue, dans un escalier, révèle soudain certaines tares, certains fléchissements de visage et de silhouette" (some unexpected mirror, at the end of a street, on a stair, reveals certain defects, certain sags in the face or the figure) (86). This comparison to the unexpected encounters of the street further points out a desire for flânerie—for a kind of liberating mobility associated with the urban landscape that was not available to women in the way that it was to men. Like the unexpected mirror, the fixity of Max's gaze is suffocating, preventing her from taking in air, from continuing to *flâner:* "Mais dès que je me penchais pour boire un peu le vent faible, chargé du musc amer des anciennes feuilles décomposées, je sentais le regard de mon amoureux se poser, assuré, sur toute ma personne" (But as soon as I leaned in to drink the light wind charged with the bitter musk of decomposing leaves, I felt the assured gaze of my lover descend upon my whole person) (130). Indeed, Max's gaze proves more powerful and dangerous than the mirror, because it threatens to undermine Renée's own point of view. Their perspectives are pitted against each other, just as his gaze seemed to want to extinguish hers during the kiss. Max wants to marry Renée, tempting her with the notion that "tu serais prise" (you would be taken) (173) and no longer alone; yet for her marriage symbolizes confinement and the dissolution of self. She asks herself: "Je pourrais donc finir paisiblement ma vie, blottie dans sa grande ombre?" (Could I thus finish my life peacefully, curled up in his large shadow?) (174).

The drama of rebirth suggested by Renée's name takes place in the final section of the novel, when writing merges with vagabondage, the travels that mobilize her gaze and bring her further from the crippling stasis of the mirror.[96] This last section, which partly comprises the letters Renée writes to Max when she is traveling with her dance company, stages in its epistolarity an explicit return to written expression. Renée's voice shifts here from being that of a character speaking to herself and her mirror, to being that of the wielder of a pen who transmits her thoughts to others.[97]

In her epistolary exchange with Max in this final section Renée mentions lesbian sexuality, in reference to her friend, Amalia Barally, whom she encounters during her trip. Without exaggerating the importance to the overall narrative of this lesbian character, who is referred to in three passages in the final section, I would like to call attention to Amalia's symbolic relationship to Renée's writing process in the context of female autobiographical fictions and the conflict suggested between heterosexual desire and female authority. Amalia brings to light the discursive barriers between men and women, stemming from their different relationships to language: the very thing that enrages Renée Vivien's San Giovanni and forces Renée Néré to choose silence. After mentioning Amalia's presence in a letter, Renée comments on Max's adverse reaction:

> Il s'y souvient, mal à propos, que ma camarade Amalia Barally n'aimait pas les hommes. Il n'a pas manqué, en être "normal" et "bien équilibré" qu'il est, de flétrir un peu, en la raillant, ma vieille amie, et de nommer "vice" ce qu'il ne comprend pas. A quoi bon lui expliquer? . . . Deux femmes enlacées ne seront jamais pour lui qu'un groupe polisson, et non l'image mélancolique et touchante de deux faiblesses, peut-être réfugiées aux bras l'une de l'autre pour dormir, y pleurer, fuir l'homme souvent méchant, et goûter, mieux que tout plaisir, l'amer bonheur de se sentir pareilles, infimes, oubliées. . . . A quoi bon écrire, et plaider, et discuter? Mon voluptueux ami ne comprend que l'amour. (211–12)
>
> [He remembers, unfortunately, that my friend Amalia Barally didn't like men. As the "normal" and "well-balanced" person that he is, he didn't fail to put my old friend down a little in mocking her, and to label as "vice" that which he doesn't understand. What good is it to explain to him? . . . Two intertwined women will never be for him anything other than a saucy couple, and not the melancholy, touching image of two weak creatures, perhaps taking refuge in each other's arms to sleep, to cry, to flee the cruelty of men, and to savor something better than any pleasure: the bitter happiness of feeling similar, frail, forgotten. . . . What good is it to write, plead, discuss? My pleasure-seeking friend can understand only love.]

Max's actual words are inscribed here in quotation marks, visually enforcing their separation from Renée's own language. Amalia is a symbol of Max's insufficiency as an interlocutor and as a reader, as well as of the need for female refuge from the dangers of the patriarchal desiring gaze—a refuge previously symbolized through Renée's own writing. Amalia's role transcends her individuality; she is representative of a larger ideal of love between women, of the unnamed *deux femmes enlacées,* and of the perceived incompatibility of heterosexuality and communication. Like Pougy's Flossie, she is a figure of the transcriptual mode, and like Vivien's Eva as well, the possibility of an ideal addressee. The correspondence between the lesbian relationship and Renée's relationship to writing is underlined by the shared vocabulary drawn on for both. Like Renée's writing, female love is a refuge to which men will never have access. As a metaphor for Renée's literary needs, the lesbian couple signals the relational aspect of writing as a form of transcriptophilia—a privileged connection between two people, reader/addressee and writer, and through which female identity receives affirmation. "L'amer bonheur de se sentir pareilles" is in that sense like Renée's bittersweet pleasure of rediscovering herself in her text, as she describes it: "tel mot suffit à recréer l'odeur, la couleur des heures vécues" (a word recreates the odor, the color of hours past) (31).

Renée's final mention of Amalia is significant as a perspectival shift that signals Renée's self-authorization as a vagabond. A few letters later, Renée sends Max a photograph of herself taken by Amalia, a last effort to force him to see her the way she would like to be seen, or, in other words, to see what she sees. She supplies a description: "M'y trouvez-vous assez noire, assez petite, assez chien perdu, avec ces mains croisées et cet air battu?" (Do you find me rather dark and small, like a lost dog, with my folded hands and that beaten look?) (219). As an aspect of Renée's flânerie, Amalia represents, then, the creation of an alternative, feminized point of view, an alternative spectacle, for which Renée would control the narration and the context. In the process, the lesbian relationship becomes a metaphor for the woman's nurturing and affirming relationship to herself, like Renée and her third novel. The narcissism of this relationship is mitigated by its relevance to the dynamics of female autobiographical writing, and to this novel in particular: the possibility of the woman's representing herself, providing the narration and focalization with which to contextualize her own to-be-looked-at-ness and thus somehow control the way she is read, as well as finding a format in which to express what she sees.

The final paragraphs of the novel read like a manifesto, addressed to a second person "tu" but no longer in epistolary form.[98] Through the "tu" Max blurs back to his original identity as one of the many admirers ogling Renée (she calls him "cher intrus" [dear intruder]), a male spectator capable of providing her with fleeting and ultimately unfulfilling pleasures. At this point Renée links her visual vigilance to her critical voice and finally incriminates the male spectator threatening the subjective possibilities of her flânerie. She thus stakes out once and for all her own viewing position by announcing: "les plus beaux pays de la terre, je refuse de les contempler, tout petits, au miroir amoureux de ton regard!" (I refuse to contemplate the most beautiful lands of the earth as tiny images refracted through the mirror of your adoring gaze!) (247). Through this declaration, she firmly rejects the male desiring gaze as a point of departure for female subjectivity, refusing love as a palliative to her subordinate position in a patriarchal desiring economy and incriminating his scopophilic desire as an obstacle to the possibility of her seeing for herself. At this point, too, Renée recognizes herself as "vagabonde, et libre" (a vagabond, and free) (248), linking the text we are reading to the one she is writing. Indeed, in the clarity of vision that returns here, predicted by the unveiling of the spectators from the stage, the shift from spectacle to writer is enacted as Renée's authority is reclaimed. The first-person voice of Renée's letters merges with that of the narrator, but this voice has turned itself outward, to address a reader. The gap between seeing and narrating is finally closed: vision becomes narrative as Renée asserts her status as author and spectator; the spectacle becomes a text; the fantasy of female flânerie is realized as the *fille publique* becomes as a writer.

The novels by Pougy, Vivien, and Colette that I have presented bring into sharper relief the importance of autobiographical writing in its particular role in female self-authorization. Marginalized figures often enter dominant discourses by writing autobiographically; much writing by francophone African writers, for example, follows this path, perhaps because to be a writer of fiction depends in part on the possibility of identifying with a textual representation of the self. Autobiographical writing enabled Pougy, Vivien, and Colette to construct an initial discursive position, a platform from which to perform their disruptive literary acts. At the same time, their autobiographical texts pose forceful critiques of the structures beyond their literary frameworks that provided obstacles to women's self-expression and intellectual recognition. Perhaps as a result of their marginalization from dominant literary movements, these authors present autobiography as a realm of experimentation, through which style and genre are mixed in creative and original ways, from Vivien's pastiche of music, poetry, letters, and narrative to Colette's merging of epistolary and diary forms. While they engage many naturalist and decadent themes, their novels artfully resist the overarching symbolics and narrative structure of these dominant literary movements. In the next two chapters, in contrast, I consider examples of women posing similar critical questions while explicitly adopting the male-authorized discourses of naturalism and decadence. The question then becomes: can the master's tools dismantle the master's house?

3

Virility and the Intellectual Woman

OR, CAN A WOMAN BE A NATURALIST?

Although the success of women authors at the fin de siècle was enough to unsettle many men in the profession, those who criticized women's literature found comfort in their perception that this writing limited itself to the traditionally feminine domains of love and romance. It was acceptable, after all, for women to write about matters of the heart, and to focus on the inner struggles posed by romantic relationships. In this vein Jules Bertaut comes to the following conclusion: "La femme est faite essentiellement pour aimer, c'est là le plus puissant et le plus habituel de ses instincts. Traduisez en art: la femme est faite pour chanter l'amour. Neuf fois sur dix, le sujet de ses romans ou de ses poèmes sera l'amour, encore l'amour, toujours l'amour!" (Woman is essentially made for loving; that's the most powerful and habitual of her instincts. Translated into art, one could say that woman is made for singing of love. Nine times out of ten, the subject of her novels and poetry will be love, more love, always love!).[1] Another well-known literary critic, Jean Ernest-Charles, offered a similar opinion in 1902. He describes women's romance writing as instinctive, for women naturally write about love, and they write practically in spite of themselves (*à leur insu*), bypassing the intellectual step entirely.[2] These comments dovetail with the widespread belief that women could write only autobiographically. Writing about love was simply another means of writing about the self. Most important, perhaps, the essentialist reduction of women's writing to their instinctive inclination to romance permitted a facile distinction from male authors. According to this logic, men's allegedly superior talent and ability to address wider-reaching, rational, and philosophical subject matter stemmed implicitly from their virility. Ernest-Charles, for one, insists on this distinction: he accepts women as writers to the extent that they produce true women's works, defined as "une littérature délicate et pure" (a pure and delicate literature).[3]

In fact, fin-de-siècle women novelists did often write about love and romance, centering their stories on the emotional drama of female heroines in the development of a relationship with a man.[4] But these authors' literary circumscription within the world of romance was not a result of genetic predisposition, as fin-de-siècle male critics would have it. Instead we can view this trend as a byproduct of the culturally entrenched assimilation of intellect with virility. Linguistically speaking, to be a writer at the fin-de-siècle was to be a man; the term *écrivain* was (and still is in France) grammatically gendered as masculine. A woman who wrote was something different, lesser—a *femme de lettres* or a *bas-bleu,* terms that held negative associations throughout the nineteenth century and well into the twentieth. Following prevailing cultural views, Barbey d'Aurevilly described the woman writer as not just an intellectual puzzle but a physiological one: "Est-elle d'organes, de cerveau, et même de main, lorsqu'il s'agit d'art, capable des mêmes oeuvres que l'homme?" (When it comes to art, is she capable with her organs, her brain, and even her hands, of the same works as man?), he asks.[5] His answer was indeed a resounding no, a conclusion upheld by nineteenth-century medicine. Women's minds and bodies were considered utterly different from men's and thus by implication incapable of producing serious literature.[6] Viewed as naturally emotional and ill-equipped to exert intellectual effort, women were thus culturally and medically predetermined to limit their writings to love stories; indeed, this was the only domain in which writing was not seen as entirely threatening to femininity.

Broadening the feminized domain of love and romance to address larger social, philosophical, religious, or scientific issues in a novel, then, went against the very notion of the woman writer as she was understood at the fin-de-siècle. The seeming contradiction in terms whereby not only female authorship but femininity itself was in tension with intellectual authority was at the heart of the challenge Marcelle Tinayre, Lucie Delarue-Mardrus, and Rachilde faced. All three women actively engaged the dominant male-authorized literary discourses of the late nineteenth century, writing novels in the styles of naturalism (Tinayre and Delarue-Mardrus) and decadence (Rachilde).[7] Each of these writers challenged the exclusive link between virility and intellect and sought to attach intellectual authority to women's experiences—including but not limited to affairs of the heart. These efforts are staged both through the stories the authors tell and the ways in which they tell them, that is, in their adaptations of the discourses of naturalism and decadence. In addition, the circumstances surrounding the publication and reception of Tinayre's and Rachilde's novels dramatically reveal the fin-de-siècle reading public's difficulty in assimilating a woman writer who did not, as it were, write like a woman.

CAN A WOMAN BE A NATURALIST?

Nowhere are virility and intellectual authority linked more explicitly than in the discourse of naturalism as theorized by Zola himself. In his 1880 essay "Le Roman expérimental," Zola describes the scientific method that determines his naturalist project as masculine and virile, in contrast to the weak, sentimental, effeminate ways of romanticism.[8] This gendered hierarchy pervades his description of the naturalist goal of scientific mastery. In "Lettre à la jeunesse," he writes: "Applaudir une rhétorique, s'enthousiasmer pour l'idéal, ce ne sont là que de belles émotions nerveuses; les femmes pleurent, quand elles entendent de la musique. Aujourd'hui, nous avons besoin de la virilité du vrai pour être glorieux dans l'avenir" (Applauding a turn of phrase, becoming enthusiastic over an ideal, these are but beautiful nervous emotions; women cry when they hear music. Today we need the virility of the true in order to be glorious in the future).[9] In this chapter, I consider how two women challenged the "virility of the true" in naturalist novels of their own. In both Marcelle Tinayre's *La Maison du péché* and Lucie Delarue-Mardrus's *Marie, fille-mère,* the authors take on the role of naturalist scientists; in their experimental novels, however, the obstacle to scientific truth is the ignorance of and insensitivity to women's experiences and to women's potential as fully realized human beings.

As discussed in Chapter 1, a central concern of Zola's naturalist science was to discern the truth of female sexuality, depicted through Nana's uncontainable body as a source of contamination and degeneration. As products of a female-authorized science, the novels here challenge this view of the female body. The foremost mind/body struggle that takes place in these texts, then, is the implicit one between the woman writer and the female body she will attempt to free from its conventional incrimination by naturalist science. Tinayre and Delarue-Mardrus effectively wrest intellectual authority from virility by suggesting, in separate ways, that naturalism's most essential blindness is its misogyny, which ultimately prevents it from arriving at scientific truth. Love and romance, though offset through naturalist discussions of instincts and temperament, are not wholly absent in these novels, whose audience was predominantly female. By unsettling naturalism's biases, however, these texts offer a rare challenge to its patriarchal hegemony as they shift the focus of its scientific lens.

Why speak through naturalism in the first place, given its inherent hostility to women? Perhaps because Zola treated so many "women's issues" in his novels: prostitution, infertility, rape, menstruation, lesbianism, childbirth, hysteria, to name but a few. Like the vast array of nineteenth-century medical literature written for a popular male audience, in which the effects of female venereal disease, or the symptoms of a hysterical seizure, were outlined in clinical detail, Zola's treatment of these subjects was scientific and diligent, and often not for the faint of heart. Ironically, whether women agreed with his point of view or not, Zola's writing provided a vocabulary and a mode of speaking that was a useful starting point for those wishing to examine female sexuality from their own perspective; in this sense, his discourse enabled their counterdiscourses. We have already seen how Liane de Pougy confronted Zola's image of the courtesan in her own self-portrait. Tinayre and Delarue-Mardrus went even further in adapting, challenging, and transforming Zola's naturalism, explicitly and implicitly, in novels that offer what we might call a "feminized" science—a notion that for Zola would have surely been a contradiction in terms.

DANGEROUS DISCOURSE: MARCELLE TINAYRE'S *LA MAISON DU PÉCHÉ*

Born Marguerite-Suzanne-Marcelle Chasteau in 1870 in the Limousin region of France, Tinayre came from a line of educated women. The most prominent of these was her mother, Louise Chasteau, a teacher and a writer who, under various pseudonyms, published pedagogical texts, novels, short stories, and a newspaper column.[10] Tinayre was one of two women to sit for the baccalaureate in 1899, which she passed with honors.[11] Two weeks later she married the engraver and painter Julien Tinayre, a coupling that helped introduce her to the Parisian world of writers and artists. She went on to publish over thirty novels between 1895 and 1945 and give birth to four children (one of whom did not survive). Like many of her female peers, Tinayre also practiced journalism, writing for a variety of women's periodicals, including Marguerite Durand's *La Fronde* and the popular *Mode pratique,* as well as for more high-brow literary journals such as *Le Temps.* A self-described feminist, she spoke out on women's rights, from equality in the workplace and education to the right to love outside of marriage. She published two novels under the pseudonym Charles Marcel before coming into her literary own with the publication of *Avant l'amour* in 1897. The novel's acclaim in Juliette Adam's *Nouvelle Revue* led to its publication in volume by the *Mercure de France.* In fact, as literary critic for the journal *Mercure,* Rachilde reviewed the novel. Although she objected to what she perceived as Tinayre's claiming of political rights for women, she applauded the novel as further demonstration that women writers did not always write about themselves.[12] Even greater success for Tinayre came with *Hellé* in 1899, which received the Prix de l'académie.[13] But it was the 1902 *La Maison du péché,* one of the year's best-selling novels, that firmly established Tinayre's reputation both in France and abroad.[14] Indeed, James Joyce devoted an enthusiastic tribute to *La Maison du péché* in the October 1, 1903, edition of the Dublin *Daily Express*—the only piece he ever wrote on a French novel in this venue.[15] The novel was widely recognized as reaching beyond women's literature, addressing philosophical and moral problems traditionally found in more "virile" domains.[16]

La Maison du péché tells the story of Augustin de Chanteprie, a fatherless Catholic youth raised by his austere mother and his devout preceptor, Elie Forgerus. When the young Parisian widow and artist Fanny Manolé comes to town, Augustin attempts to lead her down the path of church doctrine by sharing his religious views. In the process, the two become engaged in a steamy love affair and plan to marry. Augustin, however, is haunted by Fanny's sexual liberty, which challenges all the church has taught him. He fears falling into the same trap as his notorious great uncle, a libertine who had an affair with a dancer named Rosalba-Rosalinde and who once lived in the house where Augustin now lives (hence the novel's title). Encouraged by Forgerus, he breaks off the relationship to return to his faith, only to fall ill, mentally and physically. The novel ends on his deathbed, as his friends and family bear witness to his gruesome demise.

Tinayre's naturalist novel conducts a Zolian experiment by staging a confrontation between two people from different backgrounds and different temperaments, introducing the engine of desire and recording the tragic dramatic consequences in richly realist detail. In the essay "Le Roman experimental," where he outlines his scientific theory of the novel, Zola follows the teachings of the physiologist Claude Bernard, whose words he calls more "virile" than any others. Zola thus describes the naturalist novel as a means to a scientific, and perhaps metaphysical, end: "pénétrer le pourquoi des choses, pour devenir supérieur aux choses" (to penetrate the why of things, in order to rule over them).[17] (In *Le Docteur Pascal* this process is reformulated as "tout dire pour tout connaître pour tout guérir" [to say everything in order to understand everything in order to cure everything]).[18] He asks, "Puisque la médicine, qui était un art, devient une science, pourquoi la littérature elle-même ne devient-elle pas une science, grâce à la méthode expérimentale?" (Since medicine, which was an art, is becoming a science, why doesn't literature itself become a science, thanks to the experimental method?).[19] Dorothy Kelly has demonstrated how two of Zola's novels, *Le Docteur Pascal,* the story of a scientist, and *La Faute de l'abbé Mouret,* the story of a priest, display the gendered structure of his scientific process as a fantasy of male mastery. Tracing the fascinating parallels between these two novels, Kelly argues that the two professions are intimately linked in Zola's oeuvre.[20] The amorous tensions between the scientist Pascal and his niece Clotilde mirror those between the priest Serge and the young Albine; in both texts, women are depicted as spoilers of scientific and religious projects, threatening the purity of these pursuits.

As a doomed love story between woman and priest, Tinayre's novel bears some obvious relationships to *La Faute.* As in Zola's text, religious discourse about sexuality overlaps with naturalist depictions of the dangers of the female body: both stereotype femininity as a source of temptation and a force of destruction, weighing its generative power against its morbid possibilities. But as Tinayre restructures the naturalist science experiment—changing both the nature of the players and the outcome—she updates and transforms Zola's naturalist model. Her novel suggests that the greatest threat to naturalist science and to Catholicism is not women but misogyny: the refusal to hear women's voices, and the notion of female sexuality as something to be either cured or expunged.

Tinayre's use of the free indirect style allows familiar fin-de-siècle anxieties about female sexuality to intrude on the text without her directly articulating them through the voice of her narrator. Her style may also have camouflaged her critique from more conservative readers, while at the same time distinguishing her writing from the moralizing rhetoric of many nineteenth-century sentimental novels, where the narrator's opinions are explicitly conveyed.[21] According to Halina Suwala's formulation, Zola's narration is characterized by "impersonality," through which the narrator adopts the voice of certain characters and sometimes an entire neighborhood.[22] Mimicking Zola's narrator, Tinayre's voice blurs with those of her characters, making it difficult to assign an authorial point of view. Without quotation marks, for example, the narrator passes in and out of Forgerus's conscience, where he worries about his pupil's sexual future: "Bientôt l'impure Ennemie viendrait rôder autour de cette âme en fleur" (Soon the impure Enemy would come to lurk around this blossoming soul).[23] In Forgerus's imagination, the drama of original sin is infused with an anxiety about the female body that is colored by naturalist language: "Oui, la femme conçoit dans le péché; la concupiscence d'Eve passe avec son sang et son lait, dans la chair de l'Adam futur" (Yes, woman conceives in sin; the lust of Eve passes with her blood and milk, into the flesh of the future Adam) (36).[24] Here he is very much like Zola's Archangias in *La Faute,* who expresses disgust for the reproductive process. Forgerus's statement is first remarkable for its reversal of biblical anthropology. Eve does not emerge from Adam's rib; instead, like Zola's Gervaise, she is the original matriarch, giving birth not to Cain but to Adam. Furthermore, Eve's sin is not simply a spiritual condition—as in the Christian tradition—but a disease that she passes on through her flesh; original sin becomes original pathology, like Zola's *fêlure,* the image of degeneration that travels through the Rougon-Macquart taking on different symbolic meaning in each context. It also recalls the *plaie grave* figured as the source of contagion in Zola's explanation of Bernard's scientific method, the hidden, originary wound that results in a complex illness. Both figures can be traced to the female anatomy in Zola's oeuvre.[25]

In using naturalism's imagery to describe Catholic doctrine, Tinayre reveals their shared assumptions. When the time is right, Forgerus offers Augustin the following educating words, in which he makes no distinction between illicit and honorable love: "Une Eve innocente et corrompue nous apparaît toujours, et nous devons lutter contre elle. . . . Dans le mariage, comme dans l'amour illégitime, la femme est l'ennemie de l'homme, et le saint qui pèche sept fois par jour, pèche six fois à cause d'elle" (An innocent and corrupt Eve always appears to us, and we must struggle against her. . . . In marriage, as in illegitimate love, woman is the enemy of man, and the saint who sins seven times a day sins six times because of her) (63). In this explanation of Catholic doctrine, marriage does not necessarily purify sexuality: a man can sin by lustfully desiring his wife. In equating all women with Eve, Forgerus reduces femininity to sexuality, which, in the convention of his era, can lead men to their own destruction.

Forgerus acts as a double in the text for Augustin's equally devout mother, Thérèse Angélique de Chanteprie. Religious and maternal adoration are conflated, as Augustin's own religious fervor is rooted in his unhealthy mystification of his mother: "Mère, Reine, et par-dessus tout, Sainte!" (Mother, Queen, and above all, Saint!) (31). In turn, Forgerus's devotion to Augustin is inspired by his own mother's choice to deliver him to God "plutôt qu'à la rivale, la maîtresse ou l'épouse" (rather than to the rival, the mistress, or the spouse) (36). Divine love is a substitute for both carnal love and incestuous desire, and these pre-existing familial tensions predispose Augustin to sexual temptation. Madame de Chanteprie shares Forgerus's view of femininity and expresses a discomfort with her own corporeality that propels her religious devotion. Even the most virtuous woman who has never stepped out of maternal bounds in her own sexual behavior regards her own femininity with disdain. Upon realizing the extent of Augustin's involvement with Fanny, and thus his betrayal of the church, she blames herself: "Hélas! j'ai été femme, et j'ai été mère. . . . Ce qui sort de la boue retourne à la boue: le fils de la femme retourne à la femme" (Alas, I was a woman, and I was a mother. . . . What comes from mud returns to mud: the son of woman returns to woman) (309). Tinayre merges biblical thematics here (from dust to dust) with naturalist vocabulary, where *boue* (mud) and *fange* (mire) are synonymous with moral depravity. The use of the *passé composé* for "j'ai été femme" suggests that religious virtue is incompatible with femininity: it is achieved after having been a woman and a mother. The narrative describes Mme de Chanteprie's anguish: "Elle découvrit le mystère de sa vie, l'inguérissable plaie qui saignait encore après vingt ans de veuvage, et que les baumes mystiques n'avaient pu cicatriser" (She discovered the mystery of her life, the incurable wound that still bled after twenty years of widowhood, and which mystical balms had not been able to heal) (309). Once again mixing a Zolian vocabulary with the thematics of mysticism, the narrator suggests that Mme de Chanteprie has infected her son with that inescapable disease of sexuality.

The ideas about sexuality that are woven throughout Tinayre's character sketches do more than simply develop these vibrant figures: through Tinayre's lens they demonstrate the force of a certain hegemonic discourse as it acts on powerless bodies. Fanny—and later Augustin—are victimized in the novel by the violent power of language itself in its disjunction from their physical and emotional reality. Before she even begins her relationship with Augustin, Fanny—known as "la créature," a term from Christian vocabulary—is thought to be a prostitute because of her commitment to male friendships and refusal to cater to provincial conventions of feminine behavior; she rides a bicycle, for example. Information about Fanny begins to circulate throughout the village, freely and viciously, without always being linked to any specific informant. This sourceless gossip enables the villagers to assume the worst, which authorizes them to conclude: "Sa gueuse l'a perverti, démoralisé. . . . M. le Curé dit qu'elle est la Bête de l'Ecriture, cette femme-là" (His tramp has perverted him, demoralized him. . . . The parish priest says that she is the beast from the Bible, that woman) (283). Tinayre thus dissolves the distinction between religious discourse and village gossip, suggesting that both are self-propelled forces equally removed from reality.

As an unmarried independent woman seeking romance, Fanny certainly has the necessary features of a naturalist *femme fatale,* a figure of illicit female sexuality. Yet in Tinayre's text, she is a subversive figure in another sense, constantly undermining by her complex individual reality the ideology—naturalist and Christian—that attempts to stereotype her as a female sexual transgressor. She is depicted as amoral rather than immoral, a kind of pure soul, untainted by religious education or philosophical reflection: "La vie éternelle! Fanny Manolé n'y songeait guère. Aucun souci de métaphysique ne lui gâtait le très simple bonheur d'exister. Les hypothèses des philosophes ne l'intéressaient pas beaucoup plus que les certitudes des croyants" (Eternal life! Fanny Manolé hardly thought about it. No metaphysical worry spoiled the simple happiness of existence. The hypotheses of philosophers did not interest her much more than the certainties of believers) (127). Tinayre thus signals the opposition between Fanny's natural existence and the constructed moral systems used to explain the world. Fanny does not understand that "on eût fondé des systèmes de moral sur la vertu purificatrice de la douleur" (moral systems have been founded on the purifying virtue of pain) (127); Christianity is depicted as a system, something to be learned through the books with which the priests attempt to convert her, as opposed to being linked to life experience. On the level of narration, we can note Tinayre's distance from the romance novel, where the narrator is typically intimately allied with the female protagonist. Here, however, the narrator is placed intellectually above Fanny; her innocent ignorance is a factor in the science experiment that Tinayre is conducting as a naturalist writer.

Tinayre's novel demonstrates the way that moral systems are inscribed in language, through semantics that create an obstacle between male and female relationships. Augustin is troubled by his feelings for Fanny because they contradict the terms by which he has been taught to understand women. Forgerus's lessons have made him frightened of " 'l'animal féminin' " (the female animal). At the same time, he realizes that "Fanny ne représentait pas 'l'animale féminine,' ni même la séductrice, ni l'épouse. Elle était seulement une âme" (Fanny didn't represent the "female animal," or even the seductress, or the spouse. She was simply a soul) (119). Augustin struggles here to assimilate the reality he witnesses using the language with which his education—social and religious—has equipped him. While he is capable of rejecting inappropriate labels—*animal, séductrice, épouse*—he ultimately chooses the most neutral term he can find, *âme,* from within this religious vocabulary. The fin-de-siècle association suggested by this term, however, is Sister Thérèse de Lisieux's best-selling *Histoire d'une âme*—the story of a nun devoted to self-sacrifice and the service of God. Augustin's use of this term for Fanny seems almost ironic in this context, underlining the extreme connotations built into the religious vocabulary, leaving no way to speak of a woman in more nuanced terms. On another level, this brief passage refers indirectly to the prototypical struggle of the woman writer attempting to analyze female sexuality through fin-de-siècle discourse: her first challenge is on the level of vocabulary, to find terms that are not packed with negative implications. This struggle is linked to Tinayre's very identity as a woman writer, a profession itself tainted by the terms meant to describe it, since both *bas-bleu* and *femme de lettres* have negative connotations in fin-de-siècle French. By staging this struggle through her male protagonist, Tinayre underlines one of the fundamental messages of her novel: that both men and women can be harmed by the inscription of misogyny in discourse.

Fanny is confronted directly with this discursive problem in conversations with her long-time friend Georges Barral, who is estranged from his wife but wants neither to divorce nor to remarry. Nonetheless, Georges tries to persuade Fanny to become his mistress, since everyone already assumes she is "une femme d'amour" (a woman of love). Georges's naïve interpretation of this label clashes with Fanny's more sophisticated understanding of the transformative power of social categories. "Une femme d'amour, c'est une fille" (A woman of love, that's a prostitute) (89), Fanny explains, understanding the figural sense of this derogatory label, and, unlike Nana, immediately penetrating to the real discursive consequences of being talked about. But Georges disagrees emphatically. For him, "une femme d'amour" is simply "une femme qui aime l'amour, une femme qui est faite pour l'amour" (a woman who loves love, a woman who is made for love) (89). And, he adds, "Soit dit sans vous offenser, ma chère, vous représentez exactement ce type de femme, au physique et au moral" (Let it be said without offending you, my dear, you represent exactly that kind of woman, physically and morally) (89). For Georges, situated comfortably on the other side of the double standard, Fanny's sexual liberty makes her his ideal partner in crime. Indeed, this conversation points to the critical relationship between social position and discursive power. Georges sees the designation "femme d'amour" as innocuous and possibly even liberating semantics; he is in a position of interpretation and manipulation of meaning. Fanny, however, recognizes her position within the label, as the object of discourse and not its speaker; she understands the danger and humiliation of being caught in such a category and reacts to Georges's suggestion with horror.[26]

Some time later, Georges explains to Fanny: "Vous êtes seule, et dans le monde parisien, la femme qui n'est à aucun homme, amant ou mari, est à tous les hommes. . . . On le croit du moins, et on le dit" (You are alone, and in the Parisian world, the woman who belongs to no man, lover or husband, belongs to all men. . . . People believe this at least, and that's what they say) (259). The word *on,* free from agency, signals the unchecked authority of public discourse. Minutes later, Georges attempts to force himself physically on Fanny and reveals the power of this discourse on the imagination. Desperate for a physical relationship, he buys into the public view of Fanny, allowing the discourse to erase the individual as it transforms the way he views reality.

Despite Tinayre's careful demonstration of women's vulnerability to linguistic categories, ultimately it is not Fanny who receives the punishing effects of this discourse but Augustin himself. As the novel progresses, Augustin cannot remain immune to the beliefs about sexuality plaguing him in both religious and secular life. His ideas about Fanny are continually conflated with ideas about femininity in general, such that "Fanny, c'était une femme et c'était la femme" (Fanny was a woman and she was woman) (168). This statement represents one of the dangers of essentializing discourse, be it that of Catholicism or of fin-de-siècle literary criticism. There is no means of distinguishing between the individual and the collective. Later Augustin's downfall is attributed to the fact that "une femme était venue qui résumait en elle toutes les séductions et tous les dangers du siècle" (a woman had arrived who incarnated all the seductions and all the dangers of the century) (233). The individual woman thus becomes the scapegoat for the problems of the whole society, regardless of her actual guilt or innocence.

When Augustin is separated from Fanny for several days before their planned marriage, the association of sin and femininity reenters his imagination, and he becomes embroiled in nightmares about his lover that mimic the public's existing view of her as a temptress. Reacting to her total indifference to religion, Augustin conjures up his beloved as an instrument of the devil. He becomes obsessed with demonic images of Fanny—infected by them—such that "son imagination malade enfantait des monstres féminins, goules et succubes, qui ressemblaient à Fanny" (his sick imagination gave birth to feminine monsters, ghouls and witches who resembled Fanny) (301). In the midst of this descent into madness, Forgerus, Augustin's former preceptor, returns to town, summoned by Mme de Chanteprie, to rescue his protégé from the diabolical woman he has been warned about. Upon reading a letter by Fanny, however, he is shocked by the disjunction between his preconceived notions of her, constructed through his interpretation of Augustin's passion and what the villagers had said. His idea of Fanny as a "Mangeuse de coeurs" ("Devourer of Hearts") (312) had developed out of the perfect intersection between village gossip and church doctrine. The role of Fanny's letter in dismantling these notions signals the critical role of women's writing as a mechanism of discursive subversion. Indeed, Fanny's writing itself takes on an important role in the novel. As Augustin becomes less stable emotionally, holding fast to Christian tradition, Fanny's letters continue to appear. Augustin need not even read them; in their mere material presence they hold great symbolism ("des morceaux de la vie de Fanny, et de cette vie inconnue qu'il avait tant désiré connaître" [pieces of Fanny's life, and of that unknown life that he had so wanted to know] [352]) and threaten to undermine all Christianity has taught him, reminding him of the woman he loved. The threat of their content is underlined by his reaction: to continue his faith, he burns them feverishly. When Forgerus finally meets Fanny (Fig. 4), he is again shocked, expecting to see "La Furie, la Gorgone." Instead, he is struck by her intelligence and sensitivity, but this surprise has no consequence in his behavior.

Despite her use of naturalistic images to describe Catholic ideas of femininity and thus her suggestion of complicity between these two perspectives, Tinayre ultimately relies on naturalist science to mount a critique of Catholic restraints on human behavior. In keeping with Zolian tradition, Fanny and Augustin's desires are represented as the result of a variety of forces and circumstances over which they have little if any control: human instincts, heredity (particularly for Augustin, "fils d'un tuberculeux et d'une névropathe, rejeton d'une race épuisée par des mariages consanguins" [son of a victim of tuberculosis and a neurotic woman, scion of a race exhausted by incestuous marriages] [379]), and milieu. Augustin's battle is overdetermined by several factors: the tension between his libertine uncle and the tainted history of his residence (*la maison du péché* [the house of sin])[27] and his devout mother and upbringing, as well as his conception "dans la haine de l'amour" (in the hatred of love) (319).

Catholicism, however, is presented as a dangerously outmoded system to artificially control human nature. During the confrontation between Forgerus and Fanny, this critique comes to the fore in Tinayre's narration, as she describes Forgerus's trepidation in the face of genuine emotion:

> Mais il ne se demanda pas s'il n'avait pas commis une sorte de crime contre la nature, en violentant la conscience d'Augustin, en substituant sa propre volonté à la volonté du jeune homme. L'idée qu'Augustin et Fanny devaient seuls, d'un plein accord, libres de toutes influences étrangère, disposer de leurs personnes et de leur destinée, cette idée subversive et choquante n'effleura même pas l'esprit de M. Forgerus. (339)
>
> [But he didn't wonder whether he might have committed a kind of sin against nature, in violating the consciousness of Augustin, in substituting his own will for the will of the young man. The idea that Augustin and Fanny should alone, in full agreement, free from all outside influence, be responsible for their selves and their destiny, this subversive and shocking idea did not even cross Mr. Forgerus's mind.]

Forgerus and the Catholicism he stands for represent, then, a kind of violence against nature and against milieu—the two central forces of human behavior in naturalism's vision. As Forgerus urges Augustin to leave Fanny and return to the faith, it is revealed that "[il] n'avait connu les passions que dans les livres" (he knew of passion only from books) (323). Forgerus's ideas about sexuality stem not from experience but from what he has read, and Tinayre's feelings about his reliability are etched in his name, suggesting forgery. These ideas prove to be no more sophisticated than the rumors and gossip exchanged among villagers.

In addition to working against Augustin's desires, Catholicism makes him into an anachronism (just think of his name), as he reflects on himself as "étranger parmi les hommes de son âge et de son pays. . . . A quoi étais-je bon dans ce siècle?" (stranger among the men of his age and country. . . . What good was I in this age?) (318). Trapped between his Catholic upbringing and his passionate desires, he feels a sense of displacement and alienation. He eventually concludes: "A quoi servent des gens comme nous? Que font-ils dans ce siècle? Où est leur place? Dans le cloître ou dans le cimetière" (What good are people like me? What are they doing in this age? What is their place? In the cloisters or in the cemetery) (319).[28] These questions become even more suggestive when considered as a commentary on the plight of female protagonists in French fiction, for this choice between the cloisters and the cemetery is essentially the one offered young women who stray from the conventional path of marriage, from *La Princesse de Clèves* to *Madame Bovary* to *Nana.* Indeed, as the text draws to an end, Augustin follows what was a typical path for a female protagonist in the French novel: he is sent off to a convent, described as one of the "hopitaux d'âmes" (hospitals for the soul) (320), recalling the term he chose for Fanny and thus further feminizing him. As the novel closes, his hysteria intensifies, moving from neurotic anxieties to its physical manifestation in devastating illness. He thus lives out the dénouement traditionally reserved for the sexually aberrant female protagonist.

Indeed, like the female hysteric that Janet Beizer has documented in fin-de-siècle fictions, Augustin's withering body becomes a vehicle for the text's own message. Yet Tinayre dramatically alters the traditional paradigm, by having a woman writer inscribe her message on a male body, and it is a radically different message from Zola's, because it bypasses the sexual tension fundamental to this relationship.[29] In this instance, naturalist clinical descriptions of death do not assert mastery over the female body but instead call into question the link between virility and authority. By sacrificing the male body to this cause, Tinayre calls attention to the dangers of sexual discourse for both men and women, without ever inculpating her victim. On the contrary, Augustin becomes a Christ-like figure, sacrificed for the sins of others.

On his deathbed Augustin is described as "le masque aux joues creuses, à la peau grise et flétrie, aux narines pincées. . . . Le chagrin, le remords, les pratiques de l'ascétisme, une violence méthodique faite à la nature, avaient ruiné ce pauvre corps que la maladie, espérée peut-être, achevait de consumer" (the mask with sunken cheeks, gray and wilted skin, pinched nostrils. . . . Sorrow, remorse, the practices of ascetism, a methodical violence done unto nature, had ruined this poor body that sickness, wished for, perhaps, was finishing consuming) (373). Like Zola, who studied pathology to enhance his descriptions, in describing Augustin's death Tinayre relies on naturalist clinical detail to underline the effects of his sexual alienation as violence against nature:

> Pâle d'une pâleur verdâtre dans le blanc cru des oreillers, il avait la bouche violette, les yeux caves, et ses prunelles élargies, profondes, reflétaient déjà toute l'horreur de la nuit éternelle où il entrait. Ses mains, tâtonnantes, pétrissaient les plis du drap . . . et des gouttes de sueur glacée tombaient de son front. (400)

[Pale with a greenish pallor against the harsh white of the pillows, his mouth was violet, his eyes sunken, and his enlarged dark pupils already reflected all the horror of the eternal night he was entering. His hands, groping, kneaded the folds of the sheet . . . and drops of icy sweat fell from his forehead.]

The description of Augustin's death calls up Nana's decomposing body, which bore the signs of her sexual degradation. Yet it is not Augustin's sexuality that has destroyed him. Unlike Nana's eyes, memorably gouged out by her disease, which present a final and definitive evacuation of her limited subjectivity, Augustin's accusing stare lays the blame beyond the body and its subversive desires: "Son regard seul vivait encore, son regard conscient, lucide, chargé de rancune farouche. Et ce regard, allant de madame Angélique aux Courdimanche, et des Courdimanche aux absents, qu'il voyait, semblait dire: "Qu'avez-vous fait de moi?" (Only his gaze remained alive, his conscious, lucid gaze, charged with ferocious rancor. And this gaze, going from Mrs. Angélique to the Courdimanches, and from the Courdimanches to those who were absent, but whom he saw, seemed to say: "What have you done to me?) (400–401). With this frozen gaze, Augustin's withering corpse announces the devastating power of discourse to act on bodies and to brutally determine their fates. Yet in using naturalist paradigms to incriminate Catholic misogyny, Tinayre places herself in uncertain literary terrain, where she is both writing and unwriting naturalism. On one hand, her critique of Catholic views of female sexuality is also a critique of naturalist misogyny, which shares the same mythology that demonizes femininity. On the other hand, Tinayre revives naturalism—stripped of this misogynist ideology—to offer an even more global critique of Catholicism's restraints on human behavior.

Let us return now to Zola's theoretical essay on the experimental novel, in which he describes in clinical terms the link between social disintegration and anatomy, through the notion of the circulus:

Le *circulus* social est identique au *circulus* vital: dans la société comme dans le corps humain, il existe une solidarité qui lie les différents membres, les différents organes entre eux, de telle sorte que, si un organe se pourrit, beaucoup d'autres sont atteints, et qu'une maladie très complexe se déclare.[30]

[The social *circulus* is identical to the vital *circulus*: in society as in the human body, there is a solidarity that links the different limbs, the different organs, such that, if one organ rots, many others are infected, and a very complex illness presents itself.]

Zola's goal in the *roman expérimental* was to identify this social circulus, which functions like a rotting organ. In his slippage between the physiological and the social, however, he ended up locating the *plaie grave* (serious wound) in the female anatomy, thus assigning a vital origin to social problems and inscribing misogyny at the core of his ideology. Tinayre, however, unlike Zola, identifies a *circulus social,* a real social cause infecting different tiers of society through the collective imagination: misogynist discourse about female sexuality. Tinayre portrays this discourse as a crime against nature that causes Georges to assault Fanny, the villagers to harangue her, and Forgerus to destroy the love between her and Augustin. Ultimately, this discourse acts on Augustin's body, destroying it like a disease.

As a *roman experimental,* then, *La Maison du péché* leads us to a different kind of originary wound at the base of the social upheaval witnessed in the novel. Tinayre inscribes the destructive lesion, the *fêlure* or *plaie grave,* not in the female anatomy but in discourse itself, be it naturalist or Catholic. Ideas, systems of thought, the putting of sex into discourse are more dangerous and powerful than sex itself, as Tinayre exposes the discrepancy between these discourses and human reality, and the inscription of these discourses within a power hierarchy. In the process, she suggests that misogyny is in contradiction to naturalism's understanding of human behavior, by pointing to its roots in mythology and in religion—which holds a tenuous position in naturalism—rather than in human behavior or science. It is as if misogyny were naturalism's own *fêlure,* the breaking point, or corrupting influence of its own discourse. The naturalist science experiment is doomed in this sense to failure—there is no mastery gained over destructive forces as the novel closes. Although misogyny is inculpated through Augustin's morbid gaze, it is not uprooted as an agent of destruction. Fanny has also disappeared as the text closes; the woman artist must look for passion and fulfillment elsewhere.

Tinayre's experiment with the discourse of naturalism did of course have its own rewards. *La Maison du Péché* received widespread critical acclaim in the years following its publication and was widely hailed as a masterpiece.[31] It sold well and insured her financial independence for years to come. Tinayre was recognized by many critics as a rarity among the throngs of women writers at the turn of the century: a woman who could engage in the traditionally masculine domains of philosophy and morals. To be a woman in this territory, however, required a delicate and sometimes precarious balance of gender roles. Unlike the women discussed in Chapter 2 who boldly embraced unconventional female identities, Tinayre was not interested in fully rejecting traditional notions of femininity as a means of voicing resistance to patriarchal structures. She was a wife and mother and carefully cultivated a public image that reconciled bourgeois femininity with female professionalism. Thus a (woman) reporter for the *Gil Blas* described her as follows: "Si Madame Marcelle Tinayre est un écrivain de grand talent, une lumineuse intelligence, qui revendique hautement le titre de féministe, elle sait rester adorablement femme et mère et rendre aimable ce féminisme" (Although Madame Marcelle Tinayre is a talented writer with luminous intelligence and she unabashedly claims the title of feminist, she knows how to remain adorably feminine and motherly, and to make this feminism likable).[32]

The challenges of being both a writer (*un écrivain de grand talent*) and a woman (*adorablement femme et mère*), rather than simply being a *bas-bleu* or a *femme de lettres,* are demonstrated first in the reception of Tinayre the novelist and second in the reception of her most admired novel. In January 1908, *Le Temps* leaked a rumor that Tinayre was to be nominated as a *chevalier* for the French Legion of Honor.[33] Although she would not be the first woman writer to enter this bastion of French patriarchy established by Napoleon to reward service to the nation, most female awardees in the recent past had been nuns or *cantinières*—women who, when charged with bringing food and water to soldiers, had often been caught in or had risen to combat.[34]

In this era of mass press, the drama of Tinayre's possible nomination played out on the front pages, where she was depicted alternately as a publicity hound and a victim of a vulturous media. The controversy began when, following the leak to *Le Temps,* several newspapers treated the nomination as a fait accompli and ran pieces on the author, complete with portraits and interviews detailing her response. *Le Temps* followed up with a letter from Tinayre in which she joked that she would prefer a strand of pearls to the traditional red ribbon attached to the medal. In this coquettish response, she mused on how the ribbon would look on her and worried that she would be taken for a *cantinière.* The days following the appearance of this letter and the other interviews saw the publication of over a hundred articles in the French press, the majority of which opposed Tinayre's nomination, criticizing her mockery of French tradition. These articles took issue with women writers, feminism, and less often, with Tinayre's writing. The outpouring was sparked in part by an early article in the *Gil Blas* by Jean Ernest-Charles, who accused her of seeking out the nomination through an orchestrated publicity campaign, a theme that reverberated in later articles and echoed a popular criticism of women writers as inappropriate seekers of publicity.[35] When the official list of nominees was finally released a week later, Tinayre's name was notably absent.

One astute female critic seems to have captured the essence of Tinayre's downfall. Writing in the *Gil Blas,* Régine Martial comments on the double-bind of contemporary *femmes de lettres* who do not want to deny their femininity. She writes: "Mme Tinayre . . . s'est certainement dit, après sa nomination: 'si je leur dis des choses sérieuses je vais les embêter.' Alors elle . . . s'est mise à jouer au cerceau avec la croix de la Légion d'honneur" (Madame Tinayre must have said to herself, after her nomination, "I'll annoy them if I talk about serious things." So she decided to play hula-hoops with the cross of the Legion of Honor).[36] In other words, Tinayre attempted to give her audience what she thought they wanted: a professional woman who was still *adorablement femme.* But the feminine role she put on was demeaning to the public's idea of the Legion of Honor. Ultimately, the public's ambivalence about women writing was put to the test, and Tinayre was identified as an ordinary *femme de lettres* after all, unworthy of this prize.

In the first place, however, Tinayre's nomination seemed to have stemmed from critical appreciation for her virility, a sentiment that outlived the controversy of her lost nomination. For Paul Flat, Tinayre signals the possibility of female artistic merit beyond that of her female peers, and he goes so far as to compare her style to that of Flaubert. He asserts that Tinayre and Flaubert share: "Le même procédé de composition par portraits détachés . . . , par descriptions de nature, isolées en apparence, mais liées intimement aux minutes pathétiques du drame" (The same method of composition through individual portraits . . . , through descriptions of nature, seemingly isolated but intimately linked to the emotional moments of the drama).[37] Flat's challenge in making this argument is in part semantic, and thus similar to the challenge Augustin faced in assimilating Fanny. Tinayre becomes a kind of critical conundrum precisely because of her talent, which Flat finds impossible to describe in feminine terms. Indeed, Tinayre is virtually indescribable because she is a *femme de lettres* who is also a good writer, or in Flat's terms, who writes like a man:

> Sous une enveloppe féminine elle dissimule un tempérament viril, le seul réellement viril que nous comptions dans notre littérature féminine, et la meilleure preuve que j'en puisse apporter, c'est que son art littéraire, aussi bien dans sa conception première que dans sa réalisation, présente ce double caractère de la virilité créatrice: il est *objectif,* étrangement objectif, et il sait être *intellectuel.*[38]

> [Within a feminine envelope she hides a virile temperament, the only truly virile one that we have in our women's writing, and the best proof that I can bring is that her literary art, as much in its initial conception as in the realization, shows this double aspect of creative virility: it is *objective,* strangely objective, and it knows how to be *intellectual.*]

Objectivity and intellect are the signs of the virile writer, as opposed to the *transposition de moi* that is the sign of feminine writing. To be a good writer is to be a male writer.[39] Similarly, Martin-Mamy describes Tinayre in her youth as a woman who was "*très femme,* très vivante, qui jette sa pensée sur le papier parce que sa pensée et le débordement de ses sensations l'entraîne" (*very womanly,* very lively, who throws her thoughts onto paper because her thoughts and the excess of her feelings lead her to do so). As she matured, however, Martin-Mamy explains, experience rendered Tinayre's talent "plus profond et plus *viril*" (deeper and more *virile*).[40] Ironically, for Flat the greatest mark of this virility is Tinayre's inversion of traditional gender roles, when she makes Fanny into Augustin's sexual *initiatrice.* In a strange twist, then, Tinayre's rejection of the link between virility and authority through the destruction of her male protagonist landed her the label of virile. So ingrained is the association between virility and intellectual prowess that when it is expunged from the male character it is passed on to the female author.

Flat's reading of *La Maison du péché,* however, ignores its subversive critique of Catholic and naturalist misogyny, seeing instead a battle between the passions and the soul, where the conquest of the latter leads to the protagonist's death. He thus misses the subtle distinction Tinayre makes between sexuality and the discourses denigrating sexuality; in her view, it is the latter that are dangerous. To better understand Flat's embrace of Tinayre's writing, one can consider his conclusion, where he articulates his anxiety about women writers through a discourse of social conservatism that weaves together Freudian and Darwinian notions of sexuality. He sees sexuality as an engine of this conservatism by preserving the race through the instinct to reproduce. Essential to this process are the social forces of morality, order, and religion, which insure the functioning of the cycle. Flat does not distinguish between these forces, grouping them together under the category of metaphysical influence, in whatever form it takes. Women writers constitute a threat to this process by challenging their traditional roles in the family. Flat singles out Tinayre, however, comparing her text to *Madame Bovary,* which he sees as moral because Emma sought help from the church. His harsh critique of the moral neglect in women's writing is tempered by the following footnote: "Ma seule réserve est pour Marcelle Tinayre, de qui l'art objectif se rapproche si étrangement de la conception virile" (My only reservation is for Marcelle Tinayre, whose objective art comes so strangely close to virile conception).[41] Flat's lauding of *La Maison du péché* is related to the novel's inscription in the tropes of naturalism, a movement itself indebted to Darwinism and a precursor to Freud. Tinayre's text speaks through a Zolian social conservatism faithful to a biological model of natural generation based on human instincts. Her critique of misogyny strips from Zola's own ideology the fear associated with female sexuality, thus reinvigorating the model. Fanny, after all, wanted to marry Augustin and presumably have a family with him. Despite the polemics of the novel to which Flat seems oblivious, Tinayre's heroine was prepared to take on a traditional feminine role within marriage and firmly rejected the more subversive possibilities offered by her libertine friend Georges.

Returning to the question of the Legion of Honor, we can now better understand the problems that Tinayre's comments created. Tinayre had been appreciated because of her intellectual virility. Ironically, however, her coquettish comments gave voice to fin-de-siècle conceptions of femininity that her novels resisted and that her writing masked. Through the press, the public was reminded of Tinayre's actual sex and of a femininity that was incompatible both with intellect and with the Legion of Honor, thus undermining her candidacy. Tinayre's lengthy career, however, took many steps to right this wrong, both before and after the affair of the red ribbon. In 1934, Tinayre was elected vice president of the Société des Gens de Lettres, another male bastion of French society. Long before that, though, she made a more lasting contribution to women's authorial status. In 1904, upon the rejection of fellow writer Myriam Harry for the Prix Goncourt on the basis of her sex, Tinayre joined other women writers in establishing a gender-blind literary prize. This award, originally known as the "Vie heureuse," later became the Prix Fémina and remains today one of the most prestigious literary honors a French person, male or female, can receive.[42]

THE SEX OF SCIENCE: LUCIE DELARUE-MARDRUS'S *MARIE, FILLE-MÈRE*

Lucie Delarue-Mardrus's first novel, *Marie, fille-mère* (1908) adds another layer to Zola's legacy for women writers as the author adopts the male-authorized, positivistic tropes of naturalism to propose a new theory of female sexuality.[43] Her novel is a rewriting of Zola's *La Bête humaine* from a female perspective—that is, a naturalist novel ultimately determined by the forces of female sexual desire. Vernon Rosario has described *La Bête humaine* as novelizing a dominant theme of nineteenth-century medical literature and fiction—the fear of an irrational, disorderly female sex. From this perspective, Zola's novel stages the desire to master the primitive female sexual beast through the exploration of Jacques Lantier's murderous impulses against women.[44] Through Delarue-Mardrus's female-focused optic, the novel offers an alternative to fin-de-siècle science, developing a theory of sexual behavior that forefronts the woman's sexual experience and provides alternative moral conclusions to those dictated by contemporary medical doctrine. Although she published in the *Fronde,* like many of her fellow women authors Delarue-Mardrus considered herself antifeminist and refused any connection to the women's rights movement. Her writing, however, challenges patriarchal structures and calls attention to injustices against women—in this novel, sexual ones—making the feminist label appropriate in its modern usage.

The youngest of six daughters, Delarue-Mardrus was born in Normandy in 1874.[45] She received a liberal education and benefited from her well-to-do family's extensive library. At the age of twenty-six, she married the wealthy Egyptian Joseph-Charles Mardrus, who had become a minor celebrity after translating the *Mille et une nuits* into French. Delarue-Mardrus initially exploited the exoticism of this coupling. She learned Arabic while traveling with her husband and frequently had herself photographed in oriental garb as a means of marketing her travel writing for French newspapers (Fig. 5).[46] In her memoirs, Delarue-Mardrus described her meeting of Joseph-Charles as "un coup de foudre intellectuel" (intellectual love at first sight) and her delight in having found an admirer of her poetry.[47] Indeed, the man whom she would refer to in her private writings as "Oeil"[48] was interested in fully exploiting her literary talent in a way not unlike Colette's Willy. She was devastated, however, by Joseph-Charles's decision to divorce her for his mistress in 1915 and felt she had lost her most ardent supporter.[49] In her memoirs, Delarue-Mardrus also describes her early passion for girls. Later, as part of an elite group of women writers, she mingled in the Tout-Lesbos, yet she never fully embraced lesbianism. She had friendships with Renée Vivien (Delarue-Mardrus and her husband are depicted in *Une Femme m'apparut*) and Colette; her relationship with Natalie Clifford Barney is described in her 1930 novel *L'Ange et les pervers.*[50]

Delarue-Mardrus's literary career began in the early 1900s with poetry published in the *Revue Blanche,* a radical journal that included Léon Blum and Alfred Jarry as contributing editors, and in which Mirbeau published his *Journal d'une femme de chambre.* Her first collections of poetry enjoyed only a limited success. In her memoirs, Delarue-Mardrus laments the positive attention received by her rival, the Countess Anna de Noailles, whose first collection of poetry, *Le Coeur innombrable,* was published in 1901 at the same time as her own *L'Occident.* Noailles's much-adored public persona overshadowed Delarue-Mardrus's, and the countess's poetry was lauded in the press, to the exclusion of Delarue-Mardrus's.[51] At the outset of her career, Delarue-Mardrus seemed more interested in critical appreciation than financial success. She writes of being scandalized by the money she received for her first published articles in *La Fronde:* "Je n'arrivais pas à comprendre qu'un travail de l'esprit pût se métamorphoser en trois pièces d'or" (I couldn't believe that intellectual work could transform into three pieces of gold).[52] Delarue-Mardrus was far more successful in her fiction writing than in her poetry, and by 1914 was one of the most highly paid and highly sought after female novelists in France. By the time of her death at age seventy-one she had published twelve collections of poetry and over forty novels, two of

Figure 4. Photograph of Lucie Delarue-Mardrus in Carthage, by Joseph-Charles Mardrus. In *Mon amie Lucie Delarue-Mardrus*, by Myriam Harry (1946). (Image courtesy of the General Research Division, The New York Public Library, Astor, Lenox and Tilden Foundations.)

which were adapted for film.[53] *Marie, fille-mère* first appeared in serial form in *Le Journal* in 1908, and without much of a critical following enjoyed great popular success, especially with female readers.[54] Unfortunately, like Tinayre's, Delarue-Mardrus's originality has eluded modern critics, and current recognition of her work has been limited almost entirely to anthological mention rather than scholarly analysis.[55]

Delarue-Mardrus's sense of rivalry with other women writers continued with the publication of *Marie, fille-mère.* She recalls in her memoirs that both Noailles and Gérard d'Houville had also just published their first novels, and that with *Marie* the Parisian public was disappointed not to find "un troisième portrait en pied de l'auteur par lui-même" (a third full-length self-portrait by the author herself). Instead, following the naturalist traditions of Zola and the Goncourts, Delarue-Mardrus had turned her attention to a class that was not her own: she chose to write "la triste histoire de la bonne qui me servait" (the sad story of the maid who worked for me), following in the spirit of *Germinie Lacerteux.*[56] The novel recounts how the life of the seventeen-year-old Norman farm girl Marie is disrupted by her brutal sexual initiation at the hands of a rich neighbor, *le fils* Budin. It is in some sense a sexual coming-of-age story, tracing Marie's life from before her first sexual encounter and the initial awakening of her libido, through her rape, pregnancy, marriage, eventual discovery of sexual pleasure, and the sexual rivalry that leads to her death. Links to naturalism and to Zola's oeuvre in particular are evident throughout this text, from her depiction of the peasant class to her attention to dialect. The influence of naturalism on Delarue-Mardrus's methodology is notable as well: the author spent a month doing research in a hospital in preparation for the childbirth scenes she would vividly detail.

In fact, Delarue-Mardrus appropriates the tropes of naturalism to develop a narrative voice that is in tension with reigning scientific and medical authority. Perhaps she did so because naturalist discourse allowed her to adopt the authority of science while still describing the violence of nature, thus making it possible to authoritatively acknowledge the most horrific aspects of what was considered women's natural role. Zola's writing in particular, in its graphic representations of sexuality, menstruation, childbirth, and disease, did not always make a distinction between the natural and the abject and did not circumscribe all of nature's forces as morally just. *La Faute de l'abbé Mouret* in particular showcases this tension between the natural and the moral. Ironically enough, Zola's often gruesome depictions of female sexuality, his demonstration that, in Jean Borie's terms, "la fécondité est abominable, puisque l'accouchement est une diarrhée" (fertility is abonimable because giving birth is diarrhea)—that is, what is traditionally considered the most misogynistic aspects of his prose—may have made it possible for Delarue-Mardrus to employ a scientific literary discourse to critique nature's injustices against women.[57]

In the novel's opening pages Marie's nubile femininity is depicted in blissful communion with the nature surrounding her, recalling descriptions of Désirée and Albine in *La Faute.* Indeed, as in Zola's novel, what initially appears to be a celebration of nature later comes to reveal nature's insidious conspiring. Marie's closeness to nature announces the way that she will be submerged by its relentless cycles. Thus, on the day of her first encounter with the young Budin, she happily communes with the flowers. But this bliss is only the harbinger of her fatal destiny: "Ce fut à ce moment d'inconsciente exaltation, à ce moment d'adolescence, de virginité, d'innocence parfaite dans la solitude et les fleurs que Marie rencontra son destin" (It was at this moment of unconscious exaltation, at this moment of adolescence, virginity, and perfect innocence in solitude and flowers that Marie met her destiny).[58]

In her youthful innocence, Marie is perfectly ignorant.[59] This ignorance is repeatedly set in opposition to the voice of the narrator, who announces in authoritative language the tragic fate that awaits Marie. In the midst of describing the first encounter between Marie and *le fils* Budin, for example, the narrator interjects:

> Comment devineriez-vous, Marie, vous qui vous sentez encore une fillette insignifiante, pareille à tant d'autres enfants des fermes, que vous êtes une proie délicieuse, debout au milieu des fleurs, et que votre jeunesse toute rouge tente déjà depuis longtemps le fin mâle blond qui vous considère, avec une envie brutale de vous renverser? Savez-vous que c'est un amoureux que vous avez devant vous, et qu'un amoureux est un ennemi? (12)
>
> [How would you guess, Marie, you who feel yourself to be still an insignificant little girl, similar to so many other farm girls, that you are a delicious prey, standing amid the flowers, and that your rosy youth has already been tempting for a long time the delicate, blond male who is considering you with a brutal desire to knock you over? Do you know that it is a lover that you have before you, and that a lover is an enemy?]

This scientific voice reducing humans to animals describes the fated encounter between male and female that dooms Marie while exculpating her of guilt. The impact of the author's alternative sympathies resonates in the narration itself. Even as Delarue-Mardrus embraces a positivistic outlook and subscribes to a theory of instincts, her writing refuses the pretense of objectivity normally assumed in naturalist prose. Unlike that of Tinayre, her narration embraces sentiment and pathos, infusing these new elements into a scientific discourse through an omniscient, unified narrative voice that contrasts with Zola's generally diffuse points of view.[60] Her narrator, though anonymous and impersonal, is a feeling and compassionate one, whose sympathies steer the polemic of the novel.

The link to *La Bête humaine* is immediately evident from the vocabulary of this early passage, where Marie is described as a delicious prey, like the female victims in Zola's novel. Yet the narrator's comments point to a fundamental break from Zola's theories of sexuality. In *La Bête humaine,* female guilt is the ultimate instigator of male aggression—some primordial unnamed sin that fuels male predatory desire. Jacques Lantier's female prey in *La Bête humaine* are always already guilty. Delarue-Mardrus, however, uses a similarly behavioralist understanding to insist on Marie's total innocence. Marie's most basic quality is her ignorance, contrasted with the scientific authority of the narrator:

> Elle ignorait que le désir est un chasseur sans pitié. Elle ne s'était jamais demandé pourquoi toutes les femelles animales, plus intelligentes que les filles, commencent par fuir les mâles après les avoir appelés à cause qu'une sorte de peur les talonne devant la fatalité de l'amour. Elle n'avait jamais réfléchi que cette fuite était peut-être beaucoup moins une coquetterie qu'un instinct d'éviter le rôle douloureux de perpétuer l'espèce. Elle ne savait pas qu'il y a de la lutte dans l'amour et de l'assassinat dans la possession, qu'il y a d'un côté l'attaque et de l'autre la défense, et que l'homme, plus cruel que tout autre bête, est agité dans sa jeunesse par la sourde envie de terrasser la femme comme un adversaire plus faible. (20)
>
> [She was ignorant of the fact that desire is a pitiless hunter. She had never asked herself why all female animals, more intelligent than girls, start by fleeing males after having called them because a sort of fear spurs them before the fatefulness of love. She had never considered that this escape was perhaps much less coquetry than the instinct to avoid the painful role of perpetuating the species. She did not know that there was struggle in love and assassination in possession, that there is on one side attack and the other defense, and that man, more cruel than any other beast, is agitated in his youth by the secret desire to throw down woman as a weaker adversary.]

This passage summarizes a major aspect of Delarue-Mardrus' novel, as a feminized—some would say feminist—science of sex. At the same time, it points to the fault line of her critique: the tension between fatalism and faith in science at the heart of the novel. Delarue-Mardrus presents a fatalistic naturalist view of what is to befall her protagonist: ignorant of all these problems, Marie will be unable to avoid "le rôle douloureux de perpétuer l'espèce" (the painful role of perpetuating the species); she will succumb to nature's cycles, both *la lutte dans l'amour* and *l'assassinat dans la possession,* purely as a result of her femininity in the face of the bestial forces of masculine desire. Despite this fatalism, however, by pointing to the behavior of female animals whose instincts incline them to flee, Delarue-Mardrus suggests that knowledge may also be power. Marie's failing seems to be her lack of reflection ("elle ne s'était jamais demandé"; "elle n'avait jamais réfléchi"; "elle ne savait pas"). While detailing the natural struggles humans share with animals, the narrator also acknowledges our intellectual capacity to learn from these struggles. Female animals instinctively flee; female humans can learn to do so to avoid their painful role.

The goals of Delarue-Mardrus's science may never become explicit in the novel, but her criticism is unmistakable as she opposes a sentimentalized naturalist description of childbirth to that of the patriarchal medical establishment. The harrowing details of Marie's labor are described, again through a naturalistic optic that insists on the animal bases of humanity, with sympathy for the female "victim." In fact, these scenes find their precedent in Zola's oeuvre, in the excruciating description of Louise's childbirth in *La Joie de vivre* (1884). Marie's labor begins when she is alone in a field, consumed in agony: "De droite et de gauche, Marie se roule dans la paille et le fumier avec des cris étouffés, des cris d'indignation contre la souffrance. Elle sent bien que ce n'est que le commencement, que l'abomination va empirer encore" (Tossing right and left, Marie rolls in the hay and the manure with smothered cries, cries of indignation against suffering. She senses rightly that this is only the beginning, that the abomination will get worse yet) (146). She eventually makes it to the hospital, where the process is completed. The physical and emotional experiences of the mother, narrated in detail, are dramatically set in contrast to the science that is actually taught in the same hospital:

> Elle est là, la femme, cet être pâmé. Sa face ruisselle de sueur, ses narines sont pincées, sa bouche ouverte; et tout son être crie: "A l'aide!"
>
> Et elle ne sait pas que, dans l'hôpital, plein des victimes de la nature, se trouve une salle de cours, où un maître aux yeux profonds, tout possédé par le génie du mâle ordonnateur, développe, devant des jeunes gens attentifs assis en amphithéâtre, ses magnifiques pensées sur la maternité, leur enseigne, avec des gestes frémissants d'éloquence, cette sorte de grand poème physiologique qu'il a conçu à force d'avoir assisté, pendant les longues années de sa jeunesse, à l'agonie de celles qui accouchent. (156)

> [She is there, this swooning woman. Her face streams with sweat, her nostrils flare, her mouth is open; and her whole being cries: "Help!"
>
> And she doesn't know that in this hospital full of nature's victims there is a classroom where a dark-eyed instructor, fully possessed by the

ius of the commanding male, develops his magnificent thoughts on ernity in front of attentive young people sitting in a lecture hall, his gestures trembling with eloquence, this sort of great physiological poem that he conceived of by having been present, during the long years of his youth, at the agony of those giving birth.]

What is perhaps most interesting about this passage is the fact that the disjunction between Marie's experience and what the instructor is teaching does not stem from his ignorance: he has witnessed numerous births. Instead, the challenge to the professor's lesson comes through Marie's perspective: her singular first-hand experience undermines the authority of his scholarly conclusions. The irony here is that Delarue-Mardrus's own authority came not from experience (she herself had no children) but from observation—one month spent in the labor ward disguised as a medical student. Yet she uses this experience to identify with the female individual rather than the detached voice of science. The gendered nature of this identification is paramount. By juxtaposing these two voices of authority, Delarue-Mardrus suggests that even when placed in the same position as the male scientist-doctor, the female observer will not necessarily produce the same form of science; thus sentiment and pathos become relevant to scientific inquiry. In this case, the narrator's feminized science privileges the woman's experience of suffering over the interpretations of the male doctor, the "mâle ordonnateur."

This alternative perspective, which valorizes the woman's suffering in the natural world, calls attention to the moral and political functions of science that precipitate its gender biases. In fact, Delarue-Mardrus is not challenging the fundamental essentialist premises of the system held up by male authority—that sexual behavior is a natural phenomenon, based on instincts and shared by all humanity—or the actual physiological mechanisms of this phenomenon. Instead, she is challenging the interpretation of the sexual function within a patriarchal moral-scientific context in which childbearing is sanitized and glorified as woman's most essential contribution to society.

The political implications of the scientific discourse of sex—and this moral-scientific context—manifested themselves at the fin de siècle in a wide variety of hygiene manuals and texts addressed to a popular audience put out by the medical and religious establishments. In these texts, sex roles are clearly delineated, and sexual behavior is coded for hygienic, moral, and political value. The vast majority of such texts were written by men, for men. Even many texts written for women speak through a patriarchal perspective that underlines the man's authority over the female body. This perspective is already made apparent, for example, in *Hygiène pratique des femmes* (1854), by A. Reinvillier, a doctor at the Faculté de Paris. In the preface to this text ostensibly written for a female readership, the author remarks: "La femme est le sujet le plus intéressant, le plus compliqué, et peut-être le plus important qu'il ait été donné à l'homme d'observer" (Woman is the most interesting, most complicated, and perhaps the most important subject that has been given to man to observe).[61] This voyeuristic pleasure linked to male scientific authority helps to explain why even texts not destined for a female audience devoted pages upon pages to detailing female maladies.

At the turn of the nineteenth century, the notion of hygiene was discursively linked to morality and had been for some time, such that in medical parlance "l'hygiène morale et sexuelle" (moral and sexual hygiene) constituted a standard category. In part, medical texts sought to compensate for a danger caused by the eroticization of contemporary literature, something warned against in the influential doctor Charles Féré's *L'Instinct sexuel* from 1899, and in Seved Ribbing's *L'Hygiène sexuelle et ses conséquences morales,* translated from the Swedish in 1895, where Zola is identified as the prime example of literature encouraging depravity. Medical doctrine insisted on ideals of a "natural" sexuality that uniformly enforced cultural norms and upheld political objectives: in this view, woman's natural and divine purpose was to procreate, through the institution of marriage. Many medical hygiene texts offer descriptions of marriage and its benefits to French society and personal well-being that promote the national goal of population increase. In Auguste Debay's popular *Hygiène et physiologie du mariage,* the author lists among the tragic consequences awaiting the unmarried: "la folie, l'épilepsie, l'hypocondrie, la manie, l'hystérie, la passion utérine" (madness, epilepsy, hypochondria, mania, hysteria, uterine passion).[62] Marriage, in contrast, "est le seul moyen de coordonner l'instinct génital et de l'assujettir à un but moral" (the only way of directing the genital instinct and subjecting it to a moral goal).[63] Marriage and its incumbent procreation are coded as natural, while alternatives take on monstrous proportions. What is natural is by definition also divinely sanctioned. Thus writes the physician and best-selling medical writer Pierre Garnier: "La copulation est rendue si voluptueuse dans la généralité des cas en vue du but élevé et divin de la procréation" (Copulation is rendered so pleasurable in the majority of cases due to the elevated and divine goal of procreation).[64]

The moral import of sexual hygiene was always implicitly if not explicitly linked to the ongoing crisis of France's declining population. In texts like Alexandre Mayer's *Des Rapports conjugaux considérés sous le triple point de vue de la population, de la santé, et de la morale publique*—another nineteenth-century bestseller—the procreative goal is again emphasized and its alternatives labeled unhealthy and unnatural. Mayer writes: "Nous avons prouvé par l'anatomie et par la physiologie, que la femme est créée et mise au monde, pour perpétuer l'espèce d'abord" (We have proved by anatomy and by physiology that woman is created and put into the world first for perpetuating the species) and later: "La nature n'a rien créé sans but. Un organe sans emploi, une fonction physiologique sans utilité, sont des choses qui répugnent à l'esprit" (Nature has created nothing without a goal. An organ without use, a physiological function without utility, these things are repugnant to the mind).[65] Procreation within marriage is thus glorified as a natural, moral, and political ideal through which human sexuality realizes its divine purpose; the horrors of sexuality—equally fascinating to the medical profession—result from straying from this goal.

Delarue-Mardrus's challenge to this kind of discourse becomes clearer as her text continues, mocking the arrogance of the professor:

> Il s'exalte. Il souligne d'un geste péremptoire les paroles qu'il prononce. Sa voix scande presque religieusement le mot qu'il a trouvé, le Rythme.
> Il dit: La nature est admirable, messieurs!
> Il dit: Sachez que la femme n'est vraiment épanouie qu'après le troisième allaitement.
> Il dit: La femme qui n'enfante pas n'est qu'un bel écran vide; elle est une manière de monstre. (156–57)
>
> [He becomes excited. With a peremptory gesture he emphasizes the words that he utters. His voice chants almost religiously the word that he has found, the Rhythm.
> He says: Nature is admirable, gentlemen!
> He says: Know that woman has not really flowered until after the third nursing.
> He says: The woman who does not have children is only a beautiful empty screen; she is a kind of monster.]

These conclusions depict the professor's exploitation of a position of power in a conversation between men (note the address to "messieurs"). The professor's remarks echo the moralizing sentiments of medical marriage manuals, in his insistence that female procreation is necessary, and that a woman who chooses not to fulfill this function is pathological and monstrous. Yet the reader has just witnessed a far more monstrous scene, which we are reminded of immediately as the narration continues: "Marie, écartelée, sanglante, comme les autres, avait senti que l'effort naturel qu'elle faisait pour chasser d'elle cette tête d'enfant plus dure qu'une énorme pierre, lui molestait tout le dedans de son corps" (Marie, torn apart, bloody, like the others, had felt that the natural effort that she had made to rid herself of that baby's head which was harder than a huge rock, molested the whole inside of her body) (157).[66]

This passage has political undertones as well, showcasing the post-1870 imperative for French mothers to produce healthy boys.[67] By juxtaposing scientific discourse with the detailed description of the mother's suffering, Delarue-Mardrus calls into question the moral and political imperatives of a science that gives little weight to the woman's experience. By depicting the brutal pain of the female victim even as she describes it as an "effort naturel," she suggests that what is most natural is perhaps neither just nor moral. From this perspective she criticizes religion as well for similarly masking the horrors of women's natural processes, demonstrating like Tinayre the unexpected collusion of scientific and religious discourses. Commenting on the suffering of women in labor, she asks: "Est-ce qu'il n'était pas nécessaire, dès les premiers temps du monde, d'envelopper dans une formule religieuse la chose révoltante?" (Hasn't it been necessary since the beginning of time to cloak the revolting thing in a religious formula?) (156).

Through the story of Marie's sexual maturation, Delarue-Mardrus develops an entire theory of sexual desire that is clearly influenced by Zola's formulations yet departs from his model in important ways. As earlier discussions show, in its depiction of how instincts determine human sexual behavior, *Marie, fille-mère* demonstrates its indebtedness to *La Bête humaine,* where Zola offers a vivid description of the violent, animalistic mechanics of male sexuality. Indeed, Delarue-Mardrus invokes this genealogy in her repeated use of the word *bête* to describe Marie's submission to her desires, and in her depiction of the uncontainable forces of sexual desire. Delarue-Mardrus's most significant innovation, however, may be in the role she attributes to the female *instinct sensuel,* whose forces ultimately determine the novel's progress.

After Marie's first encounter with *le fils* Budin, in which he kisses her, she is overwhelmed with a distinctly nonsexual emotion: "Trop jeune pour ressentir aucun émoi sensuel, elle continue à se nourrir d'une sentimentalité inconsciente et douce. Il ne lui est pas encore venu à l'idée de se demander pourquoi elle aime ce fils Budin" (Too young to feel any sensual emotion, she continues to thrive on an unconscious, gentle sentimentality. The idea has not yet occurred to her to ask why she likes this son of Budin) (27). This sentimental attachment, in Delarue-Mardrus's theory, is a first step in the sexual awakening of the female subject. The emotional reactions feed the atavistic urges and nature's grand plan. Indeed, nature seems to heighten Marie's emotion, predicting her sexual initiation as "la chaleur vibre au-dessus du pré, un parfum stupéfiant environne Marie" (the warmth vibrates over the meadow, and an overwhelming scent surrounds Marie) (30). This perfume intoxicates her, inciting her to take pleasure in being "jeune, fraîche, immaculée, et d'aimer" (young, fresh, immaculate, and in loving) (30). At the same time, the overcharged atmosphere diminishes her fear, "pour ne laisser subsister en elle que la grande joie du rendez-vous proche" (such that she continues to feel only the great joy of the coming rendez-vous) (30). This passage again recalls Zola's *La Faute* (as well as Thomas Hardy's *Tess of the D'Urbervilles*) in its evocation of nature's fervent erotic energy. One remembers in particular the active role of the Paradou in encouraging Serge to consummate his desire for Albine. The innovation here, however, is that nature's apparent affiliation with the feminine is only an illusion; in fact, nature is preparing Marie for a violent rape.

Indeed, Marie's path to knowledge takes place through disturbing violence, narrated in detail from her perspective. The following description is discursively significant because of the counterdiscourse in which it is included and this discourse's dependence on the authority of female experience:

> Le coeur de Marie bat avec tant de violence qu'elle peut à peine crier. Une révélation foudroyante lui apprend tout le drame de l'amour. Elle comprend que l'homme est un animal comme les autres, et que son gentil amoureux va la couvrir comme elle a vu les taureaux couvrir les vaches dans les prés de son enfance. Une terreur immense l'a saisie tout entière. . . .
>
> Elle veut se débattre. Une épaule lourde et vêtue lui écrase la figure. Marie, étouffée, malmenée, annihilée par l'épouvante, jette tout à coup un cri plus martyrisé, plus indigné, plus terrifié que les autres. Des pleurs jaillissent de ses yeux, tout son corps se tend, s'arc-boute pour protester.
>
> Le garçon est muet, implacable, haletant. Marie, maintenant, pousse des sanglots de rage impuissante. Et, soudain, se mêle à sa clameur bâillonnée celle plus courte, plus saccadée, de son agresseur. Marie se tait presque pour l'écouter. Une nouvelle stupeur la terrasse. Va-t-elle devenir folle de tout cela?
>
> Brusquement, l'étreinte a cessé. Le garçon s'est tu. L'étau desserré désemprisonne Marie, renversée dans le désordre des jupons saccagés. (35–36)

> [Marie's heart beats with so much violence that she can barely cry out. A powerful revelation teaches her the whole drama of love. She understands that man is an animal like the others, and that her sweet lover is going to lie on her just as she saw the bulls lie on the cows in the meadows of her childhood. An immense terror seizes her entirely. . . .
>
> She wants to fight. A heavy, clothed shoulder smashes her face. Marie, suffocating, manhandled, annihilated by terror, lets out suddenly a more martyred, more indignant cry, more terrified than the others. Tears spurt from her eyes, her whole body tenses, arches in protest.

The boy is mute, implacable, panting. Marie now lets out sobs of powerless rage. And, suddenly, her muzzled clamor mixes with the shorter, halting one of her aggressor. Marie almost becomes quiet to listen to him. A new stupor overcomes her. Will she go mad from all this?

Abruptly, the embrace ceases. The boy quiets. The tightened vise releases Marie, overturned in the disorder of ransacked skirts.]

Delarue-Mardrus frames the rape as an emotionally complex experience for Marie, who, in the midst of her terror, discovers of her own sexual organs: "elle sentait mieux cette place creuse d'elle-même, cette douloureuse cachette de sa chair qu'elle n'avait jamais soupçonnée encore" (she sensed better that hollow place in herself, that painful hiding place of her flesh that she had never suspected) (36). Despite her pain, in her confusion, Marie ends up naïvely returning to *le fils* Budin, having forged an intimate connection to him that will ultimately aggravate her pain.

Following this aggressive act Marie becomes a female *bête humaine.* Her sexual initiation marks her departure from rational decision making; from that moment on she obeys the call of nature, and her body's urges take precedence over her thoughts. Marie finds herself pregnant and is sent to Paris to escape her father's wrath. There she experiences humiliation because of her altered state, until finally she gives birth, confirming her link to the animals she has raised on the farm. The birth of her son, Alexandre, introduces another internal transformation, the emergence of the "bête maternelle" (159). Delarue-Mardrus's description of the awakening of instincts in Marie challenges prevailing medical and religious thought, which posited that the woman's instincts guided her to procreation from an early age. Marie is not initially guided by any maternal instinct that determines her fate and bonds her to the father and to her child. Instead, nature ensures that she is bonded to her male partner through a rape, and only after the child is born is her maternal attachment formed.

The second part of the novel picks up five years after the birth of Alexandre. Marie is working at a fruit store, and Alexandre is extremely attached to her but believes her to be his aunt. Marie is pursued by the Sicilian Natale Fanella, who eventually persuades her to marry him, despite his strong sense of rivalry with the child.[68] This marriage leads to the final phase of Marie's sexual development, the discovery of pleasure, on which the novel ultimately turns. Marie's second sexual initiation, as it were, begins as a kind of rape. (In fact, because of lack of sexual education, many women experienced their first marital intercourse as a kind of rape. I examine this fact further in the novels that address women's right to pleasure in Chapter 5.) Natale's forceful exertion reminds her of her earlier experience, and she is consumed with terror. Yet in the midst of this terror, Marie begins to feel something different:

> Un gémissement semblable à ceux qui lui arrachait jadis la douleur de mettre son fils au monde monta de sa poitrine. Ses yeux s'étaient révulsés sous les paupières lourdes. Une transe aussi intense que celles de l'enfantement, mais délicieuse, venait de traverser tout son être, sous le coup de poignard du baiser. Maintenant, elle était comme une assassinée sur laquelle le meurtrier s'acharne. . . . Sa chair, qui, jusqu'alors, s'était ignorée, venait de s'éveiller, comme il arrive souvent aux femmes les plus glacées, lorsqu'elles ont eu un enfant. Le démon du plaisir se dressait en elle. Une énergie nouvelle, formidable, venait de lui naître. En vérité, cette surprise était la plus foudroyante de toutes celles que le destin lui avait apportées. (266)

> [A moan rose up from her chest similar to those extracted long ago by the pain of bringing her son into the world. Her eyes had rolled upward under her heavy eyelids. A trance as intense as the ones from labor, but delicious, had just traversed her whole being, under the stabbing thrust of the kiss. Now she was like an assassinated woman whom the murderer hounds. . . . Her flesh, until then ignorant, had just awoken, as it often happens to the most frigid women when they have had a baby. The demon of pleasure arose in her. A new, formidable energy had just been born to her. In truth, this surprise was the most striking of all those that fate had brought.]

As in *La Bête humaine*, pleasure is linked here to death, and sexual desire is inherently violent. Yet Delarue-Mardrus's description far surpasses Zola's in detail (one remembers Séverine and Jacques: "Ils se possédèrent retrouvant l'amour au fond de la mort" (They possessed each other discovering love at the depths of death) (298). Here, the violent and murderous images are related to an explicit physical experience; even if there is no specific mention of Marie's anatomy, the physical pleasure of her flesh is invoked. Furthermore, this experience is not overshadowed by the couple's union, as it is in Zola's text; instead, the entirely singular, physical experience of the female partner alone is described.

The social implications of Marie's pleasure are inscribed within this very moment. The passage continues:

> Au moment où, pâmée, elle attendait l'éclair de joie inouie et finale que son corps prévoyait, elle entendit Natale haleter sur sa bouche:
> —Qui aimes-tu l'mieux? Moi ou le gosse?

> —Ah! toi, toi! sanglota-t-elle malgré elle. Et d'une voix vaincue, rauque, monotone, elle répéta sans le savoir:
> —Je t'aime . . . je t'aime . . . ah! je t'aime. (267)
>
> [At the moment when, swooning, she awaited the flash of extraordinary and final joy that her body anticipated, she heard Natale pant against her mouth:
> —Who do you love more? Me or the kid?
> —Ah! You, you! She sobbed despite herself. And in a vanquished, husky monotone, she repeated unaware:
> —I love you . . . I love you . . . ah! I love you.]

Pleasure, then, becomes the locus of Marie's power struggle, the means of her submission to the domineering male. In this light, the images of murder take on symbolic value, and one remembers the narrator's earlier mention of "l'assassinat dans la possession" (20); pleasure seems to imply the death of the woman's free will, as she becomes enslaved to the one who satisfies her. At the same time, however, pleasure allows Marie to be reborn, a physical awakening that saves her from being fully subsumed by her lover's violent embrace.

After these moments of sexual intimacy, Marie is consumed by guilt as her maternal fidelities return. Her victimization once again stems from her limited intellectual capacities, contrasted with the narrator's scientific authority: "La pensée de Marie s'essayait péniblement à une analyse trop difficile pour son cerveau" (Marie's thoughts painfully attempted an analysis too difficult for her mind) (271). The narrator explains what has gone awry: normally, the *instinct sensuel* precedes the *instinct maternel,* such that fidelity to the husband supercedes fidelity to the child, avoiding the kind of conflict she is experiencing. Knowledge, in this instance, may even have saved her; perhaps she would not have married had she been aware of this "scientific" reality. Alas, however, Marie has not been forewarned, and again her ignorance is emphasized, with the reminders that "elle ne savait pas" (she did not know) and "elle ignorait" (she was unaware) (271). As a result, like Zola's degenerative *fêlure,* "la plaie inguérissable du désir avait été ouverte en elle" (the incurable wound of desire had been opened within her) (273). The discovery of pleasure, the awakening of the *instinct sensuel,* so closely related to the death instinct, signals her own demise.

The originality of Delarue-Mardrus's theory of instincts should be recognized. Prevailing scientific doctrine downplayed the existence of sensual instincts in the female; such feelings, if they were to be kindled in normal women, were subordinate to maternal instincts. Yet the force binding Marie to her husband is not duty but an open and natural wound of desire. Further, Delarue-Mardrus's recognition of the force of the sensual instinct and her pitting of it against maternal drives, as well as her giving equal weight to the roles of "amante" (lover) and "génitrice" (progenitor) (271), sets her theory apart from established views of "normal" female sexuality. Indeed, Marie's desire is figuratively born out of the sexual encounter—"une énergie . . . venait de lui *naître*"—further underlining the tension between these competing roles.

Marie's knowledge of her own physical capacities determines the novel's final conflict and dénouement. For the first time, she seeks sexual experience. Fleeing by train to her parents' farm, she is consumed with sexual desire and, upon arriving, begins a brief affair with her original lover, *le fils* Budin. When she finally returns to Natale, still sexually unsatisfied, she submits to him willingly. Marie's behavior, stemming purely from instinct and natural urges, leads her not to procreation but to the taking of multiple partners in search of satisfaction. Disturbed by Natale's terrible jealousy of Alexandre, Marie finally admits that he is her son and further wounds him by admitting that she has been adulterous since their marriage. Marie's admissions are introduced as the mark of her sexual maturity and self-knowledge: "Elle, l'innocente, la faible de jadis, la maternité et le plaisir l'avaient accomplie. Elle avait tout su du secret féminin; elle était en possession de sa puissance. Ni son corps, ni son coeur n'avaient plus de mystère pour elle" (She, the innocent one, the weak one of long ago, maternity and pleasure had made complete. She knew the secrets of femininity; she was in control of her power) (352). Outraged, Natale kills Alexandre; Marie, linked to her son by a powerful maternal bond that proves even stronger than the sensual one, dies simultaneously.

On one level, then, the novel ends with violence that stems from a conflict between men, following Zola's anthropology where the woman is in Jean Borie's terms "une proie qu'on arrache aux autres" (a prey that one snatches from others) (47). In *La Bête humaine,* the assassination of the male rival is disrupted at the last moment, and the female love object is murdered instead. *Marie, fille-mère* enacts a similar slippage: Marie's admissions lead Natale to kill Alexandre, whose death results in her own simultaneous death. Natale's act expresses his aggression toward both rivals, the child and the father. Yet I believe Delarue-Mardrus's conclusion must be read slightly differently, accounting for the more active role of the woman, in this instance, Marie. The self-knowledge linked to Marie's admissions suggests that the real rivalry was with Marie herself, and that she was in fact the object of Natale's rage. With Marie as an independent sexual entity, the true threat to Natale is Marie's own power over her body and the realization that her sexual pleasure can come from other sources. The notion of pleasure as a means of power over men seems confirmed in the following poem, "Cri des femmes dans la nuit" (Cry of women in the night), which Delarue-Mardrus published just two years after her novel:

> Votre amour masculin forme de votre haine
> Ne nous laisse pour liberté
> Que le cri naturel de la maternité . . .
> Vous avez bien voulu que nous fussions des mères
> Vous, les maîtres, vous, les plus forts
> Mères, mais non pas amantes tout entières
> Parce que vous craignez le cri de notre corps
> Vous êtes trop humains pour nous trop animales
> La bête féminine aime en toute saison . . .
> Oui, soyez orgeuilleux de posséder les femmes
> Mais elles sont comme la mer
> Et toute la ferveur de vos petites âmes
> Ne satisfera point l'océan de leur chair.[69]
>
> [Your masculine love, shape of your hate
> Leaves us for freedom
> Only the natural cry of maternity . . .
> You so wanted that we would be mothers
> You, the masters, you the stronger ones
> Mothers, but not lovers entirely
> Because you fear the cry of our body
> You are too human for us who are too animal
> The female beast loves in every season . . .
> Yes, be proud to possess women
> But they are like the sea
> And all the fervor of your little souls
> Will never satisfy the ocean of their flesh.]

The *bête féminine* mentioned here is the alternative to the *bête maternelle;* she is a woman aware and in control of her sexual needs.

Despite the active role Marie may have had in inciting Natale's anger, she is still considered fundamentally a female victim of nature's male biases as the novel closes:

> Créature sans défense contre la fatalité physiologique qui pèse sur les femmes, elle meurt comme elle a vécu, victime du désir masculin. Un homme avait commis le crime de lui imposer un enfant, un autre homme

> a commis le crime de tuer cet enfant. Toute la vie de Marie a tenu entre ces deux gestes. Au coup de foudre du viol a succédé pour elle celui de la maternité, au coup de foudre du plaisir celui de la mort. (356)
>
> [Creature without defense against the physiological fate that weighs on women, she dies as she lived, victim of masculine desire. A man had committed the crime of imposing a child on her, another man had committed the crime of killing this child. Marie's whole life held between these two gestures. Maternity followed the lightning bolt of rape for her; death followed the lightning bolt of pleasure.]

In French the term "coup de foudre" connotes love at first sight; here this meaning is undermined, suggesting instead a violence utterly devoid of emotion. With this synopsis of Marie's sexual history, we return to the fundamental question. Does the scientific-naturalist analysis of the woman's plight—so inherently critical—offer any possibility for female salvation? In other words, does Delarue-Mardrus's Zolian science experiment lead to some kind of mastery where Tinayre's could not? The explicit fatalism of this anthropology seems to suggest not: at least within the novel, knowledge does not lead to power. As the novel comes to a close, Marie's increased knowledge is tempered by an increase in other sociobiological factors overdetermining her fate. As Natale's aggression intensifies, Delarue-Mardrus seems to offer more and more naturalist and implicitly Zolian explanations for Marie and Natale's marital conflicts, which are exacerbated by their incompatible races and their lower-class origins. Ultimately, the couple's main obstacle is this lowly blood, making them even more susceptible to nature's forces: "chez [les instincts] du peuple, la bête humaine est restée farouchement entière et les concessions sont presque toujours impossibles: d'où ces violences aveugles . . . chaque jour parmi eux" (in the instincts of the working class, the human beast remains ferociously intact and concessions are almost always impossible: hence these blind acts of violence . . . every day among them) (336). These explanations seem to exculpate Natale, such that his murderous act is universalized as "le geste de sa race" (the gesture of his race) (354). By incriminating men, class, and nature, Delarue-Mardrus leaves few options besides a grim fatalism in which women can do no more than simply become aware of their impending doom.

Yet as with Zola, even if Delarue-Mardrus's characters themselves are without hope, the novel's own project as a scientific achievement is not necessarily a failure. Indeed, the significance of Delarue-Mardrus's novel may lie more in the strength of her narrator than in the weakness of her protagonist, a role that only complied with pre-existing structures of the traditional naturalist plot. Among the most important breaks from naturalist convention in Delarue-Mardrus's novel is the fact that her point of view is not diluted through the free, indirect style. The narrative voice is not filtered through any character or characters, in effect signaling the profound absence of such empathetic figures in Marie's world. To understand better the import of the novel's feminist implications, we can link this voice to the author herself. Delarue-Mardrus's self-proclaimed antifeminism must be understood in the context of Belle Epoque politics. Like many of her female literary peers, she did not embrace the political fight for women's rights; but her books may have offered hope to women who found in them compassion for their previously untold suffering.[70] By softening science with *sensibilité,* the narrator of her novel appeals to a specifically female audience (readers of popular novels) while still suggesting that maternity was innately brutal. Her message, couched in this form, acted as a kind of literary consciousness-raising that directly challenged the moral hegemony of fin-de-siècle French discourse. The ramifications of such a challenge were realized by Delarue-Mardrus herself: she steadfastly refused to become a mother, instead dedicating herself to writing. But more dramatically, there is evidence that Delarue-Mardrus's writing spoke directly to women in need of the kind of scientific compassion she develops in this novel. While disguised as a medical student at a local hospital, Delarue-Mardrus churned out a new chapter of *Marie, fille-mère* each week for the Friday edition of *Le Journal.* One morning, a woman suffering complications from a difficult labor recognized the author from her image in the newspaper. Delarue-Mardrus recounts the incident in her memoirs without commentary:

> —"C'est vous?" Me dit-elle au milieu de ses affres. "Je lis *Marie, fille-mère,* vous savez! On me met de côté les numéros du *Journal* pour que je continue l'histoire quand je serai remise."
>
> Le lendemain, elle était morte. (158)

> ["Is it you?" She asked me in the midst of her throes of anguish. "I'm reading *Marie, fille-mère,* you know! They're putting aside the issues of the *Journal* for me so that I can finish when I'm better."
>
> The next day, she was dead.]

This human encounter stands in stark contrast to the cold medical proclamations documented within the novel, most likely observed in that very hospital. Perhaps in some way, the woman's knowledge that her plight had been recognized and that she was not alone mitigated the tragedy of her death, offering a first feeble step in the process of creating a science sensitive to women's experience.

Challenges to traditional gender roles in fin-de-siècle women's novels were not always recognized as such by critics. At the same time, however, female readers may have noticed that some of these books depicted women's lives in radical new ways. This dissonance in the way women's books were received seems especially true for those who voiced their challenges through what were traditionally patriarchal literary discourses. We can see it, for example, in the reception of both Tinayre's and Delarue-Mardrus's naturalist fictions. For many fin-de-siècle critics, these women's rejection of conventional romance formulas and style suggested a kind of virile writing, bringing them mainstream critical acclaim in addition to their popular success. Ironically, as literary critic for the *Mercure,* Rachilde described *Marie, fille-mère* as "très fort, très masculin" (very strong, very masculine) and went on to applaud its author as a true "homme de lettres."[71] Such readings ignore these writers' efforts to construct a specifically female intellectual authority. Other readers, however, like the patient quoted above, may have recognized Tinayre and Delarue-Mardrus as speaking to their own circumstances and likely appreciated their subversive vision of a world where women's experiences could influence scientific truth and religious dogma. The complex place of the woman writer within this matrix is exhibited perhaps most vividly here by Rachilde herself: in the comment above, she ventriloquizes a patriarchal discourse that recognizes intellect only in terms of virility, even as she herself offered up endless subversions of women's roles in her own novels.

4

Can a Woman Be a Decadent?

RACHILDE, GENDER, AND THE MALE BODY

Il n'y a pas de littérature féminine. *Il y a des écrivains.* Leur sexe importe peu.

[There is no women's writing. *There are writers.* Their sex matters little.]

—Rachilde, 1931

Rachilde was born Marguerite Eymery in 1860, near Périgueux in southwest France.[1] She adopted her pseudonym while in her teens, after participating in a séance in which she claimed to be visited by a sixteenth-century Swedish nobleman. Like many of her female peers, Rachilde benefited from the burgeoning mass press and gained her initial literary muscle through journalism. After moving with her mother to Paris in 1878, she began working at *L'Ecole des femmes,* a journal edited by a maternal cousin. Thanks to her maternal family's relative affluence and literary connections, she was soon mingling with many influential fin-de-siècle figures, including the actress Sarah Bernhardt, the writer Catulle Mendès, and Arsène Houssaye, a well-known novelist who would facilitate the publication of her first novel, *Monsieur de la nouveauté,* in 1880. By her own telling, Rachilde first became involved with the decadents through a chance encounter at a café in Paris, which she describes in the autobiographical preface to her novel *A mort* (1886).[2] She then became part of a group that included Albert Samain, Paul Adam, Jean Moréas, Félix Fénéon, Jean Lorrain, and Laurent Tailhade, among others. Rachilde acknowledged a certain debt to naturalism and Zola, but like her decadent peers, she rejected naturalism's privileging of reason and social reality over the creative imagining of new worlds.[3]

Aside from Colette, whose place in the French canon has long been fixed, Rachilde is the only author in our study to have gained substantial critical attention in the past twenty years in both the United States and Europe; a new translation of *Monsieur Vénus* has recently been published by the Modern Language Association, and the first two English-language biographies of her appeared in 2001. This academic recognition is a belated postscript to Rachilde's initial acceptance by her decadent peers, who praised her adaptation of decadent themes. Upon reading *L'Animale* in 1893, Jean Lorrain lauded his friend's accomplishments in a personal letter: "Ma chère amie, je viens de lire le livre le plus pervers, le plus malsain, et le plus cruellement détraqué que je connaisse" (My dear friend, I have just read the most perverse, unhealthy, and cruelly disturbed book that I know), he writes, listing attributes prized by decadent writers.[4] Despite his avowed disdain for the *bas-bleus,* Barbey d'Aurevilly admired Rachilde as a "distinguished pornographer" and Maurice Barrès called her "Mademoiselle Baudelaire."[5] Rachilde was welcomed in the male literary circles of the avant-garde, regularly published in *Le Décadent,* and maintained friendships with many influential fin-de-siècle writers, who frequented her salon. In 1889, she married Alfred Vallette (notably after having earned literary success on her own), who co-founded the *Mercure de France,* a journal with which she enjoyed a special relationship.[6] As part of the artistic elite of Belle Epoque Paris, Rachilde mingled in overlapping circles with many other successful women writers, while vehemently rejecting her identity as one.[7] She was an early and consistent supporter of Colette, one of the only women to attend her Tuesday salons, and a friend of Natalie Clifford Barney.[8] As literary critic for the *Mercure,* she reviewed much of her female peers' writing, including, remarkably, works by every author in this study, with the possible exception of Odette Dulac; her critiques ranged from scathing to laudatory, showing neither preference for nor discrimination against women writers as a whole.[9]

Rachilde offers, then, a case study of how one woman managed to speak through the dominant discourses of her time. How was she able gain acceptance by her male peers while still putting forth images of powerful, if disturbing, figures of female creativity during a period when intellectual authority was linked—seemingly inextricably—to virility? In what follows I argue that Rachilde's success hinged on a series of ambiguous collaborations with forms of male authority, from Francis Talman, the supposed co-author of the first edition of *Monsieur Vénus,* to Maurice Barrès, who facilitated the reception of the French edition with his preface, to, more broadly speaking, the discourses of medicine and of decadence themselves, whose tropes she finessed even as she undermined their symbolic structures. I consider two of Rachilde's best-known novels, *Monsieur Vénus* (1884) and *La Jongleuse* (1900), as relentless attacks on masculinity and male bodies, suggesting that Rachilde's collaboration with decadence was also a means of dismantling the symbolic structures of virility, thus delegitimizing the masculine prowess that supposedly determined and authorized cerebral might.[10] In both novels, the agent of destruction is a female creative figure allied implicitly with the author's own voice. In other words, the image of the woman writer in these texts is generated in part through the annihilation of male power.

Rachilde was certainly not the first fin-de-siècle author to attack virility in fiction. For male authors of the period, the perceived frailty of the male body was a source of much anxiety: images of pathetic, cuckolded men abound in their writing. Yet these images ultimately reinforced the virility of the male authors who invented them, since the *femmes fatales* who preyed on such weak male characters were nearly always punished by their texts' end. Violence in these texts was most often wreaked on the female body, leaving the men corporally intact, empowering male-authorized discourse, and affirming the widespread extratextual association between virility and intellect in the nineteenth-century imagination. Perhaps the most vivid example of this appears in Barbey d'Aurevilly's short story "A Dinner of Atheists" from *Les Diaboliques* (1874), an influential decadent text that can be read as a parable warning of the dangers of desire. The story ends with the frustrated Major Ydow dipping the pummel of his sword in hot wax and sealing the sex of his former lover, just as she sealed the letter in which she revealed the ambiguous paternity of her dead child.[11] This sexual mutilation avenges the woman's discursive and sexual power over her male suitors and reminds us of the terrifying link between female sexual freedom and female knowledge in the fin-de-siècle imagination. Ydow's act compensates for the double humiliation of the men in the story—a humiliation of male minds, unable to attain La Rosalba's knowledge, and of male bodies, whose virility was undermined by her infidelity. In *Monsieur Vénus* and *La Jongleuse,* however, the female body, so often mutilated in nineteenth-century fiction and morselized by nineteenth-century science, is displaced and preserved intact, thanks in large part to the unusual machinations and triumphs of a highly original female creative force that subverts the terms of sexual warfare.

RACHILDE AND THE WOMAN QUESTION

Between 1891 and 1914, more than thirty feminist publications emerged in France, including Marguerite Durand's influential *La Fronde,* which began in 1897.[12] During this same period, Paris was host to at least ten international feminist congresses.[13] In its diverse forms, feminist activism was on the rise

Figure 5. Portrait of Rachilde by Margaret van Bever. Frontispiece for *Rachilde, by Ernest Gaubert* (Paris: E. Sansot et cie, 1907). From the series Les Célébrités d'aujourd'hui. (Image courtesy of the General Research Division, The New York Public Library, Astor, Lenox and Tilden Foundations.)

in France, and its progress could be monitored in changes to laws regarding education, divorce, and women's property, even though suffrage—a principal goal of many turn-of-the-century feminists—would not be achieved for decades to come. Although many of Rachilde's texts—and much of her behavior—appear to challenge traditional gender roles, Rachilde did not identify with this wave of feminism or with women writers as a group.[14] Rachilde's relationship to feminism as a political movement has never been in question; she ridiculed it throughout her life, beginning in her teens when, as a reporter for the local newspaper, she mocked speakers at local feminist conferences.[15] But the relationship of Rachilde's work to feminist ideals—that is, the question whether her writing challenges patriarchal hierarchies—is one of the slipperiest and most persistent issues facing her contemporary critics. Many scholars have asked whether the gender reversals in her novels are meant as attacks on decadent views of sexuality or whether they simply cleverly reproduce misogynist strategies. While recent criticism has generally favored a more subversive reading, scholars continue to note signs of ambivalence that put this subversion into question.[16] Although Rachilde's value in this study is not as a feminist spokesperson, her critique of gender roles is relevant to the extent that it helps us to appreciate the challenges of expressing female intellect in a male-dominated literary discourse and the significance of her heroines' aggressive behaviors.[17]

The major obstacle to addressing this question stems from the suggestiveness of Rachilde's personal behavior, which did not conform to fin-de-siècle conventions of femininity. Indeed, Rachilde never fully identified with other women, perhaps because her intelligence, talents, and independence left her little in common with what were perceived as the traditional traits of the "inferior sex." As Catherine Ploye explains, "la femme capable de s'affirmer dans un rôle non traditionnel devient autre chose qu'une femme et n'a donc que faire de l'émancipation des femmes" (the woman able to take on a nontraditional role becomes something other than a woman and thus has no interest in the emancipation of women).[18] Rachilde seemed to carve out a place for herself beyond the traditional poles of masculinity and femininity, but she always refused the political implications of her gestures. As she explains in her 1928 essay "Pourquoi je ne suis pas féministe": "J'ai toujours agi en individu ne songeant pas à fonder une société ou à bouleverser celle qui existait. . . . Si je consens à être une exception (on ne peut pas faire autrement dans certains cas) je n'entends pas la confirmer en prenant mes personnelles erreurs pour de nouveaux dogmes" (I have always acted as an individual not thinking of founding a society or of upsetting the one that existed. . . . If I consent to be an exception [one cannot do otherwise in certain cases] I don't mean to encourage this by taking my personal errors for new dogmas). Indeed, Rachilde did not see her individualism as a political act. In the same essay she writes: "Non, je ne suis pas féministe. Je ne veux pas voter parce que cela m'ennuierait de m'occuper de politique" (No, I am not a feminist. I do not want to vote because it would bore me to deal with politics).[19] This is an important point: Rachilde saw no relationship between herself and a movement that was concerned with the political issues mentioned above.[20] But this resistance to the feminist label should not prevent us from recognizing the ways in which Rachilde's writing may have interrogated relationships among sexuality, language, and power that much later feminist theorists would explore explicitly. As Mary Louise Roberts has argued, resistance to patriarchal structures was expressed at the turn of the century "as a diverse language, in which feminism is simply one dialect."[21] Rachilde, under her gender-neutral pseudonym, often cross-dressing in her early years and using business cards that read "Rachilde, homme de lettres" (Rachilde, man of letters), spoke through her own highly original dialect of resistance, as did her female protagonists.

GENDER TROUBLE

Monsieur Vénus, Rachilde's second novel and first literary *succès de scandale* was originally published in Belgium in 1884, where it was promptly banned. It did not appear in France until five years later, when it was published with a mollifying preface by Maurice Barrès, which I consider more closely in the next section. The novel is filled with the images of fin-de-siècle deviance popularized by medical research that resurfaced constantly in a literature that fed on science's most provocative ideas. *Monsieur Vénus* tells the story of the gender-bending hysteric Raoule de Vénérande's seduction of the effete florist Jacques Silvert. Once Jacques has become Raoule's "mistress," they marry, overturning conventions of both class and gender in the process. In the meantime, Jacques's sister Marie resorts to prostitution, and Raoule's jilted lover, the macho soldier Baron de Raittolbe, alternates between satisfying his urges with Marie and fielding Jacques's own advances. Finally, Raoule becomes jealous and orders Raittolbe to fight Jacques, who dies in their duel. The novel closes with the image of Raoule alternating between male and female attire as she amorously interacts with a wax effigy of her dead lover.

Despite Rachilde's apparent rejection of the limitations of binary gender categories, I would argue that the novel is propelled fundamentally by a kind of gendered warfare: the wily female Raoule against the macho, lusting soldier Raittolbe and the frail, impotent Jacques, who will ultimately be sacrificed. This underlying dynamic is made clear in a chapter that appeared in the Belgian 1884 edition but was later edited out. The Belgian edition was not signed by Rachilde alone; it also bore the initials F.T., supposedly referring to a young journalist named Francis Talman, whom the author claimed to have met while fencing. According to Rachilde, Talman convinced her that she needed his collaboration, so that he could fight on her behalf if there were a duel resulting from the novel's publication. Rachilde was the sole author of the 1889 French edition, however, and an editorial note explains that Talman's contributions were edited out.[22] I am not convinced, however, that Talman existed in reality any more than did the Swedish nobleman who was Rachilde's namesake, since the only evidence that either of them were real is Rachilde's own testimony. Rachilde tells the story of meeting Francis Talman in a letter to the literary critic Auriant.[23] But Rachilde had a history of inventing different motives for her fiction. In the preface to *A mort,* she describes *Monsieur Vénus* as inspired by her feelings for Catulle Mendès, which she claims provoked temporary paralysis. She also claimed to have written it as a publicity stunt. In a letter to the poet Robert de Sousa, she offers a more sentimental explanation, saying that the idea for the novel grew out of her trauma at watching her mother beaten by her father.[24] No other publications by Talman have ever been located, nor did anyone ever attempt to claim credit for coauthoring *Monsieur Vénus.*[25]

The chapter that Rachilde later disavowed, on one hand, offers a manifesto against gender disparity in sexual relationships that it is hard to imagine a man of her generation executing. It is also intimately linked in style, decadent thematics, and vocabulary to the rest of the novel. On the other hand, it is didactic and abstract, reflecting a less mature authorial voice, and perhaps for these reasons it was later eliminated, by agreement of "author and editor."[26] Clearly Rachilde ultimately did not want to be known as the author of chapter 7, which by 1938 (ten years after the publication of her essay "Pourquoi je ne suis pas féministe") she viewed, in line with the feminist ventures of her female contemporaries, as "le comble de tous les ridicules" (the height of silliness) in a book that she had also now declared "mauvais" (bad).[27] Her husband, Alfred Vallette, never cared for the novel and had mocked chapter 7, a fact that may have contributed to her distancing herself from it in later years.[28] If it was indeed Rachilde's writing, it offers a rare glimpse of the polemical ideology driving the young author of *Monsieur Vénus.* Real or imagined, the collaboration with Francis Talman is part of Rachilde's complex entanglement with male-authorized discourse, whose power she cleverly exploited as she built her reputation. It is in fact part of a series of ambiguous alliances with male figures that make up the intra- and extratextual history of this novel. Rachilde's own justification for Talman as a means of her own self-protection may be most revelatory: Talman may have been simply a phantom whose male signature—rather than his fencing skills—provided the young author initial security in publishing her subversive writing.

The chapter in question begins:

> L'homme assis à sa propre droite sur les nuées d'un ciel imaginaire a relégué sa compagne au second rang dans l'échelle des êtres.
> En cela, l'instinct du mâle a prévalu. Le rôle inférieur que sa conformation impose à la femme dans l'acte générateur, éveille évidemment une idée de joug d'asservissement.
> L'homme possède, la femme subit.[29]
>
> [The man seated on her own right in the clouds of an imaginary sky has relegated his companion to second rank on the scale of beings.
> In this, the male instinct has prevailed. The inferior role that woman's form imposes on her in the procreative act evidently gives rise to an idea of the yoke of slavery.
> Man possesses, woman submits.]

Protesting the different male and female sexual roles necessitated by the obligations of the *l'acte générateur* (and in this, the author was using the idiom of popular medical literature), the narrator offers a solution that involves the rejection of "the pact of procreation" and the embrace of a decadent return to practices of antiquity:

> L'homme est matière, la volupté est femme, c'est l'éternelle inapaisée.
> N'est-ce pas à cette disparité profonde, monstrueuse antithèse, qu'il faut demander le secret des ardeurs stériles, seuls fruits d'accouplement sans nom?
> Oublions la loi naturelle, déchirons le pacte de procréation, nions la subordination des sexes, alors nous comprendrons les débordements inouïs de cette autre prostituée qui fut l'antiquité païenne.[30]
>
> [Man is matter, pleasure is woman, she is the eternally unappeased.
> Isn't it from within this profound disparity, this monstrous antithesis, that one should seek the secret of sterile passions, the only fruits of a coupling that has no name?
> Let's forget about natural law, let's rip up the pact of procreation, let's deny the subordination of the sexes. Then we will understand the unheard of excesses of that other prostitute that was pagan antiquity.]

In this new world order, "la volupté est femme" (pleasure is woman). And thus the path of the novel is paved, as the narrator proclaims: "Dans l'irradiation d'une aurore vengeresse, la femme entreverra pour l'homme la possibilité d'une fabuleuse chute" (In the radiance of this vengeful dawn, woman will glimpse the possibility of a fabulous downfall for man).[31] Raoule de Vénérande is to be this woman, making man's downfall possible.

Chapter 7 makes clear that Raoule and Jacques are fundamentally representatives of male and female categories, and that Rachilde's subversions, in the name of *la femme,* have implications for women as a whole. The text goes on to explain that man's downfall will take place through Raoule's possession of Jacques: "Elle inventera des caresses, trouvera de nouvelles preuves aux nouveaux transports d'un nouvel amour et Raoule de Vénérande possédera Jacques Silvert" (She will invent caresses, will find new proofs in the new transports of a new love and Raoule de Vénérande will possess Jacques Silvert) (94).[32] It is unclear whether the "elle" that heads this sentence refers to Rachilde, her female protagonist, or women in general. As the narrator describes it here, the woman's revenge links the intellectual with the sensual and thus ties the female protagonist to the female author. Raoule's triumph over "l'instinct du mâle" (male instinct) will take place through a sexual subversion that is also a creative process. The description of sexual inventiveness, which triply emphasizes newness ("de *nouvelles* preuves aux *nouveaux* transports d'un *nouvel* amour"), presages Raoule's desire to "créer une dépravation nouvelle" (create a new depravity), which maps onto the decadent author's eternal quest for new discoveries. In this vision of the world, sexual creativity and female intellect are inseparable as the narrator compares the vacuousness of male sexuality to the woman's position: "Pour celle-là, au contraire . . . l'action des sens s'étend au domaine intellectuel, l'imagination s'éveille aux aspirations sans bornes" (For the woman, on the other hand. . . . the acts of the senses extend to the intellectual domain, the imagination awakens to limitless aspirations).[33] (To me, this sentence in particular seems to belie Talman's authorship.) While for the male lover "tout est dit" (everything has been said), for the female "de nouvelles joies" (new joys) are still a possibility.[34]

This declaration of war between the sexes suggests a unity between women that is utterly absent in the rest of the novel. Raoule is in eternal conflict with her overly religious Tante Elisabeth and is even more disgusted by any associations with Jacques's prostituting sister, Marie. Indeed, Raoule's triumph over Jacques will be a unique and profoundly individual one that may have theoretical value for *la femme* but has no bearing or relevance to any other specific women. As Raoule explains this elitist ethic to Raittolbe earlier in the novel, she hinges her sexual originality in pseudofeminist foundations that align Raoule the female artist with Rachilde her creator, both of whom define themselves as women only to the extent that they are exceptional:

> Je représente ici, dit-elle . . . l'élite des femmes de notre époque. Un échantillon du féminin artiste et du féminin grande dame, une de ces créatures qui se révoltent à l'idée de perpétuer une race appauvrie. . . . J'arrive à votre tribunal, députée par mes soeurs, pour vous déclarer que toutes nous désirons l'impossible, tant vous nous aimez mal.[35]

> [I represent here, she said . . . the elite of the women of our generation. An example of the female artist and the feminine grand lady, one of those creatures who revolts at the idea of perpetuating an impoverished race. . . . I arrive at your tribunal, deputized by my sisters, to declare to you that we all desire the impossible, for you love us so badly.]

Notably echoing the promises of the excised chapter 7, Raoule rejects the obligation to procreate and announces her desire for the *impossible*—a term that highlights her social and linguistic position outside existing modes for speaking about female sexuality and thus also harks back to the mention in that chapter of "couplings that have no name."

Perhaps the greatest irony in *Monsieur Vénus* is that the elite representative of female artistry is considered by those around her to be mentally ill: she is diagnosed early on with hysteria.[36] By the 1880s, hysteria had become a veritable phenomenon, and its most popular purveyor, Jean-Martin Charcot, a Parisian celebrity. Widespread discussion of the disease was fueled by a vibrant popular press that generated volumes of medical treatises written for a largely male audience. These texts blurred the line between fiction and science: the slim paperback issues from the "Bibliothèque populaire des connaissances médicales," which featured a volume on hysteria (along with others on syphilis, pederasty, and impotence), displayed advertisements for *romans passionnels* alongside those for other medical works and racy postcards.

In part as a result of the extensive discussion of the disease, medical definitions of hysteria were remarkably elastic, making it easy to diagnose any erratic female behavior as hysterical. Charcot worked against this popular perception through his scientific classifications of hysterical symptoms.[37] Yet so extensive was the popular view of the disease that in 1885, Charcot applauded his disciple Paul Richer for writing a treatise that sought to dispel the notion of hysteria as "un Protée qui se présente sous mille formes et qu'on ne peut saisir aucune" (a Proteus that appears in a thousand forms, none of which can be grasped).[38] Several women writers satirize the pervasiveness of the hysteria diagnosis in their novels, in scenes where male doctors rush to this dire conclusion to explain any female malady.[39] Rachilde is more subtle in her manipulation of this phenomenon, using the looseness of the diagnosis to her own creative advantage. She exploits hysteria's lack of determinacy to reinvent the disease as an illness so subversive that it challenges the very patriarchal system in place to diagnose and contain such deviance. At the same time, the text camouflages this subversiveness in familiar decadent vocabulary. Rachilde's text thus functions on two levels: for much of the novel one can read Raoule as a hysteric, according to an ideology that categorizes all female sexual deviance as hysterical. But if one recognizes the full ramifications of Raoule's actions, one sees that her behavior represents a sexual identity that cannot be contained or categorized by fin-de-siècle medical discourse. These terms thus become empty labels that allow Raoule the freedom to act as she wishes—and her behavior, in its deviation from conventional femininity, is inevitably described as hysterical.

The twentieth-century feminist response to the question of hysteria might be summarized very broadly as following two general trends: the first, exemplified in varied and nuanced criticism by such scholars as Gladys Swain, Ruth Harris, Elaine Showalter, and Martha Noel Evans, for example, examines the gender hierarchy of the medical profession and its victimization of women through history and literature; in this light, the hysteria diagnosis is revealed to have unfairly silenced women who threatened the social order.[40] The other trend takes a more psychoanalytic perspective, seeing hysteria, in Carol Smith-Rosenberg's terms, as a desperate "flight into illness." From this perspective radical French feminists like Hélène Cixous, Catherine Clément, and Luce Irigaray recognize hysteria as a form of female resistance.[41] Irigaray, for example, recognizes the revolutionary potential of the hysteric, as a "culturally induced symptom."[42] Irigaray's hysteric herself deliberately assumes the feminine role, carrying on a charade of feminized suffering to, in her words "convert a form of subordination into an affirmation, and thus begin to thwart it."[43]

From her unique temporal position, writing in the midst of the golden age of hysteria while Charcot was at the peak of his career, Rachilde, through her use of hysteria, presciently incorporates elements of both of these future trends. In the first instance, her ironic portrayal of the disease points to its capacity to silence women from a young age. Although always a strong-willed child, Raoule de Vénérande lived a life of relative normality until the fateful moment when she began to read, around the age of fifteen: "Vers ce temps, une révolution s'opéra dans la jeune fille. Sa physionomie s'altéra, sa parole devint brève, ses prunelles dardèrent la fièvre, elle pleura et elle rit à la fois" (Around this time, a revolution took place in the young girl. Her expression changed, her words became brief, her eyes darted feverishly, she laughed and cried at the same time) (40).[44] This description is highly suggestive of hysteria to the fin-de-siècle reader, likely to be familiar enough with the topic to recognize at once such generic symptoms of the era's most well-known illness. Almost immediately a doctor is summoned to the house to make the following prediction for Raoule:

> Quelques années encore, et cette jolie créature que vous chérissez trop, à mon avis, aura, sans les aimer jamais, connu autant d'hommes qu'il y de grains au rosaire de sa tante. Pas de milieu! Ou nonne, ou monstre! Le sein de Dieu ou celui de la volupté! Il vaudrait peut-être mieux l'enfermer dans un couvent, puisque nous enfermons les hystériques à la Salpêtrière! (40–41)

> [A few more years, and this pretty creature whom you cherish so, in my opinion, will have known as many men as there are beads on her aunt's rosary without ever loving them. No middle ground! Nun or monster! The bosom of God or that of sensuality! It might be better to lock her up in a convent, since we lock up hysterics in the Salpêtrière!]

In this early conclusion, the two possible diagnoses for a woman who refuses traditional female roles (e.g., marriage, which is the first suggestion the doctors make) are laid out in their full simplicity: a total repression of sexuality or its total embrace.

Upon the doctor's pronouncement of Raoule's condition, the narrative continues: "Il y avait dix ans de cela, au moment où commence cette histoire . . . , et Raoule n'était pas nonne" (It had been ten years since, at the moment that this story begins . . . , and Raoule was not a nun) (41). The narrator deliberately implies, then, that Raoule has gone the other route—that of *volupté, hystérie,* and *vice:* she has become a hysterical monster.

Rachilde takes advantage of these symptoms as literary openings that create the traditional premise for decadent intrigue, and to a certain extent her text reads as what Emily Apter has called "pathography"—that fin-de-siècle gray area between literature and clinical study that played on the fluidity between science and fiction, in this instance, the case history of female sexual pathology.[45] Raoule's hysterical symptoms are indeed rather well documented at this point in the novel, as Janet Beizer, who recognizes in the novel "unmistakable citations of the teachings of Charcot," has demonstrated.[46] After her first meeting with Jacques, for example, Raoule is seen reproducing the *arc de cercle* pose made famous by Charcot's iconographies; in a state of excitation, she lies "la tête en arrière, le corsage gonflé, les bras crispés, avec de temps à autre un soupir de lassitude" (head back, swollen bodice, arms tensed, with from time to time a sigh of lassitude) (34). Another description of her, as "folle comme les possédées du Moyen Age qui avaient le démon en elles et n'agissaient plus de leur propre attitude" (crazy like the possessed women of the Middle Ages who had the demon in them and no longer acted of their own accord) (176), explicitly speaks through the discourse used to explain hysteria. Furthermore, Raoule is predisposed to this illness because of her family history: a father described as "un de ces débauchés épuisés" (one of those used-up debauched men) and a mother who had had "les plus naturels et les plus fougueux appétits" (the most natural and impetuous appetites) before hemorrhaging to death after giving birth (39). As Charcot's own theories held (and as Zola had so imaginatively elaborated), heredity was the ultimate reason for mental degeneracy. With a perverse father and a mother with the unfortunate combination of healthy appetites and a weak constitution, Raoule is physiologically predisposed to illness.

Yet at the same time as Rachilde mimics the discourse of medicine and dominant ideologies determining female sexual behavior, she stages the production of this discourse in its reductiveness and circularity, thus suggesting a more subversive use of hysteria as a means of strategic mimicry. We have already seen the first doctor's rush to judgment of the adolescent girl, immediately recommending her exile from society. Later Raoule's frustrated former lover Raittolbe promises himself "qu'il ne reviendrait jamais chez cette hystérique, car, selon ses idées, on ne pouvait qu'être hystérique dès qu'on ne suivait pas la loi commune" (that he would never come back to that hysteric, for, according to him, once one no longer followed common rules one could only be hysterical) (65). Just like the doctor, Raittolbe is unable to see beyond the preexisting societal categories that define a woman when she steps out of bounds. Paradoxically, according to this definition of the hysteric as a woman who "no longer followed common rules," Raoule's individuality is erased when she stops acting like everybody else; deviance is normalized and contained through the generic category of hysteria. At the moment she begins to act as an independent sexual being, she is seen as a hysteric. Hysteria in this context appears to be just the kind of radical individualism that Rachilde herself associated with the artistic elite. Indeed, for much of the novel hysteria seems to liberate Raoule from conventional feminine roles, thus functioning as a mode of resistance to patriarchal structures.

In fact, despite Charcot's best efforts to rigorously classify the disease, it has been argued that the common trait linking the multifarious nineteenth-century ideas about hysteria was its indeterminacy, manifested in an inability to define the disease.[47] In 1889, the doctor Joseph Grasset, author of the *Dictionnaire encyclopédique des sciences médicales,* complained that hysteria was "l'article de ce Dictionnaire le plus difficile à faire *clair* et *court*" (the article in the dictionary that was hardest to make *clear* and *concise*) and called the disease "un véritable protée qui se présente sous autant de couleurs que le caméléon" (a veritable Proteus that shows as many colors as the chameleon).[48] Dr. Zabé, writing for a general audience in his *Manuel des maladies des femmes* from 1884, claimed: "Les caractères de cette maladie, véritable caméléon, sont si fugaces, si variables, qu'elle est pour ainsi dire indéfinissable" (The features of this illness, a veritable chameleon, are so ephemeral, so variable, that it is undefinable, so to speak).[49] The overlapping vocabulary here (Charcot was writing against the protean notion of hysteria, a term Grasset also invokes, and both Grasset and Zabé call hysteria a chameleon) suggests that these terms were circulating in the mass press, becoming catchphrases or clichés to describe the popular diagnosis. The prominent doctor Legrand du Saulle admits in his treatise: "Il est peu de maladies dans le cadre nosologique qui comptent des formes aussi multiples . . . que l'hystérie" (There are few illnesses within a nosological framework that have as many forms . . . as hysteria).[50] The doctor in Jules Claretie's novel *Les Amours d'un interne* offers a similar description: "Une définition, c'est toujours difficile. Je vous dirai plutôt que l'hystérie n'est point. . . . Ça peut être érotique—pour donner raison au vulgaire—ça peut être sombre, ça peut être mystique, ça peut être tout. C'est, si vous voulez, l'exagération de tout" (A definition, that's always hard. I will tell you instead that hysteria is not. . . . It can be erotic—to agree with the masses—it can be somber, it can be mystical, it can be anything. It is, if you will, the exaggeration of everything).[51] It was not a far leap from this to the allegation by the popular medical writer known as Dr. Caufeynon that the hysteric's behavior was so eccentric as to "faire pâlir les creations des romanciers les plus inventifs" (make the creations of the most inventive novelists pale in comparison).[52] It seems to me that Rachilde exploits this aspect of the overdetermined illness—the *ça peut être tout*—at the same time as she paints her protagonist with its most identifiable symptoms. Raoule's diagnosis of hysteria thus gives all those familiar with it the comfort of medical and discursive authority, while it justifies her deviant behavior in whatever form it takes. In other words, once Raoule has been diagnosed as hysterical, there are no longer any preconceived limits to her behavior.

Indeed, in much of the novel one has the sense that Raoule is less victim of a disease than beneficiary of a discursive loophole that grants her sexual autonomy and permission to reinvent herself outside of gender norms.[53] Hysteria, the disease that supposedly makes its victims "femme plus que les autres femmes" (more womanly than other women) according to one critic's 1880 formulation, enables Raoule to reinvent just what it means to be a woman.[54] Many critics have noted Rachilde's prescient relationship to postmodern gender theory.[55] Beyond simple reversals, I would argue, Rachilde's depiction of Raoule in particular can be seen as an early attempt at, to borrow Judith Butler's term, "making gender trouble."[56] Raoule's behavior constantly probes at the unwritten rules of gender construction, primarily through her use of language, by defying the linguistic structures that inscribe gender in speech. "Je suis *amoureux*" (I am *in love*) (85) she declares in her usual fashion of substituting the masculine ending for the feminine one and demanding others to do the same. By interrupting the signifying process, this subversive speech upsets the discursive stability of sexual difference and points to the critical role of language in the social construction of gender. Gender conventions in language function only as long as the speakers are willing to follow the rules. What Raoule reveals is that these rules are easily modified without totally disrupting communication; not only does she identify linguistically in the masculine but her behavior inspires others to participate in this reversal. Her chaste aunt, generally horrified by Raoule's impropriety, has long referred to her niece as "mon neveu"; the homophobic Raittolbe calls his potential lover "mon cher ami" (my dear friend) as opposed to the feminine "ma chère amie"; and Jacques succumbs fully to the charade, becoming wife to her husband. As Dominique Fisher has suggested, this manner of speaking becomes a kind of discursive transvestism mimicking Raoule's cross-dressing. Linguistic gender, like clothing, is revealed as something you put on; the inscription of gender in language is thus distanced from the physical being speaking, undoing the supposedly natural relationship between the two. Raoule's use of masculine endings, like drag in reverse, cannot fully mask her anatomical sex, nor does it intend to; instead, it dramatizes the disjunction between sex and gender, by calling attention to the latter's contingency.[57]

Although Jacques incarnates a femininity that is in opposition to his sex, Raoule is the real gender artist, orchestrating the gender-bending dynamics that transform him ultimately into her "wife." Yet even this identity as an artist seems to be safely linked to Raoule's diagnosis as hysteric. According to nineteenth-century medicine, hysterics were given to fits of delirium and were thus naturally creative. Caufeynon writes: "L'hystérique ment sans but, sans raison, pour le plaisir, c'est dans le mensonge, le culte de l'art pour l'art" (The hysteric lies without a purpose, without a reason, for pleasure, the cult of art for art's sake is in lying).[58] Indeed, the most distinguishing characteristic of Raoule's sexual dysfunction is the creativity exhibited through her desire to craft her own sexual identity. In addition to her penchant for painting nudes, Raoule studies her lovers, comparing them to books in her library and thus underlining the links between passion, intellect, and creativity: "Il est certain, monsieur, que j'ai eu des amants. Des amants dans ma vie comme j'ai des livres dans ma bibliothèque, pour savoir, pour étudier. . . . Mais je n'ai pas eu de passion, je n'ai pas écrit mon livre, moi!" (It is certain, sir, that I have had lovers. Lovers in my life like I have books in my library, for knowledge, for studying. . . . But I have not had a passion, I have not written my book!) (85). Her relationship with Jacques is to be this sexual creation—her passion and her book—and in her quest she feeds him drugs and transforms her bedroom into an erotic palace. What happens on the canvas of Jacques's body, then, is also symbolic of Rachilde's own literary project: Raoule is also writing Rachilde's book, as it were.

Raoule's movement between male and female identities expresses her desire for the "impossible" announced earlier, a desire that demands a language that does not yet exist. Through the interactions between Raoule and Raittolbe, Rachilde confronts her protagonist with the fin-de-siècle labels meant to contain her deviance. Raittolbe first recognizes that Raoule is not a typical woman and thus calls her hysterical. But this label, once probed, proves unsatisfying, leading Raittolbe to scurry through other possible terms with which to describe his friend's behavior. At a certain point, Raittolbe thinks he has finally recognized Raoule's elusive identity. He exclaims excitedly: "Sapho! . . . je m'en doutais. Continuez, monsieur de Vénérande, continuez, *mon* cher ami!" (Sapho! . . . I thought as much. Continue, Mr. De Vénérande, continue, my dear [male] friend!) (84). Believing he finally has figured out that she is a lesbian, and that this would explain her bizarre sexual tastes, he sounds almost relieved. But Raoule quickly undermines him by announcing: "Vous vous trompez monsieur de Raittolbe; être Sapho, ce serait être tout le monde!" (You are mistaken Mr. De Raittolbe; to be Sapho, that would be so common!) (85).[59] By self-consciously refusing to be like *tout le monde,* she guards against being defined by any pre-existing category, whether it be lesbianism or prostitution. Raittolbe's attempts to label Raoule more specifically prove fruitless, and he leaves the conversation frustrated and dizzy. This episode shows that Raoule's behavior cannot be assimilated by fin-de-siècle vocabulary, largely because of the juggling of gender ("adoptons *il* ou *elle,* afin que je ne perde pas le peu de bon sens qui me reste" [let's use *he* or *she,* so that I don't lose the little bit of good sense I have left] [91]); her *nouvelle dépravation* will be completely new, such that Raittolbe can only exclaim that she is "le Christophe Colomb de l'amour moderne!" (the Christopher Columbus of modern love!) (88). Through its undefinability, hysteria essentially becomes medically meaningless for Raoule, serving instead as a vehicle of invention; it seems to contain within it the possibility for female self-definition, a liberating possibility within this fin-de-siècle context.

A WOMAN'S VENGEANCE

In the second half of the novel, the progress of Raoule's creative passion takes a violent turn on the landscape of the male body. Jacques, "dont le corps était un poème" (whose body was a poem), becomes Raoule's oeuvre, on whose body she inscribes her desires. He is the so-called hysteric's ultimate revenge: the sensual art project presaged in the eliminated chapter that symbolizes Raoule's sexual and intellectual authority. Violence and destruction, likewise predicted in this chapter through images of broken scepters and prostrate men ("l'homme a dépouillé sa force, brisé son sceptre" [man has stripped his strength, broken his scepter] (94) are fundamental to the creation of Raoule's oeuvre, signaling the voice of Rachilde's own critique of the discourse to be destroyed in the process. In Raoule's absence, the frustrated Raittolbe beats Jacques. Seeing the traces of Raittolbe's presence on her lover's body, Raoule continues this violence, brutally scratching and biting Jacques' already wounded flesh: "D'un geste violent, elle arracha les bandes de batiste qu'elle avait roulées autour du corps sacré de son éphèbe, elle mordit ses chairs marbrées . . . [et] les égratigna de ses ongles affilés" (With a violent gesture, she ripped off the bandages that she had rolled around the sacred body of her ephebe, she bit his mottled flesh [and] scratched it with her sharpened nails) (145). But Raoule's collaboration with Raittolbe is really her undoing of his inscription as she deliberately reopens Jacques's wounds and replaces the signs of Raittolbe's presence with her own sadistic signature ("il faut que j'efface chaque cicatrice sous mes lèvres" [I must erase each scar with my lips] [144]). In an act of powerful vengeance, she inscribes the mark of her alternative sexuality on the unsuspecting canvas of the male body, and in so doing erases the work of her apparent collaborator.[60] Indeed, Raoule's authorial gesture mirrors Rachilde's literary collaboration with the discourses of decadence, using them as a landscape for her novel while undermining them between their own lines. As the female artist appropriates the male body, Rachilde effectively explodes the link between virility and intellectual authority. After revising Raittolbe's inscription on her lover's body, Raoule announces to him: "Jacques n'est plus qu'une plaie; c'est notre oeuvre" (Jacques is but a wound; he is our work) (156). By embracing the slippage between the *plaie* and the oeuvre Raoule places her art in a kind of negative space traditionally associated with female sexuality, recalling Zola's own vivid vocabulary. Her creative endeavor takes place at the breaking point of male authorized discourse, where the male imagination confronts its limits. At the same time, by describing Jacques as "notre oeuvre," she refuses sole authorship, labeling him instead a collaboration.

Raoule's creative vengeance does not stop with her sadistic inscription. It seems her masterpiece can be achieved only with Jacques's total destruction, when he is killed by Raittolbe in a duel. Like Tinayre's *Maison du péché,* the novel thereby ends with a reversal of narrative convention, with the death of the male hero as a result of his sexual deviance, as opposed to the conventional expulsion of subversive female sexuality in the interest of narrative closure.[61] With Jacques's death at the hands of Raittolbe, Raoule once again revises her partner's work. We are told: "Le soir de ce jour funèbre, Mme Silvert se penchait sur le lit du temple de l'Amour et, armée d'une pince en vermeil, d'un marteau recouvert de velours et d'un ciseau en argent massif, se livrait à un travail minutieux" (The night of this tragic day, Madame Silvert leaned over the bed of the temple of love, and, armed with silver tweezers, a velvet-covered hammer and a sterling silver scalpel, began a delicate task) (224–25). The delicacy of this task is revealed in the next and final chapter, when a wax effigy is described, made up of the products of this labor:

> Sur la couche en forme de conque . . . repose un mannequin de cire revêtu d'un épiderme de caoutchouc transparent. Les cheveux roux, les cils blonds, le duvet d'or de la poitrine sont naturels; les dents qui ornent la bouche, les ongles des mains et des pieds ont été arrachés à un cadavre. (228)
>
> [On the seashell-shaped bed . . . rests a wax mannequin covered with a transparent rubber skin. The red hair, the blond eyelashes, [and] the gold hair of the chest are natural; the teeth that ornament the mouth, [and] the nails on the hands and feet were torn from a corpse.]

This mannequin, later described as a "chef d'oeuvre d'anatomie" (masterpiece of anatomy) (228), is Raoule's final masterpiece, adorned with Jacques's own hair, teeth, and nails.

Unlike in Barbey's story, wax, rather than sealing and silencing the female sex, becomes the material of female creativity. But wax has other cultural affiliations as well. Raoule's "Monsieur Vénus" evokes the wax models known as anatomical venuses used to teach medicine in the nineteenth century. These lifelike models were equipped with removable internal organs and often boasted real human features, such as long hair and eyelashes; their sleepy expressions sometimes suggested a sensual presence that their artifice belied.[62] As Jann Matlock has demonstrated, the association between wax venuses and the scientific display and voyeuristic exploration of disease, particularly in women, is revealed in the mythology surrounding the Musée Dupuytren, the Parisian pathological anatomy museum, rumored to display likenesses of the most gruesome maladies. This museum was closed to the public (contributing to its mythology) but a fake replica of it was featured in a traveling fair of waxworks in the 1880s that tapped into the nineteenth-century thrills of medicine. Visitors are invited in, in the interest of fighting, as the poster says, "ignorance that leads to debauchery."[63]

Raoule's wax Venus plays vividly—and morbidly—on these popular associations, further mocking the medical profession that diagnosed her hysteria. Indeed, Charcot also used wax models beginning in the 1870s, when he would cast his patients' bodies in wax. These models contributed to the iconography of the Salpêtrière, without having a clear medical purpose. Considered in the context of these medical practices, Raoule's wax model, though it is a creation made by a supposed hysteric, stands in the tradition of medical convention and thus aligns the patient with the doctors themselves. In effect, with Rachilde's final montage, the distinction between doctor/scientist and hysteric is permanently blurred; traditional medical practice is pathologized and pathology aestheticized, as Raoule the hysteric/artist becomes overseer of her anatomical model. The limits of the hysteric's behavior are so uncircumscribed that they allow her to assume the position of medical authority, and in so doing subvert the very mechanisms that make her diagnosis possible. Her monstrous, necrophilic power is tied to the medical profession's own complicity in aestheticizing sickness, making male-authorized medical discourse her unwitting collaborator in this final "masterpiece of anatomy."

The mouth of Raoule's creature is transformed into the primary means of physical stimulus by a spring hidden inside the thighs: "un ressort, disposé à l'intérieur des flancs, correspond à la bouche et l'anime" (a spring, set up inside the hips, corresponds to the mouth and animates it) (228). It is apparently this substitute for the masculine sex organ that now enables Raoule to be satisfied physically, in an existence that moves beyond genital sex. It is worth noting that in the original 1884 edition, this spring corresponded not only to the mouth but to a mechanism between the legs, thus more literally replacing the male organ.[64] Living as both male and female, alternating gender in her attire, Raoule seems at last to have found a way to live her full double-sexuality independent of the outside world. In this rebellious autonomy, she has also released herself from discursive bounds, realizing a kind of emancipatory ideal from sexual categories. With the voices of Raittolbe and Jacques eliminated and no doctor in sight, the text leaves no linguistic or scientific resources to assimilate this genderless creature who ultimately resists fin-de-siècle labels.

And yet, however tempting it is to read Raoule's sexual and artistic freedom as symbolic of Rachilde's intellectual freedom, neither Raoule nor Rachilde completely separates herself from male authority as the novel closes. In fact, the text ends with the acknowledgment of another collaboration. The enigmatic last sentence explains: "Ce mannequin, chef d'oeuvre d'anatomie, a été fabriqué par un Allemand" (This mannequin, a masterpiece of anatomy, was created by a German) (228), reducing Raoule to a partner in the creation of this masterpiece—and by implication Rachilde as well. This terse final reference suggests a nod to E.T.A. Hoffmann, the German creator of another famous nineteenth-century automaton, the wooden doll Olympia from his 1817 short story "The Sandman."[65] Linking herself to the author of a fantastic story about a sexual relationship between man and doll, whose underlying theme of castration anxiety is invoked in the theme of detached eyeballs, Rachilde mitigates the newness of Raoule's perversions, while situating herself in a well-established male tradition. By aligning herself with Hoffmann, she downplays her own originality; at the same time, her male automaton has challenged the heterosexual, patriarchal psychodynamics that propel Hoffmann's famous tale (which would later be the basis of Freud's 1919 essay on the uncanny). Thus, once again, the collaboration with male authority is also the tacit reminder of the extent to which she has transformed and remade his creation.

Rachilde's ambiguous alliances with male authority continue with the publication history of the novel. On its initial publication in Belgium, *Monsieur Vénus* was deemed pornographic; its author was fined and sentenced to two years in prison. Rachilde avoided this punishment by staying in France, where the scandal reverberated to the extent that she was forced to hide her copies of the novel. André David describes the public reaction as follows: "Ce livre avait intrigué et étonné: on inventa des légendes. . . . Le *Gil Blas* déclara que c'était un livre obscène. . . . Les femmes en défendirent la lecture à leurs maris" (This book had intrigued and surprised: legends were invented. . . . The *Gil Blas* declared that it was an obscene book. . . . Women forbade their husbands to read it).[66] In this ironic twist, novel reading—which in *Monsieur Vénus* leads to Raoule's illness—is now seen as dangerous for men. It is not surprising that readers would be unsettled by the novel's intimidating protagonist. The preface in the original Belgian version of the novel states briefly: "Nous prévenons nos lecteurs qu'au moment où ils coupent ces premiers feuillets, l'héroïne de notre histoire passe peut-être devant leur porte" (We warn our readers that at the moment that they cut open these first pages, the heroine of our story might be passing in front of their door). Not long after, Rachilde began an enigmatic relationship with Maurice Barres.[67] He later volunteered to write a preface to *Monsieur Vénus,* published with the 1889 French edition, which helped launch Rachilde's lengthy literary career.

In his introduction, Barrès identifies the barrier to the novel's reception: readers seemed to have been threatened not simply by the content of the novel and its nontraditional ending but by the unfamiliar fact of a woman skillfully constructing this story of sexual deviance. Barrès dispels public anxiety by describing Rachilde as "une jeune fille de vingt ans" (a young woman of twenty) suffering from "la maladie du siècle" (the illness of the age)—that is, from the same malady as Raoule, hysteria.[68] Barrès is perfectly aligned with contemporary medical doctrine that associated creativity and imagination in women with hysteria, such that what in men would be considered skills in women became symptoms. Female creativity must be diagnosed. With this in mind, Barrès encourages the reader to view the text not as a carefully crafted psychological drama but as a fascinating byproduct of mental illness:

> Les jeunes filles nous paraissent une chose très compliquée, parce qu'elles sont gouvernées uniquement par l'instinct. . . . Rachilde, à vingt ans, pour écrire un livre qui fait rêver un peu tout le monde, n'a guère réfléchi; elle a écrit tout au trot de sa plume, suivant son instinct.[69]
>
> [Young girls seem to us something very complicated, because they are governed solely by instinct. . . . Rachilde, at the age of twenty, hardly reflected in writing this book that makes everyone dream a bit; she wrote it all at the run of her pen, following her instinct.]

By describing the author as "une nerveuse" (a neurotic) and "une fièvreuse" (a feverish girl) and by calling the novel "le spectacle d'une rare perversité" (the spectacle of a rare perversity), Barrès uses the same discursive short-cuts as Rachilde to render the seemingly subversive into something identifiable and familiar. The reader, Barrès writes, is no longer being challenged by a skillfully defiant writer but instead is witnessing the fantasies of the hysteric, whose threat is further diminished by her young age. "Fantaisie pleureuse d'une isolée, excentricité cérébrale, mais qui intéresse le psychologue, le moraliste et l'artiste, *Monsieur Vénus* est un symptôme très significatif" (The weepy fantasy of an isolated girl, a cerebral eccentricity, but of interest to the psychologist, the moralist and the artist, *Monsieur Vénus* is a very significant symptom).[70] The reader is placed in a position of authority—that of the psychologist, moralist, and artist—where he should not feel threatened by what is described as the ignorant object of his enlightened gaze. By stripping Rachilde's novel of its subversiveness with these explanations, Barrès's preface mimics the strategies of the decadent and naturalist writer who must disempower the sexual deviant he has created by the time he reaches his final paragraphs. In the process, Rachilde is transformed into a product of the decadent imagination rather than a creative force in and of herself, and the traditional fin-de-siècle paradigm of male writer/doctor/scientist to female subject is comfortably reinstated. Ironically, by diagnosing the author as a young hysteric, Barrès assumes readers are more comfortable with a Raoule than a Rachilde; at the end of the nineteenth century, female discursive authority is much more of a social threat than pathological sexual deviance: the woman writer is more terrifying than the hysteric.[71]

One must wonder why Rachilde would allow Barrès to offer such a loaded introduction to her novel. In fact, their correspondence reveals it to have been a publicity stunt in which Rachilde was complicit. Barrès promised to write twenty beautiful pages in which he would explain "comment et en quoi ce livre-là est un chef d'oeuvre" (how and in what ways this book is a masterpiece); Rachilde edited these pages before they were published.[72] Rachilde, in the spirit of her time, apparently believed that there is no such thing as bad publicity. Furthermore, Barrès's essay only reproduces the dogmas and reading strategies already inscribed in Rachilde's text through her use of clichéd notions of female sexuality. By deeming her novel the perverse creation of a hysterical woman, he transforms what might have been construed as frightening and unique into the realm of the familiar. In this clever alternative to censorship, the novel and its author are permitted to exist in all their transgressive glory; their threat is masked by their categorization in the context of fin-de-siècle commonplace. The appropriateness of the label hysteric seems to have been irrelevant to Rachilde: what she recognized was its usefulness.

In fact, this preface also echoes Rachilde's denigrating self-description from the year before in the autobiographical preface to *Madame Adonis,* where she describes herself as a "hysteric of letters" and her writing as a physical rather than reflective process.[73] Echoing the animosity directed against women writers of her generation, her self-description is shockingly misogynist; yet at the same time, it invites an ironic and playful reading that thereby undermines the misogyny. Barrès's preface reestablishes the collaboration with male authority found within *Monsieur Vénus,* while accomplishing a similar goal. By linking her female signature to his male one, Rachilde seems to suggest that there is nothing particularly feminine or feminist about her writing, thus distilling this particular threat and protecting herself from unwanted association with the *bas-bleus;* a closer look, however, reveals that everything subversive about her novel comes from the powerful female protagonist overthrowing her unprepared male partners and orchestrating gender warfare. From a modern perspective, it starts to look like an early form of radical feminism.

Ironically, through her outrageous attack on the structures of virility, Rachilde becomes the quintessential decadent. The fact of her being a woman only adds another layer of transgressiveness to her text. Yet, as the reception of her novel reveals, to be a female decadent, Rachilde had to shield certain aspects of her subversiveness from her readers, who read her for her conformity to her male peers. Her female signature had to become part of the fiction of her text, an extra frame of the narrative to be interpreted through the reassuring voice of a male author. Rachilde the writer is reduced in this context to nothing more than a decadent character herself, a product of the intersection between female creativity and female pathology in late nineteenth-century culture. And this is ultimately why it was essential that her *femme fatale* triumph, for Rachilde knew too well that as a woman writer she was as much *femme fatale* as *femme de lettres.* She thus allows her authorial identity to be pathologized, knowing full well that safely within the novel the category of hysteria is challenged, while the power of the hysteric—and by extension the woman writer—is amplified.

BEYOND THE PLEASURE PRINCIPLE: RACHILDE'S *LA JONGLEUSE*

Rachilde's attack on virility continues in *La Jongleuse* (1900), where once again, the construction of the female artist, in this instance Eliante Donalger, coincides with the de(con)struction of the male love interest, Léon Reille. As a *jongleuse,* a term that recalls medieval storytelling techniques, Eliante is the figure of the female artist, the inscription of the woman writer herself in the text. A creative figure who orchestrates the sexual humiliation of her male suitor, Eliante is in no small measure a kindred spirit to Raoule. Unlike Jacques, however, Léon does not experience physical bodily harm. Instead, the very symbolic structures of his sexuality are relentlessly challenged by Eliante's unusual desiring mode. Again, Rachilde's female artist seems fundamentally incompatible with the conventions of heterosexuality as her autoerotic pleasure poses new questions about the very possibility of being a female artist in a patriarchal world.

As the novel opens, Léon, a young medical student, stands in Eliante's salon, eyeing the mysterious older woman whom he has been surreptitiously ogling for some time. His profession is not irrelevant: in this novel Rachilde will again demonstrate the ultimate impotence of medical discourse. Already in this first scene, Eliante's impenetrability is contrasted with Léon's naïve desire, which is fueled by its frustration. Léon is initially infuriated by Eliante's audacity: having remarked his interest, she invites him to accompany her home. Her recognition of his amorous intentions leads him to self-righteous denial: "Je ne suis pas amoureux de vous . . . si j'en ai l'air! . . . Vous me semblez un object curieux, et cela m'amuse de vous regarder de près . . . derrière la vitrine. Pas envie de toucher . . . ni d'acheter, je vous jure" (I am not in love with you . . . if I look like it! . . . You seem to me a curious object, and it amuses me to look at you up close . . . behind the glass. No desire to touch . . . nor to buy, I swear to you).[74]

By comparing Eliante to "un objet curieux" Léon proclaims his desire to fetishize her, a perversion that is thematized throughout the novel. As a medical problem, fetishism—a term borrowed from the field of anthropology—was first documented and described by doctors in the 1880s and 1890s in France and was identified by Foucault as the "master perversion" of this period. In 1887 Charcot's student Alfred Binet published "Fetishism in Love," naming the perversion Charcot and Magnan had already described in detail.[75] Fetishism was linked to impotence, understood as the male's need to compensate for his sexual inadequacy by overvaluing a particular feature or object. In other words, the fetishist seeks phallic reinforcement from an external source, in an inherently narcissistic cycle. Freudian theory complicates this process by linking it to the child's denial of castration, against which it provided a safeguard.[76]

Fetishism is one of decadent literature's favored perversions. In a discourse dominated by images of weak men and *femmes fatales,* it offers the male subject comfort before the woman's castrating menace.[77] Rachilde's reference to this perversion is thus perfectly consistent with the conventions of decadent writers like Maupassant, Huysmans, Lorrain, and Péladan. Rachilde's text, however, subverts convention in the creation of an erotic female figure who refuses fetishistic identification, constantly forcing the male subject to recognize his own sexual inadequacy. The reading that follows demonstrates again how Rachilde made a tool of decadent literature into a debilitating weapon against male power, which strengthened in turn her own authority as a decadent writer.

The thread of fetishistic imagery begins to be woven in the first paragraphs of Rachilde's novel, where Eliante is first described as a "statue de marbre" (a marble statue) like the one she resembles in the anteroom of her house: "La glace ne reflétait que la statue de marbre, là-bas, une nymphe tenant une torchère, et ici, la silhouette obscure de la femme immobile, également statue, deux jumelles se tournant le dos" (The mirror only reflected the marble statue, there, a nymph holding a torch, and here, the obscure silhouette of an immobile woman, equally statuesque, two twins with their backs turned) (26). (Later she will confirm this mimetic link by introducing Léon to her late husband's collection of miniature marble statues, all uncannily in her likeness.) Léon's comparison of Eliante to an *objet curieux* behind glass a few pages later calls up this original image of the mirror. The comparison places him symbolically before the mirror; indeed, rather than disavowing his desire, as was his apparent intention, his fetishization of Eliante redefines it as a means of affirming his own phallic power, and thus as essentially narcissistic. In fact, his initial interest in Eliante was in the pursuit of conquest: "Il se sentait éperdument entraîné vers une *conquête* peut-être possible, sinon facile" (He felt passionately drawn to a possible *conquest,* if not a simple one) (29).

The hopelessness of Léon's pursuit is confirmed by the end of this first chapter, when the true *objet curieux* is unveiled: a human-sized alabaster vase that is the sole object of her affections. As she stands caressing the vase, Léon becomes anxious, and they engage in a debate about pleasure that, like the rest of the novel, sets in opposition the dynamics of male and female desire. Léon has already admitted that he just wants to have sex with her and move on with his life ("Je vous veux, tout simplement. . . . Donnez-moi ce que je désire, et flanquez-moi ensuite à la porte, ça me sera bien égal" [I want you, simply put. . . . Give me what I desire, and then throw me out the door, it will be fine with me] [42]). He now becomes even more frank: "Croyez-moi, chérie, [he says], on n'est pas amoureux d'autre chose que de soi" (Believe me, honey, one is not in love with anything other than one's self) (49), confirming the narcissism associated with his fetishistic tendencies. For Eliante, in contrast, "ce n'est pas le but, le plaisir; c'est une manière d'être" (pleasure is not the goal; it's a way of being) (49). This statement subverts the teleological processes determining the Freudian notion of desire. To confirm her freedom from men and her rejection of physical union, she demonstrates her capacity to achieve physical satisfaction with the alabaster vase:

> Sans un geste indécent, les bras chastement croisés sur cette forme svelte, ni fille ni garçon, elle crispa un peu ses doigts, demeurant silencieuse, puis, l'homme vit ses paupières closes se disjoindre, ses lèvres s'entr'ouvrirent, et il lui sembla que des clartés d'étoiles tombaient du blanc de ses yeux, de l'émail de ses dents; un léger frisson courut le long de son corps,—ce fut plutôt une risée plissant l'onde mystérieuse de sa robe de soie,—et elle eut un petit râle de joie imperceptible, le souffle même du spasme. (51)
>
> [Without an indecent gesture, her arms chastely crossed over the svelt form that was neither male nor female, she clenched her fingers a little, staying silent, then the man saw her closed eyelids open, her lips part, and it seemed to him that starlight fell from the whites of her eyes, from the enamel of her teeth; a slight shudder ran the length of her body,—it

> was more a flurry wrinkling the mysterious wave of her silk dress,—and she had a little groan of imperceptible joy, the very breath of orgasm.]

In this moment of pleasure Eliante realizes a decadent ideal of an autonomous sexuality, free from the enslaving forces of nature. At the same time, this passage can be seen as Rachilde's most obvious subversion of phallic hegemony in what is probably the most explicit description of female orgasm to be found in a decadent text.[78] The subversion of decadence can be found at the level of plot as well: Eliante's satisfaction of desire in the novel's first chapter undermines the teleology of desire as engine of narrative.[79]

The fundamental subversiveness of this scene of female pleasure is in its relationship to Léon's own desire. His desire determines the narrative, for Eliante is on some level desire-free, having discovered the happy rhythms of sexual autonomy. The narrative is most often focalized through Léon's gaze; through his eyes Eliante appears statuelike and impenetrable, and through his eyes the orgasm is witnessed. Rachilde's description of Eliante's encounter with the vase is subversive perhaps because of the way that pleasure becomes visible, and this visibility—on Eliante's body and traversing her silk dress—undermines Léon's own voyeuristic pleasure. After Eliante climaxes, the narrator explains: "Ou c'était la suprême, la splendide manifestation de l'amour, le dieu vraiment descendu dans le temple, ou le spectateur avait devant lui la plus extraordinaire des comédiennes, une artiste dépassant la limite du possible en art" (Either it was the supreme, splendid manifestation of love, the god really descending into the temple, or the spectator had in front of him the most extraordinary of actresses, an artist bypassing the limits of what is possible in art) (51). Léon chooses to believe the latter and comforts himself in leaving by thinking to himself: "Rideau!" (Curtain!) (52). If Eliante were acting, as her name's reference to Molière suggests, perhaps this performance could be seen as a kind of limit case of female specularity: the eroticized woman performer as object of the male voyeuristic gaze, and the orgasm representing for the man an affirmation of his own sexual prowess. Yet the male observer experiences no such satisfaction, because he is all too aware that he is excluded from the equation. Voyeurism is threatened by the preponderance of visual evidence undermining what the viewer seeks to confirm.

After Eliante's initial "performance," Léon is frustrated by her visual impenetrability: he is unable to interpret the signs that are present before him, because they do not refer to him. Eliante's appearance refuses fetishization, because it relates to her sexuality rather than to his. Eliante is constantly cloaked, for example, in a dark robe that hides most of her body. After declaring that her dress scares him, Léon begs her to take it off: "Dégantez votre cou, vous étouffez, il me semble. . . . Moi, ça me fait froid . . . et vous ça doit vous faire trop chaud" (Unfasten the neck, you are suffocating, it seems to me. . . . As for me, it makes me cold . . . and it must make you too warm) (41). Léon's mistake is in constantly seeing his own condition reflected in the object of his desire. This practice is at the heart of the decadent fascination with castration, through which women's perceived lack reflects on male sexual identity. The absurdity of his position is underlined by his conclusion that Eliante must want to be raped. In other words, he is unable to understand her beyond the stakes of phallic mastery. In fact, Eliante is not hiding anything; her sexuality is very clearly and provocatively on display, if only Léon could see beyond phallic terms. Eliante's dress is an extension of her physicality—"Elle releva sa jupe, elle releva ses paupières" (She raised her skirt, she raised her eyes) (28)—and is thus metonymically linked to her pleasure. As she experiences pleasure with the vase, the spasms of her body and clothing are indistinguishable: "un léger frisson courut le long de son corps,—ce fut plutôt une risée plissant l'onde mystérieuse de sa robe de soie" (a slight shudder ran the length of her body—it was more a flurry wrinkling the mysterious wave of her silk dress) (50–51). In addition, as Eliante removes her gloves, on some level she unveils her sexual organ—the body part most linked to her sexual gratification; Léon, however, cannot fully appreciate the significance. Rather than fetishize Eliante's hand, which would have been a way for him to enter into her sexual equation, he examines it with his medical gaze and determines that she is ill or a drug user: "Il examinait ce joli morceau de chair avec les yeux d'un expert en l'art de découvrir des tares physiques" (He examined this pretty piece of flesh with the eyes of an expert in discovering physical flaws) (34). The narrator seems to be mocking Léon's use of medicine to mitigate his sexual reaction to her. We are reminded of the relationship of the medical gaze to the dynamics of spectacle and performance, both part of a heterosexual scopic desiring economy. In this instance, the medical gaze sublimates sexual desire.

Léon's initial frustration does not prevent him from returning to Eliante's home, still longing for sexual satisfaction. This time Eliante allows him into a room that no other man has entered since her husband's death. This highly suggestive scene is Rachilde at her best, alternately playful and horrifying. The templelike chamber is worthy of Des Esseintes in its décor, filled with potential fetishes: furs and silks and heads of exotic animals; it is the room exactly as it appeared five years earlier on the ship her husband, Henri Donalger, commanded. Léon demands to see a portrait of this man, and Eliante complies, removing a Moroccan leather wallet from a jewel-encrusted cabinet. The narrative follows Léon's gaze: "L'étudiant en médecine ne put s'empêcher de remarquer que le portrait du défunt se trouvait à l'abri des indiscrétions comme une pièce anatomique" (The medical student could not stop himself from remarking that the portrait of the defunct was located in a place sheltered from indiscretions, like an anatomical part)

(112); the corporeal, if not yet explicitly phallic, function of the portrait is thus established through its metonymic link to a "pièce anatomique."

Naomi Schor has argued that Marie-Madeleine de Lafayette's *Princesse de Clèves,* Germaine de Staël's *Corinne,* and George Sand's *Indiana* are all intertextually related through a shared portrait scene that "stages the violation by the male gaze of the female protagonist's private space and the protagonist's discovery therein of a portrait, his own and/or that of another masculine figure." The first instance is a famous scene in *La Princesse de Clèves* where the princess, alone in her pavilion, admires a portrait of the Duc de Nemours, while he spies on her from the garden. In Staël's novel, Oswald finds a portrait of himself in Corinne's bedroom; in Sand's novel, Raymon, after making love to Noun in Indiana's bedroom, discovers a portrait of Ralph, his rival. According to Schor, each of these scenes by women authors works to "unsettle man's secure relationship to his own image and the representational system it underwrites."[80] With Léon's entry into Eliante's bedroom, Rachilde offers a final addendum to this tradition by having her female authorial figure confront her suitor with a series of images that undermine his narcissism. Like Sand's Raymon, Léon is met with the image of his rival that is altogether disconcerting:

> Malgré les précautions du photographe, qui avait placé son personnage sous un vélum de colonnade antique, le défaut de ce visage s'apercevait tout de suite et retenait le regard de telle façon qu'on ne s'occupait guère du reste. Le commandant Donalger avait eu la moitié du nez emporté, soit par un coup de fusil ou de sabre, soit par un accident de machine, une chaudière ayant éclaté près de lui. (112)
>
> [Despite the precautions of the photographer, who had put his subject under the awning of an antique colonnade, the defect of this face was readily apparent and held one's gaze in such a way that one didn't care about the rest. Commander Donalger had lost half of his nose, whether by a gun shot or a saber, or by an accident with a machine, a boiler having exploded near him.]

The inscription of the photographer's gaze in this passage is significant because it underlines the relationship of the object of the gaze to the person looking; despite the photographer's ostensible control over the image, this object, the face with its defect,controls the gaze and "retenait le regard" (holds the look). The commander is wholly determined by this lack, the absent nose. Thus, the portrait that Léon sees, rather than affirming the masculine prowess of his rival and satisfying his fascination with the previous lover of his present love-object, provides nothing but the image of castration, lack of virility, and weakness. The morselized "pièce anatomique" that Léon anticipated is in this sense absent. Furthermore, it is significant that the commander's disfigurement is not a birth defect. It is the mark of a physical failing, which, by its indeterminate origins only multiplies the extent of his fallibility. Donalger's weakness is not a source of comfort for the rival; instead, Léon wants to affirm his own virility by seeing a strong counterpart who demands his even stronger prowess. The rival's weakness is something the current lover wants to be the first to prove, as we see in *Indiana:* after Raymon views the picture of his ostensible rival, he declares that were he Indiana's husband, "I wouldn't have consented to leave [the picture] here unless I had cut out the eyes."[81] This assertion channels his jealous rage into a violent fantasy of emasculation. Léon's experience before the portrait of Henri precludes such a possibility; the eyes, as it were, are already removed. He can only respond in pity, and that response is in itself emasculating.

Castration, to repeat, was a central fantasy of the decadent imagination. But this fantasy was most often explored through the safety of the fetish, thus masking the underlying anxiety around the possibility of castration. Bernheimer argues that Freud's theory of the Medusa's head was a product of the same fantasies that provoked the decadent fascination with the figure of Salomé.[82] The significance of this mythology to our text is suggested by the presence of the decapitated animal heads decorating Eliante's boudoir. In some sense, as Eliante hands Léon "une tête d'officier," she is Salomé, castrating woman, handing him the head of John the Baptist and thus re-playing a decadent theme explored in the paintings of Moreau and the texts of Huysmans, Mallarmé, Flaubert, and Wilde.

A closer look, however, reveals that Eliante is not so much holding up the decapitated head, and thus the fetish, or that which will insure the comforting stiffening in Freudian terms, as the thing that is usually masked, the lack itself. We have here a repetition that undermines the fetish's functioning. The head, itself ostensibly symbol of and mask over phallic lack, instead displays and calls attention to that lack. The centrality of this lack to the scene of viewing is underlined by Eliante herself, who comments "cela ne se voit pas beaucoup sur ce portrait-là" (you can't really see it in this portrait) and promptly hands over another portrait, sketched by a friend at the time of accident:

> Et elle lui passa une feuille de papier jaunie où se reproduisait la même tête, seulement, cette fois, tout à fait horrible. Cela ressemblait à une charge, à quelque macabre plaisanterie. La face, imberbe, exhibait un sanglant tronçon où les cartilages se distinguaient formant l'entrée des narines, qui n'existaient plus qu'à l'état de bouillie. Stoïquement, les lèvres souriaient, intactes et railleuses, essayant de porter beau ce masque

épouvantable, se moquant de sa hideur, n'ayant même pas l'air d'en souffrir. (112–13)

[And she passed him a yellowed piece of paper where the same head was reproduced, only this time, completely horribly. It resembled a caricature, some macabre joke. The face, beardless, showed a bloody section where one could distinguish the cartilage forming the entrance to the nostrils, which existed only in a state of pulp. Stoically, the lips smiled, intact and laughing, trying to handsomely wear this frightening mask, making fun of its hideousness, seeming not even to be bothered.]

Once again, a repetition forces us—and more important, Léon—to confront this lack directly like the Medusa's head in Freud's essay. That Henri's lack is discursively likened to the female genitals is striking. The bloody nose forms an entrance, with lips framing it. As Barbara Spackman has argued, "the Medusan moment of the revelation of 'woman's castration' " constitutes "the essential decadent scene."[83] Yet here, this revelation is displaced onto the male body. In addition, Eliante's removal of the portraits from cabinets within cabinets covered in jewels borrows from thematics and imagery of female sexuality that use fetishes to mask what Freud paradoxically called "the fact of female castration."

Indeed, in Freudian theory, decapitation must inevitably refer to the phallus through fetishism. The mutilated female genitals must be covered up, masked, veiled. Eliante is constantly unveiling, revealing what is behind the fetish, the mask, the cabinets. She thus valorizes castration, giving it an unmasked textual locus, representing lack in and of itself. If anything, she fetishizes these portraits, abandoning heterosexual dynamics as she invents her own perversion: male castration as a means of affirming her own non-phallic sexuality. This gesture is all the more subversive in that her embrace of castration is necessarily threatening to her male counterpart. By embracing lack within a patriarchal desiring economy and thus refusing fetishization, Eliante manages to defer the phallus indefinitely. The portrait of Henri forces Léon to confront the fact of female lack, the presence of female genitals, and his own implied phallic lack, rather than allowing him the comforts of the fetish.

The exotic animal heads turn out to be among Henri's possessions and reveal his excessively fetishistic collecting. As Eliante's tour of her boudoir continues, she introduces Léon to a collection of statues that bear a remarkable resemblance to herself. Indeed, Henri Donalger had commissioned them during his absence from his wife; they thus act as fetishes, compensating for Eliante's absence. Yet Léon is not titillated by the other man's fetish, even though he has already informed us that he wanted to consider Eliante as "un objet curieux." Instead, he is horrified: "Enlevez tout cela . . . vite . . . ôtez tout, vous m'entendez, ou je brise d'un seul coup de pied tout ce petit monde infernal" (Take all this away . . . quickly . . . take it all, you hear me, or I will smash with one kick this whole infernal world) (121).

Like Oswald, who was troubled by the presence of bracelets made of hair next to the portrait of another man in Corinne's bedroom, what disturbs Léon might be described as "the uncanny doubling of the fetish, for this multiplication works to undermine the uniqueness of the phallus and to underline its infinite substitutability."[84] Similarly for Rachilde, the multiple markers of the emasculated husband's sexuality threaten Léon's ability to see himself differently through his own attempts to fetishize Eliante. In Freudian terms, Henri's fetishes confirm the link between a multiplication of phallic symbols and castration. Rachilde's repetition of the fetish suggests a radical sequel to Staël's strategy. In Rachilde's novel, the proliferating fetishes—Henri's statues—are both the image of Eliante and, according to psychoanalytic theory, substitutes for the phallus itself. But Eliante is already described as a statue; as an *objet curieux* she is impenetrable, her sphinxlike personality suggesting castrating power. The chain of representation—statue referring to woman referring to statue—undermines the stability and comfort of fetishization; again, Léon is unable to achieve scopic satisfaction with Eliante. Thus Henri's miniatures, rather than affirm phallic centrality, broadcast phallic failure through their place among an endless multiplication of similar images.

I return now to the original scene of pleasure with the alabaster vase, where symbols of castration abound. The vase is initially compared to a man, "un vase d'albâtre de la hauteur d'un homme" (an alabaster vase the height of a man) and its physical features are offered in detail: "Le pied, très étroit, lisse comme une hampe de jacinthe, surgissait d'une base plate et ovale . . . atteignait, à mi-corps, les dimensions de deux belles jeunes cuisses hermétiquement jointes et s'effilait vers le col" (The foot, very narrow, smooth like a scape of hyacinth, surged from a flat oval base . . . attained, mid-way, the dimensions of two beautiful young thighs hermetically joined and tapered toward the neck) (46). At the juncture of these thighs there is an absence: "Ce col s'évasant en corolle faisait songer à une tête absente, une tête coupée ou portée sur d'autres épaules que celles de l'amphore" (This neck flaring out in a corolla made one think of an absent head, a head cut off or worn on other shoulders than those of the amphora) (46). This "absent head" is perhaps none other than Henri's "tête d'officier," which itself reveals another glaring absence. Indeed, the word *tête* is mentioned three times in the portrait scene, in one instance appropriately following "le col raide" (the stiff neck). Once again, the multiplication of the absent fetish is striking, expanding the absence of the phallus through the missing heads, which themselves have missing noses, in Eliante's chosen objects of desire, as the vase and the portrait themselves refer to one another. Like Salomé holding the head of John the Baptist, Eliante holds the alabaster vase—and its conspicuous lack of a head. Yet unlike Salomé, who, in decadent views, wants what she lacks, Eliante seems to want an affirmation of her own lack (still figured within a decadent, i.e., patriarchal, fantasmatic view). As in the portrait scene, this lack is what is valorized, rather than fetishized; the only fetishization, which is of the vase itself, seems to affirm lack rather than mask it. Yet Léon is not initially disturbed by the vase; instead he is "séduit par cette apparition de l'adorable chasteté de la ligne" (seduced by this apparition of the adorable chastity of the silhouette) (46). Nor is he even terribly horrified by the gruesome pictures of Henri; he feels pity for the couple. Léon's reactions betray his own identification with what he sees; Eliante confronts the desiring male with his own castrated image, but narcissism wins out over horror. Only when the possibility of his physical satisfaction is eliminated does he become scandalized; in this context the role of the vase and the statues becomes clearer—in Eliante's desiring economy they are not fetishes, or affirmations of the man's phallic power, but extensions of Eliante's own decidedly nonphallic sexuality.

Léon is the first man since Eliante's husband to enter her bedroom, but he does not enter illicitly, as do Lafayette's, Staël's, and Sand's male protagonists; instead, Eliante invites him in. Herein lies Rachilde's important twist on this topos, making her critique more radical in its consequences than that of her predecessors. Rachilde's subversion of Léon's relationship to his phallic power is magnified by the role that Eliante plays in its undermining. As a *jongleuse,* Eliante represents female creative power in the novel. In this context it is significant that Eliante manipulates the portrait scene; symbolically the woman writer inscribes herself in the text, forcing the man to confront his own state of castration. Eliante tells Léon in one of her letters that she does not know how to write ("je veux bien vous écrire, seulement, *je ne sais pas*" [I want to write to you, only, *I don't know how*] [83]), meaning perhaps that she communicates best in other ways. Melanie Hawthorne's interpretation is that "Eliante's response to the masculine appropriation of the pen is not anxiety, but an escape to a different way of signifying, one which remains invisible to those who cannot read the body."[85] Eliante's relationship with Léon thus demonstrates the same kind of discursive gestures that Lafayette, Staël, and Sand perform but taken to a new level by the role Eliante herself plays in the subversion: like these writers, Eliante, juggler and epistolary maven, takes control of the desiring man's relationship to his own image, but she refuses him the comforts of the fetish, forcing him to see himself as powerless and castrated by confronting Léon with missing noses and decapitated vases. To the extent that Léon experiences a specular identification with the vase or the portraits, this narcissism is stripped of its grounding phallicism: the act of looking no longer affirms his sexual power.

Léon believes that Eliante is, like most women, hysterical: "Eliante est un cas pathologique, c'est une femme nerveuse, superstitieuse, un peu folle" (Eliante is a pathological case, she's a nervous woman, superstitious, a little crazy) (155). Medical authority thus becomes an alternative form of fetishism, masking Léon's sexual impotence. Eliante's neurosis seems to be tied in Léon's eyes to her discursive abilities; hysterical women have a propensity for invention. Thus, what she writes is assumed to be fiction: "Il est certain que vous avez l'art des lettres d'amour comme vous avez l'art de jongler avec des chinoiseries ou des couteaux" (It is certain that you have the art of love letters just as you have the art of juggling with Chinese pieces or knives) (170). Eliante learned to write from Ninaude, the Creole maid-servant that looked after her during her marriage. Her first love letter was written to her husband, who demanded that she write him one.Terrified, Eliante turned to Ninaude, who taught her the secret to satisfying him:

> Petite Mada, cria-t-elle, regardez voir par la fenêtre! C'est le printemps de France, n'est-ce pas, il y a des roses, il y a du soleil, il y a du ciel chaud. Il faut lui écrire tout ça et lui dire que vous aimez tout ça *parce que c'est son image,* que vous êtes heureuse de le voir là dedans maintenant qu'il est loin. . . . Ça lui fera plaisir. (179)

> [Little Mada, she cried, look out the window! It's spring in France, is it not, there are roses, there is sunshine, there is a warm sky. You must write him all this and tell him that you love all this because it is his image, that you are happy to see him in it now that he is far away. . . . It will give him pleasure.]

Ninaude voices here what Lafayette, Staël, and Sand present in their novels: men find pleasure in the spectacle of their own desirability. Like that of Nemours, Henri's *jouissance* will come not from the image itself but from observing Eliante's taking pleasure in the image. Yet Eliante's feelings are a fabrication, a signal of the written word's power to manipulate men's pleasure. In another important repetition, we can see this as a version of the portrait scene, preceding the one with Léon, as Eliante offers Henri an image of himself through her writing. Likewise, Henri's affirmation of phallic power through narcissistic identification with his desirability is based itself on a false construction, the manipulations of the female imagination, which create only the illusion of his desirability. Rachilde's text has no explicit intertextual links to her female predecessors, yet could we read Eliante's Creole origins and her relationship with Ninaude as a wink to her fellow Creole Indiana, whose cherished servant Noun also taught her (albeit inadvertently) about romantic deceit?

The lesson here is not far from the one found repeatedly in the memoirs of the *fille publique.* To write within the bounds of patriarchal desire, Rachilde seems to suggest, is foreign to the dynamics of female pleasure. Women's writing must find another mode of satisfaction, perhaps in a new relationship between reader and writer that would avoid this narcissistic relationship. Indeed, the social critique bound up in Rachilde's playful staging of male narcissism and her indebtedness to more sentimental tropes come to light as the formidable heroine recounts her past.[86] Despite Eliante's radical independence, her *femme fatale* personality is tempered by the presence of a certain vulnerability, even fearfulness, regarding heterosexual desire. Describing her marriage at a young age, she writes:

> En ce temps-là, je ressemblais à un petit chat sauvage qu'on aurait un peu écrasé en lui marchant dessus, sans le vouloir, et j'aurais souvent désiré qu'on m'achevât, car je ne pouvais m'imaginer que c'était ça *le bonheur.* (172)
>
> [At that time, I resembled a savage little cat that one might have crushed by walking on, without meaning to, and I would often wish that someone finish me off, for I could not imagine that this was *happiness.*]

At the age of eighteen, Eliante believed that a wife's obligation was to focus entirely on her husband—"Il faut que je pense à mon mari!" (I must think of my husband!) (173)—and to project her desire—however imaginary it might be—back to him; at this point Ninaude recognizes Eliante's preoccupation with her husband's desires as fear in disguise. In this brief sketch of Eliante's youth, Rachilde portrays marriage in service of male narcissism, at the expense of female imagination. After her husband's death, Eliante seemingly more than makes up for her past submission to male naricissistic needs. Yet her forceful autonomy is, by her own admission, linked to a pervasive fear: "j'ai peur de l'amour des hommes qui est mortel" (I fear the love of men that is mortal) (149). In fact, Eliante believes she caused her husband's death, which stemmed from his rampant jealousy. Regardless, her persistent disdain for union expresses a refusal of submission and a fear of male aggression. Surprised in the bedroom, she throws a knife at Léon and then explains: "Vois-tu, c'est plus fort que moi, l'idée qu'on va me surprendre . . . me violer . . . je ne peux pas endurer ça" (You see, it's stronger than me, the idea that I am going to be caught unawares . . . raped . . . I cannot endure that) (147). Léon has already suggested that rape must be what his enigmatic love-object truly wants. Heterosexual intercourse is portrayed by Rachilde as a kind violation, rape, *écrasement,* where the woman is necessarily subject to the narcissistic desires of the male.[87]

At a certain point in their epistolary exchange, Eliante imagines a conversation she could have had with Léon: " 'Femme, a-t-il dit en riant, nous ne parlons pas la même langue' " (Woman, he said laughing, we do not speak the same language) (213). The language that they do not have in common is that of pleasure and desire. Yet obstinate Léon continues to insist on Eliante's desire for him, despite her insistence that she wants him to marry her niece, Missy, and then she will disappear. The extent of Léon's blindness and Eliante's devotion to her fantasy is confirmed in the final pages of the novel, where Léon thinks he is finally realizing his desire with Eliante but is in fact making love to Missy in the absolute darkness of Eliante's bedroom. He becomes aware of his mistake only the next morning, when a gleeful Eliante kills herself with her juggling knife before the couple's astonished eyes. Despite the sexual perversions detailed in the novel, Léon's night of passion with Missy is noted with the conventional series of ellipses meant to suggest the kind of intimacy whose description was beyond the scope of the decadent novel:[88]

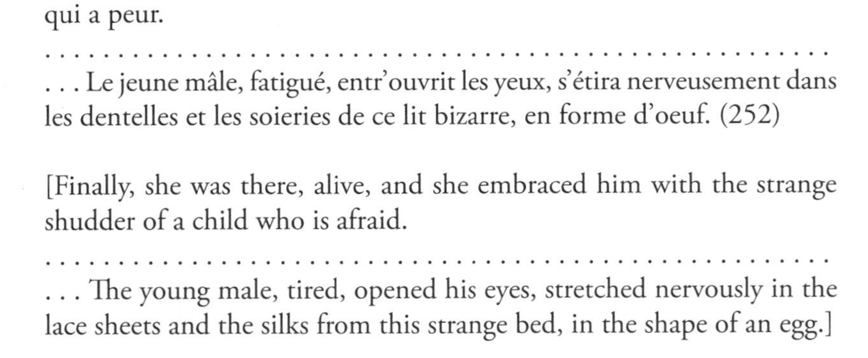

> Enfin, elle y était, vivante, et elle l'enlaça avec un étrange frisson d'enfant qui a peur.
>
> . . . .
>
> . . . Le jeune mâle, fatigué, entr'ouvrit les yeux, s'étira nerveusement dans les dentelles et les soieries de ce lit bizarre, en forme d'oeuf. (252)
>
> [Finally, she was there, alive, and she embraced him with the strange shudder of a child who is afraid.
>
> . . . .
>
> . . . The young male, tired, opened his eyes, stretched nervously in the lace sheets and the silks from this strange bed, in the shape of an egg.]

Marc Angenot has suggested that the use of ellipses to elide the moment of intimacy was intended to "masquer, de détourner le regard des pratiques sexuelles (et contraceptives) de la bourgeoisie et de 'problèmes' sexuels réels" (to mask, to turn the gaze away from the sexual [and contraceptive] practices of the bourgeoisie and from "real sexual problems").[89] In Rachilde's novel, however, the textual lacuna playfully mocks at literary convention; the goal here is most likely not to protect bourgeois norms. Instead, the heterosexual act comes to appear more perverse than the other erotic forms the novel presents, linking Léon, "le jeune mâle," in a bed shaped like an egg, to a base animal sexuality. We remember Henri's fetishes, which Léon called "les emblèmes de la prostitution conjugale" (the emblems of conjugal prostitution)

(121). Marriage (the end result of Léon and Missy's tryst) is represented as a form of prostitution, where the female is eminently substitutable. Eliante, in contrast, "joyeuse d'une joie surnaturelle" (joyous with a supernatural joy), escapes from all this and achieves a spiritual apotheosis worthy of the decadent ideal by finally transforming her life into art.

To summarize, then, Rachilde's discursive gesture in this novel: the phallus is not eliminated as a central image in the desiring male's self-definition. Instead, it is refigured, by its indeterminacy and perpetual referentiality, in such a way as to call attention to its status in the imaginary, as a symbol of power fulfilling a fundamental psychological need or lack. Léon's and Henri's repeated recourse to fetishism reflects this persistent psychological flaw. With a female artist as agent of this subversion, Rachilde challenges once again the foundational discursive relationship between virility and intellectual authority. The refusal to subject Eliante's enigmatic sexuality to any kind of scopic scrutiny, or to situate it in a single, visually discrete organ, is also a refusal of the fin-de-siècle teleology that posits the female sex as the bearer of the text's ultimate secrets. Unlike Delarue-Mardrus, Rachilde does not offer a theory of female sexuality. Instead, she demonstrates where it is not located (a patriarchal scopic, phallocentric desiring economy, or under Léon's gaze) and only points to the locus of pleasure (somewhere within Eliante's "cuisses jointes hermétiquement" (hermetically joined thighs).

Free of the theoretical constraints of feminist criticism, Rachilde offers what can be recognized anachronistically as a kind of feminist fantasy in which female pleasure is privileged and a sexual alternative to a patriarchal desiring economy is vividly imagined. Yet Eliante's joyful suicide, following declarations of her desire to travel to distant exotic lands ("J'irai retrouver mon pays, le royaume de mes songes! La chaleur!" [I will go find my country, the kingdom of my dreams! Warmth!] [251]) only confirms the nonexistence of this imagined utopia, and the radical incompatibility of her bodily rhythms with the bourgeois desiring economy in which she lives. Moreover, to underline the social implications of Rachilde's discursive gesture that are so often obscured by her own antifeminist declarations, Eliante's self-empowered suicide can be seen as the completion of a wish fulfillment that began in the early days of her marriage: she desired then that her life be taken from her, unwilling to believe "que c'était ça *le bonheur*" (that this was *happiness*) (172). This disillusion, recounted in a rare instance of sentimentality for Rachilde, is similar to the shared starting point for the novels I consider in the next chapter. For the group of women writers that follows, the failings of sexual relations, particularly within marriage, are the impetus to an entirely new analysis of female pleasure and its emotional consequences for the thinking woman.

5

The Right to Pleasure

SEX AND THE SENTIMENTAL NOVEL

In the late eighteenth century, medical science disposed of the long-held notion that female orgasm was necessary for procreation. The fact that a woman could conceive without pleasure was finally recognized. As a result, as Thomas Laqueur has argued: "the independence of generation from pleasure created the space in which women's sexual nature could be redefined, debated, denied or qualified."[1] And so it was throughout the nineteenth century in France. In the second half of the century, a new subspecialty began to emerge in the field of medicine that would come to be known as sexology—the scientific study and classification of sexual behavior. Sexology slowly shifted the medical lens from physiology to psychology: scientists began to emphasize behavior over bodily functions, transcribing patients' own descriptions of their problems in search of clues to understanding sexual behavior.[2] Drawing on a century of medical research into perversion and sexual dysfunction, this almost exclusively male discipline sought to understand, and by implication control, complex human sexual impulses.[3]

In this chapter I present novels in which women writers embrace the separation between pleasure and procreation as an opening into a bold examination of female sexuality. In these texts, pleasure is totally unhinged from its physiological associations, depicted instead as a critical element to the development of a mature female identity and as a necessary tool for self-knowledge. Following and sometimes anticipating the trends of sexologists such as Richard von Krafft-Ebing, Alfred Moll, Magnus Hirschfeld, and Havelock Ellis, whose works were widely read in France, as well as their

French influences in figures such as Alfred Binet, Henri-Etienne Beaunis, Auguste Forel, and Charles Féré (who cited Krafft-Ebing, Moll, and Ellis before their works were available in translation), the women authors in this chapter recognized that the implications of sexuality extended beyond the genitals to a person's emotions and sense of self. Their novels, however, demonstrate a very different understanding of the relationship between the female mind and body than that of male doctors, thus presenting an alternative to sexology, authorized by women's experiences. Nineteenth-century medical doctrine emphasized the potentially dangerous relationship between the female mind and body. Intellectual and emotional exertion were said to lead directly to physical illness and infertility.[4] The energy of the *esprit*, which included the mind and the heart, was meant to be directed inward, to sublimate the dangerous bodily drives that threatened women's fragile constitutions.[5] In fact, it was widely believed that passion itself was dangerous to women, and that excess pleasure would impede procreation.[6] The novels in this chapter demonstrate a forceful rejection of such entrenched notions. For the authors here, the female body has needs that are essential to the happiness of the *esprit*. By critically confronting and grappling with these bodily needs, female protagonists insure their own well-being. Indeed, in these novels, the body's pleasures are revealed to be intimately linked to the development and fulfillment of the emotional life of the mind.

The scientific discourse of sex has been plagued historically by a gender imbalance, through which male scientists privileged the study of female bodies. Throughout the nineteenth century the expression of the erotic was becoming increasingly fundamental to both literary and scientific expositions of the self.[7] Women figured most often as objects of this exploration, however, rather than subjects in their own right. For women themselves, the examination of sexual behavior was not yet an accepted means through which to develop self-knowledge. Many of the texts I consider in the preceding chapters offer exceptions to this rule: they portray women exploring sexuality and sexual identity in the context of female character development. The texts I present here, however, are unique in their focus on the sexual act itself, which represents a break from the stylistic conventions of naturalism and decadence and a more dramatic literary link to sexological discourse.[8] In what follows, I propose that for these women authors, the structures of the sentimental novel offered an alternative to the sexological case-study and the popular medical hygiene text as a tool for bringing into relief the psychological and physiological consequences of sexual behavior. In examining sexual behavior and in attempting to articulate women's sexual experiences in as precise terms as possible, the aim in these novels is not to control sexuality by delineating what is appropriate or inappropriate; rather, the discussion of sexuality offers women a means of gaining control over their own bodies. Just as Marcelle Tinayre and Lucie Delarue-Mardrus feminized naturalist science with their empathy for women's experience, these authors bring the male-dominated scientific discourse of sex into the feminine domain of the sentimental novel. The result is novels that, while not explicitly scientific, offer critical analyses of women's sexual experiences in various forms.

What I call the sentimental novel here is a cross between the fin-de-siècle female-authored romance novel as defined by Diana Holmes and the nineteenth-century sentimental novel described by Margaret Cohen. Holmes situates romance novels' critical importance "in their purposeful and explicit reflection on the meaning of love, and on how it may be reconciled with other female desires such as those for personal integrity and independence."[9] The novels at issue here, however, reflect not so much on the meaning of love and on a single romantic relationship, as Holmes also specifies, as on the meaning of sex. Cohen's description of the nineteenth-century sentimental novel, while based on novels from the middle of the century, thus helps capture the broader emotional drama of the narratives I examine. On the level of plot, Cohen describes the sentimental novel as portraying a protagonist caught between conflicting moral imperatives: collective welfare—a duty to society such as marriage and family—and individual freedom—happiness, love, passion.[10] The emphasis is on the internal emotional consequences of this conflict, in contrast to the wider social arena depicted in nineteenth-century naturalist and decadent novels.

The late nineteenth-century sentimental novel has also been seen as a veiled pedagogical instrument, through which woman learned her proper role in society.[11] What the novels here reveal, however, is that just what constituted that role was very much in flux at the turn of the nineteenth century. Anna de Noailles's *Le Visage émerveillé,* Gyp's *Autour du mariage,* Colette's *L'Ingénue libertine,* and Odette Dulac's *Le Droit au plaisir* demonstrate new lessons about femininity learned through the exploration of sexual pleasure, thus offering fresh pedagogical models. They reveal how women-authored sentimental novels, whose readership was almost exclusively female, provided a forum for analysis of female sexuality, and thus a means to develop a female erotic self through women's own sexological insights. Holmes argues that the romance novel allowed middle-class women to address some of the issues raised by contemporary feminism. My argument is in some sense the opposite: that these sentimental sexological novels allowed women to address issues that were not being raised by contemporary feminism, and that would not be considered in a feminist context until much later on.[12]

SEX AND SENSIBILITY: ANNA DE NOAILLES'S *LE VISAGE EMERVEILLÉ*

> Pense plutôt au devoir qu'au plaisir.
>
> [Think of duty rather than pleasure.]
>
> —Association du mariage chrétien, *De l'Education morale de la femme: Conseils à une jeune fille,* 1864

> L'amour n'est point précisément et uniquement un plaisir: les plaisirs même qu'il peut donner ne durent qu'un moment; les tourments qu'il amènent peuvent durer toute la vie. Ce n'est pas ainsi qu'en parlent les romans, c'est pourquoi les romans n'apprennent pas bien l'amour. Non, l'amour n'est pas seulement un plaisir, . . . il est surtout un devoir.
>
> [Love is not at all precisely and uniquely a pleasure: the pleasures that it can give only last a moment; the torments that it leads to can last a lifetime. Novels do not speak of it this way, and that is why novels do not teach about love well. No, love is not only a pleasure, . . . it is above all a duty.]
>
> —Edouard Montier, *Le Mariage, lettre à une jeune fille,* 1919

Before becoming a novelist, the countess Anna de Noailles enjoyed great success as a poet, beginning with her collection *Le Coeur innombrable.* Her aristocratic roots paved the way for an adoring reception by the Parisian literati, provoking jealousy among her less fortunate female peers.[13] She was a favorite of Belle Epoque high society, and of a Parisian press as interested in her beauty as in her poetry. Over the years, she would also become friendly with Francis Jammes, whose influence has been noted in her writing, as well as André Gide, Marcel Proust, Anatole France, and Maurice Barrès, all of whom offered high praise for her literary talent.[14] After the success of her first novel, *La Nouvelle espérance,* which first appeared in serial form in *La Renaissance latine* in 1903, Noailles's second novel, *Le Visage émerveillé,* was published directly by Calmann-Lévy in 1904. The story of a young woman's discovery of sexuality within the walls of a convent, the novel received rave reviews from Proust, Cocteau, Jules Renard, and Colette. A few, however, criticized its mixing of religion and sensuality; one critic went so far as to suggest alternative titles: "*La Religieuse s'amuse* ou *Une Demi-vierge au couvent*" (*The Nun has Fun* or *A Semi-Virgin at the Convent*), comparing it

Figure 6. Caricature of Anna de Noailles by A. Berrere, in *Fantasio*, August 15, 1906. (Image courtesy of the Bibliothèque Nationale de France.)

to Marcel Prévost's provocative novel ten years earlier.[15] Despite Noailles's consistent critical success and her receipt of several major awards including prizes from the Académie française and the Legion of Honor, she is remembered today chiefly as a vibrant literary personality rather than for her extensive literary contributions.[16]

Noailles was certainly not the first author to write about a voluptuous nun; Diderot's 1760 *La Religieuse* had surprised and shocked readers with its own transgressive intrigue many years before. Within the social and literary context of the fin de siècle, however, the setting of *Le Visage émerveillé* takes on special significance. In naturalist and decadent traditions, the convent symbolizes the sublimation of sexuality. It is used more traditionally in Marcelle Tinayre's *La Maison du péché,* a novel with which this one was often compared, as a place to escape sexuality, a kind of sexual safe haven. Thus Augustin de Chanteprie is sent to a convent by his family to escape Fanny Manolé's perceived seduction; this is one of the options considered to curb Raoule de Vénérande's behavior as well. Indeed, the convent is on the margins of fin-de-siècle textuality, a place into which characters disappear and become unnarratable, according to a convention that reaches all the way back to *La Princesse de Clèves.* What is interesting to readers and writers of this period is the conflict faced by the religious person within the secular world: in Tinayre's novel, the preceptor Forgerus encountering Fanny; or how in Rachilde's *Monsieur Vénus,* Tante Elisabeth, would-be nun, struggles with Raoule de Vénérande's perversity. In Rachilde's text, Elisabeth exists as a character only when she leaves the convent to care for Raoule; when Raoule marries Jacques, she disappears into religious life without a trace. Similarly, Augustin's months spent in the cloisters are left undescribed. We read simply: "La longue retraite achevée. . . . M. de Chanteprie était sorti du cloître, comme d'un hôpital" (The long retreat finished. . . . Mr. De Chanteprie had come out from the cloisters, as if from a hospital)[17]—a comparison that affirms the shared roles of religious and medical discourses in policing sexuality.

By situating her story of sexual awakening within the convent, Noailles allows herself a clean slate, where the rules governing society do not apply. Here the innocent teenager Sister Sainte-Sophie is wooed by a young painter, Julien. They engage in secret trysts until Julien attempts to persuade Sainte-Sophie to leave the convent and join him. Horrified by this seeming betrayal, Sainte-Sophie confesses to the head nun and chooses her independent life in the convent over Julien's proposal. Within this simple plot, the discovery of pleasure is represented as a fundamental step in female psychological development, a means of gaining self-knowledge and the authority to make personal choices.

The generic tensions of the novel underline its critical import as a subtle exploitation of various novelistic traditions. At the same time, the text's sentimental and romantic leanings, which suggest its inscription within a traditionally feminine domain, help to mask a subversiveness that has never been fully recognized. The text consists of Sainte-Sophie's diary entries over the course of a year, thus exposing the inner workings of a young girl's mind. Although thematically linked to Zola's *La Faute de l'abbé Mouret* and to Tinayre's *La Maison du péché, Le Visage émerveillé*'s representation of nature and behavior is more romantic than naturalist; indeed, Noailles's representation of the joys of the convent—or what her fellow writer and friend Henri de Regnier describes as her depiction of "le plaisir de la contrainte" (the pleasure of constraint)—is similar to Stendhal's depiction of the "prison heureuse" (happy prison).[18] Yet if the novel can be called romantic, it is by a refiguring of romantic tropes through which the sensual wins out over the sublime. In this sense it seems to affirm the observation of Jean Larnac, who argued in his 1929 history of French women writers, "Le romantisme de 1830 avait libéré le coeur des femmes; celui de 1900 a libéré leurs sens" (The romanticism of 1830 had liberated women's hearts; that of 1900 liberated their senses).[19]

I suggest that this novel has as much in common with nineteenth-century genres as with a certain kind of Enlightenment travel literature, where the naive language of the noble savage is able to shed light on experiences that are burdened with cultural associations in conventional discourse, blinding interlocutors from the plain meaning of the words.[20] Indeed, this is the place of the female sexologist at the fin-de-siècle: a foreigner in male-dominated territory. Noailles's ingenue is Sister Sainte-Sophie, whose journal records her discovery of sexuality. Having entered the convent before having had any sexual experience (and, unlike Diderot's Suzanne, of her own accord), Sainte-Sophie has neither the vocabulary nor the sophistication to offer anything beyond a superficial interpretation of the sexual relationship into which she enters. Yet for the more sophisticated reader, her simple language and naïveté effect a defamiliarizing relationship with the practices of sexuality, both exposing some of Julien's audacity and allowing her to define a relationship that in another context would be overdetermined by cultural standards for love and marriage. Noailles's novel might then be seen as a kind of experiment: how does the removal of social influences help us to understand better the relationships between love (*amour*) pleasure (*volupté*) and female independence? Like certain Enlightenment novels, this novel focuses on the disjunction between the protagonist's own conclusions and prevailing social norms, creating an emotional tension that also links it to the nineteenth-century sentimental novel.

The religious setting and thematics of the novel reflect the imbrication of religious aesthetics with various other discourses at the turn of the century.

Christian images of religious blood and sacred hearts permeate nineteenth-century romantic literature, inspiring images in the writings of Chateaubriand, Hugo, and Musset, to name a few.[21] In addition, female sexuality and religion were curiously joined in medical and literary discourses. Both Charcot and Richer, for example, drew on devotional vocabulary and spiritual associations in classifying the stages of hysterical attacks.[22] Feminine mysticism was also depicted in the Goncourt brothers' *Madame Gervaisais,* a novel that largely fleshed out their belief that religion was "une partie du sexe de la femme" (part of women's sex).[23]

These associations help to explain why religious doctrine and belief are not at stake in Noailles's novel. Her young heroine is drawn to the convent for aesthetic rather than ascetic reasons. In the opening pages, religious devotion is already laced with sensuality, as Sainte-Sophie watches Sister Catherine, whom she admires because "elle est belle quand elle prie" (she is beautiful when she prays).[24] Observing Catherine's devotion, she addresses God, praising a spiritual union that is both aesthetic and sensual: "Seigneur . . . [l]es bouts de ses doigts, sa bouche, la toile délicieuse et votre corps divin faisaient un groupe admirable" (Lord . . . the ends of her fingers, her mouth, the delicious drapes and your divine body made an admirable grouping) (2). Sainte-Sophie's discovery of sexuality within the convent is therefore not completely incongruous with the novel's setting, and the religious vocabulary employed emphasizes the spiritual and the aesthetic, rather than the ascetic. Clues about Sainte-Sophie's own religious prioritization can be found in her relationship with other characters. She respects the *mère abbesse* more than any other nun, although the *mère*'s religious fervor is less than that of some of the other sisters. She also criticizes the chaplain, whom she finds less compassionate and less intelligent than the doctor who comes to treat the girls (51). Indeed, medical authority is used to challenge religious authority. When the chaplain boasts to the doctor of the stigmata on Sister Catherine's hands, he responds: "Nous avons à l'asile d'Orthez une jeune fille un peu exaltée, qui a cela aussi, comme votre sainte. On la soigne, elle guérira" (We have an excitable young woman at the Orthez Asylum who has the same thing, like your saint. We are treating her, and she will be cured) (74).

Furthermore, as the novel progresses, Sainte-Sophie's ethos leads her to reject religious principles. This ethos again links her to an Enlightenment tradition: Sainte-Sophie's journal reveals that she believes only in what she knows to be true from her own experience. She relies on her own emotional and physical sensitivity to make determinations, thus exhibiting a *sensibilité* reminiscent of eighteenth-century literary figures such as Zilia in Françoise de Graffigny's *Lettres d'une péruvienne* and Usbek in Charles de Montesquieu's *Lettres persanes.* In fact, Sainte-Sophie's epistemology bears some resemblance to the eighteenth-century sensationism popularized by Condillac, which posits that all of our knowledge comes from our sensations. John O'Neal explains that sensationism "enabled all individuals to challenge the sometimes arbitrary authority of those in positions of power and led to the establishment of a new authority, the authority of experience."[25] This is, surprisingly, the authority to which Sainte-Sophie subscribes, even within the convent. Her faith in God is challenged by her faith in her own body. Initially, she is troubled by her feelings for Julien, vowing to avoid "le péché terrible" (the terrible sin) (84) and praying to God to cure her of a desire she understands only as illness (43). Yet once Sainte-Sophie consummates her desire, she abandons the language of sin altogether. She writes instead: "Je suis heureuse. Ah! qu'importe tout l'univers, tout le péché! . . . Au fond de l'être une divine perle s'émeut! et la sensation même c'est cette perle" (I am happy. Ah! Who cares about the whole universe, all the sin! . . . At the depths of one's being a divine pearl is roused! And that pearl is sensation itself) (91). Indeed, this physical experience allows her to question the very notion of sin, if God has created the body to experience pleasure. "Ce n'est pas de notre faute" (it's not our fault), she pleads to God. "C'est comme cela que vous nous avez faites" (You have made us like this) (100). Her own physical experiences take precedence over the laws of the church.

Sainte-Sophie's naïveté is developed in her first journal entries, as she recounts in a childlike voice the prettiness of the gardens around her and her love for the *mère abbesse.* The attempt to demonstrate her innocence with respect to her own body at times borders on the absurd:

> Je sais que je suis jolie, que je suis jeune, je le sens. Je sens ma vie et ma jeunesse à chaque minute; je sais que j'ai, sous ma robe droite, mon corps qui est doux, mes jambes qui ont des mouvements. Je n'y avais jamais pensé. Je croyais que des religieuses ne sont toujours que des religieuses; mais maintenant je sais que, quand elles n'ont plus leur robe, ni leur linge, elles sont nues. (39–40)
>
> [I know that I am pretty, that I am young, I feel it. I feel my life and my youth at every minute; I know that under my stiff dress I have a soft body, legs that move. I had never thought about it. I thought that nuns were always just nuns; but now I know that without their dress or their underwear, they are naked.]

This description, shortly before her first physical encounters with Julien, marks the beginning of Sainte-Sophie's sexual self-discovery. Julien has already begun to flirt with her; the recognition of her own corporeality seems to result from his desiring glances.

In general Julien's statements are relayed uncritically in the text, for Sainte-Sophie is not equipped to interpret his efforts at seduction. But to the more sophisticated reader, they appear transparent from the beginning. Sainte-Sophie's repeated insistence that she does not understand what he means only underlines the power imbalance. It is as if Sainte-Sophie, like the Enlightenment traveler in a foreign land, had to learn a new language. Julien, for example, offers her his "Prière à l'amour" (Prayer to love), which recounts the various gifts and sacrifices he will make for love, from all the wonders of nature to the expanses of time. Although Sainte-Sophie admits that much of this text escapes her understanding, its implications are clear to the reader. The prayer ends with the following paragraph:

> Et je vous offre, Amour, comme rose dernière et plus belle, et pour que soient éternellement charmées vos sensibles oreilles, le son le plus brûlant, le plus voluptueux, qui n'est pas la voix de Juliette à son balcon, ni la tendre plainte d'Iphigénie, mais le divin éclat d'or que fit, en se brisant, la chaîne étroite des pieds de Salambô [*sic*]. (82)

> [And I offer you, Love, as a last and most beautiful rose, so that your sensitive ears will be eternally charmed, the most burning and pleasureful sound, which is not the voice of Juliet on her balcony, nor the tender moan of Iphigenia, but the divine burst of gold that the tight chain of Salambô's (*sic*) feet made when breaking.]

The crowning symbol of ideal love is found not in spiritual romances but in Flaubert's decadent novel, when the breaking of the gold chain marks Salammbô's loss of virginity to Mâtho. In other words, the *rose dernière et plus belle* of love is sexual intercourse. Julien's less than pure motives are underlined by the dissimulation of this corporeal desire in ethereal aestheticized poetry that Sainte-Sophie struggles to understand. The selfless discourse of love disguises a selfish desire for eros.

Although Julien attempts to seduce Sainte-Sophie with this romantic vocabulary, it is almost entirely lost on her. For him, "La poésie est la vérité du monde" (Poetry is the truth of the world) (111); he lends her *Les Fleurs du mal,* which frightens her: "Tous les désirs ressemblent, dans ce livre, à de grandes blessures, et l'amour c'est la torture, le supplice" (All the desires in this book resemble great wounds, and love is torture, anguish) (110). In contrast, all that Sainte-Sophie knows comes from what she feels and experiences. Outside of society, love is nothing more than an idea, and like religion, is true only in so much as it can be confirmed by experience. She derives strength and joy not from its mythic power but from her own physical pleasures, which she describes repeatedly. This effort in itself—to articulate the physical experience of pleasure—is informed and influenced in

Noailles's text by the prevailing medicalization of sexuality through sexology, while at the same time serving as an antidote to this discourse by inserting women's emotional needs into its explication.

At first Sainte Sophie attempts to communicate her experiences to Sister Catherine. She sees the possibility of Catherine's relating to what she has felt because Catherine has stigmata on her hands; she thus recognizes the relationship between Catherine's sensualized relationship with God and her own heterosexual experience: "O ma soeur Catherine qui avez dans les mains de chères blessures, comprenez-moi il y a des plaisirs du coeur que l'on ne peut pas dire; des plaisirs du coeur qui ressemblent justement à vos mains" (Oh Sister Catherine who has on her hands dear wounds, understand me. There are pleasures of the heart that one cannot speak; pleasures of the heart that resemble precisely your hands) (107). The *plaisirs du coeur* are compared to an unquestionably physical experience, suggesting that they are more likely *plaisirs du corps.* Later she imagines encouraging Catherine to have this incomparable experience: "Vous verrez, on ne pense à rien, on ne se tourmente de rien; vous aurez tant de petits flammes rouges dans votre tête, que ce sera plus beau que le soleil sur des vitraux rouges . . . et après, ma soeur, on ne se tourmente pas non plus, parce que c'est fini, et qu'on voit bien que tout, autour de nous, est resté pareil" (You will see, you do not think about anything, you aren't bothered by anything; you will have so many little red flames in your head, that it will be more beautiful than sunshine through red stained-glass windows . . . and afterward, my sister, you're not disturbed anymore either, because it is over, and you see very well that everything around you has stayed the same) (114). It is clear in this description that Sainte-Sophie is describing a discrete sensation, rather than a continuing emotion. Ultimately, the physical experience effaces any other intellectual connection:

> Rien ne fait peur, ni l'idée du châtiment, ni l'idée de la mort et de la mort éternelle. La volupté, c'est un moment silencieux et haut comme une voûte infinie. . . . Toute l'âme se porte d'un côté et de l'autre côté du plaisir comme un vent soyeux qui se balance entre deux rangées d'oeillets. . . . Quelle paix! On ne craint plus la mort, et si le couvent, le monde entier, tout le plafond de la chambre s'effondraient, on penserait: Qu'importe! comment le saurais-je, mon âme ne peut rien percevoir que ce qui lui vient de soi-même. (120–21)

> [Nothing is scary, not the idea of punishment, nor the idea of death or eternal death. Pleasure is a silent, elevated moment like an endless arch. . . . The whole soul sways from one side of pleasure to the other like silky wind swinging between two rows of flowers. . . . What peace! You no longer fear death, and if the convent, the whole world, the ceiling of

the room collapsed, you would think: What does it matter! How would I even know, since my soul can perceive only what comes from itself.]

The word *âme* is used rather subversively here and throughout the text in the effort to specify the experience of physical pleasure. Borrowed from religious discourse, the word often suggests in romantic literature a sublimation of the erotic for the spiritual. One is reminded of the fin-de-siècle best-seller *Histoire d'une âme,* the autobiography of Sainte Thérèse de Lisieux, in which the author describes her self-sacrifice and spiritual devotion to God. The term *âme* has feminine connotations, the pure soul that contrasts with the baseness of the body, which it is meant to control. One is reminded also of Tinayre's Augustin's description of his beloved Fanny as "simply a soul" in his attempt to challenge the villagers' accusations. But in Sainte-Sophie's writing, the *âme* represents not the female spirit but an actual female physical body part, an imaginary sexual locus where erotic sensation is felt (closer, then, to Nhine's *âme* in *Idylle saphique*). Later, she describes the *âme* as "le dernier secret physique, . . . la place de l'être où afflue le sang le plus sensible" (the last physical secret, . . . the place of the being where the most sensitive blood rushes) (182); the image of blood underlines the *âme*'s contrast to the stigmata. Noailles's use of the soul as the site of erotic sensations is different from the use of the soul in other eighteenth- and nineteenth-century sentimental novels—a feminine genre—where it is also associated with an enhancement of erotic pleasure. Margaret Cohen offers examples from Rousseau's *La Nouvelle Héloise* and Claire de Duras's *Edouard,* where, "the move beyond the material negates sensual pleasure to the benefit of erotic intensification."[26] In these examples, the soul figures metaphorically. Duras's Edouard, for example, exclaims that "this angel penetrated my soul entirely."[27] In Noailles's text, however, the *âme* functions as a metonym, linked to an actual part of the body, and the sensual and material are privileged above the sublime, confirming Larnac's depiction of a *romantisme de sens.*

This physical experience is Sainte-Sophie's primary discovery in the novel. She devotes extensive journal entries to attempting to describe her newfound pleasure and is consumed by the idea that some of her sisters remain ignorant of the joys of "le seul bonheur du monde" (the only happiness in the world) (113). The emphasis on physical sensual experience demonstrates Sainte-Sophie's epistemological process, in the spirit of the Enlightenment tradition. In the *Traité des Sensations,* Condillac argues that the sensations are essential to man's understanding of the world he inhabits. Such is the trajectory of Noailles's novel, as a sentimental novel determined by a radical sensationism, where sexuality enables the female subject to make choices about her conflicting moral imperatives. This process should also be considered in the light of contemporaneous debates about girls' premarital knowledge about sexuality. Léon Blum argued in his widely read *Du mariage* from 1907 that for both men and women, premarital sexual education and experience would insure more lasting marriages; the feminists Nelly Roussel and Madeleine Pelletier engaged similar issues in political speeches.[28] In reading Gyp, Colette, and Dulac in the next section of this chapter, we see just how powerless this lack of information made some women. In a fundamental sense, then, *Le Visage émerveillé* is about a young woman making an informed decision about her future. After confessing to the *mère abbesse,* Sainte-Sophie sits in her room contemplating her new knowledge: "Je m'enferme avec vous et je meurs, rayon incomparable, qui êtes le souvenir et le désir—qui êtes la connaissance—la connaissance du bien et du mal et leur goût confondu" (I shut myself up with you and I am dying, incomparable ray of light, you are memory and desire—you are knowledge—the knowledge of good and evil and their mixed up taste) (182). This knowledge—the knowledge that came all too belatedly to Lucie Delarue-Mardrus's Marie—is now a part of Sainte-Sophie, and she begins to consider her past physical experience as a way of determining her future.

What is perhaps most interesting in Sainte-Sophie's decision is that she does not ultimately choose between Julien and God, despite the contrast between corporeal and spiritual pleasures developed throughout the text. In fact, Julien himself is surprisingly irrelevant to Sainte-Sophie's choice; instead, she chooses between the world Julien wants to lead her into and the one she is currently in. On one hand, Julien's increasingly ill-tempered behavior is recounted faithfully, as if to prepare the reader for Sainte-Sophie's ultimate rejection of him. She tells of his angrily breaking the rosary on her belt, in a jealous gesture that recalls the image of Salammbô's broken chains from his prayer to love. Julien's idea of love hides ulterior motives of possession. Yet although Noailles provides these incriminating details for the discerning reader, Sainte-Sophie herself is not really critical of Julien's behavior; she emphasizes her forgiveness of him and describes inequality between men and women as "une part profonde de la volupté" (a deep part of sensual pleasure) (193). But what exactly is this injustice? Sainte-Sophie does not really elaborate. In fact, the fruits of her sexual discoveries seem almost entirely unrelated to her emotional bond.

Sainte-Sophie's choice to stay in the convent helps us to recognize the significance of her sexual self-knowledge as an affirmation of independence. Absent are any romantic ideals of eros as blissful union; Sainte-Sophie's physical experiences are strikingly solitary, a fact underlined by her own synopsis of *la volupté* quoted earlier: "mon âme ne peut rien percevoir que ce qui lui vient de soi-même" (my soul can perceive only what comes from itself) (121)—a perfect evocation of the sensationist ethos. In this context

Sainte-Sophie's choice of the convent becomes clear, as an affirmation of this same independence and self-sufficiency elucidated through her sexuality. Indeed, she chooses the convent over Julien because the convent seems more a factor in her pleasure than Julien himself. After he proposes to take her away, she writes:

> Je ne pourrais, mon couvent, vivre sans vous. Le bonheur, la passion tendre et vénéneuse, les belles voluptés, c'est vous qui les avez faites pour moi si précieuses et si abondantes, Solitude! Les caresses reluisantes comme l'argent et l'or et plus mélodieuses que toutes les harpes, c'est vous qui les polissiez pour moi, qui les accordiez pour moi dans l'ombre. (132)
>
> [My convent, I could not live without you. Happiness, tender and poisonous passion, beautiful pleasures, it is you who made these things so precious and abundant to me, Solitude! Caresses that gleam like silver and gold and are more melodious than any harp, it is you who polished them for me, who tuned them for me in the shadows.]

Although she cannot imagine life without the convent, later she will succeed in imagining life without Julien.

Sainte-Sophie is unable to reconcile her need for independence with socially acceptable forms of love.[29] She explains: "J'ai tout de suite compris que la femme et l'homme ne sont pas pareils devant l'amour" (I understood right away that woman and man are not alike in love) (202). Her physical experience assures her of her own subjecthood, her own self-determined power, and enables her to choose the convent. Had love made her dependent on Julien—as one might imagine it would have in society, or in a typical sentimental novel—she would not have been able to imagine life without him. Furthermore, rather than rejecting eros, Sainte-Sophie rejects its social consequences—the world that Julien proposes as an alternative to the convent, and the jealousy and possessiveness that followed their physical closeness. Her sensationist ethos thus enables her to avoid submission to a partner who has already revealed himself to be selfish, jealous, and possessive.

Sainte-Sophie's rejection of the social consequences of sexuality and her fidelity to the female world of the convent links this text to another early-modern literary discourse: the utopian fantasies of seventeenth-century women writers who wrote of feminocentric worlds in which they could enjoy freedom outside of courtship and marriage. Indeed, in Lafayette's *La Princesse de Clèves,* as well as in the letters of Anne-Louise de Montpensier, the convent and Christian ideals of austerity were promoted less for religious reasons than for the fact that their moral codes conformed to challenges to patriarchy developed in these writings.[30] Like the Princesse de Clèves, many of Sainte-Sophie's sisters have sought the convent's *repos* (rest) as a means to escape the sexual turmoil of the public world. Sainte-Sophie's embrace of solitude as the key to *volupté* upholds this antisocial imperative. Montpensier imagined a Christian female community where she would be sovereign, to escape the slavery of marriage. Similarly, Sainte-Sophie writes: "Moi seule ici je suis la reine, je suis oisive et langoureuse et les autres sont des eclaves qui travaillent. Quand Julien m'a demandé si je ne le suivrais pas un jour, si je n'irais pas vivre avec lui pour toute la vie . . . je lui en ai voulu; comment a-t-il supposé qu'on pouvait accomplir un sacrifice aussi grand, aussi impossible?" (I alone here am the queen, I am lazy and languorous and the others are slaves who work. When Julien asked me if I wouldn't follow him one day, if I wouldn't go live with him for the rest of my life . . . I was mad at him; how could he have thought that I could make such an impossibly large sacrifice?) (133)

Finally, to best appreciate the significance of the novel's setting, one has to consider the literary and social conventions that it leaves out—the discursive structures outside the walls of the convent. Noailles wrote her novel at a time when women's bodies were a continuous source of literary and scientific fascination. The female body was subject to a science controlled almost entirely by men, and based on men's interpretations of women's behavior. By relying on female sensibility and resuscitating a sensationist aesthetic, Noailles gave her cloistered heroine a power over her own body that was nowhere available in the "real world." Sainte-Sophie makes decisions based on her personal happiness, without consulting a father or a husband. This is the ultimate meaning of her setting: the possibility for a self-determined epistemology, for the woman to learn directly from her body without mediation, and the possibility—unavailable to her female peers, as Blum, Roussel, and Pelletier argued—of making an informed decision about her sexual future. In this light, the subtle polemic of the novel can be recognized in terms of a feminist sexology that acknowledges a woman's need to understand her own sexual desire and to translate it into recognizable terms, in order to make informed decisions about her future.

MARRIAGE AND THE FEMALE ORGASM: GYP'S *AUTOUR DU MARIAGE*, ODETTE DULAC'S *LE DROIT AU PLAISIR*, AND COLETTE'S *L'INGÉNUE LIBERTINE*

> "O femmes! . . . cédez aux besoins de votre mari pour mieux vous l'attacher. Malgré votre aversion momentanée pour les plaisirs qu'il sollicite, efforcez-vous de le satisfaire, agissez de ruse et simulez le spasme du plaisir.

> [Oh women! . . . give in to the needs of your husband to make him more attached to you. Despite your momentary aversion to the pleasures he solicits, force yourself to satisfy him, act with cunning and simulate the spasm of pleasure.]
>
> —Auguste Debay, *Hygiène et physiologie du mariage: Histoire naturelle et médicale de l'homme et de la femme mariés dans ses plus curieux détails,* 1874

> Certes, votre femme ne doit pas, sans raison sérieuse, se refuser à vous; elle doit même, dans une certaine mesure, vous sacrifier son repos et ses goûts; mais, d'autre part, votre femme n'est pas une chose, un jouet dont vous pouvez user jusqu'à l'abus, au gré de vos caprices.
>
> [Certainly, your wife must not refuse you without serious cause; she must, to a certain extent, sacrifice her rest and her tastes for you; but, on the other hand, your wife is not a thing, a toy that you can abuse, following your caprices.]
>
> —Edward Montier, *L'Amour conjugal et paternel. Lettre à un jeune mari,* 1919

> If a woman's mind develops normally, and if she is properly educated, her sexual desire is limited in intensity. If it were otherwise, the whole world would be a vast bordello where marriage and family life would be impossibilities.
>
> —Richard Von Krafft-Ebing, *Psychopathie sexuelle,* 1895

Although medical and hygiene manuals proliferated throughout the fin de siècle and female sexuality was discussed in newspapers and novels, young bourgeois women were taught surprisingly little about their bodies and had little access to explicit sexual education. The extent of this lack of information is humorously documented in Gyp's *Autour du mariage,* a dialogue novel that met with astounding success. The novel was first serialized in the somewhat racy journal *La Vie parisienne* and then published in book form by Calmann-Lévy, where it went through over ninety editions.[31] Best remembered for her right-wing political views and fervent anti-Semitism, Gyp was a reluctant female role model with ambiguous feelings about what women's social roles ought to be. The only child of aristocratic parents who divorced during her youth, Gabrielle Marie-Antoinette de Riquetti de Mirabeau married and had three children before turning to writing for financial reasons: her husband had squandered the proceeds of her dowry.[32] Like Rachilde, Gyp referred to herself as "homme de lettres" and occasionally cross-dressed. She quickly became a shrewd connoisseur of the new print culture, which she used "to create and perform various fantasy versions of herself."[33] To the author's great surprise, the protagonist of *Autour du mariage,* the plucky young Paulette, became a feminist heroine, admired by female readers as an independent, charismatic model of a new femininity.[34]

In the chapter entitled "Les Conseils d'une mère" (A mother's advice), Paulette initially shocks her mother by announcing that she is marrying chiefly "pour m'amuser" (to have fun).[35] Madame d'Hautretan attempts to steer her daughter down a more austere path and prepare her for the wedding night. Echoing the rhetoric of popular hygiene manuals, she explains: "Je te demandais . . . si tu serais contente d'avoir des enfants . . . parce que c'est le but . . . naturel . . . du mariage" (I asked you . . . if you would be happy to have children . . . because it's the natural . . . goal. . . . of marriage) (27). Her comments are generously peppered with ellipses, demonstrating her discomfort with even speaking on the topic. Believing her daughter to be naïve, she wants to warn her about the demands of sexual intercourse. She thus continues: "Il faut . . . pour remplir . . . consciencieusement ce but . . . te soumettre à tout ce que voudra ton mari . . . quelque pénible que cela puisse te paraître" (You must . . . in order to conscientiously . . . fulfill this goal . . . submit to everything your husband wants . . . however painful it might seem to you) (28). Paulette tries not to laugh, and her mother continues: "J'espère, mon enfant, que cela ne te sera pas . . . pénible. . . . Ce que tu éprouveras sera plutôt . . . de l'étonnement que . . . autre chose. . . . (Elle s'éponge le front)" (I hope, my child, that it will not be too . . . painful for you. . . . What you will feel will be more . . . surprise . . . than anything else. . . . [She wipes her brow]) (29). Just as Mme d'Hautretan is struggling to complete her description, Paulette interrupts her and assures her, "je sais tout ça" (I know all that) (29). Kissing her shocked mother, she says, "Que veux-tu, maman? Nous devinons aujourd'hui ce qu'il fallait vous apprendre autrefois, c'est le progrès!" (What do you want, Mom? We guess today what you had to learn before, that's progress!) (29).

When Paulette is sitting around with her friends later on, however, her true ignorance and genuine trepidation come to light. Asked whether she knows what to expect, she responds: "je le sais . . . vaguement" (I know about it . . . vaguely) (45). Just then, her married friend hurriedly leaves, unwilling to supply the information the others desire from her. "Elle respecte le secret professionnel!" (She respects the professional secret!) Paulette explains. Another friend comments that if women really understood what to expect,

Figure 7. Photograph of Gyp. (Print Collection, Miriam and Ira D. Wallach Division of Art, Prints and Photographs, The New York Public Library, Astor, Lenox and Tilden Foundations.)

half of them would not get married in the first place (46). The anxiety surrounding the powerlessness of these young women is telling. One friend recounts the following anecdote:

> Il y a six mois, j'ai fait semblant d'accepter M. de X . . . qui voulait m'épouser. . . . Je pensais: "On me dira . . . on m'expliquera . . . enfin je saurai . . . et cela me servira peut-être à choisir pour tout de bon!" Alors, il a fait sa cour consciencieusement, ce pauvre garçon! Et puis, un beau jour, j'ai dit à maman: "Maman, je voudrais bien savoir en quoi consistent les devoirs du mariage? . . ." Et maman m'a répondu: "Mon enfant, c'est ton mari qui se chargera de te les expliquer; tout ce que je puis te dire, c'est que tu dois te soumettre à 'tout' ce qu'il te demandera." (51–52)
>
> [Six months ago, I pretended to accept Mr. X's marriage proposal. . . . I thought: "They will tell me . . . they will explain to me, finally I will

> know . . . and maybe that will help me to really choose!" So, he courted me conscientiously, the poor guy! And then, one fine day, I said to my mom: "Mom, I really want to know what the duties of marriage are? . . . And Mom answered me: "My child, it's your husband who will be in charge of explaining them to you; all I can tell you is that you have to submit to "everything" he asks of you.]

Not surprisingly, when Paulette is asked whether she is afraid following this confession she readily admits that she would rather have a tooth pulled.

Paulette's knowledge, it turns out, consists almost entirely of what she has read in *Monsieur, madame et bébé,* Gustave Droz's best-selling pseudo-memoir of courtship, marriage, and parenthood, the first edition of which appeared in 1866. Paulette confesses—to her new husband's great shock—to having read this book surreptitiously in *La Vie parisienne,* the somewhat salacious journal in which this novel itself was serialized.[36] But this book, which tested the limits of social standards, offers little more than a description of a woman in a similarly ignorant position, and her new husband's awkward challenges in their new marriage. It is hardly the reassuring tell-all Paulette would have wanted.

The long-desired secrets of the sexual encounter are finally revealed on the wedding night, following which Paulette remarks: "Ce n'est que ça! . . . Je ne comprends pas qu'on fasse des folies pour ça!" (That's all it is! . . . I can't believe that people go crazy for that!) (94). Paulette's reaction is more relief than disappointment, but it is a noteworthy passage because it replays a scene that appears in several other female-authored novels from the same period. Earlier, we saw how Rachilde's Eliante was inspired by post-wedding-night disappointment to reject her husband, refusing to believe that "c'était ça, *le bonheur*" (this was *happiness*). Another version of this scene occurs in the popular novelist Jeanne Marni's 1889 *Amour coupable.* In this novel, the bride finds herself savagely bruised on her wedding night after an encounter that she describes as "un viol légal" (a legal rape). Her description echoes those of Eliante:

> Elle resta étendue près de lui, écoutant sa respiration bruyante, n'osant faire un mouvement dans la crainte de frôler ses jambes . . .—C'est donc ça le mariage! Un homme ronflant près d'une femme qui pleure![37]
>
> [She stayed stretched out next to him, listening to his noisy breathing, not daring to make a move for fear of touching his legs . . .—So that's marriage, then! A man snoring next to a woman crying!]

Marc Angenot singles out this passage as defying realist and naturalist conventions by depicting the marriage bed. He therefore places this novel in a separate, generic category: the *roman féministe,* where "occasionnellement, fugitivement, un certain *indicible* du discours social s'y exprime, spécialement dans ces romans écrits par des dames qui se diffusent aux niveaux 'moyen' et 'populaire' de grande diffusion" (occasionally, fleetingly, a certain unspeakable element of social discourse is expressed, especially in these widely distributed "popular" and "middlebrow" novels written by women).[38]

In this section, I consider two novels that I believe belong to this subgenre, Colette's *L'Ingénue libertine* and Odette Dulac's *Le Droit au plaisir,* in the light of Gyp's *Autour du mariage.* Following Angenot's lead, I believe that these novels contain a sexual discourse that defied generic conventions; Angenot's category of "roman féministe," however, is problematic. Feminism was burgeoning in France during the period in which these novels were written and was concerned with a variety of contemporary social issues, but it was rarely associated with sexual liberation.[39] Many activists in the feminist movement wrote novels, especially in the first decades of the twentieth century. Among them were Madeleine Pelletier, Nelly Roussel, and Harlor.[40] In addition, many women novelists had some connections with the feminist movement and touched on these subjects. Colette Yver wrote several novels about girls and women in the educational system; Marcelle Tinayre often wrote about equality in marriage, as did Louise-Marie Compain.[41] Yet these novels rarely explicitly portray sexuality or speak specifically about women's bodies.

We can categorize many of the novels of the authors cited above in terms of what Margaret Cohen has labeled the *sentimental social novel,* a variation of the sentimental novel and of what David Owen Evans calls the *roman social.* Cohen has described the subgenre of the sentimental social novel, of which George Sand is the most famous author, as focusing on "the suffering of individuals in dominated social positions," and often on the injustices of marriage.[42] Gyp's, Marni's, Colette's, and Dulac's novels differ from these in that they target sexual relationships, while neglecting more conventionally feminist attacks on the social institution of marriage and eliminating the moralizing rhetoric that often accompanied them. Another subgenre that bears some ressemblance to Angenot's "roman féministe" is the sentimental novel about sexual freedom, such as Camille Pert's *Les Amoureuses* (1895) and *Les Florifères* (1898), Jane de la Vaudère's *Les Demi-sexes* (1897), and Adrienne de St-Agen's *Les Amants féminins* (1902).[43] In two of these novels, women have their ovaries removed so that they can have sex more freely and in the last three texts, the heroines are ultimately condemned for their behavior. The moral lesson taught is that sexual liberation leads to pathology.

The novels by Colette and Dulac are a hybrid genre, merging the sexual explicitness of *littérature boulevardière,* on the fringes of pornography, with the social polemic and critical discourse of the sentimental social novel. Their critical discourse distinguishes them from low-brow writing in much the same way that today's women's magazines differ from Harlequin romances or soft porn: though the sexual content may be just as explicit, the critical distance and register render one type of text more legitimate than the other. In this context, they might be renamed *sentimental sexological novels;* the social injustice at stake in the sentimental social novel is transformed in these texts to a sexual injustice: the absence of female pleasure in the marital relationship. Like many of the novels addressed in this book, these novels are feminist only in an anachronistic sense: they signal a modern sensibility by positing sexuality as a site of women's self-knowledge and self-empowerment, even though this power is limited to the private sphere.

Gyp's Paulette is disappointed after her wedding night, and she is fairly clear about what the problem is. When her husband tries to make love to her, she repeatedly pushes him away. He worries that sex is painful to her, but she responds: "Mon Dieu, pénible n'est pas précisément le mot, ça ne m'amuse pas, voilà tout. C'est votre faute, c'est toujours trop la même chose" (My God, painful is not quite the word, it's no fun for me, that's all. It's your fault, it's always too much of the same thing) (119). When he protests, she exclaims: "Je suis sûre que ça pourrait bien être plus varié!" (I'm sure that it could be more varied!) (119). Later, seeking to inspire her husband to new heights of romance, she suggests that he love her like a mistress rather than a wife. But Paulette still cannot make her husband understand, and so she turns to a more physical explanation, confessing: "Je ne suis pas aussi . . . insensible que vous le croyez . . . J'ai la conviction que je puis . . . vibrer à un moment donné. . . . Le tout est de trouver quelqu'un qui sache s'y prendre . . . eh bien, tâchez que ce soit vous!" (I am not as . . . unfeeling as you think. . . . I have the sense that I could . . . vibrate at some point. . . . The thing is to find someone who knows how to set about making it happen . . . well, try to make sure that it's you!) (180).

Paulette's lack of satisfaction with the physical relationship is the impetus for all that follows; the fun she is looking for in marriage is sexual, and when she does not find it, she seeks flirtations elsewhere. Ultimately, she leaves her husband, and a sequel, *Autour du divorce,* follows her shenanigans as she tries to obtain a divorce. But once she is divorced, her husband becomes more attractive to her, and the second novel ends with their reuniting. Whether she finds sexual fulfillment, however, though suggested, remains unclear. Indeed, the sexual disappointment that fuels Paulette's initial rejection of her husband is not really mentioned in the second novel. At the end of her pre-wedding-night conversation with friends, Paulette had promised to fill them in, finally, on what she would discover: "Elles ne quittent Paulette qu'après lui avoir fait promettre solennellement qu'elle leur 'écrira' tout ce qu'elles désirent savoir" (They do not leave Paulette until after having made her solemnly promise to "write" to them everything they want to know) (55). But Paulette does not fulfill this promise, and on this level at least, Gyp does not quite write the book that Paulette and her friends are dying to read. Yet even if the novel is ultimately conservative in its affirmation of marriage, it makes a strong statement about what is necessary to insure a lasting one. When Paulette returns to her husband, it is with increased knowledge of men, her body, love, and intimacy. The suggestion then, is that sexual satisfaction depends, at least in part, on a certain sophistication and experience in the woman.

Paulette has kindred spirits in the heroines of Colette and Dulac's novels. These women take Paulette's disappointment to another level by actively pursuing adultery. *L'Ingénue libertine* was published in 1909 under the name Colette Willy and has received minimal critical attention. It combines two previously published ventures: *Minne* (1904) and *Les Égarements de Minne* (1905). The first half follows the adolescent Minne's active imagination as her cousin Antoine pines after her; the second half tells of Minne's marriage to Antoine, to fulfill her mother's dying wish. Here I discuss only the second half, which can be summarized as Minne's quest to achieve an orgasm by any means necessary.

Little is known about Odette Dulac, who began her career as a successful singer and music-hall dancer, known for her performances at the Chat Noir and Folies Bergères. The *Dictionnaire de biographie française* recounts that she left the stage in 1904, "ayant perdu sa beauté et sa voix" (having lost her beauty and her voice).[44] In 1908 she published *Le Droit au plaisir,* followed by nearly a dozen more novels over the next three decades. An Art Nouveau poster of her as a dancer by Leonetto Cappiello, the prolific advertising artist of the Belle Epoque, is housed in Paris's Musée de la Publicité (Fig. 9). This brief biography links Dulac, along with Gyp and Colette, to the new women described by Mary Louise Roberts whose theatrical performances and literary ventures constituted a form of resistance to patriarchal structures of femininity. While they often rejected the feminist movement, the new women of the Belle Epoque supported themselves financially and offered models of a newly independent female identity removed from the conventional roles of wife and mother. *Le Droit au plaisir* contains the letters exchanged between the Marquise Marcelle de Rouvray and the actress Claire Prelly, who knew each other as girls in a convent. In the letters, the reunited friends frankly discuss marriage, adultery, and the search for sexual pleasure.

The adulterous liaisons pursued by the protagonists of both Colette's and Dulac's novels are linked to an initial disappointment on the wedding

Figure 8. Poster of Odette Dulac by Leonetto Cappiello, 1901. (Image courtesy of Les Arts décoratifs, Musée de la Publicité, Paris. Photo by Laurent Sully Jaulmes.)

night. The description of this disappointment in Colette's novel justifies Minne's various adulterous liaisons:

> Au cri aigu de Minne blessée, Antoine avait répondu par une manifestation idiote de joyeuse gratitude, de soins émus, de dorlotements fraternels. . . . Elle claquait tout bas ses dents et ne pleurait pas. Elle respirait avec surprise cette odeur d'homme nu. Rien ne l'enivrait, pas même sa douleur—il y a des brûlures de fer à friser qui sont autrement insupportables—mais elle espérait mourir, sans trop y croire. . . . Son mari tout neuf, son ardent et maladroit mari s'étant endormi, Minne avait tenté, timidement, de s'évader des bras encore fermés sur elle.[45]

> [To the sharp cry of wounded Minne, Antoine had responded with an idiotic manifestation of joyous gratitude, excited efforts, and fraternal fondling. . . . Her teeth were chattering and she did not cry. She was surprised to breathe the smell of a naked man. Nothing excited her, not even her pain—there are curling iron burns that are far more intolerable—but she wanted to die, without really believing it. . . . Her brand new, passionate and awkward husband having fallen asleep, Minne tried timidly to escape from the arms still enclosing her.]

Like Eliante as a young bride, Minne apathetically ponders death here as an alternative to her new life. Marriage itself is seen as a kind of prison, but less because of its social restrictions on women's behavior (as in Sand's *Indiana,* for example) than for its ungratifying sexual dynamics. Dulac's Marcelle offers a similar story in a letter to Claire:

> Mon mariage fut deux jours après dans une chambre du palace hôtel de la Riviera, devant un décor merveilleux, avec des fleurs sur tous les meubles. Mon mari, reposé, les yeux brillants, la parole tendre, le geste hardi. . . . Et ce fut l'initiation . . . pas brutale, bien que douleureuse. Lui s'excusant—un peu paternel—de devoir sa joie à ma souffrance, et me promettant, dans l'avenir, des délices sans nom! Hum! Hum! A vrai dire, je l'attends encore, ce "plaisir" dont les littérateurs parlent toujours et dont la recherche nous fait patientes et soumises aux désirs de notre époux. Je me suis bien souvent dit en . . . conjuguant le verbe aimer: Ce sera peut-être pour aujourd'hui! Les yeux fermés, immobile, analysant mes sentiments, j'ai guetté le frisson . . . mais le paradis me resta fermé.[46]

> [My marriage was two days later in a room in the palace hotel of the Riviera, beautifully decorated with flowers placed on all the furniture.

> My husband was relaxed, his eyes sparkling, speaking tenderly but moving aggressively. . . . And that was the initiation . . . not brutal, however painful it was. He excused himself—a little paternally—to have had his thrills at my suffering, and promised me untold pleasures in the future! Well! Well! Actually, I am still waiting for it, this "pleasure" that writers always talk about and that the quest for makes us patient and submissive to our husbands' desires. I have often said . . . in conjugating the verb to love: Maybe it will be today! With my eyes closed, not moving, analyzing my feelings, I lay in wait for the thrill . . . but paradise remained closed to me.]

This experience is all the more dramatic because of the "complicité de silence" that Marcelle has also confronted. She describes an earlier meeting with a prospective suitor where she is embarrassed to admit what she has read, later remarking: "Vous voulez que nous ayons une opinion et vous savez qu'on ne nous permet pas de nous renseigner" (You want us to have an opinion and you know that we are not allowed to educate ourselves) (16). Claire expresses similar frustration when her mother refuses to enlighten her about sex. She writes: "Je savais beaucoup de choses, mais le fait essentiel et final, le mystère, que les hommes—dans leur formule de demande—prétendent exquis et divin, je n'arrivais pas à me le représenter" (I knew a lot of things, but the essential and final fact, the mystery that men claim to be so exquisite and divine when they ask for it, I could just not imagine what it was) (35).

In offering this justification for the adulterous explorations of their protagonists, both novels separate themselves from the bawdiness of *littérature boulevardière.* The sexual elements of these plots are not presented in the interest of salaciousness. Instead, adultery is committed to combat an initial injustice, and in this sense follows the codes of the sentimental social novel. In addition, adultery functions differently here than in the nineteenth-century sentimental novel, where the heroine is typically drawn to it because of an uncontrollable attraction to a man besides her husband, but never because of a premeditated desire for sexual fulfillment. Furthermore, the search for an orgasm that determines the plots of both novels forces the protagonists into a critical relationship with their own bodies as well as with the discourses determining them. From this standpoint these texts differ from both conventional sexological and sentimental writings. The critical distance of Dulac's Marcelle is evident in this first passage, as she refers to the pleasure described by "les littérateurs." Presumably she is speaking of sentimental writing for women, whose pedagogical import Angenot has underlined; Marcelle's reference reminds us that this is not the kind of writing we are reading here. It is also worth noting the mention of pain in both descriptions of the wedding night, a factor that is notably absent in both scientific and literary discussions of heterosexual intercourse. Even in the detailed anatomical accounts that accompany the sexological expositions of Beaunis and Krafft-Ebing, for example, there is no examination of the woman's physical pain. By recognizing it in their descriptions, Colette and Dulac, like Delarue-Mardrus, valorize women's suffering as essential to determining the moral implications of her sexual behavior.

The impact of the sentimental writing alluded to in Dulac's text on the female imagination and the woman's self-conception is underlined further in Colette's novel, where Minne fears there is something medically wrong with her because of her failure to experience what she has read about so extensively. She initially blames Antoine for this condition, assuming it to be the result of the unexpected pain of her wedding night: "C'est sa faute, je parie, si je ressens autant de plaisir que . . . ce strapontin. Il a dû me fausser quelque chose de délicat" (It's his fault, I bet, if I feel as much pleasure as . . . this folding chair. He must have messed up something fragile) (124). This sense of physical impairment prevails much later on as she imagines demanding of her lover: "Guérissez-moi! Donnez-moi ce qui me manque, ce que j'appelle si humblement, qui me ravalera au rang des autres femmes!" (Heal me! Give what is missing, what I so humbly call for, which will restore me to the level of other women!) (149). Minne implicates the source of her information: popular novels that romanticize sexual intimacy:

> Elle ouvre un volume tout moite d'encre fraîche et relit: "Leur étreinte fut à la fois une assomption et un paroxysme. Adila rugissante enfonça ses ongles aux épaules de l'homme, et leurs regards exacerbés se croisèrent comme deux poignards empennés de volupté. . . . Dans un spasme suprême, il sentit sa force se dissoudre en elle, tandis qu'elle, les paupières révulsées, dépassait d'un envol les sommets inconnus où le Rêve se confond avec la sensation." (149)[47]

> [She opens up a volume all damp from fresh ink and rereads: "Their embrace was at once an assumption and a paroxysm. Roaring Adila dug her nails into the man's shoulders, and their intense looks met like two daggers feathered with pleasure. . . . In a supreme spasm, he felt his strength dissolve into her, while she, eyes rolled upward, flew past unfamiliar summits where Dreams mix with sensation."]

Again, this reference generically distinguishes Colette's novel from the one cited, while problematizing the pedagogical aspect of women's sentimental novels. Furthermore, through this quotation, Colette frames the representation of sexuality that her novel and Dulac's undermine. The image presented here is of blissful union, sexual intercourse as a metaphor for the merging of the man and woman into one, physical desire as a realization of spiritual love. Colette and Dulac demystify this romantic cliché by separating physical satisfaction from love; for both protagonists, one has nothing to do with the other. The sexual act, even when physically enjoyed by both partners, is an experience of divisiveness. Thus, Claire tells Marcelle of her first orgasm:

> Quand il accomplit les rites du sacrifice païen . . . je sentis dans tout mon être le frisson nouveau . . . j'avais ouï la grande voix de la chair! Cela s'est passé sans cri, sans délire de paroles, parce que je n'aimais point cet homme; mais mon corps mûri par le temps, mes nerfs tendus par la vie, avaient accompli cette mise au point de mes sens. Tu as bien compris, Marcelle, mon âme n'avait eu aucune part à cette évolution. (92)
>
> [When he had finished the rites of the pagan sacrifice . . . I felt in my whole being the new shudder; . . . I had heard the great voice of the flesh! It happened without a cry, without the delirium of words, because I did not love this man at all; but my body, ripened over time, my nerves fraught from life, had accomplished this sharpening of my senses. You surely understand, Marcelle, that my soul did not have any part in this evolution.]

Claire explains her ability to achieve this pleasure as a result of her physical maturity; love is split from desire. This realization that love and sex are separate further distinguishes this story from sentimental novels, where love and passion are subsumed under one heading, and more often than not, love justifies passion. The separation of the *âme* from what the body is experiencing also marks the development of Claire's critical relationship to her body. The absence of emotional involvement is underlined by her partner's unsuspecting exclusion from this experience. Misunderstanding her sudden change of temperament, he flees, "croyant avoir commis une maladresse" (thinking he had committed some act of clumsiness) (93). Thus, the sexual act is stripped of its symbolics of union; rather than an experience of similitude, it is an affirmation of separateness. Herein lies an important aspect of these quests for pleasure: for these female protagonists, the orgasm is a refusal to lose oneself in the other, to sacrifice one's selfhood to the couple. For Minne, then, the search for orgasm is a way of exercising her independence from her mother's wishes and of expressing her own will. It is the realization of her desperate wedding night plans, during which she frantically plotted a way to undo "l'erreur profonde d'avoir épousé cette espèce de frère" (the profound error of having married this kind of brother) (125).

The significance of the quest for orgasm as liberty is developed even more clearly in Dulac's novel. Marcelle says as much to Claire when she privileges freedom over her curiosity for the "petit 'frisson' " (the little "shudder"). What she is really seeking, she insists, is "La liberté, tu m'entends celle du corps et de l'esprit" (Freedom, you understand, that of the body and the mind) (102). In linking physical and mental satisfaction, Marcelle points to a fundamental paradox of these protagonists' quests. Although the novels demystify the sentimental union of love and pleasure and show them to be separate entities, they also express a nostalgic longing for such a union, which remains an ideal. Thus, Claire is disappointed in her lover, who gives her physical satisfaction but is confused by her emotional reaction. What is subversive, then, is the choice of targeting the sexual deficiency as the essential key, rather than following the conventions of the traditional sentimental novel and pursuing love outside of marriage. A modern sensibility is evident in this privileging of the body as a site of female oppression and emancipation. The medical discourse that subtly enters both texts perhaps offers an explanation for this change. Minne sees herself as medically suffering, perhaps as a result of the pervasive cultural link between deviant female desire (outside of marriage) and pathology. Similarly, Marcelle's adulterous leanings bring her to the doctor. After falling in love with a mysterious Don Juan–type known as "L'Abeille" (The Bee), she writes:

> Ma santé, d'ailleurs, s'altère. Des insomnies creusent mes orbites et alanguissent mes membres; je me lève courbaturée et le docteur m'ordonne du bromure. Il diagnostique: Hystérie. Cela me met hors de moi! Alors, c'est une maladie que de désirer l'assouvissement de sa chair? L'homme qui n'a point trouvé de secret pour ressusciter ses forces défaillantes a toujours une drogue pour éteindre l'ardeur des nôtres. (148–49)
>
> [My health, on the other hand, is changing. Insomnia digs into my eye sockets and makes my limbs feeble; I get up aching and the doctor prescribes me bromide. He diagnoses: Hysteria. That drives me crazy! So it's a sickness to desire the satisfaction of the flesh? Men who haven't found the secret to curing their own impotence always have a drug to extinguish our passion.]

Marcelle offers a commentary here on medical constraints on the female body, alluding to the widespread belief in the dangers of excessive female pleasure as well as the continuing pervasiveness of the hysteria diagnosis. Her remarks go beyond social critiques of marriage and demonstrate why sex and not love is at stake in the novel. The critique that continues, in its didactic explicitness, recalls Sand's literary polemics, while displacing the blame from the institution of marriage to the more far-reaching dynamics of heterosexual desire:

> Oh! ma rage contre l'injustice et l'ironie sociale! Parce que la femme est un être faible, c'est elle qui doit refreiner la bête humaine et ne jamais rien laisser paraître de la douleur de ses morsures. Il faut que ses formes soient belles, que sa chair resplendisse, qu'elle soit ferme et saine, mais si le parfait équilibre de sa santé réclame des étreintes vigoureuses ou nouvelles, on la déclare demi-folle. (149)

> [Oh! My anger against injustice and the irony of society! Because women are weak, they are the ones who have to put the brakes on the human beast and never reveal the pain of its biting wounds. Women must have beautiful figures, their skin must be radiant, firm and healthy, but if balancing their perfect health demands new, intense kinds of passion, they are declared half mad.]

The political language employed here points to the significance of the title, *le droit au plaisir,* which suggests pleasure as a political right. In the light of the reference to the *bête humaine,* Marcelle can be seen as implicitly calling into question naturalist explanations of sexual behavior that exculpate the man who cannot control his instincts, while incriminating women who express sexual desire. Instead, her argument links naturalism—in its assumption of sexual instincts—to a social justice argument predicated on personal responsibility and civil rights.

Both Minne and Marcelle experience their first orgasm in the arms of their husbands, underlining that in these novels the institution of marriage itself is not at stake. Marcelle's husband suspects her of having an affair; when he discovers she is innocent (she has decided against having an affair with "L'Abeille"), they return home with relief:

> Il me sembla que dans ma chair, s'éveillait toute une région de sensibilité nouvelle—comme si des nerfs engourdis se décidaient à souffrir doucement—, puis tout mon être se crispa et se détendit. . . . Quand le marquis me dit très fier: "Enfin! tu as vibré!" j'avais encore la figure douloureuse et les yeux ravis. (192)

> [It seemed to me that a whole region of new sensitivity was awakening in my body—as if overstimulated nerves had decided to suffer gently—then my whole body tensed and then released. . . . When the Marquis said to me very proudly: "Finally! You came!" I looked pained but delighted.]

The derailed affair is significant as an impetus to this moment: Marcelle's satisfaction can be seen as logically resulting from a new emotional maturity. That this long-awaited pleasure is laced with pain seems to predict the inevitable: although initially Marcelle and her husband become lovers, he eventually betrays her by having an affair. This rift is perhaps announced in the passage above, where the Marquis's comments undermine any suggestion of romanticism. Physical pleasure is no guarantee of spiritual union.

The novel ends years past this point, as the two friends continue a correspondence imbued with bitter resignation. Pleasure has been recognized as a woman's right, but one that is in conflict with society's structures. Thus Marcelle can only anticipate her own daughter's future "marital initiation" as an inevitable crisis. "Mais comment la persuaderai-je de cette vérité que l'homme ne respecte que ses martyres et qu'il n'a crucifié Jésus que pour pouvoir l'adorer ensuite?" (But how will I convince her of the fact that men respect only martyrs and that they crucified Jesus only to be able to worship him after?) she asks. "Le plaisir est une juste redevance de la chair; nous y avons toutes droit, mais . . . il est dangereux de forcer sa volonté." (Pleasure is a just accounting of the flesh; we all have the right to it, but . . . it is dangerous to force its will) (253). The religious vocabulary that pervades this lament signifies at once her resignation to prevailing social (sexual) norms and her refiguring of Christian sexual morality. The woman here is not the traditional source of original sin but a martyr who must sacrifice her own pleasure for social good. In this sense, *Le Droit au plaisir* conforms to the codes of the sentimental novel, where "what builds . . . is an increasingly crushing sense that the conflict between collective welfare and individual freedom is inevitable."[48]

What, however, are we to make of Colette's dénouement, which appears to be a rather facile happy ending? When they are away on vacation together, after months of Minne's adulterous meanderings and Antoine's increasing jealousies, their marital intimacy finally results in crescendoed satisfaction. The narrative suggests they will now live happily ever after, since Minne's desire has been quenched:

> [Minne] n'envie plus rien, ne regrette plus rien. La vie vient au-devant d'elle, facile, sensuelle, banale comme une belle fille. Antoine a fait ce miracle. Minne guette le pas de son mari, et s'étire. Elle sourit dans l'ombre, avec un peu de mépris pour la Minne d'hier, cette sèche enfant quêteuse d'impossible. Il n'y a plus d'impossible, il n'y a plus rien à quêter, il n'y a qu'à fleurir, qu'à devenir rose et heureuse et toute nourrie de la vanité d'être une femme comme les autres. (249)

> [(Minne) no longer wants anything, no longer regrets anything. Life comes to her, easy, sensual, as banal as a beautiful girl. Antoine made this miracle. Minne listens for her husband's steps and stretches. She smiles in the dark, with a little disdain for the Minne of yesterday, that tough girl seeking the impossible. There is no more impossible, there is nothing left to seek, there is only blossoming, becoming rosy and happy and enriched from the pride of being a woman like everyone else.]

From this passage it would seem that the sentimental sexological novel elides its middle name in this conclusion, simply following a pre-Sand sentimental moralizing model that, as in Gyp's novel, finds peace in the home front. In such novels, the heroine's internal conflict was compounded by her husband's virtue. Similarly here, Antoine is never incriminated; he is just the unfortunate victim. Minne's ultimate orgasm thus resolves the conflict simply, allowing Minne the pleasure she is due within the bounds of marriage, and perhaps thereby protecting Colette's novel from censorship.

Yet this dénouement, despite its facile facade, is simmering with subversion beneath the surface. First, there is no moralizing voice guiding the reader in Colette's novel, which allows for a certain ambiguity usually precluded by the presence of the conventional rhetoric of the genre. In addition, Colette's redemption of marriage privileges physical pleasure above love; this physical satisfaction saves the marriage. This is a striking message, offered with minimal salaciousness, that confirms the sexological significance of the novel. The importance of the wife's pleasure in marriage, especially in preventing adultery, was recognized in many of the sexual and moral hygiene manuals of the period. This message is transformed in the context of Colette's novel, where pleasure is not something granted by the husband to rein in his wife but an experience that the mature woman (that is, the woman who has gained physical knowledge of her body) is ready to accept from her partner. Indeed, sexual satisfaction becomes a defining element of female maturity—Minne has become a woman, happy "d'être une femme" (to be a woman), just as Marcelle laments "avoir été femme si tard et si peu" (having been a woman so late and so little) (50), and then, after experiencing orgasm says "je me sens tout à fait femme" (I feel completely womanly) (222). The positing of sexual experience as a definition of femininity is a product of the circular relationship between patriarchal discourse and female identity that women reclaim in these novels.

The resolution of the marriage bonds, however, even as it is glorified, seems to suggest something less than a happy ending, as the quirky and rebellious Minne dissolves into a doting housewife in the novel's last phrases:

> Minne, demie-nue, frotte sa tête décoiffée à la manche d'Antoine, d'un geste amoureux de bête domestiquée. Elle bâille, lève vers son mari la flatteuse meurtrissure de ses yeux d'où s'est enfui le mystère. (251)
>
> [Minne, half-nude, rubs her rumpled hair against Antoine's sleeve, with the loving gesture of a house pet. She yawns, raises her pretty black and blue eyes, now lacking in mystery, to her husband.]

It is hard not to read a criticism of marriage in this description, where Minne's devotion to her husband is symbolized through her becoming a house pet, devoid of mystery. While certainly to some this image of wifely submission is an ideal, to others, including those who had any sympathy for the eccentric heroine, the banality described in this passage is the displaced tragic ending of the sentimental sexological novel. The lack of moralizing rhetoric interpreting this conclusion fosters its ambiguity.

The underlying subversiveness of Colette's novel is further borne out in the description of Minne's orgasm, which continues in the representation of physical pleasure as an isolated and isolating experience, rather than a blissful union of souls. As in Dulac's text, this description emphasizes the separate experiences of the two parties. Minne's pleasure at first seems the accident of two people engaged in separate and solitary enterprises. Remembering the advice of a school friend, Minne begins to sigh, "Ah! Ah!" and is startled to feel "une angoisse progressive, presque intolérable" (a progressive anguish, almost intolerable) squeeze her throat (249). Then, in the midst of this descent into *jouissance,* Antoine is immobilized, such that Minne's pleasure seems almost autoerotic, while Antoine watches, helpless. Finally, she reminds him of his role ("Va donc!" [Go ahead!]) and he consumes himself with the pursuit of her pleasure; indeed, his own satisfaction is not even mentioned, though safely assumed. Colette's remarkable extended description of female orgasm offers a repudiation of the romantic satisfaction it seemingly represents, in that short of portraying joyous union of husband and wife, it suggests the process by which the woman slides into a submissive role. Minne's physical release is coupled with her emotional one. The orgasm literally transforms her: "Enfin elle tourna vers lui des yeux inconnus et chantonna: 'Ta Minne . . . ta Minne . . . à toi.' " (Finally she turned unfamiliar eyes to him and chanted: "Your Minne . . . your Minne, yours.") (249), recalling Marie's rapid subjugation in Delarue-Mardrus's novel. One can only remark the violence of the whole experience, described as *une angoisse* during which, her head shaking side to side, she is compared to "une enfante atteinte de méningite" (a child afflicted with meningitis) (249) and then, nails digging into her husband, "[elle] semblait en proie à un enfantin désespoir" ([she] seemed in the grip of a childlike despair) (249).[49] Looking ahead to *La Vagabonde*'s Renée Néré, for whom sexual desire is described as the opening of a wound, and who reviles marriage for its constraints on women, the pleasures of Minne's orgasm come to look like pain in disguise. Marital bliss, from this perspective, is a sentimental literary fallacy undermined implicitly between its own lines.

Colette's, Dulac's and Gyp's descriptions of the path to female pleasure all conflict with the conclusions of contemporary sexologists as well as with the descriptions presented in nineteenth-century popular medical texts. Auguste Debay, for example, offers a clinical list of causes of "anaphrodisie," or frigidity, including masturbation, genital disease, alcoholism, malnutrition, prolonged study, deep thinking (*méditations profondes*), and excess emotion in the 1862 edition of his extremely successful *Hygiène et physiologie du mariage*. According to this view, women's minds can be involved in their sexuality only in a negative, obstructive way. In general, female sexual desire is downplayed in medical texts, while its excess is linked to disease and infertility. Thus, the German sexologist Krafft-Ebing writes in the 1895 French edition of *Psychopathia Sexualis:*

> If a woman's mind develops normally, and if she is properly educated, her sexual desire is limited in intensity. If it were otherwise, the whole world would be a vast bordello where marriage and family life would be impossibilities. . . . Women, however, are more sexual than men. Their need for love is greater, and it is continuous rather than periodic, but this love is more psychological [*psychique*] than sensual.

On one hand, according to Krafft-Ebing, the healthy wife does not need sexual pleasure to be satisfied, for "wives see marital intercourse more as a mark of affection than as a form of sensual satisfaction."[50] On the other hand, more and more doctors did acknowledge women's sexual needs, even if they were considered lesser than their husbands; yet this acknowledgment was predicated on a notion that men must maintain control over these needs. Thus, the medical causes of frigidity are abandoned as doctors highlight the husband's role. In this vein, J. P. Dartigues claims that the majority of adulterous women are led to other men by sexually incompetent husbands; Seved Ribbing makes women's sexual behavior the husband's responsibility; and the medical writer Dr. Désormeaux cites men's "ignorance and negligence" as the primary cause of "froideur" in his contribution to the popular series Bibliothèque sexuelle.[51] Years later, the British sexologist Havelock Ellis would address the problem of frigidity, or "the persistent absence of sexual desire and sexual feeling" as follows:

> The chief reason why women are considered "frigid" lies less in themselves than in men. It is evident that while in men the sexual impulse tends to develop spontaneously and actively, in women, however powerful it may be latently and more or less subconsciously, its active manifestations need in the first place to be called out. That, in our society, is normally the husband's function to effect. It is his part to educate his wife in the life of sex; it is he who will make sex demands a conscious desire to her.[52]

The ramifications of these conclusions underline the import of women novelists' explorations of female pleasure. On one level, Gyp, Colette, and Dulac concur with medical authority by depicting their husbands as hapless brutes, whose ignorance of their needs drives them nearly to adultery. But by unilaterally situating female sexuality in the man's control, the medical texts enforce patriarchal structures and remind us of the role of scientific discourse in determining under what conditions sexual desire is appropriate. "Normal" women experience desire only with men's help; others, like Dulac's Marcelle, are considered hysterical, or *demi-folle.* As forms of countersexology, Colette's and Dulac's novels offer a completely different picture of women's sexual pleasure by weighing their physical satisfaction against their emotional fulfillment and autonomy.

Surprisingly, none of these texts seemed to offend, despite their explicit engagement of sexual activity; none was censored or charged with obscenity; their frank discussion of female sexuality inspired no public debate.[53] I believe this reception is due primarily to their circumscription within a feminized arena. The sentimental novel, destined for a female readership, constituted in this sense a continuation of the private sphere. When women wrote these novels, as they did increasingly at the fin de siècle, the sphere was even more delimited: a conversation between women. This fact is underlined by Dulac's epistolary novel, which literally takes the form of such a conversation (in contrast to the conversation between men that was common to most medical literature). Thus, within the safely feminine confines of sentimental fiction, women could offer this alternative sexology to each other. Another important factor protecting the subversiveness of these novels was their inherent conservatism. Noailles's Sainte-Sophie ultimately rejects her unbridled sexuality; Gyp's Paulette returns to her husband, as do Dulac's Marcelle and Colette's Minne. Indeed, the subversive undertones of Colette's ending are easily missed within the seemingly facile ending, where marital order is restored. This conservatism seems to have allowed its authors to voice audacious attacks on bourgeois sexual mores free of critical consequences.

Perhaps because of the contemporary blindness to their subversion, critics have failed to recognize the political import of these novels and the ways in which they begin to develop a modern feminist sensibility. Within these circumscribed conversations between women, the authors take a tentative yet significant step toward a renunciation of patriarchal sexual relationships, even as they preserve the patriarchal structures of marriage. Furthermore, in their focus on the body—the domain of male medical authority—their novels offer a clear and compelling example of the hysteric's revenge as defined at the outset of this study: as a means for women to claim control of their bodies by determining their own meanings in defiance of gender-biased medical doctrine. Nowhere is such a gesture more explicit than in Odette Dulac's depiction of Marcelle, who begins her joint path of sexual exploration and self-analysis after rejecting her doctor's diagnosis of female sexual desire as a symptom of hysteria.

Conclusion

Now that the century has turned once again, French women have entered nearly all professions and women writers abound. Yet the dream of intellectual equality still faces barriers, some as impermeable as the French language itself. The following passage appeared in an essay from the June 22–28, 2000 edition of the *Nouvel observateur* by the weekly columnist Delfeil de Ton:

> Une dame magistrat vient d'être nommée procureure générale. Générale avec un e et procureur avec un e. . . . Ah, c'est subtil, une langue. Des femmes de lettres se désignent comme écrivaines. Je vous fiche mon billet, pourtant, que le plus beau compliment qu'on pourrait faire serait d'écrire, de l'une ou l'autre d'entre elles, que "*cette écrivaine est un véritable écrivain.*" Grand écrivain, le rêve de l'écrivaine.[1]

> [A woman magistrate has just been named a director of public prosecutions (*procureure générale*). *Générale* with an e and *procureure* with an e. . . . Ah, a language is subtle. Women of letters call themselves "écrivaines" (writers, with the feminine e ending). I bet you my bottom dollar, however, that the best compliment one could give would be to write about one of them that "*this* écrivaine *is a true* écrivain." Great *écrivain,* the dream of the *écrivaine.*]

This journalist's comment demonstrates that many of the tensions complicating the fin-de-siècle woman writer's self-image continue to dominate one hundred years later. The term *écrivaine* exemplifies these tensions. On one hand, the feminine *e* suffix affords women writers legitimacy in a profession in which their grammatical difference symbolized patriarchal exclusion. The word *écrivaine* did not exist originally because there was no such thing as a female *écrivain;* its invention actualizes women's overcoming of a barrier that was not simply linguistic. On the other hand, this same suffix separates *écrivaines* from their male counterparts, placing them in a feminized category that still bears the burden of all sorts of unwanted associations—the remnants of those voiced decades earlier by Jules Bertaut, Paul Flat, and Barbey d'Aurevilly. The dream of the contemporary French woman writer thus seems similar to that of Rachilde's Raoule de Vénérande a century ago, who sought a language that effaced gender but that also allowed her to benefit from both male and female sexual identities. Like many of her female peers, Rachilde (who first identified herself as a *homme de lettres*) wanted to be both a woman and a writer, without either label transforming the connotations of the other.

Rachilde's vision of a literary existence beyond gender, however, was far from reality at the fin de siècle. As the numbers of women writers grew, the preoccupation with the *bas-bleus,* a politically loaded term signaling masculine women abandoning their wifely duties, and thus patriotic duties as well, reinforced the sense of crisis surrounding female authorship. Women's novels lay in the shadow of their female authors, whose femininity preoccupied male critics, startling Barbey d'Aurevilly with the "odor di femina," for example. "N'étaient-elles pas femmes avant tout?" (Weren't they women first and foremost?) Bertaut asks, reading women's gender as linked to a shared temperament imagined as "une sorte de fatalité à laquelle elles n'ont pas encore pu échapper" (a kind of fate [read: fatal flaw] that they have not yet been able to escape).[2] Medical doctrine backed these presumptions, inscribing femininity in a biologically inferior brain, prone to emotion and even hysteria if not properly employed. Indeed, the female mind constituted a threat to the body, able to thwart women's procreative role if not properly regulated.

At a time when the possibility of female intellect was very much in question, women's writing was nearly always read through the female signature itself. Because of the equation between women's writing and the "transposition of the self,"[3] the slippage between the female author and her text was even more likely. The term *littérature féminine* starkly encapsulates this problem: referring to women's writing (as opposed to writing for women), literally translated it means "feminine literature." In other words, the novels themselves take on the gender of their authors and all its unwanted associations, directing critics away from the novels' content. (Such is also true for the term *roman féminin,* as well as for Charles Maurras's influential treatise on *le romantisme féminin.*)

Paradoxically, because of the blindness to the ideas women expressed in their writings and the innovations they demonstrated, they may have been able to write more freely than men about controversial subjects, as exemplified by the novels by Gyp, Dulac, and Colette discussed in Chapter 5, with their explicit engagement of female pleasure. At the same time, the inability of critics to engage women's work on any serious level beyond their gendered signature may help to explain the effacement of what André Billy called the "triomphe de la femme" from literary history. In the era of the mass press, the legacy of a book was insured in part by the sensation that it made and by the resonance of its content with the dominant cultural voices who responded to it. *La littérature féminine* did create a sensation at the fin de siècle, stirring up a loud cultural debate, but this debate centered on the fact of female authorship rather than on individual literary contributions. When books did evoke their own controversy, attention was repeatedly guided back to the author. Thus Rachilde's scandalous *Monsieur Vénus* may have escaped censorship in France by highlighting the role of the young female author. Barrès's preface to the French edition turned attention away from Rachilde's subversive imaginings to the fact of the author's frail, hysterical femininity. But Marcelle Tinayre's nomination to the Legion of Honor was deterred by the failure of her public persona to assuage cultural anxiety about female authorship.

Women authors themselves often contributed to this focus on their public identity, as they shrewdly manipulated the workings of the press to enhance their own publicity. Whether appearing on postcards, in newspaper photographs, or on cigarette boxes, many if not most of the women considered here exploited the commodification of their images as a means to professional success. Their increased visibility only added to the sense that there were throngs of women writing, threatening to outnumber their male counterparts. This celebrity may have helped inscribe prominent personalities like Liane de Pougy, Anna de Noailles, and Gyp in the cultural history of the Belle Epoque, while contributing to the lessened legitimacy of their literary contributions.

In the shorthand of Belle Epoque literary criticism, femininity was associated with inferiority, excess of emotion, narcissism; virility with objectivity, clarity, and quality.[4] These associations limited the tools with which women's writing could be analyzed, such that even when it was to be praised it was nearly always done in these highly gendered and weighted terms. Good women's writing was wholly separate from good writing in general. In a 1905 collection of commentary by contemporary writers (all male, except Rachilde), the novelist Marcel Schwob applauds what he describes as a revolutionary new literary point of view: "le point de vue féminin" (the female point of view).[5] This praise for women's literature at first seems to upend virility's role as sole gauge of literary quality, yet it does not release itself from the essentializing gendered terms of the equation. Like the notion that women write in spite of themselves, their writing gushing forth without apparent reflection, the appreciation for the female point of view implicitly belittles the individual accomplishments of women authors by grouping them together under this limited rubric. Schwob's praise does not in this sense significantly contradict Bertaut's assertion that "nulles individualités ne sont moins dissemblables entre elles que les femmes de lettres" (no individuals are less dissimilar than women writers).[6]

In response to their readers' tendency to generalize about them as a group, women writers resisted functioning as one. Beyond their individual friendships with one another, the writers examined here rarely formed gender-based literary alliances and for the most part eschewed the feminist movement. Constructing their own unique identities through bold personal choices, women like Colette, Gyp, Renée Vivien, and Rachilde risked social ridicule by embracing independence and nontraditional roles. At the same time, the separate political agenda of the contemporary feminist movement alienated many women writers, preventing an alliance between two avenues of dissent that could have benefited from unity; such an alliance could have brought attention to the largely ignored political import of many women's novels. Indeed, if fin-de-siècle women writers had found a political or literary movement with which to align themselves and that could have supplied them with added theoretical backing, then perhaps their subversions would not have been so quickly eclipsed by prevailing essentializations about their sex.

In considering the elitist individualism of so many of these women authors, I have wondered how literary history might have been different if they had banded together. What if Colette, Rachilde, and Lucie Delarue-Mardrus, for example, had formed a literary movement, theorizing together the rejection of gender binarisms, or challenging the associations between virility and intellectual authority through a broader literary agenda? Or what if Renée Vivien, Colette, Natalie Clifford Barney, and Liane de Pougy had written a manifesto against patriarchal sexual structures, positing lesbianism as an intellectual choice? What other women—or men (Jean Lorrain?)—would have joined them, hinging further success on the notorious celebrity of this clan rather than on distancing themselves from the category of *bas-bleus?* How might such gestures have brought attention to these women's ideas? Unfortunately, the refusal of fin-de-siècle women writers to articulate a literary agenda—shared or otherwise, or to define the goals of their writing, meant that male critics were able to define it in their own biased terms (that of *littérature féminine*).[7] This dynamic began with the critics of the early 1900s—Flat, Bertaut, Ernest-Charles, Maurras, Bonnefon—and continued in future generations with Jean Larnac's influential history of women's writing in 1929 and André Billy's 1951 reflections on the period. For all of these critics, the discussion of fin-de-siècle *littérature féminine* is dictated by the presumed link between virility and intellectual authority; the feminine, in its difference from the masculine, is invariably presumed to be lesser.

The gathering momentum of women writers as a literary presence in the 1900s was disrupted by World War I. The political upheaval of the war may have foiled the progressive acceptance of the French woman writer as an intellectual force, reinvigorating a conservatism in French society that stigmatized women who took on public roles. The war crystallized preexisting anxiety about gender roles around the changes resulting from the prolonged absence of thousands of soldiers whose jobs were left to fill. In turn, a new dichotomy emerged, furthering discrimination against female intellect. In the new terms, the pleasure-seeking, selfish *femme moderne* was a direct threat to the *mère de famille.*[8] The tension between these two female stereotypes is vividly represented in Henry Fèvre's 1925 *L'Intellectuelle mariée,* which depicts the horrific consequences of marriage to a *femme moderne,* in this case a female philosopher whose selfish intellectual interests overshadow her patriotic duty to procreate in order to compensate for military losses. The protagonist's eventual pregnancy plays out as a penance for the dismal, bloody death of her veteran husband as a result of defending his wife's honor; motherhood is thus a cure for her selfish femininity.[9] The novel suggests the impact of the war on the question of female intellect, which is buried by this author within sociocultural anxieties about masculinity, and masked once again by a patriotism preoccupied with the nation's birthrate.

Despite the stubborn individualism of the authors examined here and their failure to speak as a group, a thread links the subversive undertones of their novels. In all of these texts, women prioritize the mind as they challenge the place of the female body in patriarchal discourse and social structures. Taken together, their works reveal a shared intellectual struggle that brought together women as seemingly diverse as the courtesan Liane de Pougy and the devoted mother Marcelle Tinayre, a confluence promoted by the eclectic social circles of Belle Epoque Paris, where these women were sure to cross paths. Delving into these authors' lives I have discovered that they were not nearly as different as their legacies might suggest. Liane de Pougy struggled to separate herself from her reputation as a pleasure-seeker and devoted herself in later years to her husband, Georges Ghika; Tinayre was disappointed with her own choice of husband and carried on several affairs that challenge the pristine domestic reputation she astutely cultivated.[10] What I have also discovered is the possibility that numerous other novels and writers took part in these subversions, suggesting myriad paths for future study. Rachilde alone wrote over sixty books, most of them novels, publishing well into the 1940s; the trajectory of her oeuvre as a whole has not been fully considered. Other women writers have surfaced in my research, demanding further inquiry—Myriam Harry, Daniel Lesueur, Gérard d'Houville, Louise-Marie

Compain, Colette Yver, Jeanne Marni, Camille Pert, to name but a few. Much work remains to be done in the field to determine the relationships between these authors' works and those of the authors I present, including the hundreds of their novels that I could not consider here. The fin-de-siècle *littérature féminine* remains to be fleshed out, so that these women's novels may finally speak for themselves, rather than through the lens imposed on them by their contemporary critics.

Not until well after World War II did French women writers begin to flourish in earnest, announcing the birth of modern French feminism with Simone de Beauvoir's call for female self-determination. Recognizing the bias of the gender binarism that privileged masculine over feminine, women writers finally began to protest the prevailing hierarchy. With the notion of *écriture féminine,* women's writing was productively polemicized as women changed the terms of the debate. Unlike the generation of 1900, women writers from Hélène Cixous and Monique Wittig to Marguerite Duras and Annie Leclerc broached the question of gender difference and theorized femininity, defining the literary process both in terms of their sex and against its inscription in a patriarchal hierarchy. What then, is the relationship of fin-de-siècle women writers to their feminist descendents? The resistance to gender norms depicted by the novels considered here comes in multiple forms, but it nearly always located the female body as a site of disruption of these norms, whether through cross-dressing, the embrace of lesbianism, the drama of childbirth, or the pursuit of pleasure. Partnered with an emphasis on the intellect as a means to overcome sexual injustice, these writings anticipate the relationship between writing and sexual liberation that accompanied the increase in French women's authorship following Beauvoir. And yet, for the most part, the writers of the Belle Epoque did not announce the feminist implications of their subversion, making it apparent only to those who were looking: presumably the female readers who may have found in their novels models of alternative forms of femininity. But seen through a contemporary feminist optic that recognizes resistance to gender inequality through a plurality of forms, these novels present a clear and prescient voice of dissent whose significance to French literary history merits recognition.

Notes

INTRODUCTION

1. Rachilde, *Monsieur Vénus* (1889; reprint, Paris: Flammarion, 1977), 5. See Chapter 4 for a discussion of Barrès's preface and his relationship to Rachilde.
2. Renée Vivien, *Une Femme m'apparut* (1904; reprint, Paris: Régine Deforges, 1977), 102, 99. Vivien published another version of this novel in 1905. The differences between the two versions are addressed in Chapter 2.
3. Marcelle Tinayre, *Madeleine au miroir, journal d'une femme* (Paris: Calmann Lévy, 1912), 212.
4. The dangers of female intellect are posited in the works of Pierre Cabanis, Julien-Joseph Virey, and Pierre Roussel, for example. See also n. 55.
5. Daumier calls women writers "bas-bleus" after the British blue-stockings. As Janis Bergman-Colter argues in her *Woman of Ideas in French Art, 1830–1848* (New Haven: Yale University Press, 1995), Daumier's woman of ideas "opportunistically [used] her fame to satisfy unnatural sexual appetites" (67).
6. Barbey d'Aurevilly, *Les Bas-bleus* (Paris: Société Générale de librairie catholique, 1878), 342.
7. Mary Louise Roberts, *Disruptive Acts: The New Woman in Fin-de-siècle France* (Chicago: University of Chicago Press, 2002), 15.
8. The canonical place allotted many of these writers has shifted dramatically throughout the centuries, reflecting political changes and changes in ideas about girls' education. See Joan DeJean and Nancy K. Miller, eds., *Displacements: Women, Tradition, Literatures in French* (Baltimore: Johns Hopkins University Press, 1991).
9. In *Tender Geographies: Women and the Origins of the Novel in France* (New York: Columbia University Press, 1991), Joan DeJean argues that women invented the French novel in the seventeenth century, and that feminist ideas were instrumental to its development as a genre that "had women as its principal architects, was read and prized equally by male and female readers, and, initially at least, was granted official status by an important faction in the largely male critical establishment" (8). Lafayette's *La Prin-*

cesse de Clèves is widely recognized as the first modern French novel, placing a woman writer at the helm of this weighty tradition.

10. In her fascinating study of nineteenth-century subgenres of the novel, *The Sentimental Education of the Novel* (Princeton: Princeton University Press, 1990), Margaret Cohen describes realism's "hostile takeover of the sentimental form" (12).
11. Naomi Schor argues that Sand embraced nonrealist practices because they were "the only alternative representational mode available to those who do not enjoy the privileges of subjecthood in the real." Schor, *George Sand and Idealism* (New York: Columbia University Press, 1993), 54. Schor's views of George Sand's canonical exclusion dovetail with Cohen's argument.
12. In *Readers and Society in Nineteenth-Century France: Workers, Women, Peasants* (New York: Palgrave, 2001), Martin Lyons writes: "Women were identified as novel-readers in the nineteenth century because lack of education was thought to disqualify them from more serious reading matter. The novel was considered entertainment for its own sake, with no important lessons to communicate, and it was therefore suitable for readers of limited education with time on their hands" (85). James Smith Allen offers another compelling history of French readership in *In the Public Eye: A History of Reading in Modern France, 1800–1940* (Princeton: Princeton University Press, 1991).
13. These statistics can be found in Géraldi Leroy and Julie Bertrand-Sabiani's excellent comprehensive study, *La Vie littéraire à la Belle Époque* (Paris: Presses Universitaires de France, 1998), 264. Another set of figures offered in this study is from the Calmann-Lévy archives. They list 243 women authors in 1902 and their 378 works from that year, an indication that the women were prolific authors. In the light of another statistic that there were 722 writers in 1899, these numbers indicate the important presence of women authors. In an essay dated May 1903, the critic Jean Ernest-Charles sarcastically refers to "les cinq cents et quelques femmes qui ont publié des romans ce mois-ci" (the five hundred or so women who have published novels this month). Ernest-Charles, "Les 'Bas-bleus' et la littérature féminine," in *Les Samedis littéraires,* 5 vols. (Paris: Sansot, 1905), 2:231. Gabrielle Houbre further analyzes the statistics of women writing at the fin de siècle in "La Belle Epoque des Romancières," in *Masculin/Féminin: Le XIXe siècle à l'épreuve du genre,* ed. Chantal Bertrand-Jennings (Toronto: Centre d'Études du XIXe siècle Joseph Sablé, 1999), 183–97.
14. A 1906 survey in the women's journal *La Vie heureuse* found that women preferred the title *femme auteur* (Leroy and Bertrand-Sabiani, *La Vie littéraire,* 266). Because of its particular associations within the French context, I have chosen to keep the term *bas-bleu* in French throughout my text rather than translate it into blue-stocking, the English term it derived from.
15. Ernest-Charles, "Les 'Bas-bleus,' " 227.
16. Jules Bertaut, *La Littérature féminine d'aujourd'hui* (Paris: Librairie des Annales Politiques et Littéraires, 1909), 8; Emile Faguet, *Je sais tout,* September 1907, quoted in Leroy and Bertrand-Sabiani, *La Vie littéraire,* 285.
17. The only woman novelist from the Belle Epoque to have been accepted into the French canon is Colette; yet her serious recognition came during the latter part of her career, after World War I. She was not inaugurated into the Legion of Honor until 1920.
18. Mary Louise Roberts deftly addresses the contradictory implications of the term *fin de*

siècle and argues that conventional metaphors of decay are insufficient to account for the interrogation of femininity during this time (*Disruptive Acts,* 1–3).

19. This inquiry complements and expands on Cohen's *Sentimental Education of the Novel,* which offers a brilliant explanation of canon formation and its relationship to the politics of why there were no great women realists.
20. Janet Beizer, *Ventriloquized Bodies: Narratives of Hysteria in Nineteenth-Century France* (Ithaca: Cornell University Press, 1994); Charles Bernheimer, *Figures of Ill Repute: Representing Prostitution in Nineteenth-Century France* (Cambridge: Harvard University Press, 1989); Bram Dijkstra, *Idols of Perversity: Fantasies of Feminine Evil in Fin-de-Siècle Culture* (New York: Oxford University Press, 1986); Jann Matlock, *Scenes of Seduction: Prostitution, Hysteria, and Reading Difference in Nineteenth-Century France* (New York: Columbia University Press, 1994).
21. Vernon Rosario, *The Erotic Imagination: French Histories of Perversity* (New York: Oxford University Press, 1997); Robert Nye, *Crime, Madness, and Politics in Modern France: The Medical Concept of National Decline* (Princeton: Princeton University Press, 1984); Alain Corbin, *Les Filles de noce: Misère sexuelle et prostitution; 19e et 20e siècles* (Paris: Gallimard, 1982); Michelle Perrot, *Les Femmes, ou les silences de l'histoire* (Paris: Flammarion, 1998); Geneviève Fraisse and Michelle Perrot, eds., *A History of Women in the West.* Vol. 4, *Emerging Feminism from Revolution to World War* (Cambridge: Harvard University Press, Belknap Press, 1984).
22. In *Sexing the Mind: Nineteenth-Century Fictions of Hysteria* (Ithaca: Cornell University Press, 1995), Evelyne Ender offers a fascinating examination of notions of the female mind in nineteenth-century gender fables of hysteria, through readings of George Sand, Henry James, George Eliot, and Freud. Her consideration of hysteria around questions of knowledge very much informs my discussion of the disease. The focus of her book, however, is on sexual difference as a literary construct rather than on the threat of the female intellect.
23. Michel Foucault, *The History of Sexuality,* vol. 1, *An Introduction* (New York: Vintage Books Edition, 1984), 67–73.
24. The term *sexology* comes from the German *sexualwissenschaft,* supposedly coined by Iwan Bloch. Sexology developed in the late the nineteenth century as a subspecialty in medicine, shifting the medical lens from physiology to an emphasis on actual behavior. In *The Erotic Imagination,* Rosario recognizes the import of fiction in shaping sexological discourse, using Zola and Huysmans as central examples.
25. For more on the relationship between medical and literary texts at the end of the nineteenth century, particularly with respect to female sexuality, see Emily Apter, *Feminizing the Fetish: Psychoanalysis and Narrative Obsession in Turn-of-the-Century France* (Ithaca: Cornell University Press, 1991), 34–40; Beizer, *Ventriloquized Bodies;* Rosario, *Erotic Imagination,* 69–111.
26. Several authors were widely read during this period without fitting into the categories of naturalism or decadence. The term *écrivain bourgeois* or *moderne* was used to describe writers such as Paul Bourget, Maurice Barrès, Henri Bourdeaux, Pierre Loti, René Bazin, Marcel Prévost, Paul Hervieu, and Anatole France. The *roman moderne* often addressed political issues, and some of these writers were known for developing the genre of the *roman à these.* Subgenres also included the *roman catholique* and the

roman psychologique. Barrès, Bourdeaux, and Bourget frequently portrayed young male heroes, often writers, learning from a master. For more on these writers, see Pierre Citti, *Contre la décadence: Histoire de l'imagination française dans le roman, 1890–1914* (Paris: Presses Universitaires de France, 1987); Anne-Marie Thiesse, *Roman du quotidian: Lecteurs et lectures populaires à la Belle Epoque* (Paris: Le Chemin Vert, 1984); Gerald Prince, *Guide du roman de langue française, 1901–1950* (Lanham, MD: University Press of America, 2002).

27. For more on the relationship between naturalism and decadence, see Charles Bernheimer, *Decadent Subjects: The Idea of Decadence in Art, Literature, Philosophy, and Culture of the Fin-de-siècle in Europe,* ed. T. Jefferson Kline and Naomi Schor (Baltimore: Johns Hopkins University Press, 2002).
28. Asti Hustvedt has summarized: "The female, the actual female body, is abhorrent because it is natural. The feminine, however, may be admired because it is duplicitous, mysterious, and finds its ultimate realization in artifice. . . . The decadent strategy attempts to empty the female body of its natural content and transform it into a feminine image that is perfectly artificial and completely external." Hustvedt, Introduction to *The Decadent Reader: Fiction, Fantasy, and Perversion from Fin-de-Siècle France,* ed. Hustvedt (New York: Zone Books, 1998), 20. Other useful references on decadence include Bernheimer, *Decadent Subjects;* Jean Pierrot, *The Decadent Imagination, 1880–1910* (Chicago: University of Chicago Press, 1981); Jennifer Birkett, *The Sins of the Fathers: Decadence in France, 1870–1914* (New York: Quartet Books, 1984); Noel Richard, *Le Mouvement décadent: Dandys, esthètes, et quintessants* (Paris: Nizet, 1968).
29. In their excellent biography, *Charcot: Constructing Neurology* (New York: Oxford University Press, 1995), Christopher Goetz, Michel Bonduelle, and Toby Gelfand describe Charcot's rise to fame in scientific and social circles, and in the popular press (217–67). See also Jan Goldstein, *Console and Classify: The French Psychiatric Profession in the Nineteenth Century* (New York: Cambridge University Press, 1987), 327–29.
30. Matlock discusses Brouillet's painting in the light of the theatricality of the Salpêtrière in *Scenes of Seduction,* 133.
31. Foucault, *History of Sexuality,* 1:101.
32. In fact, Foucault offers little factual support for his argument that homosexuality constitutes a reverse-discourse, and few details about the relationship of such a discourse to dominant discourses.
33. For a critique of Foucault's notion of the relationship between body and state, see Dorinda Outram, *The Body and the French Revolution: Sex, Class, and Political Culture* (New Haven: Yale University Press, 1989), 16–21.
34. Foucault, *Surveiller et punir: Naissance de la prison* (Paris: Gallimard, 1975).
35. Thomas Laqueur, *Making Sex: Body and Gender from the Greeks to Freud* (Cambridge: Harvard University Press, 1990), 23.
36. André Billy, *L'Epoque 1900* (Paris: Editions Jules Taillandy, 1951), 217, 221.
37. Bertaut, *La Littérature féminine,* 3. Until his death in 1959, Bertaut wrote prolifically on French literature, theater, history, and politics, including books on Balzac, George Sand, Chateaubriand, Prévost, and Napoleon. The Bibliothèque Nationale de France lists over one hundred titles of his works.
38. Paul Flat, *Nos femmes de lettres* (Paris: Perrin, 1909), 3. In addition to literary and art

criticism, Flat wrote several novels and was well integrated in literary circles. Maurice Barrès wrote the preface for his *Premier vénitiens* (1899) and Flat wrote the preface for Renée Vivien's *Dans un coin de violettes* (1910).

39. A perhaps less objective effort is offered in Ernest-Charles, "Les 'Bas bleus.' " Describing the crowds of women writers, he asks, "Quelles sont ou quelles seront les victimes de cette concurrence épouvantable? Les hommes, les femmes ou la littérature?" (Who are or who will be the victims of this frightening rivalry? Men, women or literature?) (227).
40. Bertaut, *La Littérature feminine*, 5.
41. It is unclear how much these fears were justified. Out of one hundred popular novelists documented in Thiesse's study of the *roman populaire* she counts seventeen, making 17 percent (as she puts it: "minorité, mais non négligeable" [a minority, but not negligible]). In the general writing population, she counts only 2 to 3 percent women. Thiesse, *Roman du quotidian*, 183, 39–41.
42. The term *horrible competition* (épouvantable concurrence/concurrence épouvantable) appears in Tinayre's book as well Ernest-Charles's essay from several years earlier, suggesting that this was a prevalent catch-phrase in the discussion of women writers.
43. Tinayre, *Madeleine au miroir*, 206.
44. Bertaut, *La Littérature feminine*, 6.
45. Ibid., 309.
46. Flat, *Nos femmes de lettres*, 238.
47. Charles Maurras, "Le Romantisme féminin," in *L'Avenir de l'intelligence* (Paris: Albert Fontemoing, Editeur, 1905), 249.
48. Paul Gaschon de Molènes, "Les Femmes poètes," *Revue des deux mondes*, 1842, 3; quoted in Christine Planté, *La Petite Soeur de Balzac: Essai sur la femme auteur* (Paris: Editions du Seuil, 1989), 23.
49. Alexandre Mayer, *Des rapports conjugaux considérés sous le triple point de vue de la population, de la santé, et de la morale publique* (1857; reprint, Paris: J.-B. Baillière et fils, 1874), 73, 77.
50. In 1879, liberal Republicans—many of whom were allied with feminist causes—gained the Senate and the presidency. The Camille Sée Law was passed in 1880, creating girls' secular secondary schools. By the fin de siècle, the effects of this democratization of education were beginning to be felt across social structures as the first generations of women to benefit from it ventured into professions. Françoise Mayeur offers a history of nineteenth-century advances in girls' education in relation to class structure in *L'Education des filles en France au XIXe siècle* (Paris: Hachette, 1979).
51. Flat, *Nos femmes de lettres*, II.
52. Bertaut, *La Littérature feminine*, 11.
53. Ibid., 301.
54. Sylvain Maréchal, *Il ne faut pas que les femmes sachent lire; ou, Projet d'une loi portant défense d'apprendre à lire aux femmes* (1801; reprint, Paris: Gustave Sandré, 1853), 9. Maréchal is quoted extensively in Geneviève Fraisse, *Muse de la raison: Démocratie et exclusion des femmes en France* (Paris: Editions Gallimard, 1995). Fraisse demonstrates the relationship between the formation of democracy and the marginalization of women in France.
55. Maréchal, *Il ne faut pas que les femmes sachent lire*, 32.

56. Summaries of these doctors' ideas about female reason can be found in Carla Hesse, *The Other Enlightenment* (Princeton: Princeton University Press, 2001), 132–33; Joan Scott, *Only Paradoxes to Offer: French Feminists and the Rights of Man* (Cambridge: Harvard University Press, 1996), 49; Lynn Hunt, *The Family Romance of the French Revolution* (Berkeley and Los Angeles: University of California Press, 1992), 156–58.
57. While in English the opposition is articulated either as soul versus body or mind versus body, in French the word *esprit* can encompass both soul and mind. The more specific word for soul is *âme*. Ender argues that an epistemological shift concerning interiority took place in the mid-nineteenth century, after which the configuration of mind predominated over that of soul (*Sexing the Mind*, 22, n. 31). For a philosophical history of sexuality and in particular the changing nature of the soul, see Denise Riley, *"Am I That Name?" Feminism and the Category of "Women" in History* (London: Macmillan, 1988). Geneviève Fraisse also offers a philosophical history of sexuality in Fraisse and Perrot, *History of Women in the West*, 4:48–79. Laqueur's fascinating history of sexuality, *Making Sex*, traces the relationship of body and gender "from the Greeks to Freud," as his subtitle suggests, focusing on the implications of changing notions of reproductive biology.
58. Pierre-Joseph Proudhon, *Contradictions économiques: La propriété* (1846), 2:197. Proudhon edited the journal *Le Peuple* in the 1840s, where he voiced many antifeminist sentiments. See Scott, *Only Paradoxes to Offer*, 69–78; James F. McMillan, *Housewife or Harlot: The Place of Women in French Society, 1870–1940* (New York: St. Martin's Press, 1981), 10–12, 193.
59. Fraisse, *Muse de la raison*, 49.
60. According to Jacques Donzelot's theory of the modern economy of the body, beginning in the eighteenth century, the soul (*âme*) was "called upon to account for the imperfections of bodies and conducts, to apply itself to their management through a healthy regulation of flows." Donzelot, *The Policing of Families*, trans. Robert Hurley (New York: Pantheon, 1979), 14. Woman's chief role in this economy was to be devoted to the proper functioning of her domestic role, mainly by avoiding illness that might prevent her from procreating.
61. Maréchal, 24.
62. Maréchal, *Considérant* 79 (1801 edition), quoted in Fraisse, *Muse de la raison*, 47.
63. See, for example, the physician and anthropologist Gustave LeBon's "Recherches anatomiques et mathématiques sur les lois des variations du volume du cerveau et sur leurs relations avec l'intelligence," *Revue d'anthropologie*, 2d ser., 2 (1879): 27–104. Research on genius also inscribed female intellectual inferiority in medical doctrine, in, for example, J. (de Tours) Moreau, *La Psychologie morbide dans ses rapports avec la philosophie de l'histoire ou de l'influence des neuropathies sur le dynamisme intellectuel* (Paris, 1859); Max Nordau, *Psycho-physiologie du génie et du talent*, trans. Auguste Dietrich (Paris, 1897). On the gendering of the medical profession in nineteenth-century France, see Rosario, *Erotic Imagination*, 162–63; Yvonne Knibiehler and Catherine Fouquet, *La Femme et les médecins: Analyse historique* (Paris: Hachette, 1983).
64. The psychiatrist and fin-de-siècle feminist activist Madeleine Pelletier did attempt to refute medical studies on male superiority during her training as a medical student. At the same time, she was theoretically stymied by the question of the female body

and sought a way to overcome sex altogether by encouraging chastity. See Scott, *Only Paradoxes to Offer,* 135–36, 144–45.

65. J. P. Dartigues, *De l'amour expérimental ou des causes d'adultère chez la femme au XIXe siècle: Etude d'hygiène et d'économie sociale résultant de l'ignorance, du libertinage et des fraudes dans l'accomplissement des devoirs conjugaux* (Versailles: A. Litzellmann, Librairie Médicale et Scientifique, 1877), 48. This text was part of a medical library series intended for a popular audience. These kinds of series proliferated in the second half of the nineteenth century.
66. Jean-Louis Brachet, *Traité de l'hystérie* (Paris: J.-B. Baillière, 1847), 505. Ender offers a fascinating reading of Brachet as a way of understanding nineteenth-century gendering of the female mind in *Sexing the Mind,* 31–65; Matlock uses Brachet to read Balzac in *Scenes of Seduction,* 175–78; and Beizer reads Brachet's treatise as a nineteenth-century medical narrative of hysteria in *Ventriloquized Bodies,* 32–53.
67. Modern literature on the history of hysteria is vast. In addition to the texts cited throughout this chapter, the following texts have been critical to my understanding of the disease in the context of nineteenth-century France: Georges Didi-Huberman, *Invention de l'hystérie: Charcot et l'iconographie de la Salpêtrière* (Paris: Macula, 1982); Gérard Wajeman, *Le Maître et l'hystérique* (Paris: Navarin, 1982); Elisabeth Roudinesco, *Histoire de la psychanalyse,* vol. 1, *1885–1939* (Paris: Seuil, 1984); Martha Noel Evans, *Fits and Starts: A Genealogy of Hysteria in Modern France* (Ithaca: Cornell University Press, 1991); Yannick Ripa, *Women and Madness. The Incarceration of Women in Nineteenth-Century France* (Cambridge: Polity Press, 1990); Jacqueline Carroy-Thirard, *Le Mal de morzine: De la possession à l'hystérie (1857–1877)* (Paris: Solin, 1981); Jocelyne Livi, *Vapeurs de femmes: Essai historique sur quelques fantasmes médicaux et philosophiques* (Paris: Navarin, 1984); Ruth Harris, *Murders and Madness: Medicine, Law, and Society in the Fin de Siècle* (New York: Oxford University Press, 1989).
68. Matlock reads this comment in the context of the relationship between mental illness and prostitution (*Scenes of Seduction,* 131).
69. Augustin Fabre, *L'Hystérie viscérale: Nouveaux fragments de clinique médicale* (Paris: A. Delahaye and E. Lecrosnier, 1883), 3; quoted in Mark Micale, "Hysteria Male/Hysteria Female: Reflections on Comparative Gender Construction in Nineteenth-Century France and Britain," in *Science and Sensibility: Gender and Scientific Enquiry, 1780–1945,* ed. Maria Benjamin (Cambridge: B. Blackwell, 1991), 205.
70. Mark Micale, *Approaching Hysteria: Disease and Its Interpretations* (Princeton: Princeton University Press, 1995), 23.
71. Legrand du Saulle and Briquet discuss the relationship of hysteria to menstruation, pregnancy, and menopause, for example. See Henri Legrand du Saulle, *Les Hystériques: Etat physique et état mental* (Paris: J.-B. Baillière et fils, 1883); Pierre Briquet, *Traité clinique et thérapeutique de l'hystérie* (1859; reprint, Paris: Hachette, 1975).
72. Brachet, *Traité de l'hystérie,* 63.
73. Briquet writes "La femme est faite pour sentir et sentir c'est presque l'hystérie" (Women is made to feel, and feeling is almost hysteria) (Traité clinique, 50). Commenting on this statement, Ender writes: "At this point, nineteenth-century hysteria looks very much like a parody of femininity" (Sexing the Mind, 37). Legrand du Saulle cites Briquet's contention that "L'hystérie est presque spéciale au sexe féminin, parce que,

chez lui, il existe une prédominance de cet élément affectif" (Hysteria is almost unique to the female sex, because women have a predisposition for its affective element) (Legrand du Saulle, *Les Hystériques*, 47; Briquet, *Traité clinique*, 161). Briquet goes on to say that men can have hysteria when they share this predisposition but that such an occurrence goes against the laws of society.

74. Dartigues, *De l'amour experimental*, 1.
75. Micale, "Hysteria Male/Hysteria Female," 205.
76. Bertaut, *La Littérature féminine*, 16.
77. Foucault, *History of Sexuality*, 104. The hystericization of the female body is the first of four central "strategic unities" that Foucault describes. The others are a pedagogization of children's sex; a socialization of procreative behavior; a psychiatrization of perverse pleasure (104–5).
78. Carolyn Dean, The Frail Social Body: Pornography, Homosexuality, and Other Fantasies in Interwar France (Berkeley and Los Angeles: University of California Press, 2000), 4. See also Robert Nye, "Degeneration and the Medical Model of Cultural Crisis in the French Belle Epoque," in Political Symbolism in Modern Europe: Essays in Honor of George L. Mosse, ed. Seymour Drescher, David Sabean, and Allan Sharlin (New Brunswick, NJ: Transaction Books, 1982), 19–41; Nye, Crime, Madness, and Politics in Modern France.
79. Bertaut, *La Littérature féminine*, 19; Flat, *Nos femmes de lettres*, II.
80. Briquet, *Traité clinique*, 19.
81. Brachet, *Traité de l'hystérie*, 71, 74, 75
82. Mayer wrote on topics ranging from meningitis and typhoid to the protection of children. His byline describes him as a doctor for L'Inspection Générale de la Salubrité, general secretary of the Société Protectrice de l'Enfance, and elected to *chevalier* of the Legion of Honor.
83. A later example of this is Jean Caufeynon, *Histoire de la femme* (1904; reprint, Paris: Côté-femmes, 1989), which quotes extensively from Briquet, *Traité clinique,* and Legrand du Saulle, *Les Hystériques.*
84. Mayer, *Des Rapports conjugaux*, 72.
85. Joseph Grasset (under the pseudonym Gasters), *Dans un cabinet de médecin: Pièce en un acte* (Paris: Société française d'imprimerie et de librairie, 1905), 3–4.Quoted in Goldstein, *Console and Classify*, 338.
86. Gladys Swain, "L'Âme, la femme, le sexe et le corps: Les métamorphoses de l'hystérie à la fin du XIXe siècle," *Le Débat* 24 (1983): 127.
87. The only other book to address women writers of this period as a group is Jennifer Waelti-Walters's *Feminist Novelists of the Belle Epoque: Love as a Lifestyle* (Bloomington: Indiana University Press, 1990). Waelti-Walters's book covers an impressive number of novelists and novels, organized thematically. But, the wide scope of her project does not allow her to provide context for the authors or novels she presents. Other examples of recent scholarship situating fin-de-siècle women writers in a wider context include Alison Finch, *Women's Writing in Nineteenth-Century France* (New York: Cambridge University Press, 2000), which offers an excellent survey of nineteenth-century women's literature up to 1899, including commentary on Marcelle Tinayre, Gyp, and Rachilde; Eva Martin Sartori and Dorothy Wynne Zimmerman, *French Women Writers: A Bio-*

Bibliographic Sourcebook (New York: Greenwood, 1991), which contains entries on Anna de Noailles, Colette, Lucie Delarue-Mardrus, and Rachilde; Mélanie E. Collado, *Colette, Lucie Delarue-Mardrus, Marcelle Tinayre: Émancipation et résignation* (Paris: L'Harmatton, 2003), which examines the conflicts these three writers confronted between traditional ideals of femininity and a desire for autonomy, in 1900–1914; Diana Holmes, *French Women's Writing, 1848–1994* (Atlantic Highlands, NJ: Athlone, 1996), which situates Marcelle Tinayre, Rachilde, Gyp, and Renée Vivien, among others, in the context of contemporary discourses on gender. An important addition to this list is *A "Belle Epoque"? Women in French Society and Culture 1890–1914,* ed. Diana Holmes and Carrie Tarr (New York: Berghahn Books, 2006), which was published as *The Hysteric's Revenge* was going to press.

88. Historically, French women's authorship has tended to parallel French feminist activism, even if women writers have not always been affiliated with the feminist movement. For the history of feminism in nineteenth-century France, see Claire Goldberg Moses, *French Feminism in the Nineteenth Century* (Albany: State University of New York Press, 1984); Felicia Gordon and Marie Cross, *Early French Feminisms, 1830–1940: A Passion for Liberty* (Brookfield, VT: Edward Elgar, 1996); Patrick Kay Bidelman, *Pariahs Stand Up! The Founding of the Liberal Feminist Movement in France, 1858–1889* (Westport, CT: Greenwood, 1982); Elinor A. Accampo, Rachel G. Fuchs, and Mary Lynn Stewart, eds., *Gender and the Politics of Social Reform in France, 1870–1914* (Baltimore: Johns Hopkins University Press, 1995).
89. Stephen Hause with Anne R. Kenney, *Women's Suffrage and Social Politics in the French Third Republic* (Princeton: Princeton University Press, 1984), 42.
90. See Roberts, *Disruptive Acts,* 49–71.
91. My argument here dovetails with Roberts's description of the New Woman, who rejected the feminism of her day largely because of its embrace of traditional domestic roles. Like Roberts's new women, these writers expressed their resistance to gender norms in terms that were not recognized as feminist at the time.
92. Scott's critique of the conflict between French universalism and feminism is also part of a debate with the French antifeminist historian Mona Ozouf, who maintains that universalism is part of a uniquely French identity that allows for gender differences. See Ozouf's *Mots de femmes: Essai sur la singularité française* (Paris: Fayard, 1995). This debate among French and American historians can be found in *Le Débat,* no. 87 (November–December 1995): 117–46. Because of the refusal of the women writers I consider to articulate a theory or theories of femininity and gender difference, it is not really possible to situate them within this debate. The writers here would likely agree with Ozouf that women should maintain gender differences while challenging some traditional female roles. At the same time, the complexity of their lives—and their resistance to the feminist label—can be understood in the light of the tensions between the competing values of feminism and universalism. Jo Burr Margadant describes in similar terms the female performers in her edited collection *The New Biography: Performing Femininity in Nineteenth-Century France* (Berkeley and Los Angeles: University of California Press, 2000), 24.

CHAPTER 1

1. Janet Beizer, *Ventriloquized Bodies: Narratives of Hysteria in Nineteenth-Century France* (Ithaca: Cornell University Press, 1994), 249.
2. Emile Zola, "Le Roman expérimental," (1880) in *Oeuvres complètes*, ed. Henri Mitterand, 15 vols. (Paris: Cercle du Livre Précieux, 1968), 10:1175–401.
3. Emile Zola, "Les Romanciers naturalistes" (1881), in Mitterand, *Oeuvres complètes,* 11:221.
4. Yvonne Knibiehler and Catherine Fouquet recount the history of France's first women doctors in *La Femme et les médecins: Analyse historique* (Paris: Hachette, 1983), 193–200. Women's enrollment in medical faculties often required special permission, and most of their work was limited to caring for children and women. Françoise Mayeur explains that medical faculties had been open to women since the Second Empire but that the 1880 Camille Sée Laws helped to increase the numbers of women enrolling in *L'Enseignement secondaire des jeunes filles sous la troisième république* (Paris: Presses de la Fondation Nationale des Sciences Politiques, 1977), 169. In 1881, Blanche Edwards opened a French debate on women's qualifications for the medical profession when she attempted to sit for her boards. This debate appeared in the early 1880s in medical journals as well as more general interest publications such as the *Voltaire* and tended to echo views on female intellect voiced in other contexts. An article in *Le Progrès médical* (no. 12, 1884) argues, for example, "Les femmes n'ont pas les aptitudes physiques necessaries. Elles n'ont pas non plus les qualités morales, ni les qualités intellectuelles suffisantes" (Women do not have the physical aptitude necessary [to become doctors]. They don't have the moral qualities or sufficient intellectual qualities either). Quoted in Knibiehler and Fouquet, *La Femme et les médecins,* 196.
5. Christopher Goetz, Michel Bonduelle, and Toby Gelfand, in *Charcot: Constructing Neurology* (New York: Oxford University Press, 1995), see Pierre Briquet and Charles Lasègue as Charcot's major predecessors (174–75).
6. Ibid., 211. According to Jan Goldstein, between 1841 and 1842, 648 women were admitted to the Salpêtrière and the Bicêtre hospitals, 7 of whom were diagnosed as hysterics; forty years later, between 1881 and 1882, 500 women were admitted, 89 of whom were diagnosed as hysterics, an increase of nearly 17 percent. Goldstein, *Console and Classify: The French Psychiatric Profession in the Nineteenth Century* (New York: Cambridge University Press, 1987), 322. Jann Matlock shows that during the period in between, the study of hysteria was already gaining momentum through doctors in public hospitals, who treated large numbers of women considered hysterical. Matlock, *Scenes of Seduction: Prostitution, Hysteria, and Reading Difference in Nineteenth-Century France* (New York: Columbia University Press, 1994), 129.
7. Although the extent of Zola and Charcot's relationship is unclear, an illustrated edition of Edward Drumont's *La France juive* from 1886 shows Zola seated near Charcot during a party at Alphonse Daudet's house. See Goetz, Bonduelle, Gelfand, *Charcot,* 251.
8. Zola, "Le Roman expérimental," 1189.
9. Charles Bernheimer argues that for Zola, desire disrupts the social circulus such that "the function of narrative is to cure itself of the illness of male passion so that it can return to a state of natural balance." Bernheimer, *Figures of Ill Repute: Representing Prostitution in Nineteenth-Century France* (Cambridge: Harvard University Press,

1989), 216. My reading of Zola and Nana owes a great deal to Bernheimer's analyses in *Figures of Ill Repute* as well as to Beizer's *Ventriloquized Bodies.* Bernheimer's reading is situated in the context of his study of prostitution in nineteenth-century fiction and art; he explores the dichotomy within the character of Nana between her identity as "bonne fille" and Zola's depiction of her as a ferment of destruction, arguing that Zola's heightening of this naturalist "double vision of women's sexual nature" constitutes his originality and emphasizing the fantasmatic origins of this vision (*Figures of Ill Repute,* 202). I focus on a different aspect of Zola's fantasmatic relationship to his female character, his anxiety about the female mind. In a chapter on "hysteria as source of Zola's Rougon-Macquart cycle," Beizer demonstrates the ways in which metaphors of textual generation are inscribed on the female body in Zola's oeuvre and the ways that Nana stages different narrative strategies. Although I focus on many of the same scenes that Beizer eloquently unpacks, I view Nana not as a "textually afflicted body" (*Ventriloquized Bodies,* 187) but as an acting subject threatening the author's own narrative strategies.

10. Bernheimer posits that both Nana and the Count Muffat's adulterous wife have moles with curly hairs because according to Lombroso these were signs of degeneration (*Figures of Ill Repute,* 218).
11. Emile Zola, *Nana* (1880; reprint, Garnier-Flammarion, 1968), 439; hereafter cited in text.
12. Mark Micale, "Hysteria Male/Hysteria Female: Reflections on Comparative Gender Construction in Nineteenth-Century France and Britain," in *Science and Sensibility: Gender and Scientific Enquiry, 1780–1945,* ed. Maria Benjamin (Cambridge: Blackwell, 1991), 206.
13. Although the uterine theory of hysteria had been abandoned by most doctors by the second half of the century, it prevailed in the popular imagination. See ibid., 205.
14. The English term for *fêlure,* "crack," encompasses a similar semantic field: it can refer to female genitals and to mental illness.
15. Janet Beizer describes the *fêlure* as being for Zola "not only the figure of female sexuality, but the central, driving image—a figure at once inspirational and demonic—of his writing." Beizer, "The Body in Question: Anatomy, Textuality and Fetishism in Zola," *L'Esprit créateur* 1 (Spring 1989): 57. In *Ventriloquized Bodies* she shows how Zola inscribes this figure on his female characters (169–204). She writes: "The leak in Clotilde's head—that is, her essential 'gushiness'—is part of that insistent, if suppressed, female-associated paradigm of myth, fantasy, and extravagance, which, throughout the cycle, sporadically bursts, drips, flows, or spurts through its containing (realist) cover" (173). Patricia Carles and Béatrice Desgranges also analyze the relationship between the *fêlure* and the female sex, particularly with respect to hysteria. Like Beizer, they conclude: "Faire parler le sexe des femmes, le rendre transparent à l'analyse, tel pourrait bien être le projet secret d'Emile Zola" (Make the woman's sex speak, make it transparent to analysis, such could be Zola's secret project"). Carles and Desgranges, "Emile Zola ou Le cauchemar de l'hystérie et les rêveries de l'utérus," *Les Cahiers naturalistes* 41, no. 69 (1995): 13–32.
16. Zola, "Le Roman expérimental," 1188.
17. Emile Zola, *Le Docteur Pascal* (1893; reprint, Paris: Gallimard, 1993), 147.
18. Marc Angenot relates the prevalence of the theme of prostitution to the gendering of

fin-de-siècle discourse: "La thématique prostitutionnelle confirme accessoirement que la littérature est et doit demeurer une activité essentiellement masculine—auteurs et public" (The theme of prostitution confirms secondarily that literature is and must remain an essentially masculine activity—for authors and readers). Angenot, *Le Cru et le faisandé: Sexe, discours social et littérature à la Belle Époque* (Brussels: Editions Labor, 1986) 192.

19. The boundaries in flux here include Nana's nudity itself. Zola describes her initially as "completely naked" (*toute nue*) but then offers that "une simple gaze l'enveloppait" (a simple gauze enveloped her") (53). He is noticeably ambiguous; she is both dressed and undressed, perhaps because her body and sexuality are unbound by the clothes she wears, permeating the gauzy covering, gushing forward into the audience.
20. The construction in French further permits the distillation of the men into one victim; in the possessive form, it is necessary to refer to only a single mouth, as in "la bouche irritée."
21. Nana's ability to remain untouched by her own forces of destruction is linked to her enigmatic double nature as both *bonne fille* and *femme fatale,* a dichotomy analyzed extensively in Bernheimer, *Figures of Ill Repute,* 200–233.
22. It is unclear to what extent Zola was inspired by Manet's painting entitled *Nana,* from 1877, which depicts a voluptuous Nana before a mirror, nor to what extent Manet was inspired by *L'Assommoir,* where Zola first introduces the character of Nana. Zola and Manet were friends, and Manet admits in a letter to having read the novel. Manet's painting captures Nana's position with respect to masculine desire and the male gaze: her suitor is cut off by the picture's frame, and she meets the eye of the viewer. As when she was on stage, she reverses the mechanics of looking by transforming the spectator into the spectacle. See Emile Zola, *Nana,* ed. Henri Mitterand, vol. 2 of *Les Rougon-Macquart,* ed. Armand Lanoux and Henri Mitterand (Paris: Pléaide, 1961), 1666–67.
23. This scene is foreshadowed earlier in the novel, when Muffat accompanies the prince backstage, into the suffocating coulisses where Nana's dressing room is. Here Muffat watches Nana apply her makeup: "Lorsqu'elle ferma l'oeil droit et qu'elle passa le pinceau, il comprit qu'il lui appartenait" (Once she closed her right eye and passed the brush over it, he understood that she possessed him) (157). His desire for her is a product of her self-involvement, another reflection of her own reflection.
24. Beizer sees this comment as an analogy for the reading strategies of the novel, pointing out a complex relationship between sexuality and textuality (*Ventriloquized Bodies,* 174–87).
25. Evelyne Ender, *Sexing the Mind: Nineteenth-Century Fictions of Hysteria* (Ithaca: Cornell University Press, 1995), 48.
26. Matlock eloquently compares nineteenth-century plots surrounding hysteria and those surrounding prostitution in *Scenes of Seduction.*
27. Several critics have pointed out that despite Nana's repeated acts of undressing, she always remained veiled, covered by hair or shadows or gauzy fabrics. For Peter Brooks, these barriers represent "the woman's sex as unknowable and unrepresentable," a final psychological line that Zola cannot cross but which fuels his narrative nonetheless. According to Brooks, "what is finally unrepresentable and unknowable is also the source of stories, the origin of the narrative dynamic." Brooks, *Body Work: Objects of Desire*

in Modern Narrative (Cambridge: Harvard University Press, 1993), 141, 159. Bernheimer criticizes Brooks's reading of Nana for reproducing the patriarchal mindset of the text he analyzes. See Bernheimer, "Response to Peter Brooks," *Critical Inquiry* 17 (Summer 1991): 868–74; and Peter Brooks, "Response to Charlie Bernheimer" in the same edition. In "Uncovering Nana: The Courtesan's New Clothes," *L'Esprit créateur* 25 (Summer 1985): 55, Janet Beizer describes Nana's veiled nudity as a metaphor for narrative's capacity to tell and show all.

28. Quoted in Bernheimer, *Figures of Ill Repute,* 230. Bernheimer argues that despite Zola's research into the world of the courtesan, he did not stray from his initial desire to portray Nana as "bonne fille." My reading, in contrast, reveals how the intelligence of the courtesan unwittingly surfaces in the novel.
29. In *La Cousine Bette,* Balzac leaves open this possibility for his female characters, as Matlock observes: "While the majority of the male characters in this novel, including Crevel, seem stumped by the language of women's performances, the novel invests women with knowledge of their own physiology" (*Scenes of Seduction,* 172). Perhaps this also explains why both Bette and Valérie, the two female protagonists, must be disease-ridden as the text closes.
30. Although Zola originally requested from his friend Henry Céard "an exact description, scientific and detailed, of the mortuary mask of a woman who died of smallpox," he settled for P. Toussaint Barthélemy's *Recherches sur la variole* as a reference for his own description (Bernheimer, *Figures of Ill Repute,* 214).
31. Bernheimer, *Figures of Ill Repute,* 224.
32. Vernon Rosario describes this dynamic in nineteenth-century fiction and medicine in *The Erotic Imagination: French Histories of Perversity* (New York: Oxford University Press, 1997), 163.
33. Alexandre Mayer, *Des rapports conjugaux considérés sous le triple point de vue de la population, de la santé, et de la morale publique* (1857; reprint, Paris: J.-B. Baillière et fils, 1874), 20
34. Barbey d'Aurevilly, *Les Bas-bleus* (Paris: Société Générale de librairie catholique, 1878), 342.
35. Karen Offen's fascinating article, "Depopulation, Nationalism, and Feminism in Fin-de-Siècle France," *American Historical Review* 89, no. 3 (1984): 648–76, examines women's roles in the fin-de-siècle population crisis and demonstrates the clash between feminism and nationalism in fin-de-siècle politics.
36. Mayer, *Des rapports conjugaux,* XII. There are many other examples of popular medical advice manuals that vehemently discouraged "l'onanisme conjugal" while emphasizing the centrality of procreation to a healthy marriage. See Gustave Droz, *Monsieur, madame et bébé,* 28th ed. (1848; reprint, Paris: J. Hetzel, 1868); Auguste Debay, *Hygiène et philosophie du mariage. Histoire naturelle et médicale de l'homme et de la femme mariés dans ses plus curieux details,* 78th ed. (1848; reprint, Paris: E. Dentu, 1874).
37. Alexandre Parent-Duchatelet was responsible for the first study of prostitution in France in the 1830s and thus provided the prostitute with a large part of her popular identity.
38. Jules Bertaut, *La Littérature féminine d'aujourd'hui* (Paris: Librairie des Annales Politiques et Littéraires, 1909), 307.
39. Ibid.

40. Barbey, *Les Bas-bleus,* xxii. Alain Corbin describes the representation of the prostitute's odor as a primary aspect of her association with morbidity, which he argues is one of the five images that inspire the need for her regulation. See his "Commercial Sexuality in Nineteenth-Century France: A System of Images and Regulations" in *The Making of the Modern Body,* ed. Catherine Gallagher and Thomas Laqueur, 209–19 (Berkeley and Los Angeles: University of California Press, 1987).

CHAPTER 2

1. The passage regarding the publication of "the story of a prostitute" is discussed in detail in Chapter 1. It has also been analyzed by Janet Beizer in "Uncovering Nana: The Courtesan's New Clothes," *L'Esprit créateur* 25 (Summer 1985): 55, and *Ventriloquized Bodies: Narratives of Hysteria in Nineteenth-Century France* (Ithaca: Cornell University Press, 1994), 174–87.
2. A second, revised version of *Une Femme m'apparut* that focuses more on Vivien's relationship with Natalie Clifford Barney appeared a year later, in 1905, but was not sent out to critics for review.
3. In the *Dictionnaire de l'Académie Française* of 1835, *fille publique* is included in the entry for *fille* along with *fille de joie* as a one of the "noms que l'on donne aux prostituées" (names given to prostitutes). A search of the ARTFL database (http://humanities.uchicago.edu/orgs/ARTFL/) shows that the expression *fille publique* is used in over fifty nineteenth-century French novels, including those of Balzac and George Sand.
4. This slippage was voiced most dramatically earlier in the century in Pierre-Joseph Proudhon's infamous declaration that women were fit to be either "housewives or harlots" (*courtisanes ou ménagères*).
5. Mary Louise Roberts, *Disruptive Acts: The New Woman in Fin-de-siècle France* (Chicago: University of Chicago Press, 2002), 8–15.
6. Vanessa Schwartz, *Spectacular Realities: Early Mass Culture in* Fin-de-Siècle *Paris* (Berkeley and Los Angeles: University of California Press, 1998), 16.
7. Jean Chalon, *Portrait of a Seductress: The World of Natalie Barney,* trans. Carol Barko (New York: Crown, 1979), 19–20.
8. Judith Thurman, *Secrets of the Flesh: A Life of Colette* (New York: Alfred A. Knopf, 1999), 137, 139.
9. Barney also inspired characters in Djuna Barnes's *Ladies Almanack* (1928), Lucie Delarue-Mardrus's *L'Ange et les pervers* (1930), and Radclyffe Hall's *Well of Loneliness* (1928). For more biographical information on Barney, see Chalon, *Portrait of a Seductress;* Natalie Clifford Barney, *Souvenirs indiscrets* (Paris: Flammarion, 1960); Karla Jay, *The Amazon and the Page: Natalie Clifford Barney and Renée Vivien* (Bloomington: Indiana University Press, 1988); see also the biographical references for Pougy, Vivien, and Colette, all of which contain discussions of Barney's life.
10. For a history of lesbianism in France, see Marie-Jo Bonnet, *Un Choix sans equivoque: Recherches historiques sur les relations amoureuses entre les femmes, XVIe–XXe siècle* (Paris: Denoël, 1981). Shari Benstock addresses the lesbian subculture of the Belle Epoque from the perspective of modernism in *Women of the Left Bank: Paris 1900–1940* (Austin: University of Texas Press, 1986).

11. Thurman, *Secrets of the Flesh,* 164, 196.
12. Jacob Stockinger argues that "lesbianism constitutes a significant and integral strand of Colette's work." He writes: "It was Colette who, even more than such secondary writers as Renée Vivien and Natalie Clifford Barney, successfully wrested the lesbian tradition from male authors, gave it the female perspective it had lacked for so long, and pointed the way to the modern lesbian tradition as marked out by the works of Simone de Beauvoir, Christiane Rochefort, Violette Leduc, and Monique Wittig." Stockinger, "The Test of Love and Nature: Colette and Lesbians," in *Colette, the Woman, the Writer,* ed. Erica Mendelson Eisinger and Mari Ward McCarty (University Park: Pennsylvania State University Press, 1981), 76.
13. Jean-Pierre Jacques, in his *Malheurs de Sapho* (Paris: Grasset, 1981), argues that the fin-de-siècle literary lesbian is a pure product of the male imagination. Some examples of nineteenth-century lesbianism may be found in Paquita in Balzac's *Fille aux yeux d'or,* Nana's lesbian relationship with Satin, Catulle-Mendès's *Méphistophéla,* and Baudelaire's *Fleurs du mal.* The publication of Alphonse Daudet's *Sapho, moeurs parisiennes* in the 1880s resulted in a fascination with the topic, inspiring several other novels, including Gabriel Faure's *La Dernière journée de Sapphô* (1901), Jean Richepin's *Sapphô* (1884), Maurice Morel's *Sapho de Lesbos* (1902), Paul Bourget's *Un Crime d'amour* (1886), Charles Vimaire's *Paris impur* (1889), and Henri d'Argis's *Gomorrhe* (1889). Lesbianism, known as *saphisme* or *tribadisme,* was also a subject of fascination in medical literature, although it was considered to exist far less frequently than male homosexuality. Lucienne Frappier Mazur touches on the counter role in which women writers represent lesbians in "Marginal Canons: Rewriting the Erotic," *Yale French Studies* 75 (1988): 112–28. She notes that four nineteenth-century novels—*Julie ou j'ai sauvé ma rose* (1807), *Le Roman de Violette* (1883), *Idylle saphique* (1901), and *Monsieur Vénus* (1884)—"establish a correlation between woman's will to power, her interest in lesbianism, and her avoidance of penetration, considered a form of subjection" (121).
14. Philippe Lejeune's inclusive definition of "roman autobiographique" thus applies: "J'appellerai ainsi tous les textes de fiction dans lesquels le lecteur peut avoir des raisons de soupçonner, à partir des ressemblances qu'il croit deviner, qu'il y a identité de l'auteur et du *personnage,* alors que l'auteur, lui, a choisi de nier cette identité, ou du moins de ne pas l'affirmer. Ainsi défini, le roman autobiographique englobe aussi bien des récits personnels (identité du narrateur et du personnage) que des récits "impersonnels" (personnages désignés à la troisième personne); il se définit au niveau de son contenu" (I will thus label all fictional texts in which the reader has reason to suspect, based on perceived resemblances, that the author and the character are one and the same, even though the author has chosen to deny this identity, or at least not to affirm it. Thus defined, the autobiographical novel includes personal narratives [identification between narrator and protagonist] as well as impersonal [third-person] narratives, defined by content"). Lejeune, *Le Pacte autobiographique* (Paris: Editions de Seuil, 1975), 25. One might, alternatively, consider these texts as "autofiction," as Serge Doubrovsky has defined this genre with respect to his own novel *Fils,* in which he describes his own life: "ni autobiographie ni roman, . . . au sens strict, il fonctionne dans l'entre-deux, en un renvoi incessant" (neither autobiography or novel . . . in the strict sense, it functions between the two, in a perpetual relay"). Doubrovsky, *Autobiographiques: De Corneille à Sartre* (Paris: Presses Universitaires de France, 1988), 70.

15. Jean Larnac, *Histoire de la littérature féminine en France,* 5th ed. (Paris: Editions Kra, 1929), 253–54. Larnac's comment is noted by Lynne Huffer in her study of Colette, where she also offers a useful summary of feminist critics' views on female autobiography. Huffer, *Another Colette: The Question of Gendered Writing* (Ann Arbor: University of Michigan Press, 1992), 4. Nancy K. Miller also mentions the comment in *Subject to Change: Reading Feminist Writing* (New York: Columbia University Press, 1988), 60. According to Mary Jacobus, this mode of reading women's writing, of which female critics have also been guilty, "posit[s] the woman author as origin and her life as primary locus of meaning." Jacobus, *Reading Woman: Essays in Feminist Criticism* (New York: Columbia University Press, 1986), 108.
16. Jo Burr Margadant, ed., *The New Biography: Performing Femininity in Nineteenth-Century France* (Berkeley and Los Angeles: University of California Press, 2000), 24. Margadant's book attempts to release its female subjects from being viewed narrowly as "exceptional women" according to conventional master narratives of nineteenth-century history. Instead, these women become "prisms for observing shifts in the gendering of their worlds" (25), such that those master narratives can be altered.
17. Jean Chalon, *Liane de Pougy: Courtisane, princesse, et sainte* (Paris: Flammarion, 1994), 110.
18. In *Mes cahiers bleus* (Paris: Plon, 1977), Pougy writes of her brutal indoctrination into marriage and her painful pregnancy. In Chalon's biography, he explains that when her husband found her having an affair, he shot her and then begged forgiveness. Pougy divorced him instead, leaving him with her two-year-old son in 1889.
19. Chalon claims that out of an estimated eighty thousand prostitutes, only about forty were courtesans catering to the upper echelons of Parisian society, able to hand pick their male suitors. Unlike regular prostitutes, courtesans made a living based on their individual identity. They were particularly threatening to the *haute bourgeoisie* because of their ability to mingle with the upper classes without necessarily being distinguishable. To summarize, while all courtesans were prostitutes, selling their bodies for financial gain, not all prostitutes were courtesans. See Hollis Clayson, *Painted Love: Prostitution in the French Art of the Impressionist Era* (New Haven: Yale University Press, 1991), 59–60. T. J. Clark distinguishes the courtesan from the prostitute in terms of her mythology, making her the "concentrated form of Woman, of Desire, of Modernity." Clark, *The Painting of Modern Life: Paris in the Art of Manet and His Followers* (Princeton: Princeton University Press, 1984), 110.
20. In 1889, the *Gil Blas* had a circulation of thirty to forty thousand. It was a literary journal filled with gossip and often included texts whose content was sexual or salacious. Among the writers who were published in this periodical were Maupassant, Catulle Mendès, Camille Lemonnier, Paul Bourget, and Octave Mirbeau. Marc Angenot, *Le Cru et le faisandé: Sexe, discours social et littérature à la Belle Epoque* (Brussels: Editions Labor, 1986), 87–88.
21. Because of the close connection between Lorrain and Pougy, many believed he had written her novels. This belief speaks both to assumptions about the *fille publique* and to her literary talent.
22. Virginie Sanders, "*Vertigineusement, j'allais vers les étoiles . . .": La poésie de Renée Vivien (1877–1909)* (Atlanta: Rodopi, 1991), 124.

23. Melanie Hawthorne outlines the way the novel corresponded to Pougy's real-life romantic history in "The Seduction of Terror: Annhine's Annihilation in Liane de Pougy's *Idylle saphique*," in *Articulations of Difference: Gender Studies and Writing in French*, ed. Dominique Fisher and Lawrence Schehr (Stanford: Stanford University Press, 1997), 136.
24. Sanders, *"Vertigineusement,"* 124.
25. The commentator adds: "A une époque de nette évolution vers le féminisme, et devant le succès du nouveau livre de Liane de Pougy, les détracteurs cesseront sans doute de refuser le don d'écrire à une femme qui peut l'avoir plus que tout autre, de par sa sensibilité native" (In a period of clear movement towards feminism, and in light of the success of Liane de Pougy's new book, detractors will undoubtedly cease to ignore the writing talent of a woman who, by dint of her innate sensitivity, may have more of it than anyone else). Quoted by Jean Chalon, in his preface to *Idylle saphique*, by Liane de Pougy (Paris: J-C Lattès, 1979), 7.
26. Lucienne Frappier-Mazur describes the novel as bearing "the mark of Decadent aesthetics," while at the same time offering "a counterpart to the fear and dislike of 'devouring femininity' expressed by male Decadents." Frappier-Mazur, "Marginal Canons: Rewriting the Erotic," *Yale French Studies* 75 (1988): 121. In the only recent critical article devoted to Pougy's novel, Hawthorne analyzes the logic of death subtending the text. Applying psychoanalytic terms, she argues that Pougy's ending is in fact consistent with an autobiographical reading because the novel is governed by a "logic of lack," reflecting the protagonist's state of castration and domination that ultimately determines her death and leads the author to this ending ("Seduction of Terror," 136–54).
27. Barney was engaged to a man named Will, heir to a Pittsburgh fortune. He originally agreed to her relationships with women but ultimately broke off their engagement, after which Natalie attempted unsuccessfully to procure her dowry for herself. Chalon, *Portrait of a Seductress*, 45.
28. Valtesse de la Bigne was instrumental in Pougy's rise to stardom and was a mother figure for her. See Chalon, *Liane de Pougy*, 39–40.
29. Liane de Pougy, *Idylle saphique* (1901; reprint, Paris: J-C Lattès, 1979), 6; hereafter cited in text.
30. As Nhine's double at the opening of the novel, Tesse meets her friend's searching gaze with what Sandra Gilbert and Susan Gubar have called, with respect to English literature, "the mirror of patriarchally imposed femininity." Gilbert and Gubar describe the fundamental obstacle to female literary expression in terms of the "mirror of the male-inscribed literary text." They argue that ideas of femininity have been so thoroughly constructed through male literary traditions that it is virtually impossible for women to see themselves outside of these culturally embedded tropes and images. Thus, when the woman writer attempts to reflect on herself in writing, "the essential process of self-definition is complicated by all those patriarchal definitions that intervene between herself and herself." Gilbert and Gubar, *The Madwoman in the Attic: The Woman Writer and the Nineteenth-Century Literary Imagination* (New Haven: Yale University Press, 1979), 15, 17.
31. Pougy's novel can also be compared to George Sand's 1833 *Lélia*, which Evelyne Ender describes as "the rupture between physical experience and metaphysical aspira-

tions." Ender, " 'Une femme qui rêve n'est pas tout à fait une femme': Lélia en rupture d'identité," *Nineteenth-Century French Studies* 3–4 (Spring–Summer 2001): 227.

32. Melanie Hawthorne emphasizes the literal translation of "vous n'avez rien," and reads this diagnosis as a statement of Nhine's lack as cause of her illness: "Rather than reading these words to mean 'there's nothing wrong with you,' we might take them to mean that there *is* something wrong: Annhine has *nothing* where implicitly there should be *something*" ("Seduction of Terror," 138). Hysteria is reread as castration, the problem of phallic lack, and it is Nhine's, and then Pougy's, inability to see beyond this lack that leads ultimately to the protagonist's death in Hawthorne's reading: "Perhaps finally it is not so much phallic lack as lack of imagination that proves fatal for Annhine" (154). I believe, however, that this reading obscures the nature of Nhine's internal conflict: Nhine's problem is not lack of imagination but rather its excess.
33. Jean-Louis Brachet, *Traité de l'hystérie (Paris: J.-B. Baillière*, 1847), 63.
34. For extensive analyses of this trope and its examples, see Emily Apter, *Feminizing the Fetish: Psychoanalysis and Narrative Obsession in Turn-of-the-Century France* (Ithaca: Cornell University Press, 1991); Dorothy Kelly, *Telling Glances: Voyeurism in the French Novel* (New Brunswick: Rutgers University Press, 1992).
35. Apter, *Feminizing the Fetish*, 47.
36. "What made Bernhardt's performance of Hamlet subversive was not the act itself but how it was enjoyed by women trying to dream other dreams of being female and needing models to do so." Roberts, *Disruptive Acts,* 15.
37. Chalon notes that in Barney's original version their real names are used: Natty and Liane. See his preface to *Idylle saphique,* 9–10.
38. This theme is present in Pougy's other two novels, *L'Insaisissable* from 1898 and *Myrhille* from 1899. In both autobiographical texts, the protagonists are courtesans who express similar self-loathing. In *Myrhille* the courtesan commits suicide.
39. For a feminist investigation of Freud's notion of epistemophilia, see Toril Moi, "Patriarchal Thought and the Drive for Knowledge," in *New Directions in Psychoanalysis and Feminism,* ed. Teresa Brennan, 189–205 (New York: Routledge, 1989). Peter Brooks explores the relationship between epistemophilia and scopophilia in *Body Work: Objects of Desire in Modern Narrative* (Cambridge: Harvard University Press, 1993), 96–106.
40. I am grateful to one of my anonymous readers at Vanderbilt University Press for the suggestion of this neologism.
41. Teresa De Lauretis, *The Practice of Love: Lesbian Sexuality and Perverse Desire* (Bloomington: Indiana University Press, 1994), 251.
42. Sue-Ellen Case, "Toward a Butch-Femme Aesthetic," in *Making a Spectacle: Feminist Essays on Contemporary Theatre,* ed. Lynda Hart (Ann Arbor: University of Michigan Press, 1989), 283.
43. Miller, *Subject to Change*, 186, 187.
44. Charles Bernheimer examines the use of the word *fange* in both Balzac and Sue: "The word *fange* covers the transition from the physical meaning of 'mud, slime, mire, filth' to the figurative/spiritual one of 'vice, degradation.' " Bernheimer, *Figures of Ill Repute: Representing Prostitution in Nineteenth-Century France* (Cambridge: Harvard University Press, 1989), 48. Pougy's use of this word re-inscribes a romantic theme, where the

courtesan's degradation was primarily figurative, into a naturalist description, where her body is in fact covered in filth.

45. Flossie has manipulated her life to fit the constraints of (or benefit from the advantages of?) the society in which she lives: "Il faut bien subir la loi ordinaire et naturelle de la vie, j'ai un fiancé, Nhine, ce qui me donne cette liberté relative dont je jouis à l'heure présente. . . . Un fiancé, vois-tu, m'est aussi nécessaire que de boire et de manger et de dormir, *that's all!*" (One does have to follow the ordinary, natural laws of life. I have a fiancé, Nhine, which gives me the relative freedom that I'm enjoying right now. . . . A fiancé, you see, is as necessary to me as eating and drinking, *that's all!*) (44). In an earlier episode, Will attempts to set Nhine up, out of jealousy. He lures her to his home to reveal her as nothing more than "une bonne putain" (a good whore) (123). But instead of being angered at Nhine, Flossie is horrified by Will's behavior in orchestrating the set-up.
46. In his biography Chalon writes: "Liane semble avoir pris goût à ce genre de sport. Elle a raté un deuxième suicide pour un baron allemand, puis un troisième" (Liane seemed to have developed a taste for this kind of sport. She failed a second suicide attempt for a German Baron, and then a third) (*Liane de Pougy,* 125).
47. Pougy's ambivalence is apparent in a passage written after her embrace of Catholicism. In the entry dated September 21, 1933, she writes: "I do not want to expand here on lesbianism, having already said all that I think about it in that same *Idylle saphique*—all and more. Yes, having been witness to some distressing sights, some sinister results of the practice of that vice, I wanted to drive home my opinion rather fiercely. And anyway it was necessary to do so in those days, in order to find a publisher who would consent to bring out a book on the subject." Pougy, *My Blue Notebooks,* trans. Diana Athill (New York: Harper and Row, 1979), 253.
48. Upon her husband's death, Pougy turned to religion and joined a Dominican order until her death five years later. See R. P. Rzewuski's preface to ibid., 9–21.
49. Gayle Rubin writes, for example: "Renée Vivien and Natalie Barney were unique in that they achieved and articulated a distinctively lesbian self-awareness. Their writings show that they understood who they were and what they were up against." Rubin, Preface to *A Woman Appeared to Me,* by Renée Vivien, trans. Jeannette H. Foster (Tallahassee: Naiad, 1976), vii.
50. Elaine Marks, " 'Sappho 1900': Imaginary Renée Vivien's and the Rear of the Belle Epoque," in *Displacements: Women, Tradition, Literatures in French,* ed. Joan DeJean and Nancy K. Miller, 211–27 (Baltimore: Johns Hopkins University Press, 1991). Marks encourages the reading of Vivien in the context of Nietzsche and Freud.
51. Vivien's biography can be found in Jay, *Amazon and the Page,* and Jean-Paul Goujon, *Tes blessures sont plus douces que leurs caresses: Vie de Renée Vivien* (Paris: Régine Deforges, 1986). In addition, Sanders offers extensive details about Vivien's literary career in her excellent, comprehensive study, *"Vertigineusement, j'allais vers les é toiles . . ."*
52. Vivien's *Cendres et poussières* was reviewed in *La Revue blanche* by Lucie Delarue-Mardrus, whose own first collection had also appeared in 1901, and by Stuart Merrill in *La Plume.* See Sanders, *"Vertigineusement,"* 118.
53. Sanders, *"Vertigineusement,"*120.

54. Pierre D'Hugues's comment in *La Muse française* of 1927 is in this vein: "Evidemment, l'inspiration de Renée Vivien procède d'émotions factices ou puériles, et ses plus beaux vers rendent parfois un son de mauvais aloi. Mais, dans la torture de l'amour, elle a trouvé des cris tels que, seuls, quelques poètes en ont su pousser" (Evidently, Renée Vivien's inspiration proceeds from puerile, feigned emotions, and her most beautiful verse sometimes sounds fake. But, amidst the torture of love, she has put forth cries that only a few poets have known how to produce). Quoted in Paul Lorenz, *Sapho 1900 Renée Vivien* (Paris: Julliard, 1977), 173.
55. "Une littérature dont seuls peuvent se réjouir les hystériques et les névrosés!" (a literature that only hysterics and neurotics can delight in!). Quoted in Goujon, *Tes blessures,* 275. Goujon counts 123 articles on Vivien between 1901 and 1914, most having appeared between 1903 and 1906. The prestigious *Mercure de France* contributed greatly to Vivien's reputation, having published a dozen articles on her.
56. See Sanders, *"Vertigineusement,"* 134–53.
57. Ibid., 113, 147; Barney, *Souvenirs indiscrets,* 91.
58. Thus wrote Jean de Bonnefon in *La Corbeille de roses, ou les dames de lettres* (1909), 136: "Les livres de Mlle Renée Vivien sont assez rares. Elle ne les vend pas au public. Elle permet aux profanes de les entrevoir; puis elle les retire. Et plus jamais ils ne reparaissent" (Mademoiselle Renée Vivien's books are rather rare. She does not sell them to the public. She permits profane people to catch a glimpse of them; then she withdraws them. And they never reappear).
59. Thurman, *Secrets of the Flesh,* 214; Sanders, *"Vertigineusement,"* 150; Jay, *Amazon and the Page,* 19. Six months after her death, Vivien's editor Edward Sansot published some of her poetry in the collection *Dans un coin de violettes* (Paris: E. Sansot, 1910). In the introduction, Sansot describes Vivien's brooding letters to him, begging that he tell her his true opinion of her verse. "J'ai tellement peur du ridicule" (I'm so afraid of ridicule), she writes (8). He hesitates to publish these poems as finished products, knowing how much she tended to edit and revise each one. The preface to this edition was written by Paul Flat, who, in addition to lauding Vivien as one of the greatest poets of the era, describes the press's silence around her death and the rumors of her suicide through starvation.
60. Quoted in Goujon, *Tes blessures,* 275, unfortunately without further reference: "pourquoi ces qualités [d'écrivain] servent-elles exclusivement au développement de thèses qui relèvent plus de la pathologie que de la littérature?" (why are these [literary] qualities used exclusively to develop ideas that stem more from pathology than literature?).
61. Bonnefon, *La Corbeille de roses,* 137.
62. As proof of Vivien's primary interest in a female audience, Jay demonstrates how she repeatedly reworked one of Sappho's gender-neutral poems to future admirers so that she would be in the role of Sappho "to generations of young women yet unborn, in a kind of unbroken line of female succession" (*Amazon and the Page,* 37). In another context Jay writes: "Both [Barney and Vivien] sought to reclaim for women the whole of Western literary tradition from Sappho to the Symbolists" (ibid., 92). At the same time, Vivien had help with her writing from several male advisers, including Charles-Brun, Eugène Ledrain, and her editor Sansot. See Lorenz, *Sapho 1900,* 76.
63. Jay explains: "Like other Vivien heroines, she is a virgin, untouched and untouchable,

but her sexlessness makes her no longer vulnerable to men's lust." *The Amazon and the Page,* 103

64. Renée Vivien, *Une Femme m'apparut* (1904; reprint, Paris: Régine Deforges, 1977), 99, 100; hereafter cited in text.
65. Sanders, *"Vertigineusement,"* 139–40.
66. Joan DeJean, in "Lafayette's Ellipses: The Privileges of Anonymity," *PMLA,* October 1984, 884–901, reads *La Princesse de Clèves* in terms of the tensions of public identity and female authorship and "the erasure of the woman author's authority once her text passes into the public domain." DeJean argues that Lafayette "managed to turn the absence of signature into a distinctive mark, laying claim to her fictional territory and indicating her identity as a woman writer" (887).
67. Natalie Barney took the salon to a whole new level when she began having gatherings a few years later, bringing together celebrated writers and artists of both sexes. Benstock writes: "Through her salon Barney wielded considerable power among Left Bank writers, power often employed in the service of her commitment to feminist ideals, using the salon to introduce women writers and their work to each other and to the larger public" (*Women of the Left Bank,* 9).
68. Years later, André Billy would write: "Ses vers ne rayonneront jamais de façon très étendue, leur inspiration étant frappée d'une tare d''immoralité' qui leur interdit l'audience du public moyen, mais à l'intérieur d'un cercle étroit de lettrés épris de la poésie pour elle-même, on les croit destinés à se situer très haut" (Her verse would never radiate extensively, its inspiration tainted with an "immorality" that prohibited a mainstream audience, but within a restricted circle of writers appreciative of poetry for its own sake, her poetry was believed to be destined for greatness). Billy, *L'Epoque 1900* (Paris: Editions Jules Taillandy, 1951), 227.
69. Quoted in Sanders, *"Vertigineusement,"* 147.
70. Dagmar is probably based on Olive Custance, also known as Opale, an American poet who wanted to start a lesbian colony of women poets like that of Sappho, and who had an affair with Barney. See Chalon, *Portrait of a Seductress,* 63.
71. Joan DeJean, *Fictions of Sappho, 1546–1937* (Chicago: University of Chicago Press, 1989), 283–84.
72. Unlike for the other authors in this study, biographical information about Colette abounds. Two recent examples are Thurman, *Secrets of the Flesh,* and Claude Francis and Fernande Gontier, *Creating Colette,* vol. 1, *From Ingenue to Libertine, 1873–1913* (South Royalton: Steerforth Press, 1998). They offer great detail about Colette's life during the period of writing and publishing *La Vagabonde* and chronicle the complex dissolution of Colette and Willy's relationship, which happened over several years.
73. *La Vagabonde* received three out of ten votes and lost out to Louis Pergaud for *De Goupil à Margot, histoire des bêtes.* Sylvie Massé offers a history of *La Vagabonde*'s critical reception in *Les Stratégies de discours et l'écriture des femmes au tournant du siècle: L'Expression implicite d'une parole hétérogène* (Quebec: Groupe de recherche multidisciplinaire féministe, Université Laval, 1993). She notes that the January 7, 1911, edition of *Le Temps* included a large column advertising positive reviews of *La Vagabonde* from *L'Excelsior, Comeodia,* and *Le Journal* (35).
74. See Thurman, *Secrets of the Flesh,* 166; Francis and Gontier, *Creating Colette,* 1:295.

75. On the ramifications of reading Colette as autobiography, see Miller, "Writing Fictions: Women's Autobiography in France" in *Subject to Change,* 47–64; Huffer, *Another Colette,* 3–6.
76. Colette, *La Vagabonde* (Paris: Librairie Générale Française, 1990), 27; hereafter cited in text.
77. Thurman describes Colette's pages about Taillandy as an act of parricide, akin to Kafka's letter to his father: "inspired by abandonment, artful and subversive but passionately sincere, thrilling to read in their virtuosity, excruciating in their rawness—and they exalt the tyrant's power even as they denigrate him." Thurman, *Secrets of the Flesh,* 201.
78. Thurman details this episode and its ramifications for all involved. Ibid., 171–74.
79. Laura Mulvey writes: "In their traditional exhibitionist role women are simultaneously looked at and displayed, with their appearance coded for strong visual and erotic impact so that they can be said to connote *to-be-looked-at-ness.*" *Visual Pleasure and Narrative Cinema* (Bloomington: Indiana University Press, 1989), 19.
80. Like Colette, Pougy moved between the worlds of writing and theater. Pougy expresses repeated rivalry with and jealousy of Colette in her *Blue Notebooks.* She believes Colette appeals to her readers' "latent sensuality" (July 14, 1920, 109) and feels vindicated when Henri Bidou writes a scathing review of her writing (August 1, 1920, 112).
81. Vanessa Schwartz, "Cinematic Spectatorship before the Apparatus: The Public Taste for Reality in Fin-de-Siècle Paris," in *Viewing Positions: Ways of Seeing Film,* ed. Linda Williams (New Brunswick, NJ: Rutgers University Press, 1995), 88.
82. Charles Baudelaire, "Le Peintre de la vie moderne," in *Oeuvres complètes,* vol. 2 (Paris: Gallimard, 1976), 692. For an elaboration of Baudelaire's flâneur, see also Walter Benjamin, *Charles Baudelaire: A Lyric Poet in the Era of High Capitalism,* trans. Harry Zohn (London: Verso, 1985).
83. According to Clark, two divergent representations of women existed in nineteenth-century painting: the *fille publique* and the *femme honnête* (*Painting of Modern Life,* 106–11). Anne Friedberg sees the female observer as a new category to define women in public spaces that followed the development of the department store and amusement parks. Friedberg, "The Gender of the Observer: The Flaneuse," in *Window Shopping: Cinema and the Postmodern* (Berkeley and Los Angeles: University of California Press, 1993).
84. There has been some debate about the possibility of female flânerie. Griselda Pollock argues, on one hand, that female flânerie did sometimes occur, despite prevailing prohibitions that made it unwelcome. On men and women's different possibilities of seeing in the modern urban landscape, she writes: "For women, public spaces thus construed were where one risked losing one's virtue, dirtying oneself; going out in public and the idea of disgrace were closely allied. For the man going out in public meant losing oneself in the crowd away from both demands of respectability." Pollock, *Vision and Difference: Femininity, Feminism, and the Histories of Art* (New York: Routledge, 1988), 69. On the other hand, Janet Wolff argues that the flâneuse was made impossible by nineteenth-century sexual divisions. Wolff, "The Invisible Flâneuse: Women and the Literature of Modernity," in *The Problems of Modernity: Adorno and Benjamin,* ed. Andrew Benjamin, 141–56 (London: Routledge, 1989). Anke Gleber rejects the finality of such a statement, as she searches for models of resistance to those divisions that would

help formulate a theory of female flânerie. She does not use the term *flâneuse,* because it has been used by Anne Friedberg and others to describe nineteenth-century female consumers. Rejecting this image of female consumption, she looks for alternate models of female flânerie that offer a resistant gaze and thus "an alternative to woman's status as an image, to override her cultural *to-be-looked-at-ness.*" Gleber, "Women on the Screens and Streets of Modernity: In Search of the Female Flâneuse," in *The Image in Dispute: Art and Cinema in the Age of Photography,* ed. Dudley Andrew (Austin: University of Texas Press, 1997), 79. I am proposing Colette's Renée as such a model.

85. Ross Chambers situates Renée Néré in relationship to other literary flâneurs, recognizing her as a "loiterly" subject on the boundaries of mainstream society. Chambers, *Loiterature* (Lincoln: University of Nebraska Press, 1999), 56–82.
86. This is Schwartz's way of sidestepping the issue of the gender of the flâneur (*Spectacular Realities,* 10).
87. In an article on the history of the cinematic gaze in France, Anne Friedberg argues that with the emergence of the department store, the shop window succeeded the mirror as a site of identity construction (later to be replaced by the cinema screen). Leaving behind the mirror's fixity, the shopper enjoyed "the pleasures of a temporally and spatially fluid subjectivity" that allowed her to escape from her physical body. Friedberg, Les Flâneurs du mal [1]: Cinema and the Postmodern Condition," *PMLA* 106 (May 1991): 420. Without limiting Renée's desires to the consumer role of the flâneuse, we can recognize in this transition the same move that Renée is attempting to make, beyond the imprisoning stability of the mirror to a mobilized identity, free from a physically bound subjectivity.
88. Martha Noel Evans describes *La Vagabonde* as "a text that gives the strange impression of floating in an undefinable zone between personal journal and public writing, between autobiography and fiction, between existence and non-existence." Evans, *Masks of Tradition: Women and the Politics of Writing in Twentieth-Century France* (Ithaca: Cornell University Press, 1987), 39.
89. "Le sujet apparaît alors constitué à la fois comme lecteur et scripteur de sa propre vie" (The subject appears at once as reader and writer of his own life). Paul Ricoeur, *Temps et récit,* 3 vols. (Paris: Seuil, 1983), 3:355–56.
90. Bernheimer notes that "well over a thousand versions of the Judean princess were made in Europe between 1870 and 1920" (*Decadent Subjects,* 104). Bram Dijkstra explains this fascination as follows: "Salome's hunger for the Baptist's head proved to be a mere pretext for men's needs to find the source of all the wrongs they thought were being done to them. Salome, the evil woman, became their favorite scapegoat, became the creature whose doings might explain why the millennium, that glorious world of the mind's transcendence over matter, did not loom as near as their impatient souls desired." Dijkstra, *Idols of Perversity: Fantasies of Feminine Evil in Fin-de-siècle Culture* (New York: Oxford University Press, 1986), 398. See also Charles Bernheimer and Richard Kaye, eds., *The Queen of Decadence: Salome in Modern Culture* (Chicago: University of Chicago Press, 1998); Toni Bentley, *Sisters of Salomé* (New Haven: Yale University Press, 2002).
91. In *Body Work* Brooks argues that Nana's nudity is always veiled. Referring to Muffat's observation of her before the mirror, he writes: "When we reach Nana's sex, we reach

a veil, which seems to be composed of both her pubic hair and the shadow thrown by her limbs. As in the staging of *La Blonde Vénus,* unveiling ultimately encounters a veil, which is here the ultimate veil: the woman's sex as unknowable and unrepresentable" (141). Janet Beizer and Naomi Schor have argued that the veiling of Nana in this scene is a kind of fetishism, denying phallic absence. See Beizer, *Ventriloquized Bodies,* 183; Schor, *Zola's Crowds* (Baltimore: Johns Hopkins University Press, 1978), 101–2.

92. See Bernheimer, *Figures of Ill Repute,* 157–99; Pollock, *Vision and Difference,* 70–79. For Pollock, the music hall is a space of sexual exchange where bourgeois men go to encounter women of another class. By virtue of her affiliation with the music hall, then, Renée becomes a *déclassée.*
93. The potential sexual debasement of Renée's position is further undermined by the economic reality. After her performance, Renée sees Max and his brother. From her perspective, it is the men who are commodified, distinguishable only as "Dufferein-Chautel 1 et 2," eminently substitutable entities. Any erotic satisfaction experienced by the men is matched by Renée's economic satisfaction: "je puis rentrer seule, serrer joyeusement ma grande coupure de cinq cents francs" (I can go home alone, happily squeezing my big five hundred franc bill) (*La Vagabonde,* 55).
94. Joan Hinde Stewart describes Renée as being "as introverted and reflexive as her name herself," adding that " 'Néré' is a nearly perfect reverse mirror image of 'Renée.' " Stewart, "Colette and the Epistolary Novel" in *Colette, the Woman, the Writer,* 44, 52.
95. Evans's description of the woman writer's relationship to language in the context of patriarchal culture's misogynist images of femininity is particularly relevant here: "The very language, indeed the only respected literary language, [women writers] have to rebut these debased and debasing images is itself the principal instrument used to construct and transmit those images. Women writers find themselves, therefore, in the precarious, emotionally damaging, and logically impossible position of having to find a way of expressing themselves by means of the very instrument that codifies their oppression" (*Masks of Tradition,* 15).
96. In her reading of women's autobiographies, Miller describes the authors' discovery of the possibility of writing as "a rebirth: the access through writing to the status of an autonomous subjectivity" (*Subject to Change,* 55).
97. It is worth remembering at this point that travel was crucial to the self-actualization of Nhine through her correspondence with Flossie; interestingly, she also expresses this inclination to escape the strains of the *fille publique* as a desire to *vagabonder.* Travel was essential to both Renée's and San Giovanni's development in *Une Femme m'apparut* as well, perhaps because it was in itself a disruptive act for an unmarried woman, undermining the stationary obligations of woman's traditional domestic role and freeing her to new kinds of experience previously associated uniquely with men.
98. The pull toward epistolarity is an important step in the self-authorization of all three female protagonists. Near the end of Vivien's novel, San Giovanni and Renée engage in a brief epistolary exchange as Renée struggles in her romantic quest. This places them, as Joan Hinde Steward has noted for Colette, in a feminine literary tradition. Like Colette's *Les Vrilles de la vigne,* it also expresses a desire for directness and absence of mediation not permitted in the typical generic framework of a novel. This desire is ex-

pressed most vividly in the final pages of *La Vagabonde,* where the boundaries between letters are elided.

CHAPTER 3

1. Jules Bertaut, *La Littérature féminine d'aujourd'hui* (Paris: Librairie des Annales Politiques et Littéraires, 1909), 302.
2. Jean Ernest-Charles, "Romans féminins: Mme Stanislas Meunier, Brada, Jacques Morian, Ivan Strannik, Rachilde," in *Les Samedis littéraires,* 5 vols. (Paris: Sansot, 1905), 2:12. Similarly, Bertaut describes women's "manque de réflexion, cette précipitation de l'écriture" (lack of reflection, the rashness of their writing) (*La Littérature féminine,* 274). Ernest-Charles started out as a lawyer specializing in literary trials. A Dreyfusard and member of the Ligue des droits de l'homme, he wrote mostly about politics before turning to literary criticism and was particularly concerned about the commercialism of women writers. Gabrielle Houbre provides details about his background and writings in "L'Honneur perdu de Marcelle Tinayre: L'Affaire de la Légion d'honneur ratée (1908)," in *Les Ratées de la littérature,* ed. Jean-Jacques Lefrère, Michèle Pierssens, and Jean-Didier Wagneur (Charente: Du Lérot, 1999), 94–95.
3. Jean Ernest-Charles, "Les 'Bas-bleus' et la littérature féminine," in *Les Samedis littéraires,* 2:234.
4. In "The Politics of Romance: Popular Romantic Fiction at the Fin de Siècle," in *New Perspectives on the Fin de Siècle in Nineteenth- and Twentieth-Century France,* ed. Kay Chadwick and Timothy Unwin (Lewiston, NY: E. Mellen, 2000), Diana Holmes describes the predominance of the romance novel among fin-de-siècle women writers. She defines this genre according to three criteria: "First, a single love relationship forms the principal dynamic of the plot. Second, the female protagonist is central, and narrative techniques construct a special relationship between reader and heroine. Third, the reader is thus offered the vicarious satisfaction of emotional and sensual desires" (125). Holmes argues that many romance novels actually provided a means to debate an oppressive model of sexual difference.
5. Jules Barbey D'Aurevilly, *Les Bas-bleus* (Paris: Société Générale de librairie catholique, 1878), xxi.
6. Cf. Jean-Louis Brachet's argument that women are incapable of literary invention because their imagination "ressemble au miroir qui réfléchit vivement les impressions qu'il reçoit" (resembles a mirror that actively reflects the impressions it receives). Brachet, *Traité de l'hystérie* (Paris: J.-B. Baillière, 1847), 74. The popular medical writer Alexandre Mayer says women must live "par le coeur" (through the heart), using their sentimentality to temper the positivistic outlook of their husbands. Mayer, *Des Rapports conjugaux considérés sous le triple point de vue de la population, de la santé, et de la morale publique* (1857; reprint, Paris: J.-B. Baillière et fils, 1874), 71.
7. The adoption of these discourses did not always prevent women's works from being read as facile romance novels. Even Rachilde's decadent *Monsieur Vénus,* the subject of Chapter 4, is read by Ernest-Charles as a typical women's novel, centered on love, despite what he acknowledges as the author's "bizarreries éclatantes" (striking eccentricities) ("Romans féminins,"13).

8. Dorothy Kelly argues: "The word virile marks Zola's scientific project as masculine. . . . The most elementary quality of the masculine is objectivity, as it opposes feminine subjectivity and sentimentality." Kelly, "Experimenting on Women: Zola's Theory and Practice of the Experimental Novel," in *Spectacles of Realism: Gender, Body, Genre,* ed. Margaret Cohen and Christopher Prendergast (Minneapolis: University of Minnesota Press, 1995), 232. David Baguley describes this general categorization in Zola's thinking: "[Zola] reduces all literature to two contending types: naturalist literature, which is allied with the scientific movement, identified with the future and characterized by a return to nature and reality; Romantic literature, which is idealistic, belonging to the past despite its anachronistic survival in the present and above all marked by rhetoric and convention." Baguley, *Naturalist Fiction: The Entropic Vision* (Cambridge: Cambridge University Press, 1990), 67.
9. Emile Zola, "Lettre à la jeunesse," in *Le Roman expérimental,* ed. Henri Mitterand (Paris: Cercle du livre précieux, 1966), 1206; quoted in Kelly, "Experimenting on Women," 232, and Janet Beizer, *Ventriloquized Bodies: Narratives of Hysteria in Nineteenth-Century France* (Ithaca: Cornell University Press, 1994), 171.
10. Details about Tinayre's family can be found in Alain Quella-Villéger, *Belles et rebelles: Le Roman vrai des Chasteau-Tinayre* (Bordeaux: Aubéron, 2000). In the 1890s, Louise Chasteau published a column called "La Vie féminine" in the bi-weekly publication *Le Journal.* Before becoming a journalist, she was director of an école normale supérieure for female teachers outside of Paris, opened by Jules Ferry to facilitate girls' education (88). No biography of Tinayre exists aside from the brief *Marcelle Tinayre* by Eugène Martin-Mamy (Paris: E. Sansot, 1909), part of the series Les Célébrités d'aujourd'hui. In addition to Quella-Villéger's text, biographical information on Tinayre can be found in Jennifer Waelti-Walters, *Feminist Novelists of the Belle Epoque: Love as a Lifestyle* (Bloomington: Indiana University Press, 1990), 31–53; Stephen Hause and Jennifer Waelti-Walters, eds., *Feminisms of the Belle Epoque* (Lincoln: University of Nebraska Press, 1994), 67; Patricia Ferlin, *Femmes d'encrier* (Paris: Christian de Bartillat, 1995), 145–85; Mélanie E. Collado, *Colette, Lucie Delarue-Mardrus, Marcelle Tinayre: Emancipation et résignation* (Paris: L'Harmattan, 2003), 105–10.
11. Quella-Villéger, *Belles et rebelles,* 114.
12. See Diana Holmes, *Rachilde: Decadence, Gender, and the Woman Writer* (New York: Berg, 2001), 85–86. Rachilde would be less generous with the 1906 *La Rebelle.* There she aligned herself with Tinayre's young daughter, who said in a magazine interview: "C'est très beau de faire des romans, mais avant de les faire, il faut apprendre à les faire et quand on les fait mal on ne gagne jamais autant d'argent que quand on les fait bien" (It's very nice to write novels, but before you do it, you have to learn how to do it, and when you do it badly you don't make as much money as when you do it well). Quoted in Claude Dauphiné, *Rachilde* (Paris: Mercure de France, 1991), 196. I consider Rachilde's relationship to other women writers more closely in Chapter 4.
13. Ferlin, *Femmes d'encrier,* 165.
14. Gabrielle Houbre, "L'Honneur perdu de Marcelle Tinayre," 90. According to Quella-Villéger, *La Maison du péché* made its author rich, bringing in forty-eight hundred francs in three months. By 1939 it had sold 83,000 copies, outpacing the 1906 La Rebelle, which had sold 64,000 copies (*Belles et rebelles,* 213).

15. Houbre, "L'Honneur perdu de Marcelle Tinayre," 90. See James Joyce, *Essais critiques* (Paris: Gallimard, 1966), 143–45.
16. Critics who saw Tinayre as moving beyond traditionally feminine subject matter include Eugène Martin-Mamy (*Marcelle Tinayre*), Paul Flat (*Nos femmes de lettres* [Paris: Perrin, 1909]), and Jean Ernest-Charles ("La Maison du péché" [October 25, 1902], in *Les Samedis littéraires* 1). Ernest-Charles is troubled by the novel's preoccupations with religion and philosophy and by the attention given to the male protagonist at the expense of the female one.
17. Emile Zola, "Le Roman expérimental" (1880), in *Oeuvres complètes*, 15 vols., ed. Henri Mitterand (Paris: Cercle du Livre Précieux, 1968), 12:1196, 1188.
18. Emile Zola, *Le Docteur Pascal* (1893; reprint, Paris: Gallimard, 1993), 147.
19. Zola, "Le Roman expérimental," 1191.
20. Kelly, "Experimenting on Women," 233.
21. For more on the rhetoric of the nineteenth-century sentimental novel, see Margaret Cohen, *The Sentimental Education of the Novel* (Princeton: Princeton University Press, 1999), 26–76.
22. Halina Suwala, *Autour de Zola et du naturalisme* (Paris: Honoré Champion, 1993), 203.
23. Marcelle Tinayre, *La Maison du péché* (Paris: Calmann-Lévy, 1903), 36; hereafter cited in text.
24. Patricia Carles and Béatrice Desgranges demonstrate the way that Zola's representation of hysteria maps onto Christian ideology throughout the Rougon-Macquart. They write: "Sanction naturelle de la faute, l'hystérie médicalise le châtiment divin" (Natural sanction of sin, hysteria medicalizes the divine punishment). Carles and Desgranges, "Emile Zola; ou, Le Cauchemar de l'hystérie et les rêveries de l'utérus," *Les Cahiers naturalistes* 41, no. 69 (1995): 21.
25. These images are discussed in depth in Chapter 1.
26. In the next chapter, I examine a different approach to undermining the power of patriarchal discourse: Rachilde allows her protagonist, Raoule de Vénérande, to be determined by denigrating categories to the extent that they allow her the kinds of freedom to which Tinayre's Georges alludes.
27. Catherine Bordeau has shown that in Zola's naturalism, the milieu has a transformative power over the body. Bordeau, "The Power of the Feminine Milieu in Zola's Nana," *Nineteenth-Century French Studies* 27 (Fall–Winter 1998–99): 96–107.
28. Forgerus's statement strangely echoes Barbey d'Aurevilly's famous conclusion, published in *Le Constitutionnel* in 1884, regarding Huysmans's *A rebours:* "Après un tel livre, il ne reste plus à l'auteur qu'à choisir entre la bouche d'un pistolet ou les pieds de la croix" (After such a book, the author's only choice is between the mouth of a pistol or the foot of the cross). In fact, Augustin shares with Des Esseintes a similar *maladie du siècle,* as he attempts to live against nature, or against the grain. An earlier precedent for this *maladie du siècle* is Chateaubriand's representation of Saint Augustin in *Les Martyrs.*
29. Tinayre's use of Augustin's body is similar to the violence against Jacques in Rachilde's *Monsieur Vénus* (which I address in Chapter 4), "whereby a male body is appropriated as a textual surface by a female creative force" (Beizer, *Ventriloquized Bodies,* 251).

30. Zola, "Le Roman expérimental," 1189.
31. Ernest Tissot effusively announced in his *Nouvelles princesses de Lettres* (Paris: Fontemoing et Cie, 1911): "Mme Tinayre a écrit un chef-d'oeuvre, un pur chef-d'oeuvre!" (Mrs. Tinayre wrote a masterpiece, a pure masterpiece!) (143).
32. Berthe Delaunay in *Le Gil Blas,* January 10, 1908, quoted in Houbre, "L'Honneur perdu de Marcelle Tinayre," 92.
33. Gabrielle Houbre deftly explains the story of Tinayre's lost honor in "L'Honneur perdu de Marcelle Tinayre," which contains extensive journalistic references from this week-long affair. The details included here are derived from her article.
34. The novelist Jeanne Loiseau, better known by her pseudonym Daniel Lesueur, was the first women author to be awarded the Legion of Honor, in 1900. For the history of women and the Legion of Honor, see Haryett Fontanges, *La Légion d'honneur et les femmes décorés, étude d'histoire et de sociologie féminine* (Paris: Alliance cooperative du livre, 1905). Danièle Déon-Bessière recounts the *cantinières*' history with the Legion of Honor in *Les Femmes et la Légion d'honneur: Depuis sa création* (Paris: Editions de l'officine, 2002), 21–25, 39–40. Gay L. Gullickson describes the controversial status of the *cantinière* during the Commune and the ways that she was caricatured by the press in *Unruly Women of Paris: Images of the Commune* (Ithaca: Cornell University Press, 1996), 89–96.
35. Ernest-Charles was a frequent critic of women's "commercialism." He accused women writers, including Tinayre, of producing numerous works in the interest of financial success while sacrificing quality. See Ernest-Charles, *Samedis littéraires,* 1:376–86, 3:125; Houbre, "L'Honneur perdu de Marcelle Tinayre," 94–95. Jules Bertaut and Paul Flat express similar concerns in their discussions of the numbers of women writers producing novels (Bertaut, *Littérature féminine d'aujourd'hui,* 12–20; Flat, *Nos femmes de lettres,* II).
36. January 18, 1908, quoted in Houbre, "L'Honneur perdu de Marcelle Tinayre," 96.
37. Flat, *Nos femmes de lettres*, 10.
38. Ibid., 151.
39. Remarking on women with literary talent, Mayer comes to a similar conclusion. Of the female creative artist, he writes: "En voyant s'allumer en elle la flamme du génie, elle a senti s'éteindre en même temps le foyer du coeur. Ce n'est plus une femme, puisque c'est un poète, un romancier, ou un peintre" (In seeing the flame of genius light up in her, she felt at the same time the hearth of her heart extinguish. She is no longer a woman, because she is a poet, a novelist, or a painter [with masculine article]) (*Des rapports conjugaux,* 72).
40. Martin-Mamy, *Marcelle Tinayre*, 12.
41. Flat, *Nos femmes de lettres*, 236.
42. Other members of this committee included Lucie Delarue-Mardrus and Anna de Noailles. See Roger Chartier and Henri-Jean Martin, eds., *Histoire de l'édition française*, vol. 4, *Le Livre concurrencé: 1900–1950* (Paris: Fayard, 1983), 249; Géraldi Leroy and Julie Bertrand-Sabiani, *La Vie littéraire à la Belle Époque* (Paris: Presses Universitaires de France, 1998), 268–72. The committee was made up entirely of women and remains so to this day. Its goal was to demonstrate women's ability to judge literature.
43. Yvonne Knibiehler describes the term *fille-mère*, meaning unwed mother, as "an affront

to the very logic of patriarchy" because it acknowledges that women can be mothers in the absence of the father. Knibiehler, "Bodies and Hearts," trans. Arthur Goldhammer, in *A History of Women in the West*, ed. Geneviève Fraisse and Michelle Perrot, vol. 4, *Emerging Feminism from Revolution to World War* (Cambridge: Harvard University Press, Belknap Press, 1984), 350.

44. Vernon Rosario, *The Erotic Imagination: French Histories of Perversity* (New York: Oxford University Press, 1997), 163.
45. For more on Delarue-Mardrus's biography and reception, see Hélène Plat, *Lucie Delarue-Mardrus: Une Femme de lettres des années folles* (Paris: Editions Grasset et Fasquelle, 1994); Pauline Newman-Gordon, "Lucie Delarue-Mardrus" in *French Women Writers: A Bio-Bibliographical Source Book,* ed. Eva Martin Sartori and Dorothy Wynne Zimmerman, 108–20 (New York: Greenwood Press, 1991); Collado, *Colette, Lucie Delarue-Mardrus, Marcelle Tinayre,* 89–98; Myriam Harry, *Mon amie Lucie Delarue-Mardrus* (Paris: Ariane, 1946); Sirieyx de Villers, *Lucie Delarue-Mardrus* (Paris: Editions Sansot, 1923); Lucie Delarue-Mardrus, *Mes mémoires* (Paris: Gallimard, 1938).
46. Collado, *Colette, Lucie Delarue-Mardrus, Marcelle Tinayre,* 91; Harry tells of Delarue-Mardrus's North African exploits in *Mon amie,* 15, 66, 112.
47. Delarue-Mardrus, *Mes mémoires,* 119.
48. Plat, *Lucie Delarue-Mardrus,* 71.
49. Harry recounts Delarue-Mardrus's disappointment and loneliness upon Joseph-Charles's departure. Delarue-Mardrus supposedly exclaimed: "Ecrire dans le vide, terminer un poème et n'avoir personne à qui le lire! Ne plus connaître un seul être au monde qui ait la curiosité de mon travail!" (Writing into the void, finishing a poem with no one to read it to! No longer knowing a soul in the world who is curious about my work!) (*Mon amie,* 78).
50. Plat describes this relationship extensively in *Lucie Delarue-Mardrus,* 99–112.
51. See Virginie Sanders, *"Vertigineusement, j'allais vers les étoiles . . .": La Poésie de Renée Vivien* (Atlanta: Rodopi, 1991), 117–19; Delarue-Mardrus, *Mes mémoires,* 123.
52. Delarue-Mardrus, *Mes mémoires,* 95.
53. The 1929 film *Le Diable au coeur* was based on Delarue-Mardrus's 1922 novel *L'ex-voto; Graine au vent* (1926) was made into a movie in 1943. Plat, *Lucie Delarue-Mardrus,* 313–14.
54. Writing in 1923, Villers described *Marie, fille-mère* as "un chef-d'oeuvre" (a masterpiece) and claimed of its author that "avec ses romans elle a conquis la première place à côté de Colette dans la littérature féminine" (with her novels she has won first place next to Colette in women's literature) (*Lucie Delarue-Mardrus,* 25–26).
55. Exceptions include the discussion of *Marie, fille-mère* in Waelti-Walter, *Feminist Novelists of the Belle Epoque,* where it is treated thematically in a chapter on maternity, and Collado's analysis of the 1912 *La monnaie de singe* in *Colette, Lucie Delarue-Mardrus, Marcelle Tinayre,* 184–201.
56. Delarue-Mardrus, *Mes mémoires,* 158.
57. Jean Borie, *Zola et les mythes; ou, De la nausée au salut* (Paris: Editions du Seuil, 1971), 64.
58. Delarue-Mardrus, Marie, *fille-mère* (Paris: Eugène Fasquelle, 1909), 10; hereafter cited in text.

59. As in Tinayre's novel, the narrator is intellectually superior to the female protagonist. This disjunction between narrator and protagonist is a difference from both the naturalist novel and the sentimental novel.
60. For more on Zola's narrative techniques and a comparison with those of other naturalist writers, see Suwala, *Autour de Zola,* 201–26.
61. A. Reinvillier, *Hygiène pratique des femmes: Guide médical pour toutes les époques de leur vie suivi de quelques considérations sur les maladies des femmes* (Paris: Bureaux du Journal *Le Médecin de la Maison,* 1854), 7.
62. Auguste Debay, *Hygiène et physiologie du mariage: Histoire naturelle et médicale de l'homme et de la femme mariés dans ses plus curieux détails,* 78th ed. (1848; reprint, Paris: E. Dentu, 1874), 10. Debay was a very successful writer who published medical texts for a popular audience on a wide variety of topics related to marriage and hygiene. See St. Le Tourneur's entry on him in *Dictionnaire de biographie française,* ed. Roman D'Amat et al. (Paris: Librairie Letouzey et Ané, 1962), 10:418.
63. Debay, *Hygiène et physiologie du mariage,* 15.
64. Pierre Garnier, *Les Anomalies sexuelles apparentes et cachées* (Paris: Garnier, 1889), 239. Garnier was the editor in chief of *La Santé publique* from 1872 to 1877 and also edited the influential *Dictionnaire annuel des progrès des sciences et institutions médicales.*
65. Mayer, *Des Rapports,* 77, 118. Zola himself expresses this sentiment with respect to the barren Pauline in *La Joie de vivre* (Paris: Garnier-Flammarion, 1974): "A quoi bon sa puberté vigoureuse, ses organes et ses muscles engorgés de sève, l'odeur puissante qui montait de ses chairs, . . . ? Elle resterait comme un champ inculte, qui se dessèche à l'écart" (What good is her vigorous puberty, her organs and muscles engorged with sap, or the powerful odor that rose up from her flesh, . . . ? She would stay like an uncultivated field that dries up on the side) (328).
66. Jennifer Waelti-Walters compares the juxtaposition of the professor's comments and Marie's labor with the scene at the agricultural fair in *Madame Bovary,* where the narrator moves back and forth between Rodolphe's seduction of Emma and the moralizing speeches of fair officials. Waelti-Walters, *Feminist Novelists of the Belle Epoque: Love as a Lifestyle* (Bloomington: Indiana University Press, 1990), 61.
67. The concern with French mothers' producing healthy babies continued to be voiced well into the twentieth century. In a religious manual on sex education entitled *Les Initiations nécessaires* (Paris: Association du Mariage chrétien, 1922), R. P. De Ganay and H. Abrand write: "Les préoccupations toujours plus actuelles d'hygiène sociale, les dangers nationaux de la crise de la natalité, le péril vénérien qui grandit, ont attiré l'attention de plusieurs gouvernements sur le problème de l'initiation sexuelle" (The current preoccupation with social hygiene, the national dangers of the crisis of the birthrate, and the growing venereal peril have attracted the attention of several governments to the problem of sexual initiation) (3).
68. Like Tinayre's Augustin and Forgerus, the name Natale is thematically inscribed in the novel, reminding us that Marie's maternity limited her choice of husband.
69. Quoted in Plat, *Lucie Delarue-Mardrus,* 129.
70. Regarding Delarue-Mardrus's political stance, Pauline Newman-Gordon concludes: "For her, the answer did not lie in subordinating femininity, but in accepting the responsibility it entailed through the uninhibited expression of feeling, intellect, and

sensuality" ("Lucie Delarue-Mardrus," 114); similarly, Plat summarizes: "Les six premiers romans de l'écrivain mettent en scène le sort douloureux des femmes de son époque, de la masse silencieuse . . . Lucie n'est pas une militante, mais une compatissante" (The writer's first six novels stage the painful destiny of women of her generation, of the silent masses . . . Lucie is not a militant, but a sympathizer) (*Lucie Delarue-Mardrus,* 135).

71. Dauphiné, *Rachilde,* 193.

CHAPTER 4

1. Three recent biographies offer a more complete picture of Rachilde in the context of her era: Claude Dauphiné, *Rachilde* (Paris: Mercure de France, 1991); Diana Holmes, *Rachilde: Decadence, Gender, and the Woman Writer* (Oxford: Berg, 2001); Melanie Hawthorne, *Rachilde and French Women's Authorship* (Lincoln: University of Nebraska Press, 2001).
2. Rachilde was not always a trustworthy historian of her own life, and her account of the history of *Monsieur Vénus* in the preface to *A mort* has been disputed. See Hawthorne, *Rachilde and French Women's Authorship*, 93–99.
3. Holmes analyzes Rachilde's debt to naturalism and Zola in *Rachilde*, 92–98.
4. Quoted in André David, *Rachilde, homme de letters: Son oeuvre, portrait et autographe* (Paris: La Nouvelle Revue Critique, 1924), 62.
5. André David includes this comment from Barbey d'Aurevilly in *Soixante-quinze années de jeunesse* (Paris: André Bonne Editeur, 1974), 42. Barrès wrote: "Mais les idées, le fond de cette extraordinaire Rachilde, qui jette sur le papier tout ce qui lui passe par la tête, appartient bien à ce siècle-ci. Cette psychologie maladive, infiniment intéressante, ces cas d'exception sont dans la fine tradition qui va de *Joseph Delorme* aux *Fleurs du mal.* Ces rêves dépravés, ces recherches, ce mélange d'affectations naïves et de vices trop réels, ce souci de se faire une figure, de jouer un rôle, tout cela c'est Mlle Baudelaire" (But the ideas, the essence of this extraordinary Rachilde, who throws onto paper everything that comes through her mind, belongs to this century. This sick and infinitely interesting psychology, these exceptional cases are in the fine tradition that goes from *Joseph Delorme* to *The Flowers of Evil.* These depraved dreams, this research, this mix of naïve affectations and all too real vices, this worry over making oneself an image, playing a role, all of this is Mademoiselle Baudelaire). Maurice Barrès, "Mademoiselle Baudelaire," *Chroniques de Paris,* February 1887, 77–79.
6. For more on Rachilde's relationship with the *Mercure*, see Claude Dauphiné, "Rachilde et Le Mercure," *Revue d'histoire littéraire de la France* 9, no. 1 (1992): 17–28; see also Dauphiné, *Rachilde, femme de lettres 1900* (Paris: Pierre Fanlac, 1985); André Billy, *L'Epoque 1900* (Paris: Editions Jules Tallandier, 1951). Rachilde is sometimes credited with a central role in the creation of the *Mercure* and its success. David writes: "Si Alfred Vallette n'était pas tombé amoureux de Rachilde, *Le Mercure de France* n'aurait sans doute jamais paru" (If Alfred Vallette had not fallen in love with Rachilde, the *Mercure de France* would probably never have appeared) (*Rachilde*, 40). See also André David, *Soixante quinze années de jeunesse* (Paris: André Bonne Editeur, 1974), 35–50, for more personal anecdotes about Rachilde's literary presence at the *Mercure.*

7. Liane de Pougy writes of sitting behind an opinionated Rachilde at the theater (February 22, 1920), in *My Blue Notebooks*, trans. Diana Athill (New York: Harper and Row, 1979).
8. Holmes, *Rachilde*, 54.
9. Dauphiné includes excerpts from these reviews in both of her biographies. Rachilde often reviewed several books by the same author as they were published, changing her opinion of the author in the process. Although she had given Marcelle Tinayre's first novel, *Avant l'amour*, a mostly positive review in 1897, she was more critical of the 1906 *La Rebelle*. See Dauphiné, *Rachilde, femme de lettres 1900*, 75.
10. Rachilde wrote over two dozen novels during the period I cover and continued publishing until the 1940s. I have chosen to examine *Monsieur Vénus* and *La Jongleuse* because these two novels are among her most well-known writings. I examine them also for the particular relationship between the male and female protagonists in these novels, the role of the female protagonists as author figures, thus revealing what was at stake for the woman writer, and the exemplary relationship of these texts to decadence. At the same time, I agree with the arguments Melanie Hawthorne and Diana Holmes make in their biographies that Rachilde's writings ought to be considered in their own context, and that more consideration should be given to her later works.
11. Mesnilgrand stabs and kills Ydow in turn, but this killing of a man by another is less significant than the fact that Mesnilgrand survives the original battle between himself and La Rosalba.
12. Maité Albistur and Daniel Armogathe, *Histoire du féminisme français du moyen âge à nos jours* (Paris: Editions des femmes, 1977), 368.
13. Ibid., 354.
14. On Rachilde's relationship with feminism, see Maryline Lukacher, *Maternal Fictions* (Durham: Duke University Press, 1994), 109–60; Catherine Ploye, " 'Questions brûlantes': Rachilde, l'affaire Douglas et les mouvements féministes," *Nineteenth-Century French Studies* 22 (Fall–Winter 1993–94): 195–207; Holmes, *Rachilde*, 69–87.
15. Holmes chronicles Rachilde's lifelong disdain for feminism in *Rachilde*, 72–82.
16. "Si Rachilde a été parmi les premières femmes à introduire des lesbiennes dans ses oeuvres et à les utiliser pour déstabiliser les frontières entre les sexes et les genres, il n'en reste pas moins que la lesbienne alimente souvent chez elle une misogynie et un antiféminisme notoires" (If Rachilde was among the first women to introduce lesbians in her works and to use them to upset boundaries between sex and gender, it is nonetheless true that the lesbian often incites in her work a notorious misogyny and antifeminism). Dominique D. Fisher, "A propos du 'Rachildisme'; ou, Rachilde et les lesbiennes," *Nineteenth-Century French Studies* 31 (Spring–Summer 2003): 297. Similarly, perhaps, Hawthorne writes: "Rachilde was not the exception that she has so often been described as. Rather, she used the claim of exceptionality as a way to exist within the status quo" (*Rachilde and French Women's Authorship*, 10). Holmes summarizes Rachilde's idiosyncrasies as follows: "reactionary yet furiously aware of the need to challenge fixed hierarchies of power; anti-feminist yet in passionate revolt against the role and identity ascribed to women; shaped by the realist tradition but equally by the anti-realist polemics of decadence, and diverging from both, particularly in the representation of gender" (*Rachilde*, 1).

17. I agree with Lisa Downing's response to the question of Rachilde's feminist reception, in which she expresses her discomfort with "critical responses which place an (impossible) burden upon writers from marginalized groups . . . to produce only positive, healthy, life-affirming representations of these groups." She argues that Rachilde should not be given the "unrealistic responsibility to represent 'Everywoman.' " Downing, "Rachilde and the Death of Gender," in *Desiring the Dead: Necrophilia and Nineteenth-Century French Literature* (Oxford: Legenda, 2003), 93.
18. Ploye, " 'Questions brûlantes,' " 198.
19. Rachilde, "Pourquoi je ne suis pas féministe," in *Leurs raisons*, ed. André Billy (Paris: Les Editions de France, 1928), 6, 83.
20. Women's bodies were generally not a feminist topic, and many feminists hinged their arguments for equality on women's contributions as wives and mothers. One exception may be Nelly Roussel, who argued for women's rights to control their fertility. See Elinor Accampo, "Private Life, Public Image: Motherhood and Militancy in the Self-Construction of Nelly Roussel, 1900–1922," in *The New Biography: Performing Femininity in Nineteenth-Century France*, ed. Jo Burr Margadant, 218–61 (Berkeley and Los Angeles: University of California Press, 2000).
21. Mary Louise Roberts, *Disruptive Acts: The New Woman in Fin-de-siècle France* (Chicago: University of Chicago Press, 2002), 9.
22. Aside from the elimination of the original chapter 7, there are minimal differences between the two editions. The history of the Belgian and French editions of *Monsieur Vénus* and their prefaces are found in *Monsieur Vénus par Francis Talman* (Paris: Fourneau, 1995). This strange text interprets literally the claim that Rachilde edited out all of Talman's contributions in the French edition and presents all changes to the later edition, from the entire chapter 7 to single prepositions, as Talman's work.
23. Auriant, *Souvenirs sur Madame Rachilde* (Paris: A L'Ecart, 1989), 29.
24. These stories are discussed in Melanie Hawhorne and Liz Constable's preface to Melanie Hawthorne's translation of the 1884 Rachilde, *Monsieur Vénus: A Materialist Novel* (New York: MLA, 2004), xviii–xx. They present the original Belgian edition of the novel, which includes Talman's supposed contributions.
25. Hawthorne and Constable, Preface, xxxi. Hawthorne describes Talman's existence as "open to debate" and discusses the suppression of part of a sentence in the final chapter of the novel as "the most interesting difference" from the later edition (*Rachilde and French Women's Authorship*, 88).
26. Auriant, *Souvenirs sur Madame Rachilde*, 29.
27. Ibid.
28. Vallette's feelings about the novel are revealed in ibid., and Alfred Vallette, *Le Roman d'un homme sérieux* (Paris: Mercure de France, 1994), 14–17.
29. Rachilde, *Monsieur Vénus: Roman matérialiste* (Brussels: Brancart, 1884), 93.
30. ibid., 93-94.
31. ibid., 94.
32. ibid., 94.
33. ibid., 93.
34. ibid., 93.

35. Rachilde, *Monsieur Vénus* (1889; reprint, Paris: Flammarion, 1977), 86; hereafter cited in the text
36. Janet Beizer argues that *Monsieur Vénus* comprises several ironizing strategies that defamiliarize fin-de-siècle conventions. See her brilliant reading of the novel: "Venus in Drag, or Redressing the Discourse of Hysteria," in *Ventriloquized Bodies: Narratives of Hysteria in Nineteenth-Century France* (Ithaca: Cornell University Press, 1994), 227–60.
37. Jan Goldstein, *Console and Classify: The French Psychiatric Profession in the Nineteenth Century* (New York: Cambridge University Press, 1987), 326–27.
38. Jean-Martin Charcot, "Préface," in Paul Richer, *Etudes cliniques sur la grande hystérie* (Paris: A. Delahaye et E. Lecrosnier, 1885).
39. In Odette Dulac's *Le Droit au plaisir* (Paris: Louis Theuveny, Editeur, 1908), for example, which I examine in Chapter 5, the protagonist, Marcelle, is tired and has trouble sleeping after discovering that her lover has betrayed her. She reports her visit to the doctor: "Il diagnostique: Hystérie. Cela me met hors de moi! Alors, c'est une maladie que de désirer l'assouvissement de sa chair? L'homme qui n'a point trouvé de secret pour ressusciter ses forces défaillantes a toujours une drogue prête pour éteindre l'ardeur des nôtres" (He diagnoses: hysteria. That drives me crazy! So, it's a sickness to desire the satisfaction of the flesh? Men haven't found the secret to curing their own impotence but always have a drug ready to extinguish our passion) (148–49). Liane de Pougy's Nhine also seems to be diagnosed with hysteria, although the term is not explicitly invoked. In diagnosing Nhine's illness, the doctor tells her "Vous n'avez rien" (You have nothing). Pougy, *Idylle saphique* (1901; reprint, Paris: J-C Lattès, 1979), 152. This diagnosis points to the way hysteria at the fin-de-siècle could mean everything and nothing.
40. See Mark Micale, *Approaching Hysteria: Disease and Its Interpretations* (Princeton: Princeton University Press, 1995); Mark Micale and Roy Porter, eds., *Discovering the History of Psychiatry* (New York: Oxford University Press, 1994); Gladys Swain, "L'Âme, la femme, le sexe et le corps: Les Métamorphoses de l'hystérie à la fin du XIXe siècle," *Le Débat* 24 (1983): 107–27; Ruth Harris, *Murders and Madness: Medicine, Law, and Society in the Fin de Siècle* (New York: Oxford University Press, 1989); Elaine Showalter, *The Female Malady: Women, Madness, and English Culture* (New York: Pantheon, 1985); Martha Noel Evans, *Fits and Starts: A Genealogy of Hysteria in Modern France* (Ithaca: Cornell University Press, 1991). There are mountains of volumes on the topic of hysteria from a variety of disciplines, and I do not mean to suggest that their valuable contributions should be reduced to this simple dichotomy.
41. Carroll Smith-Rosenberg, *Disorderly Conduct: Visions of Gender in Victorian America* (New York: Knopf, 1985); Hélène Cixous and Catherine Clément, *La Jeune Née* (Paris: Union générale d'édition, 1975); Luce Irigaray, *Ce sexe qui n'en est pas un* (Paris: Les Editions de Minuit, 1977).
42. Luce Irigaray, "Women-Mothers, the Silent Substratum of the Social Order," in *The Irigaray Reader*, ed. Margaret Whitford (Cambridge: Blackwell, 1996), 47.
43. Luce Irigaray, *This Sex Which Is Not One*, trans. Catherine Porter and Carolyn Burke (Ithaca: Cornell University Press, 1985), 76. Diane Chisolm discusses Irigaray's use of hysteria in "Irigaray's Hysteria," in *Engaging with Irigaray*, ed. Carolyn Burke, Naomi Schor, and Margaret Whitford, 264–83 (New York: Columbia University Press,

1994). Elaine Showalter in *Hystories: Hysterical Epidemics and Modern Culture* (New York: Columbia University Press, 1997), defines hysteria along these same lines, a bit more broadly: "Hysteria is a mimetic disorder; it mimics permissible expressions of distress."

44. Rachilde's representation of the symptoms of hysteria also seems to parody the *maladie du siècle* depicted earlier in the century in the works of Chateaubriand and Musset. The question of the novel and its changing relationship to hysteria throughout the nineteenth century is explored in Jann Matlock, *Scenes of Seduction: Prostitution, Hysteria, and Reading Difference in Nineteenth-Century France* (New York: Columbia University Press, 1994). Beizer explores the nineteenth-century belief that reading novels causes hysteria in girls (*Ventriloquized Bodies*, chap. 3).
45. For more on pathography as a genre, see Emily Apter, *Feminizing the Fetish: Psychoanalysis and Narrative Obsession in Turn-of-the-Century France* (Ithaca: Cornell University Press, 1991), 34–40.
46. Beizer, *Ventriloquized Bodies*, 24.
47. Beizer discusses elusive definitions of the disease in ibid., 33–40.
48. Joseph Grasset, "Hystérie," in *Dictionnaire encyclopédique des sciences médicales*, ed. A. Dechambre and L. Lereboullet (Paris: Asselin & Houzeau/Masson, 1889). Quoted in Beizer, *Ventriloquized Bodies*, 34.
49. Docteur Zabé, *Manuel des maladies des femmes* (Paris: Léon Vanier, 1884), 43.
50. Henri Legrand du Saulle, *Les Hystériques: Etat physique et état mental* (Paris: J.-B. Baillière et fils, 1883), 514. Dr. Jean Caufeynon (pseudonym of Jean Fauconney) quotes Legrand du Saulle as saying: "Une hystérique a toutes les audaces. Incapable de modérer ses vivacités passionnelles, elle peut tout oser pour faire réussir ses combinaisons, ses plans et ses machinations" (A hysteric has every audacity. Unable to moderate her passionate vivaciousness, she can dare to do anything in order to succeed in her schemes, her plans, and her machinations). Caufeynon, *Histoire de la femme* (1904; reprint, Paris: Côté-femmes éditions, 1989), 167. The fact that Caufeynon, a writer of popular medical texts for a general audience, quotes Legrand du Saulle, author of more scholarly medical treatises, is illustrative of the problem of dissemination. Ideas about hysteria were dispersed through the popular press, making it difficult for clinical researchers like Charcot to have any control over public perception. Fauconney's use of pseudonyms again underlines the fluid relationship between literary and scientific writing.
51. Jules Claretie, *Les Amours d'un interne* (Paris: Dentu, 1881), 124.
52. Caufeynon, *Histoire de la femme*, 173.
53. Dorothy Kelly provides a helpful summary of the reversals of gender roles in the novel: "Raoule sends Jacques flowers, he makes flowers. . . . He veils himself, she undresses herself. He is natural, she is degraded. She lifts him up and carries him; she is the one solicited by a female prostitute; she is challenged to a duel; she is called the 'honnête homme,' the 'monsieur,' the 'maître.' He is called the 'épouse,' the 'fiancée.' Finally, she calls him 'Mme de Vénérande.' " Kelly, *Fictional Genders: Role and Representation in Nineteenth-Century Narrative* (Lincoln: University of Nebraska Press, 1989), 150.
54. Charles Richet, "Les Démoniaques d'aujourd'hui," *Revue des deux mondes* 37 (January 15, 1880): 346, quoted in Beizer, *Ventriloquized Bodies*, 251. Ironically, Rachilde was later praised by Jules Bertaut for being, in her writing, "moins femme que les

autres femmes" (less womanly than other women). Bertaut, *La Littérature féminine d'aujourd'hui* (Paris: Librairie des Annales, 1909), 222. Diana Holmes notes this comment in "The Politics of Romance: Popular Romantic Fiction at the Fin de Siècle," in *New Perspectives on the Fin de Siècle in Nineteenth- and Twentieth-Century France*, ed. Kay Chadwick and Timothy Unwin (Lewiston, NY: E. Mellen, 2000), 122.

55. Downing invokes Judith Butler to argue that *Monsieur Vénus* "is trying to think outside gender, yet it does this—paradoxically—by playing very deliberately with the binary signifiers of gender, breaking them down and showing that they are inadequate as a system of meaning" (*Desiring the Dead*, 99). See also Dominique Fisher, "Du corps travesti à l'enveloppe transparente: *Monsieur Vénus* ou la politique du leurre." *L'Esprit Créateur*, Winter 1997, 46–57; Rita Felski, "The Art of Perversion: Female Sadists and Male Cyborgs," in *The Gender of Modernity* (Cambridge: Harvard University Press, 1995), 174–206.
56. In *Gender Trouble: Feminism and the Subversion of Identity* (New York: Routledge, 1989), 34, Butler defines gender trouble as "an effort to think through the possibility of subverting and displacing those naturalized and reified notions of gender that support masculine hegemony and heterosexist power."
57. Further probing Rachilde's anticipation of gender theory, one could consider Raoule as the heroine of the kind of fable Luce Irigaray herself might have written, through which sexual difference itself is reinvented. Like Irigaray, who argues that patriarchal language cannot translate female desire, Rachilde seems to be searching for a rearticulation of female sexuality from somewhere beyond the problematic binarism of male/female. She also anticipates Monique Wittig's project "to destroy the categories of sex in politics and in philosophy, to destroy gender in language," which targets personal pronouns as a means of moving beyond the categories of sex. Wittig, "The Mark of Gender," in *The Straight Mind and Other Essays* (Boston: Beacon Press, 1992), 81. Yet unlike the theorists she anticipates, Rachilde is not bound by theoretical consistency or practicality in her fantasyland. In fact, Butler's notion of gender as performance, a series of fabrications enacted on the body (a notion built on feminist theory) seems to describe perfectly Raoule's effortless movement between male and female identities; yet in *Bodies That Matter: On the Discursive Limits of "Sex"* (New York: Routledge, 1993), Butler describes having been criticized for implying just such a thing: the possibility of a voluntarist subject who exists apart from gender, as if "one woke up in the morning, perused the closet or some more open space for the gender of choice, donned that gender for the day, and then restored the garment at night" (x). Raoule, in contrast, appears to be the fulfillment of just such a fantasy.
58. Caufeynon, *Histoire de la femme*, 57.
59. Downing reads this passage as demonstrating the "individuality of desire" and thus the inadequacy of categories like "lesbian" (*Desiring the Dead*, 96).
60. In another link to later French feminism, these acts of reading Jacques's poetic body literalize Monique Wittig's belief in the violent effect of discourse on the body. Wittig argues that "language casts sheaves of reality upon the body," forcing it to be unified in ways that conform to heterosexual goals ("Mark of Gender," 78). Considered in this light, Raoule and Raittolbe's ravaging of Jacques can be interpreted as a discursive battle over Jacques's physical role in their conflicting desiring economies.

61. Beizer compares the appropriation of Jacques's body as a textual surface to the way female characters have traditionally been "killed into art," in Gilbert and Gubar's term (*Ventriloquized Bodies*, 250–54).
62. For a history of the medical use of waxworks in France, see Michel Lemire, *Artistes et mortels* (Paris: Editions Raymond Chabeau, 1990).
63. Jann Matlock, "Censoring the Realist Gaze," in *Spectacles of Realism: Gender, Body, Genre*, ed. Margaret Cohen and Christopher Prendergast (Minneapolis: University of Minnesota Press, 1995), 53. Viewing waxworks became a widespread cultural phenomenon at the end of the nineteenth century in such places as the popular Musée Grévin. See Vanessa Schwartz, *Spectacular Realities: Early Mass Culture in Fin-de-Siècle Paris* (Berkeley and Los Angeles: University of California Press, 1998), 89–148. The 2004 MLA edition of *Monsieur Vénus* has further contextualization of waxworks (208–9, n. 67).
64. The original, 1884 edition states: "Un ressort, disposé à l'intérieur des flancs, correspond à la bouche et l'anime en même temps qu'il fait s'écarter les cuisses" (A spring set up inside the hips corresponds to the mouth and animates it, at the same time that it makes the thighs separate) (228).
65. The theme of female automatons will also appear in the 1886 novel by Villiers de l'Isle Adam, *L'Eve future*. In this novel, Thomas Edison creates a "humanized Venus Victrix." On the relationship of this invention to wax Venuses, see Annette Michelson, "On the Eve of the Future: The Reasonable Facsimile and the Philosophical Toy" *October* 29 (Summer 1984): 3–20.
66. David, *Rachilde, homme de lettres*, 21.
67. Michael Finn traces the romantic history of Barrès and Rachilde in his "Rachilde, Maurice Barrès, and the Preface to *Monsieur Vénus*," *Romanic Review*, January–March 2000, 89–104, and has reprinted their correspondence in *Rachilde-Maurice Barrès: Correspondance inédite 1885–1914* (Brest: CNRS, 2002). This volume also includes the preface to *A mort*, a text that is otherwise difficult to find.
68. Barrès, "Mademoiselle Baudelaire," 5.
69. Ibid., 14. This description recalls Jean Ernest-Charles's contention that women write "à leur insu" (without knowing it). Ernest-Charles, "Romans féminins: Mme Stanislas Meunier, Brada, Jacques Morian, Ivan Strannik, Rachilde," in *Les Samedis littéraires*, 5 vols. (Paris: Sansot, 1905), 2:13.
70. Barrès, *Chroniques de Paris*, 3, 5.
71. The caricaturist F. A. Cazals echoed many of Barrès's sentiments in a song he performed at a party for *La Plume* in 1890: "J'suis névropathe et mon papa / Qu'était de bonn' famille / Dès mon jeune âge s'occupa / De fair' de moi sa fille. / Au jour d'aujourd'hui / J'ai déjà produit / Beaucoup plus qu'René Ghil . . . de; / Je fais des bouquins / Qui font du boucan / C'est moi que j'suis Rachilde! / A l'heur' qu'il est mes éditeurs / Me tirent à dix mille / Ça prouve que j'ai des ach'teurs / Autant que l'grand Emile. / Mais l'argent n'fait pas, / Malgré ses appas, / Le bonheur de Rachilde. / Fill' de Périgueux, / J'donnerai pas mes ch'veux / Pour tout l'or des Rothschild . . . e! / J'ai dépeint dans *Monsieur Vénus* / Un amour sanguinaire. / Barrès m'a surnommé sans plus / Mademoisell' Baud'laire. / J'aim' les animaux / Et les anormaux / Mais je crains l'accolade / Des bas bleus jaloux / Et des auteurs fous / De la *Marquis' de Sade!*" (I am a neurotic

and my father / who was from a good family / took care since I was young / to make his girl out of me. / To this very day today / I have already produced / a lot more than René Ghil . . . [de]; / I make books / that make noise / That's me, I'm Rachilde! / Right now my editors / publish me in ten thousand copies / that proves that I have buyers / as many as the great Emile. / But money can't buy / despite its appearance/ Rachilde's happiness. / Daughter of Périgueux, / I would not give my hair / for all the gold of the Rothschildes! / I depicted in *Monsieur Vénus* / a bloodthirsty love / Barrès nicknamed me no less / Mademoiselle Baudelaire. / I love animals / and abnormals / But I fear accolades / from jealous *bas-bleus* / and authors crazy about / the *Marquis' de Sade!*). Quoted in Noel Richard, *Le Mouvement decadent: Dandys, esthètes et quintessents* (Paris: Librairie Nizet, 1968), 67–68.

72. Finn, *Rachilde, Maurice Barrès*, 122.
73. The preface to *Madame Adonis* is discussed in Renée Kingcaid, "The Epithalmic Horror: Displacement in Rachilde," in *Neurosis and Narrative: The Decadent Short Fiction of Proust, Lorrain, and Rachilde* (Carbondale: Southern Illinois University Press, 1992), 111–44.
74. Rachilde, *La Jongleuse* (1900; reprint, Paris: Des femmes, 1978), 33; hereafter cited in text.
75. See Robert Nye, "Medical Origins of Sexual Fetishism," in *Fetishism as Cultural Discourse*, ed. Emily Apter and William Pietz (Ithaca: Cornell University Press, 1993), 13–30.
76. According to Sigmund Freud, the fetish is a substitute for the maternal phallus, "the woman's (mother's) penis that the little boy once believed in and . . . does not want to forgo." As such, it masks the child's aversion to the female genitals, which he sees as castrated, and constitutes "a token of triumph over the threat of castration and a safeguard against it." Freud, "Fetishism," in *Sexuality and the Psychology of Love*, ed. Philip Rieff (New York: Simon and Schuster, 1997), 205–6.
77. Charles Bernheimer argues that Freud's theory of castration and its companion perversion of fetishism reflect the extent of his influence by fin-de-siècle decadent literature, in which castration figures as the central fantasy. Bernheimer, "Fetishism and Decadence: Salomé's Severed Heads," in *Fetishism as Cultural Discourse*, ed. Emily Apter and William Pietz, 62–83 (Ithaca: Cornell University Press, 1993).
78. This scene also shows links to the 1884 version of *Monsieur Vénus*, which included a more elaborate masturbatory fantasy in the second chapter than what would be included in the later edition. It describes "la femme qui vibrait en elle" (the woman who vibrated within).
79. Huysmans's *A rebours* would offer another kind of subversion of the teleology of desire at the level of plot. See Peter Brooks's discussion of Freudian desire as narrative model in *Reading for the Plot: Design and Intention in Narrative* (Cambridge: Harvard University Press, 1984), 90–112, as well as Susan Winnet's critique of Brooks in "Coming Unstrung: Women, Men, Narrative, and Principles of Pleasure," *PMLA* 105 (May 1990): 505–18.
80. Naomi Schor, "The Portrait of a Gentleman: Representing Men in (French) Women's Writing," in *Bad Objects: Essays Popular and Unpopular* (Durham: Duke University Press, 1995), 112, 115.

81. George Sand, *Indiana* (Paris: Folio, 1984), 68. Quoted in and translated by Schor, "Portrait of a Gentleman," 125.
82. "The decadent visionary accepts Freud's phantasmatic equation 'to decapitate = to castrate' and sees women as agents of male dismemberment. Salome signifies this desire to castrate, which her dance celebrates, but she also signifies the motive for her desire, the 'natural' condition of women from the point of view of decadent male neurosis, her castration." Bernheimer, "Fetishism and Decadence," 67.
83. Barbara Spackman, "Recycling Baudelaire: The Decadence of Catulle Mendès (1841–1909)," in *The Decadent Reader: Fiction, Fantasy, and Perversion from Fin-de-Siècle France*, ed. Asti Hustvedt (New York: Zone Books, 1998), 817.
84. Schor, "Portrait of a Gentleman," 123.
85. Melanie Hawthorne, Introduction to *The Juggler*, by Rachilde, trans. Melanie Hawthorne (New Brunswick, NJ: Rutgers University Press, 1990), xxiv.
86. Diana Holmes explores Rachilde's relationship to sentimental themes in "Decadent Love: Rachilde and the Popular Romance," *Dixneuf*, September 2003, 16–28.
87. The theme of heterosexual love as violation is found in Renée Vivien's collection of short stories, *La Dame à la louve* (Paris: Alphonse Lemerre, Editeur, 1904). It is also central to arguments made decades later by the radical American feminist Andrea Dworkin, particularly in her book *Intercourse* (New York: Free Press, 1987).
88. Marc Angenot has argued: "Représenter un coït, une scène d'initimité sexuelle est impossible dans le roman du XIXe siècle, du réalisme au naturalisme" (Representing coitus or a scene of sexual intimacy is impossible in the nineteenth-century novel, from realism to naturalism). Angenot, *Le Cru et le faisandé: Sexe, discours social et littérature à la Belle Epoque* (Brussels: Editions Labor, 1986), 128.
89. Ibid., 133.

CHAPTER 5

1. Thomas Laqueur, *Making Sex: Body and Gender from the Greeks to Freud* (Cambridge: Harvard University Press, 1990), 3. See also Laqueur's "Orgasm, Generation, and the Politics of Reproductive Biology," in Laqueur and Catherine Gallagher, *The Making of the Modern Body* (Berkeley and Los Angeles: University of California Press, 1987), 1–41.
2. Overviews of the history of sexology can be found in Judith Walkowitz, "Dangerous Sexualities," in *A History of Women in the West*, ed. Geneviève Fraisse and Michelle Perrot, vol. 4, *Emerging Feminism from Revolution to World War* (Cambridge: Harvard University Press, Belknap Press, 1993), 369–98; Jan Bremmer, ed., *From Sappho to De Sade: Moments in the History of Sexuality* (London: Routledge, 1989); Lisa Downing, "From Sade to Sexology," in *Desiring the Dead: Necrophilia and Nineteenth-Century French Literature* (Oxford: Legenda, 2003); Jeffrey Weeks, *Sexuality and Its Discontents: Meanings, Myths, and Modern Sexualities* (New York: Routledge, 1985).
3. The roots of sexology can be found in nineteenth-century hygiene manuals and medical publications addressed to a popular audience, which offered increasingly detailed depictions of sexual acts and dysfunction, usually in the context of how to maintain a healthy marriage. Examples include Auguste Debay's best-selling *Hygiène et physiologie*

du mariage: Histoire naturelle et médicale de l'homme et de la femme mariés dans ses plus curieux détails, 78th ed. (1848; reprint, Paris: E. Dentu Librairie-Editeur, 1874); Alexandre Mayer's *Des Rapports conjugaux considérés sous le triple point de vue de la population, de la santé, et de la morale publique* (1857; reprint, Paris: J .-B. Baillière et fils, 1874), which went through several editions over twenty years, and Pierre Garnier's best-selling *Le Mariage dans ses devoirs, ses rapports et ses effets conjugaux au point de vue légal, hygiénique, physiologique et moral* (Paris: Garnier Frères, 1879), which went through over seventeen editions in twenty years. The moral and political imperatives of these kinds of texts were often overtly declared, as when Mayer's text condemns "l'onanisme conjugal," or methods of birth control that "altèrent la santé, dépravent les moeurs, et, en fin de temps, diminuent la *natalité*" (alter health, cause depravity, and ultimately, decrease *birth rates*) (xii).

4. Thus, the doctor J. P. Dartigues warned that "la grande fécondité de l'esprit chez la femme produit presque toujours la stérilité corporelle, ou du moins des dérangements vicieux dans les fonctions de l'utérus" (great mental productivity in women almost always produces physical sterility, or at least severe difficulties in uterine function). Dartigues, *De l'amour expérimental ou des causes d'adultère chez la femme au XIXe siècle: Etude d'hygiène et d'économie sociale résultant de l'ignorance, du libertinage et des fraudes dans l'accomplissement des devoirs conjugaux* (Versailles: A. Litzellmann, Librairie Médicale et Scientifique, 1877), 48.
5. See Yvonne Knibiehler, "Bodies and Hearts," in Fraisse and Perrot, *History of Women,* 4:325–68.
6. See, for example, Auguste Debay: "les femmes ardentes, affectées de passion utérine, sont généralement impropres à la génération" (sexually ardent women, affected by uterine passion, are generally unsuited to procreation). Debay, *Hygiène et physiologie du mariage,* 237.
7. See Vernon Rosario, *The Erotic Imagination: French Histories of Perversity* (New York: Oxford University Press, 1997), 43. Rosario argues that authentic women's voices were scarcely heard in France in a sexological context, a term that he uses broadly to include literature as well. Rosario demonstrates fiction's important role in shaping nineteenth-century medical discourse on sexuality, citing Zola and Huysmans as two primary examples. In the absence of their voices, women's experiences were ventriloquized through male authority figures in both scientific case studies and fictional renderings. A similar argument is explored from a more literary and psychoanalytic perspective in Janet Beizer, *Ventriloquized Bodies: Narratives of Hysteria in Nineteenth-Century France* (Ithaca: Cornell University Press, 1994).
8. Marc Angenot argues that representing a scene of bourgeois sexual intimacy was impossible in the nineteenth-century realist and naturalist novel because of the ideological motives that kept writers from turning their scrutinizing gaze on their own bedrooms. Angenot, *Le Cru et le faisandé: Sexe, discours social et littérature à la Belle Epoque* (Brussels: Editions Labor, 1986). Lucie Delarue-Mardrus's *Marie, fille-mère* (Paris: Eugène Fasquelle, 1909) appears to be an exception, using the tropes of naturalism to examine the role of pleasure in Marie's relationship with her husband.
9. Diana Holmes, "The Politics of Romance: Popular Romantic Fiction at the Fin de Siècle," in *New Perspectives on the Fin de Siècle in Nineteenth- and Twentieth-Century*

France, ed. Kay Chadwick and Timothy Unwin (Lewiston, NY: E. Mellen Press, 2000), 125.

10. Margaret Cohen, *The Sentimental Education of the Novel* (Princeton: Princeton University Press, 1999), 34.
11. Marc Angenot, "Des Romans pour les femmes: Un Secteur du discours social en 1889," *Etudes Littéraires* 16 (1983): 347.
12. Holmes, "Politics of Romance," 124.
13. Virginie Sanders, *"Vertigineusement, j'allais vers les étoiles . . .": La Poésie de Renée Vivien* (Atlanta: Rodopi, 1991), 117–19; Lucie Delarue-Mardrus, *Mes mémoires* (Paris: Eugène Fasquelle, 1909), 123. Biographical information on Noailles can be found in Claude Mignot-Ogliastri, *Anna de Noailles, une amie de la Princesse Edmond de Polignac* (Paris: Méridions Klincksieck, 1986); François Broche, *Anna de Noailles: Un mystère en pleine lumière* (Paris: Editions Robert Laffont, 1989); Tama Lea Engelking, "Anna de Noailles (1876–1933)," in *French Women Writers: A Bio-bibliographical Sourcebook,* ed. Eva Martin Sartori and Dorothy Wynne Zimmerman, 335–45 (New York: Greenwood, 1991).
14. For an account of Noailles's tumultuous relationship with Barrès, see Patricia Ferlin, *Femmes d'encrier* (Paris: Christian de Bartillat, 1995), 22–44. Broche recounts Noailles's first meeting with France at Proust's salon (*Anna de Noailles,* 143); she also includes some of Noailles's correspondence with Gide (158–59) and Jammes (162–69).
15. Georges Pellisier made this comment in his *Etudes de littérature et de morale* (Paris: Cornély, 1905). Quoted in Mignot-Ogliastri, *Anna de Noailles,* 199.
16. In 1931 Noailles was the first woman to be awarded the rank of commander of the Legion of Honor. Danièle Déon-Bessière, *Les Femmes et la Légion d'honneur: Depuis sa création* (Paris: Editions de l'officine, 2002), 276.
17. Marcelle Tinayre, *La Maison du péché* (Paris: Calmann-Lévy, 1903), 351.
18. Henri de Regnier wrote extensively of his good friend Noailles in his journals. See Mignot-Oliastri, *Anna de Noailles,* 195; Broche, *Anna de Noaille,* 205.
19. Jean Larnac, *Histoire de la littérature féminine en France,* 5th ed. (Paris: Editions Kra, 1929), 234.
20. In this context, perhaps, we can see a relationship to Diderot, who, like many of his contemporaries, used a female protagonist "to portray the world of sensibility and the way in which one acquires knowledge." John C. O'Neal, *The Authority of Experience: Sensationist Theory in the French Enlightenment* (University Park: Pennsylvania State University Press, 1996), 110.
21. See Frank Paul Bowman, " 'Precious Blood' in Religion, Literature, Eroticism, and Politics," in *French Romanticism: Intertextual and Interdisciplinary Readings* (Baltimore: Johns Hopkins University Press, 1990), 81–105.
22. For a more extensive investigation of this phenomenon, see Emily Apter, *Feminizing the Fetish: Psychoanalysis and Narrative Obsession in Turn-of-the-Century France* (Ithaca: Cornell University Press, 1991), 124–46.
23. Edmond de Goncourt and Jules de Goncourt, *Journal Tome I* (Paris: Editions Aricette, 1959), 334.
24. Anna Elisabeth de Brancovan, Comtesse de Noailles, *Le Visage émerveillé* (Paris: Calmann-Lévy, 1904), 2; hereafter cited in text.

25. O'Neal, *Authority of Experience*, 2.
26. Cohen, *Sentimental Education*, 57.
27. Claire de Duras, *Edouard* (1825), in *Romans des femmes du XVIIIe siècle* (Paris: Robert Laffont, 1996), 1021. Quoted in Cohen, *Sentimental Education,* 58.
28. In a 1904 review of the play *Le Droit des vierges* by Paul-Hyacinthe Loyson, Nelly Roussel writes: "I can conceive of nothing more profoundly 'immoral' than the marriage of a young woman who is absolutely ignorant of the most elementary laws of physiology, who is thrust, unknowingly, blindly, into this fearful unknown; who is handed over like a toy, like an object, to a man she doesn't love, whom she is unable to love because she is ignorant—poor thing—of the very meaning of the word 'love'!" Roussel, *Women, the Family, and Freedom: The Debate in Documents,* vol. 2, *1880–1950,* ed. Susan Bell and Karen Offen (Stanford: Stanford University Press, 1983), 178. Pelletier outlines an entire theory of sexual education for girls in her 1914 brochure, *L'Education féministe des filles.* Roussel and Pelletier are among the first French feminists to link sexual self-knowledge to women's rights and thus anticipate future feminist arguments. See Elinor Accampo, "Private Life, Public Image: Motherhood and Militancy in the Self-Construction of Nelly Roussel, 1900–1922," in *The New Biography: Performing Femininity in Nineteenth-Century France,* ed. Jo Burr Margadant, 218–61 (Berkeley and Los Angeles: University of California Press, 2000); Felicia Gordon, *The Integral Feminist: Madeleine Pelletier, 1874–1939; Feminism, Socialism, and Medicine* (Cambridge: Polity, 1990).
29. In Sainte-Sophie's inability to reconcile her need for independence with socially acceptable forms of love, the novel resembles the nineteenth-century Sandian sentimental social novel as described by Margaret Cohen, which I consider more closely later in this chapter, where a tragic ending nearly always underlines the incompatibility of the heroine's individual needs with those of society.
30. Anne Marie Louise d'Orléans, Duchesse de Montpensier, *Lettres* (Paris: Collin, 1806).
31. For more on Gyp's life and works see Willa Silverman's excellent comprehensive biography, *The Notorious Life of Gyp: Right-Wing Anarchist in Fin-de-Siècle France* (New York: Oxford University Press, 1995). On *Autour du mariage*, see especially "La Femme de 1885," 66–68. Mary Louise Roberts analyzes Gyp in the context of the *New Woman in Disruptive Acts: The New Woman in Fin-de-siècle France* (Chicago: University of Chicago Press, 2002), 152–64.
32. Silverman, *Notorious Life of Gyp,* 54.
33. Roberts, *Disruptive Acts,* 161.
34. Ibid., 67.
35. Gyp [Gabrielle Marie-Antoinette de Riquetti de Mirabeau], *Autour du mariage* (Paris: Calmann-Lévy, 1883), 27; hereafter cited in text.
36. *La Vie parisienne* was published from 1862 to 1939. Marc Angenot describes it as less bawdy and less literary than the *Gil Blas* but also snobbier, speaking the language of the leisure class (*Le Cru et le faisandé,* 90). Colette first published *La Vagabonde* in serial form in *La Vie parisienne.*
37. Jeanne Marni, *Amour coupable* (Paris: Ollendorf, 1889), 115. Also quoted in Angenot, "Des romans pour les femmes," 344.

38. Angenot, "Des romans pour les femmes," 344. Angenot sees this convention as an ideological imperative to maintain the privacy of bourgeois sexual practices. Separately, he notes the popularity of the theme of the "Nuit de noce" in stories published in the bourgeois press, including the *Gil Blas.* These are stories of wedding nights gone awry, often ending in violence. Angenot, *Le Cru et le faisandé,* 133, 104–5.
39. See Felicia Gordon and Marie Cross, *Early French Feminisms, 1830–1940: A Passion for Liberty;* Claire Goldberg Moses, *French Feminism in the Nineteenth Century* (Albany: State University of New York Press, 1984).
40. For more information on these women's political and literary endeavors, see Steven C. Hause and Jennifer Waelti-Walters, eds., *Feminisms of the Belle Epoque* (Lincoln: University of Nebraska Press, 1994).
41. Colette Yver received the "Vie Heureuse" prize for her 1907 novel *Princesses de science.* See Waelti-Walters and Hause, *Feminisms of the Belle Epoque,* 210–11. Tinayre often supported feminist causes and explicitly evokes the movement in *La Rebelle;* she also wrote for the newspaper *La Fronde.* Louise-Marie Compain's novel *L'Un vers l'autre,* which criticizes the infringement of marriage on female identity, allied her with the feminist movement. She later devoted time to women's suffrage and women's right to work. For a brief biography of Compain, see Waelti-Walters and Hause, *Feminisms of the Belle Epoque,* 133–34.
42. Cohen, *Sentimental Education of the Novel,* 129. According to Cohen, "the sentimental social novel was the main generic practice competing with realism for top literary and cultural honors in the novel throughout the 1830's and 1840's. In the discursive slippage of contemporary polemic, it was identified with a range of terms, notably as the literature of ideas, the philosophical novel, and the social novel" (121–22).
43. The sexual explicitness in *Les Demi-sexes* and *Les Amants féminins* seems meant to titillate, such that these novels might be included in Angenot's category of "littérature boulevardière"—"à la frange de la pornographie" (boulevard literature—at the fringe of pornography) or his "genre voluptueux et faisandé" (genre of pleasure and decadence) where "les curiosités sexuelles pour la femme conduisent à la folie, la déchéance, et la mort" (sexual curiosities lead to madness, degeneration, and death in women). Angenot, "Des romans pour femmes," 337; Angenot, *Le Cru et le faisandé,* 117.
44. H. Temerson, "Jeanne-Marie-Claire Latrilhe, dite Odette, Dulac," in *Dictionnaire de biographie française,* ed. Jules Balteau et al. (Paris: Librairie Letouzey et Ané, 1970), 12:58. Dulac also published under the name Odette Roche.
45. Colette, *L'Ingénue libertine* (Paris: Editions Albin Michel, 1951), 125; hereafter cited in text.
46. Odette Dulac, *Le Droit au plaisir* (Paris: Louis Theuveny Editeur, 1908), 18–19; hereafter cited in text.
47. It is interesting to note a similar passage in Erica Jong's groundbreaking 1973 novel *Fear of Flying* (1973; reprint, New York: Signet, 2003), where she quotes from a pornographic novel that one of her characters is reading: "*His hips began to move faster* [Lalah read in a histrionic voice] *as the urgency of climax approached. I felt his body pounding against mine, his stiff prick was filling every inch of my womanly canal*" (337). In both instances, the quotations from pornographic novels remind the readers that while the author's text may be transgressive, it is not pornographic.

48. Cohen, *Sentimental Education of the Novel*, 61.
49. This emphasis on the violence of the physical act further links Colette's novel to a sexological discourse, with an attention to the details of the physical experience. Dr. Henri Beaunis describes sexual climax in *Les Sensations internes* (1889): "la sensation voluptueuse envahit brusquement tout l'organisme, se traduisant par des réactions convulsives de nature variable, frissons, tressaillements, secousses spasmodiques, convulsion des globes oculaires, soupirs, sanglots, cris, râles, halètements, trismus, grincements de dents, etc., en un mot par tout un ensemble de phénomènes qui font involontairement penser au mot de Démocrite: le mariage n'a pour but qu'une petite attaque d'épilepsie" (the sensation of pleasure briskly invades the whole organism, manifesting itself in variable convulsive reactions, trembling, shivers, spasmodic shakes, convulsions of the eyeballs, sighs, sobs, cries, groans, pants, lockjaw, grinding of the teeth, etc., in other words, in an ensemble of phenomena that automatically make you think of the words of Democritus: marriage has no other goal than a little epileptic seizure) (quoted in Angenot, *Le Cru et le faisandé,* 24).
50. Richard von Krafft-Ebing, *Psychopathie sexuelle,* trans. into French from the 8th German edition by Emile Laurent and Sigismund Csapo (Paris, 1895), 17–18.
51. Dartigues, *De l'amour expérimental,* 123; Seved Ribbing, *L'Hygiène sexuelle et ses conséquences morales,* (Paris: F. Alcan, 1895), 84; Dr. Désormeaux, *L'Amour conjugal* (Paris: Librairie P. Fort, 1907), 25.
52. Havelock Ellis, *The Psychology of Sex: A Manual for Students* (1933; reprint, New York: Emerson Books, 1972), 309.
53. Silverman describes the reception of *Autour du mariage,* which brought Gyp great success, as generally warm (*Notorious Life of Gyp,* 67). The audaciousness of her protagonist was addressed within the ongoing discussion of the new, modern woman rather than in the context of sexology and women's sexual experience.

CONCLUSION

1. Delfeil de Ton, "Le Rêve de l'écrivaine," *Le Nouvel Observateur,* June 22–28, 2000, 112.
2. Jules Bertaut, *La Littérature féminine d'aujourd'hui* (Paris: Librairie des Annales Politiques et Littéraires, 1909), 8.
3. Paul Flat, *Nos femmes de lettres* (Paris: Perrin, 1909), 154.
4. Béatrice Slama elegantly traces the notion of sexual difference in the writing and reception of twentieth-century women's writing. She describes the "littérature féminine" of 1900 as being defined by both excess and lack: "Manque d'imagination, de logique, d'objectivité, de pensée métaphysique . . . ; trop de facilité, trop de facticité, trop de mots, trop de phrases, de mièvrerie" (lack of imagination, logic, objectivity, metaphysical thought . . . ; excess of facility, artifice, words, sentences, sentimentality). Slama, "De la 'littérature féminine' à 'l'écrire-femme': Différence et institution," *Littérature* 44 (December 1981): 53.
5. Georges Le Cardonnel and Charles Vellay, *La Littérature contemporaine* (Paris: Société de Mercure de France, 1905), 117.
6. Bertaut, *La Littérature féminine*, 16.

7. Slama argues that post-Beauvoir feminism and the founding of Editions des femmes marked a critical juncture in the history of women's writing: "Jusqu'alors, des hommes ont tenté de définir, de codifier une 'littérature féminine' et des femmes ont dû répondre, se situer par rapport à ces définitions" (until then, men had attempted to define, to codify 'women's writing' and women had to respond, situating themselves with respect to those definitions) ("De la 'littérature feminine,' " 58).
8. Mary Louise Roberts develops this dichotomy in *Civilization without Sexes: Reconstructing Gender in Postwar France, 1917–1927* (Chicago: University of Chicago Press, 1994) in terms of the cultural polarization of gender brought on by World War I.
9. This novel is presented in ibid., 143–47.
10. Tinayre was thought to have had several affairs with other men during her marriage. See Alain Quella-Villéger, *Belles et rebelles: Le Roman vrai des Chasteau-Tinayre* (Bordeaux: Aubéron, 2000), 184, 307, 310; Patricia Ferlin, *Femmes d'encrier* (Paris: Christian de Bartillat, 1995), 158–59; Collado, *Colette, Lucie Delarue-Mardrus, Marcelle Tinayre* (Paris: L'Harmattan, 2003), 129 n. 121.

Bibliography

Accampo, Elinor A., Rachel G. Fuchs, and Mary Lynn Stewart, eds. *Gender and the Politics of Social Reform in France*, 1870–1914. Baltimore: Johns Hopkins University Press, 1995.

______. "Private Life, Public Image: Motherhood and Militancy in the Self-Construction of Nelly Roussel, 1900–1922." In *The New Biography: Performing Femininity in Nineteenth-Century France*, edited by Jo Burr Margadant, 218–61. Berkeley and Los Angeles: University of California Press, 2000.

Albistur, Maité, and Daniel Armogathe. *Histoire du féminisme français du moyen âge à nos jours*. Paris: Editions des femmes, 1977.

Allen, James Smith. *In the Public Eye: A History of Reading in Modern France, 1800–1940*. Princeton: Princeton University Press, 1991.

Angenot, Marc. *Le Cru et le faisandé: Sexe, discours social et littérature à la Belle Epoque*. Brussels: Editions Labor, 1986.

______. "Des Romans pour les femmes: Un secteur du discours social en 1889." *Etudes littéraires* 16 (1983): 317–50.

Apter, Emily. *Feminizing the Fetish: Psychoanalysis and Narrative Obsession in Turn-of-the-Century France*. Ithaca: Cornell University Press, 1991.

Auriant. *Souvenirs sur Madame Rachilde*. Paris: A L'Ecart, 1989.

Baguley, David. *Naturalist Fiction: The Entropic Vision.* Cambridge: Cambridge University Press, 1990.

Balbus, Isaac. "Disciplining Women: Michel Foucault and the Power of Feminist Discourse." In *Feminism as Critique,* edited by Seyla Benhabib and Drucilla Cornell, 110–27. Minneapolis: University of Minnesota Press, 1987.

Balteau, Jules, Marius Barroux, Michel Prévost, Jean-Charles Roman d'Amat, Henri Tribaut de Morembert, Jean-Pierre Lobies, Rober Limouzin Lamoth. *Dictionnaire de biographie française.* Vols 10, 12. Paris: Letouzey et Ané, 1965.Barbey d'Aurevilly, Jules. *Les Bas-bleus.* Paris: Société Générale de librairie catholique, 1878.

______. Les Diaboliques. Paris: Gallimard, 1973.

Barney, Natalie Clifford. *Souvenirs indiscrets.* Paris: Flammarion, 1960.

Barrès, Maurice. "Mademoiselle Baudelaire." *Chroniques de Paris.* Paris, 1887:77–79 .

Baudelaire, Charles. "Le Peintre de la vie moderne." In *Oeuvres complètes,* vol. 2. Paris: Gallimard, 1976.

Beizer, Janet. "The Body in Question: Anatomy, Textuality, and Fetishism in Zola." *L'Esprit créateur* 1 (Spring 1989): 50–60.

_____. "Uncovering Nana: The Courtesan's New Clothes." *L'Esprit créateur* 25 (Summer 1985): 45–56.

_____. *Ventriloquized Bodies: Narratives of Hysteria in Nineteenth-Century France.* Ithaca: Cornell University Press, 1994.

Bell, Susan, and Karen Offen. *Women, the Family, and Freedom: The Debate in Documents.* Vol. 2, *1880–1950.* Stanford: Stanford University Press, 1983.

Benjamin, Walter. *Charles Baudelaire: A Lyric Poet in the Era of High Capitalism,* translated by Harry Zohn. London: Verso, 1985.

Benstock, Shari. "Authorizing the Autobiographical." In *The Private Self: Theory and Practice in Women's Autobiography,* edited by Shari Benstock and Susan Stanford Friedman, 10–33. Chapel Hill: University of North Carolina Press, 1988.

_____. "Paris Lesbianism and the Politics of Reaction, 1900–1940." In *Hidden from History: Reclaiming the Gay and Lesbian Past,* edited by Martin Bauml Duberman, Martha Vicinus, and George Chauncey Jr. New York: Penguin Books, 1990.

_____. *Women of the Left Bank: Paris 1900–1940.* Austin: University of Texas Press, 1986.

Bentley, Toni. *Sisters of Salomé.* New Haven: Yale University Press, 2002.

Bergman-Colter, Janis. *The Woman of Ideas in French Art, 1830–1848.* New Haven: Yale University Press, 1995.

Bernheimer, Charles. *Decadent Subjects: The Idea of Decadence in Art, Literature, Philosophy, and Culture of the Fin-de-siècle in Europe.* Edited by T. Jefferson Kline and Naomi Schor. Baltimore: Johns Hopkins University Press, 2002.

_____. "Fetishism and Decadence: Salomé's Severed Heads." In *Fetishism as Cultural Discourse,* edited by Emily Apter and William Pietz, 62–83. Ithaca: Cornell University Press, 1993.

_____. *Figures of Ill Repute: Representing Prostitution in Nineteenth-Century France.* Cambridge: Harvard University Press, 1989.

_____. "Response to Peter Brooks." *Critical Inquiry* 17 (Summer 1991): 868–74.

Bernheimer, Charles, and Richard Kaye, eds. *The Queen of Decadence: Salomé in Modern Culture.* Chicago: University of Chicago Press, 1998.

Bertaut, Jules. *La Littérature féminine d'aujourd'hui.* Paris: Librairie des Annales Politiques et Littéraires, 1909.

Besnard-Coursodon, Micheline. "Monsieur Vénus, Madame Adonis: Sexe et discours." *Littérature* 54 (1984): 121–28.

Bidelman, Patrick Kay. *Pariahs Stand Up! The Founding of the Liberal Feminist Movement in France, 1858–1889.* Westport, CT: Greenwood, 1982.

Billy, André. *L'Epoque 1900.* Paris: Editions Jules Taillandy, 1951.

Birkett, Jennifer. *The Sins of the Fathers.* New York: Quartet Books, 1984.

Blum, Léon. *Du mariage.* Paris : P. Ollendorff, 1907.

de Bonnefon, Jean. *La Corbeille de roses ou les dames de lettres.* Paris: Société d'éditions de Bouville et compagnie, 1909.

Bonnet, Marie-Jo. *Un Choix sans equivoque: Recherches historiques sur les relations amoureuses entre les femmes, XVIe–XXe siècle.* Paris: Denoël, 1981.

Bordeau, Catherine. "The Power of the Feminine Milieu in Zola's *Nana.*" *Nineteenth-Century French Studies* 27 (Fall–Winter 1998–1999): 96–107.

Borie, Jean. *Zola et les mythes; ou, De la nausée au salut.* Paris: Editions de Seuil, 1971.

Bowman, Frank Paul. *French Romanticism: Intertextual and Interdisciplinary Readings.* Baltimore: Johns Hopkins University Press, 1990.

Brachet, Jean-Louis. *Traité de l'hystérie.* Paris: J.-B. Baillière, 1847.

Brahimi, Denise. "Exotisme, nationalisme, socialisme chez trois écrivaines de la Belle Epoque." *L'Esprit créateur,* Winter 1997, 29–45.

Brécourt-Villars, Claudine. *Ecrire d'amour: Anthologie de textes érotiques féminins, 1799–f1984.* Paris: Ramsay, 1985.
Bremmer, Jan, ed. *From Sappho to De Sade: Moments in the History of Sexuality.* London: Routledge, 1989.
Briquet, Pierre. *Traité clinique et thérapeutique de l'hystérie.* 1859. Reprint, Paris: Hachette, 1975.
Broche, François. *Anna de Noailles: Un Mystère en pleine lumière.* Paris: Editions Robert Laffont, 1989.
Brooks, Peter. *Body Work: Objects of Desire in Modern Narrative.* Cambridge: Harvard University Press, 1993.
_____. *Reading for the Plot: Design and Intention in Narrative.* Cambridge: Harvard University Press, 1984.
_____. "Response to Charles Bernheimer." *Critical Inquiry* 17 (Summer 1991): 875–77.
Butler, Judith. *Bodies That Matter: On the Discursive Limits of "Sex."* New York: Routledge, 1993.
_____. *Gender Trouble: Feminism and the Subversion of Identity.* New York: Routledge, 1990.
Carles, Patricia, and Béatrice Desranges. "Emile Zola; ou, Le Cauchemar de l'hystérie et les rêveries de l'utérus." *Les cahiers naturalistes* 41, no. 69 (1995): 13–32.
Carroy-Thirard, Jacqueline. *Le Mal de morzine: De la possession à l'hystérie (1857–1877).* Paris: Solin, 1981.
Case, Sue-Ellen. "Toward a Butch-Femme Aesthetic." In *Making a Spectacle: Feminist Essays on Contemporary Theatre,* edited by Lynda Hart, 282–99. Ann Arbor: University of Michigan Press, 1989.
Caufeynon, Jean [Jean Fauconney, pseud.]. *Histoire de la femme.* 1904. Reprint, Paris: Côté-femmes éditions, 1989.
Chalon, Jean. *Liane de Pougy: Courtisane, princesse, et sainte.* Paris: Flammarion, 1994.
_____. *Portrait of a Seductress: The World of Natalie Barney.* Translated by Carol Barko. New York: Crown, 1979.
_____. Preface to *Idylle saphique,* by Liane de Pougy. Paris: J.-C. Lattès, 1979.
Chambers, Ross. Chambers, *Loiterature* (Lincoln: University of Nebraska Press, 1999.
Charcot, Jean-Martin. "Préface," in Paul Richer, *Etudes cliniques sur la grande hystérie.* Paris: A. Delahaye et E. Lecrosnier, 1885.
Chartier, Roger, and Henri-Jean Martin, eds. *Histoire de l'édition française.* Vol. 3, *Le Temps des éditeurs: Du romantisme à la Belle Epoque.* Paris: Fayard, 1983.
_____. *Histoire de l'édition française.* Vol. 4, Le Livre concurrencé: 1900–1950. Paris: Fayard, 1983.
Chisolm, Diana. "Irigaray's Hysteria." In *Engaging with Irigaray,* edited by Carolyn Burke, Naomi Schor, and Margaret Whitford, 264–83. New York: Columbia University Press, 1994.
Cim, Albert. *Bas-bleus.* Paris: A. Savine, 1891.
Citti, Pierre. *Contre la decadence: Histoire de l'imagination française dans le roman, 1890–1914.* Paris: Presses Universitaires de France, 1987.
Cixous, Hélène. "Laugh of the Medusa." In *The Signs Reader: Women, Gender, and Scholarship,* edited by Elizabeth Abel and Emily K. Abel and translated by Keith Cohen and Paula Cohen, 279–97. Chicago: University of Chicago Press, 1983.
Cixous, Hélène, and Catherine Clément. *La Jeune Née.* Paris: Union Générale d'Editions, 1975.
Claretie, Jules. *Les Amours d'un interne.* Paris: Dentu, 1881.
Clark, T. J. *The Painting of Modern Life: Paris in the Art of Manet and His Followers.* Princeton: Princeton University Press, 1984.

Clayson, Hollis. *Painted Love: Prostitution in French Art of the Impressionist Era*. New Haven: Yale University Press, 1991.
Cohen, Margaret. *The Sentimental Education of the Novel*. Princeton: Princeton University Press, 1999.
Colette. *L'Ingénue Libertine*. 1909. Reprint, Paris: Editions Albin Michel, 1951.
———. *Romans—Récits—Souvenirs (1900–1919)*. Paris: Robert Laffont, 1997.
———. *La Vagabonde*. 1910. Reprint. Paris: Librairie Générale Française, 1990.
———. *Le Pur et l'impur*. Paris : Aux Armes de France, 1941.
Collado, Mélanie E. *Colette, Lucie Delarue-Mardrus, Marcelle Tinayre: Emancipation et résignation*. Paris: L'Harmattan, 2003.
Compain, Louise-Marie. *L'Un vers l'autre*. Paris: P-V Stock, Editeurs, 1903.
Condillac, Etienne Bonnot de. *Traité des sensations*. 1754. Reprint, Paris: Thomas-Victor Charpentier, Editeur Scientifique, 1909.
Conley, Verena Andermatt. *Hélène Cixous: Writing the Feminine*. Lincoln: University of Nebraska Press, 1984.
Constable, Liz. "*Fin-de-siècle* Yellow Fevers: Women Writers, Decadence, and Discourses of Degeneracy." *L'Esprit créateur*, Fall 1997, 25–37.
Constable, Liz, and Melanie Hawthorne. Preface to *Monsieur Vénus: A Materialist Novel, by Rachilde*. New York: MLA, 2004.
Copley, Antony R. H. *Sexual Moralities in France, 1780–1980: New Ideas on the Family, Divorce, and Homosexuality; An Essay on Moral Change*. New York: Routledge, 1989.
Corbin, Alain. "Commercial Sexuality in Nineteenth-Century France: A System of Images and Regulations." In *The Making of the Modern Body*, edited by Catherine Gallagher and Thomas Laqueur, 209–19. Berkeley and Los Angeles: University of California Press, 1987.
———. *Les Filles de noce: Misère sexuelle et prostitution; 19e et 20e siècles*. Paris: Gallimard, 1982.
Cosslett, Tess. *Women Writing Childbirth: Modern Discourses of Motherhood*. New York: St. Martin's Press, 1994.
———. *Dictionnaire de biographie française*. Vol. 12. Paris: Letouzey et Ané, 1970.
Dartigues, J. P. *De l'amour expérimental ou des causes d'adultère chez la femme au XIXe siècle: Etude d'hygiène et d'économie sociale résultant de l'ignorance, du libertinage et des fraudes dans l'accomplissement des devoirs conjugaux*. Versailles: A. Litzellmann, Librairie Médicale et Scientifique, 1877.
Dauphiné, Claude. *Rachilde*. Paris: Mercure de France, 1991.
———. *Rachilde, femme de lettres 1900*. Paris: Pierre Fanlac, 1985.
———. "Rachilde et *Le Mercure*." *Revue d'histoire littéraire de la France* 92, no.1 (1992): 17–28.
David, André. *Rachilde, homme de lettres: Son oeuvre, portrait et autographe*. Paris: La Nouvelle Revue Critique, 1924.
———. *Soixante quinze années de jeunesse*. Paris: André Bonne Editeur, 1974.
Dean, Carolyn. *The Frail Social Body: Pornography, Homosexuality, and Other Fantasies in Interwar France*. Berkeley and Los Angeles: University of California Press, 2000.
Debay, Auguste. *Hygiène et physiologie du mariage: Histoire naturelle et médicale de l'homme et de la femme mariés dans ses plus curieux détails*. 78th edition. 1848. Reprint, Paris: E. Dentu Librairie-Editeur, 1874.
DeGanay, R. P., and H. Abrand. *Les Initiations nécessaires*. Paris: Association du mariage chrétien, 1922.
DeJean, Joan. *Fictions of Sappho, 1546–1937*. Chicago: University of Chicago Press, 1989.
———. "Lafayette's Ellipses: The Privileges of Anonymity." *PMLA*, October 1984, 884–901.

_____. *Tender Geographies: Women and the Origins of the Novel in France.* New York: Columbia University Press, 1991.

DeJean, Joan, and Nancy K. Miller, eds. *Displacements: Women, Tradition, Literatures in French.* Baltimore: Johns Hopkins University Press, 1991.

Delarue-Mardrus, Lucie. *Marie, fille-mère.* Paris: Eugène Fasquelle, 1909.

_____. *Mes mémoires.* Paris: Gallimard, 1938.

DeLauretis, Teresa. *The Practice of Love: Lesbian Sexuality and Perverse Desire.* Bloomington: Indiana University Press, 1994.

Déon-Bessière, Danièle. *Les Femmes et la Légion d'honneur: Depuis sa création.* Paris: Editions de l'officine, 2002.

Désormeaux, Dr. *L'Amour conjugal.* Paris: Librairie P. Fort, 1907.

Didi-Huberman, Georges. *Invention de l'hystérie: Charcot et l'iconographie de la Salpêtrière.* Paris: Macula, 1982.

Dijkstra, Bram. *Idols of Perversity: Fantasies of Feminine Evil in Fin-de-Siècle Culture.* New York: Oxford University Press, 1986.

Doane, Mary Anne, Patricia Mellencamp, and Linda Williams. *Re-vision: Essays in Feminist Film Criticism.* Frederick, MD: University Publications of America, 1985.

Doléris, Jacques Amédée, and Jean Bouscater. *Néo-malthusianisme, maternité et féminisme, éducation sexuelle.* Paris: Masson, 1918.

Donzelot, Jacques. *The Policing of Families.* Translated by Robert Hurley. New York: Pantheon Books, 1979.

Doubrovsky, Serge. *Autobiographiques: De Corneille à Sartre.* Paris: Presses Universitaires de France, 1988.

Downing, Lisa. *Desiring the Dead: Necrophilia and Nineteenth-Century French Literature.* Oxford: Legenda, 2003.

Droz, Gustave. *Monsieur, madame, et bébé.* 28th ed. 1848. Reprint, Paris: J. Hetzel, 1868.

Dubust de Laforest, Jean Louis. *Pathologie sociale.* Paris: Paul Dupon, Editeur, 1897.

Dulac, Odette. *Le Droit au plaisir.* Paris: Louis Theuveny Editeur, 1908.

Dworkin, Andrea. *Intercourse.* New York: Free Press, 1987.

Eisinger, Erica Mendelson. "*The Vagabond:* A Vision of Androgyny." In *Colette, the Woman, the Writer,* edited by Erica Mendelson Eisinger and Mari Wardy McCarty, 95–103. University Park: Pennsylvania State University Press, 1981.

Ellis, Havelock. *The Psychology of Sex: A Manual for Students.* 1933. Reprint, New York: Emerson Books, 1972.

Ender, Evelyne. " 'Une Femme qui rêve n'est pas tout à fait une femme': Lélia en rupture d'identité." *Nineteenth-Century French Studies* 3–4 (Spring–Summer 2001): 226–46.

_____. *Sexing the Mind: Nineteenth-Century Fictions of Hysteria.* Ithaca: Cornell University Press, 1995.

Engelking, Tama Lea. "Anna de Noailles (1876–1933)." In *French Women Writers: A Bio-Bibliographical Sourcebook,* edited by Eva Martin Sartori and Dorothy Wynne Zimmerman, 335–45. New York: Greenwood, 1991.

_____. "Renée Vivien's Sapphic Legacy: Remembering the 'House of Muses.' *Atlantis: A Women's Studies Journal* 18, no. 1–2 (1992–93): 125–41.

Ernest-Charles, Jean. *Les Samedis littéraires.* 5 vols. Paris: Sansot, 1905.

Evans, David Owen. *Le Roman social sous la monarchie de juillet.* Paris: Presses Universitaires de France, 1930.

Evans, Martha Noel. *Fits and Starts: A Genealogy of Hysteria in Modern France.* Ithaca: Cornell University Press, 1991.

_____. *Masks of Tradition: Women and the Politics of Writing in Twentieth-Century France.* Ithaca: Cornell University Press, 1987.

Federman, Lillian. *Surpassing the Love of Men: Romantic Friendship and Love between Women from the Renaissance to the Present.* New York: William Morrow, 1981.
Felski, Rita. *The Gender of Modernity.* Cambridge: Harvard University Press, 1995.
Féré, Charles. *L'Instinct sexuel.* Paris: Félix Alcan, Editeur, 1899.
Ferlin, Patricia. *Femmes d'encrier.* Paris: Christian de Bartillat, 1995.
Fèvre, Henry. *L'Intellectuelle mariée.* Paris: Albin Michel, 1925.
Finch, Alison. *Women's Writing in Nineteenth-Century France.* New York: Cambridge University Press, 2000.
Finn, Michael. "Rachilde, Maurice Barrès, and the Preface to *Monsieur Vénus.*" *Romanic Review*, January–March 2000, 89–104.
_____. *Rachilde-Maurice Barrès: Correspondance inédite 1885–1914.* Brest: CNRS, 2002.
Fischer, Henri. *Hygiène de l'enfance: De l'education sexuelle.* Paris: Librairie Ollier-Henry, 1903.
Fisher, Dominique D. "A propos du 'Rachildisme'; ou, Rachilde et les lesbiennes." *Nineteenth-Century French Studies* 31 (Spring–Summer 2003): 297–310.
_____. "Du corps travesti à l'enveloppe transparente: *Monsieur Vénus* ou la politique du leurre." *L'Esprit créateur*, Winter 1997, 46–57.
Flat, Paul. *Nos femmes de lettres.* Paris: Perrin, 1909.
Foster, Jeannette H. Preface to *A Woman Appeared to Me*, by Renée Vivien, translated by Jeannette H. Foster. Tallahassee: Naiad, 1979.
Foucault, Michel. *The Archeology of Knowledge and the Discourse on Language.* Translated by A. M. Sheridan Smith. New York: Pantheon Books, 1972.
_____. *The History of Sexuality.* Vol. 1, *An Introduction.* New York: Vintage Books, 1980.
_____. *Surveiller et punir: Naissance de la prison.* Paris: Gallimard, 1975.
_____. "What Is an Author?" In *Textual Strategies: Perspectives in Post-Structuralist Criticism.* Edited by Josué V. Harari, 141–60. Ithaca: Cornell University Press, 1979.
Fontanges, Haryett. *La Légion d'honneur et les femmes décorées; étude d'histoire et de sociologie féminine.* Paris: Alliance cooperative du livre, 1905.
Fraisse, Geneviève. *Muse de la raison: Démocratie et exclusion des femmes en France.* 1989. Reprint, Paris: Gallimard, 1995.
_____. *Reason's Muse: Sexual Difference and the Birth of Democracy.* Translated by Jane Marie Todd. Chicago: University of Chicago Press, 1994.
Fraisse, Geneviève, and Michelle Perrot, eds. *A History of Women in the West.* Vol. 4, *Emerging Feminism from Revolution to World War.* Cambridge: Harvard University Press, Belknap Press, 1993.
Francis, Claude, and Fernande Gontier. *Creating Colette.* Vol. 1, *From Ingenue to Libertine, 1873–1913.* South Royalton: Steerforth, 1998.
Frappier-Mazur, Lucienne. "Marginal Canons: Rewriting the Erotic." *Yale French Studies* 75 (1988): 112–228.
Freud, Sigmund. *Sexuality and the Psychology of Love.* Edited by Philip Rieff. New York: Simon and Schuster, 1997.
Friedberg, Anne. "Les Flâneurs du mal (1): Cinema and the Postmodern Condition." *PMLA* 106 (May 1991): 419–31.
_____. *Window Shopping: Cinema and the Postmodern.* Berkeley and Los Angeles: University of California Press, 1993.
Friedman, Susan Stanford. "Women's Autobiographical Selves: Theory and Practice." In *The Private Self: Theory and Practice of Women's Autobiographical Writings,* edited by Shari Benstock. Chapel Hill: University of North Carolina Press, 1988.
Garnier, Pierre. *Les Anomalies sexuelles apparentes et cachées.* Paris: Garnier, 1889.

_____. *Le Mariage dans ses devoirs, ses rapports et ses effets conjugaux au point de vue légal, hygiénique, physiologique et moral.* Paris: Garnier Frères, 1879.

Gilbert, Sandra, and Susan Gubar. *The Madwoman in the Attic: The Woman Writer and the Nineteenth-Century Literary Imagination.* New Haven: Yale University Press, 1979.

Gleber, Anke. "Women on the Screens and Streets of Modernity: In Search of the Female Flâneuse." In *The Image in Dispute: Art and Cinema in the Age of Photography,* edited by Dudley Andrew, 55–85. Austin: University of Texas Press, 1997.

Goetz, Christopher, Michel Bonduelle, and Toby Gelfand. *Charcot: Constructing Neurology.* New York: Oxford University Press, 1995.

Goldstein, Jan. *Console and Classify: The French Psychiatric Profession in the Nineteenth Century.* New York: Cambridge University Press, 1987.

Goncourt, Edmond de, and Jules de Goncourt. *Germinie Lacerteux.* 1864. Reprint, Paris: Flammarion, 1990.

_____. *La Fille Elisa.* 1887. Reprint, Paris: La Boîte à documents, 1990.

_____. *Journal Tome I.* Paris: Editions Aricette, 1959.

_____. *Madame Gervaisais.* Paris: Librairie Internationale, 1869.

Gordon, Felicia. *The Integral Feminist: Madeleine Pelletier, 1874–1939; Feminism, Socialism, and Medicine.* Cambridge: Polity, 1990.

Gordon, Felicia, and Marie Cross. *Early French Feminisms, 1830–1940: A Passion for Liberty.* Brookfield, VT: Edward Elgar, 1996.

Goujon, Jean-Paul. *Tes blessures sont plus douces que leurs caresses: Vie de Renée Vivien.* Paris: Régine Deforges, 1986.

Grasset, Joseph. *Dans un cabinet de médecin: Pièce en un acte.* Paris: Société française d'imprimerie et de librairie, 1905.

Gubar, Susan. "Sapphistries." In *The Lesbian Issue: Essays from SIGNS,* edited by Freedman, Estelle B. 91–110.Chicago: University of Chicago Press, 1985.

Gullickson, Gay L. *Unruly Women of Paris: Images of the Commune.* Ithaca: Cornell University Press, 1996.

Gusdorf, Georges. "Conditions and Limits of Autobiography." In *Autobiography: Essays Theoretical and Critical,* translated and edited by James Olney, 28–48. Princeton: Princeton University Press, 1980.

Gyp [Gabrielle Marie-Antoinette de Riquetti de Mirabeau]. *Autour du divorce.* Paris: Calmann-Lévy, 1886.

_____. *Autour du mariage.* Paris: Calmann-Lévy, 1883.

Harris, Ruth. *Murders and Madness: Medicine, Law, and Society in the Fin de Siècle.* New York: Oxford University Press, 1989.

Harry, Myriam. *Mon amie Lucie Delarue-Mardrus.* Paris: Ariane, 1946.

Hartog, Laura C. " 'Ces monstres antiques': La Femme prostituée et le milieu sexualisé dans les *Rougon-Macquart.*" *Excavatio* 3 (Winter 1993): 23–31.

Hause, Steven C., and Jennifer Waelti-Walters, eds. *Feminisms of the Belle Epoque.* Lincoln: University of Nebraska Press, 1994.

Hause, Steven C., and Anne R. Kenney. *Women's Suffrage and Social Politics in the French Third Republic.* Princeton: Princeton University Press, 1984.

Hawthorne, Melanie. Introduction to *The Juggler,* by Rachilde, translated by Melanie Hawthorne. New Brunswick: Rutgers University Press, 1990.

_____. *Rachilde and French Women's Authorship.* Lincoln: University of Nebraska Press, 2001.

_____. "The Seduction of Terror: Annhine's Annihilation in Liane de Pougy's *Idylle Saphique.*" In *Articulations of Difference: Gender Studies and Writing in French,* edited

by Dominique Fisher and Lawrence Schehr, 136–54. Stanford: Stanford University Press, 1997.
______. "The Social Construction of Sexuality in Three Novels by Rachilde." *Les Genres de l'Héraurme Siècle. Papers from the Fourteenth Annual Colloquium in Nineteenth-Century French Studies,* edited by William Paulson. Ann Arbor: University of Michigan Press,1989.
Hesse, Carla. *The Other Enlightenment: How French Women Became Modern.* Princeton: Princeton University Press, 2001.
Hewitt, Nicholas. "Victor Margueritte and the Reception of *La Garçonne:* Naturalism, the Family and the 'Ordre Moral.' " *Nottingham French Studies* 23, no. 1 (1984): 37–50.
Hinde Stewart, Joan. "Colette and the Epistolary Novel." In *Colette, the Woman, the Writer,* edited by Erica Mendelson Eisinger and Mari Ward McCarty, 43–53. University Park: Pennsylvania State University Press, 1981.
Holmes, Diana. "Decadent Love: Rachilde and the Popular Romance." *Dixneuf,* September 2003, 16–28.
______. *French Women's Writing, 1848–1994.* Atlantic Highlands, NJ: Athlone, 1996.
______. "The Politics of Romance: Popular Romantic Fiction at the Fin de Siècle." In *New Perspectives on the Fin de Siècle in Nineteenth- and Twentieth-Century France,* edited by Kay Chadwick and Timothy Unwin, 117–38. Lewiston, NY: E. Mellen, 2000.
______. *Rachilde: Decadence, Gender, and the Woman Writer.* New York: Berg, 2001.
Holmes, Diana and Carrie Tarr, eds. *A 'Belle Epoque'? Women in French Society and Culture 1890–1914.* New York: Berghahn Books, 2006.
Houbre, Gabrielle. "L'Honneur perdu de Marcelle Tinayre: L'Affaire de la Légion d'honneur ratée." In *Les Ratées de la littérature,* edited by Jean-Jacques Lefrère, Michèle Pierssens, and Jean-Didier Wagneur,89–101. Charente: Du Lérot, 1999.
______. "La Belle Epoque des Romancières." In *Masculin/Féminin. Le XIXe siècle à l'épreuve du genre,* edited by Chantal Bertrand-Jennings. (Toronto: Centre d'Études du XIXe siècle Joseph Sablé, 1999), 183–97.
Huffer, Lynne. *Another Colette: The Question of Gendered Writing.* Ann Arbor: University of Michigan Press, 1992.
Hunt, Lynn. *The Family Romance of the French Revolution.* Berkeley and Los Angeles: University of California Press, 1992.
Hustvedt, Asti. Introduction to *The Decadent Reader: Fiction, Fantasy, and Perversion from Fin-de-Siècle France,* edited by Asti Hustvedt. New York: Zone Books, 1998.
Irigaray, Luce. *Ce sexe qui n'en est pas un.* Paris: Les Editions de Minuit, 1977.
______. *This Sex Which Is Not One.* Translated by Catherine Porter with Carolyn Burke. Ithaca: Cornell University Press, 1985.
______. "Women-Mothers, the Silent Substratum of the Social Order." In *The Irigaray Reader,* edited by Margaret Whitford, 47–52. Cambridge: Blackwell, 1996.
Jacobus, Mary. *Reading Woman: Essays in Feminist Criticism.* New York: Columbia University Press, 1986.
Jacques, Jean-Pierre. *Malheurs de Sapho.* Paris: Grasset, 1981.
Jay, Karla. *The Amazon and the Page: Natalie Clifford Barney and Renée Vivien.* Bloomington: Indiana University Press, 1988.
Jong, Erica. *Fear of Flying.* 1973. Reprint; New York: Signet, 2003.
Joyce, James. *Essais critiques.* Paris: Gallimard, 1966.
Kaplan, E. Ann. *Women and Film: Both Sides of the Camera.* New York: Methuen, 1983.
Kelly, Dorothy. "Experimenting on Women: Zola's Theory and Practice of the Experimental Novel." In *Spectacles of Realism: Gender, Body, Genre,* edited by Margaret Cohen and Christopher Prendergast, 231–46. Minneapolis: Minnesota University Press, 1995.

_____. *Fictional Genders: Role and Representation in Nineteenth-Century Narrative.* Lincoln: University of Nebraska Press, 1989.

_____. *Telling Glances: Voyeurism in the French Novel.* New Brunswick: Rutgers University Press, 1992.

Kingcaid, Renée. *Neurosis and Narrative: The Decadent Short Fiction of Proust, Lorrain, and Rachilde.* Carbondale: Southern Illinois University Press, 1992.

Knibiehler, Yvonne, and Catherine Fouquet. *La Femme et les médecins: Analyse historique.* Paris: Hachette, 1983.

_____. "Bodies and Hearts." *A History of Women in the West,* edited by Geneviève Fraisse and Michelle Perrot. Vol. 4, *Emerging Feminism from Revolution to World War,* 325–68. Cambridge: Harvard University Press, Belknap Press, 1993.

Krafft-Ebing, Richard von. *Psychopathie sexuelle,* translated into French from the 8th German edition by Emile Laurent and Sigismund Csapo. Paris, 1895.

Lafayette, Marie-Madeleine Pioche de la Vergne, Comtesse de. *La Princesse de Clèves.* 1678. Reprint, Paris: Flammarion, 1966.

Landes, Joan. *Women and the Public Sphere in the Age of the French Revolution.* Ithaca: Cornell University Press, 1988.

Lanteri-Laura, Georges. *Lecture des perversions: Histoire de leur appropriation médicale.* Paris: Masson, 1979.

Laqueur, Thomas. *Making Sex: Body and Gender from the Greeks to Freud.* Cambridge: Harvard University Press, 1990.

Laqueur, Thomas, and Catherine Gallagher. *The Making of the Modern Body.* Berkeley and Los Angeles: University of California Press, 1987.

Larnac, Jean. *Histoire de la littérature féminine en France.* 5th ed. Paris: Editions Kra, 1929.

Laslett, Barbara, Sally Gregory Kohlstedt, Helen Longino, and Evelynn Hammonds, eds. *Gender and Scientific Authority.* Chicago: University of Chicago Press, 1996.

LeBon, Gustave. "Recherches anatomiques et mathématiques sur les lois des variations du volume du cerveau et sur leurs relations avec l'intelligence." *Revue d'anthropologie,* 2d ser., 2 (1879): 27–104.

Legrand du Saulle, Henri. *Les Hystériques: Etat physique et état mental.* Paris: J.-B. Baillière et fils, 1883.

Lejeune, Philippe. *Le Pacte autobiographique.* Paris: Editions de Seuil, 1975.

Lemire, Michel. *Artistes et mortels.* Paris: Editions Raymond Chabeau, 1990.

Leroy, Géraldi, and Julie Bertrand-Sabiani. *La Vie littéraire à la Belle Epoque.* Paris: Presses Universitaires de France, 1998.

Le Cardonnel and Charles Vellay, *La Littérature contemporaine.* Paris: Société de Mercure de France, 1905.

Livi, Jocelyne. *Vapeurs de femmes: Essai historique sur quelques fantasmes médicaux et philosophiques.* Paris: Navarin, 1984. Lorenz, Paul. *Sapho 1900 Renée Vivien.* Paris: Julliard, 1977.

Lorrain, Jean. *Femmes de 1900.* Paris: Editeur de la Madeleine, 1932.

Lukacher, Maryline. "Mademoiselle Baudelaire: Rachilde ou le féminin au masculin." *Nineteenth-Century French Studies*20 (Spring–Summer 1992): 452–65.

_____. *Maternal Fictions.* Durham: Duke University Press, 1994.

Lyons, Martin. *Readers and Society in Nineteenth-Century France: Workers, Women, Peasants.* New York: Palgrave, 2001.

Maréchal, Sylvain. *Il ne faut pas que les femmes sachent lire; ou, Projet d'une loi portant défense d'apprendre à lire aux femmes.* 1801. Reprint, Paris: Gustave Sandré, 1853.

Margadant, Jo Burr, ed. *The New Biography: Performing Femininity in Nineteenth-Century France.* Berkeley and Los Angeles: University of California Press, 2000.

Marks, Elaine. " 'Sapho 1900': Imaginary Renée Vivien's and the Rear of the Belle Epoque." In *Displacements: Women, Tradition, Literatures in French,* edited by Joan DeJean and Nancy K. Miller, 211–27. Baltimore: Johns Hopkins University Press, 1991.

Marks, Elaine, and George Stambolian, eds. *Homosexualities and French Literature.* Ithaca: Cornell University Press, 1979.

Marni, Jeanne. *Amour coupable.* Paris: Ollendorff, 1889.

Martin, Biddy. "Lesbian Identity and Autobiographical Difference(s)." In *Life/Lines: Theorizing Women's Autobiography,* edited by Bella Brodzki and Celeste Schenck. Ithaca: Cornell University Press, 1988.

Martin-Mamy, Eugène. *Marcelle Tinayre.* Paris: E. Sansot, 1909.

Massé, Sylvie. *Les Stratégies de discours et l'écriture des femmes au tournant du siècle: L'Expression implicite d'une parole hétérogène.* Quebec: Groupe de recherche multidisciplinaire féministe, Université Laval, 1993.

Matlock, Jann. "Censoring the Realist Gaze." In *Spectacles of Realism: Gender, Body, Genre,* edited by Margaret Cohen and Christopher Prendergast, 28–65. Minneapolis: University of Minnesota Press, 1995.

______. *Scenes of Seduction: Prostitution, Hysteria, and Reading Difference in Nineteenth-Century France.* New York: Columbia University Press, 1994.

Maurras, Charles. "Le Romantisme féminin." In *L'Avenir de l'intelligence.* Paris: Albert Fontemoing, Editeur, 1905.

Mayer, Alexandre. *Des Rapports conjugaux considérés sous le triple point de vue de la population, de la santé, et de la morale publique.* 1857. Reprint, Paris: J.-B. Baillière et fils, 1874.

Mayeur, Françoise. *L'Education des filles en France au XIXe siècle.* Paris: Hachette, 1979.

______. *L'Enseignement secondaire des jeunes filles sous la troisième république.* Paris: Presses de la Fondation Nationale des Sciences Politiques, 1977.

Mayne, Judith. *The Woman at the Keyhole: Feminism and Women's Cinema.* Bloomington: Indiana University Press, 1990.

McMillan, James F. *Housewife or Harlot: The Place of Women in French Society, 1870–1940.* New York: St. Martin's Press, 1981.

Merrick, Jeffrey, and Bryant T. Ragan, eds. *Homosexuality in Modern France.* New York: Oxford University Press, 1996.

Micale, Mark. *Approaching Hysteria: Disease and Its Interpretations.* Princeton: Princeton University Press, 1995.

______. "Hysteria Male/Hysteria Female: Reflections on Comparative Gender Construction in Nineteenth-Century France and Britain." In *Science and Sensibility: Gender and Scientific Enquiry, 1780–1945,* edited by Maria Benjamin. Cambridge: Blackwell, 1991.

Micale, Mark, and Roy Porter, eds. *Discovering the History of Psychiatry.* New York: Oxford University Press, 1994.

Michaelson, Annette. "On the Eve of the Future: The Reasonable Facsimile and the Philosophical Toy." *October* 29 (Summer 1984): 3–20.

Mignot-Ogliastri, Claude. *Anna de Noailles, une amie de la Princesse Edmond de Polignac.* Paris: Méridions Klincksieck, 1986.

Miller, Nancy K. *Subject to Change: Reading Feminist Writing.* New York: Columbia University Press, 1988.

Moi, Toril. "Patriarchal Thought and the Drive for Knowledge." In *New Directions in Psychoanalysis and Feminism,* edited by Teresa Brennan, 189–205. New York: Routledge, 1989.

Montier, Edward. *L'Amour conjugal et paternel. Lettre à un jeune mari.* Paris: Association du Mariage Chrétien, 1919.

_____. *Le Mariage, lettre à une jeune fille.* Paris: Association du Mariage Chrétien, 1919.
Montpensier, Anne Marie Louise d'Orléans, Duchesse de. *Lettres.* Paris: Collin, 1806.
Moreau, J. (de Tours). *La Psychologie morbide dans ses rapports avec la philosophie de l'histoire ou de l'influence des neuropathies sur le dynamisme intellectuel.* Paris: 1859.
Moroy, Elie. *La Littérature féminine définie par les femmes écrivains.* Geneva: Semaine de Genève, 1931.
Moses, Claire Goldberg. *French Feminism in the Nineteenth Century.* Albany: State University of New York Press, 1984.
Mulvey, Laura. *Visual Pleasure and Narrative Cinema.* Bloomington: Indiana University Press, 1989.
Newman-Gordon, Pauline. "Lucie Delarue-Mardrus, 1874-1945." In *French Women Writers: A Bio-Bibliographical Sourcebook*, edited by Eva Martin Sartori and Dorothy Wynne Zimmerman, 108-120. New York: Greenwood, 1991.
Noailles, Anna Elisabeth de Brancovan, Comtesse de. *Le Visage émerveillé.* Paris: Calmann-Lévy, 1904.
Nordau, Max. *Psycho-physiologie du génie et du talent.* Translated by Auguste Dietrich. Paris: 1897.
Nye, Robert A. *Crime, Madness, and Politics in Modern France: The Medical Concept of National Decline.* Princeton: Princeton University Press, 1984.
_____. "Degeneration and the Medical Model of Cultural Crisis in the French Belle Epoque." In *Political Symbolism in Modern Europe: Essays in Honor of George L. Mosse,* edited by Seymour Drescher, David Sabean, and Allan Sharlin. New Brunswick, NJ: Transaction Books, 1982.
_____. "Medical Origins of Sexual Fetishism." In *Fetishism as Cultural Discourse,* edited by Emily Apter and William Pietz. Ithaca: Cornell University Press, 1993.
_____, ed. *Sexuality: A Reader.* New York: Oxford University Press, 1999.
Offen, Karen. "Depopulation, Nationalism, and Feminism in Fin-de-Siècle France." *American Historical Review* 89, no. 3 (1984): 648–76.
O'Neal, John C. *The Authority of Experience: Sensationist Theory in the French Enlightenment.* University Park: Pennsylvania State University Press, 1996.
Osenthal, Marie. *De l'éducation morale de la femme: Conseils à une jeune fille.* Paris, 1864.
Outram, Dorinda. *The Body and the French Revolution: Sex, Class, and Political Culture.* New Haven: Yale University Press, 1989.
Ozouf, Mona. *Mots des femmes: Essai sur la singularité française.* Paris: Fayard, 1995.
Pagès, Alain. *La Bataille littéraire.* Paris: Librairie Séguieur, 1989.
Pellisier, Georges. *Etudes de littérature et de morale.* Paris: Cornély, 1905.
Perrot, Michelle. *Les Femmes, ou les silences de l'histoire.* Paris: Flammarion, 1998.
_____. "The New Eve and the Old Adam: Changes in French Women's Condition at the Turn of the Century." In *Behind the Lines: Gender and the Two World Wars,* edited by Margaret Higonnet, Jane Jenson, Sonya Michel, and Margaret Weitz and translated by Helen Harden-Chenut. New Haven: Yale University Press, 1987.
Pert, Camille. *Le Bonheur conjugal.* Paris: Librairie Universelle, 1905.
Pierrot, Jean. *The Decadent Imagination, 1880–1900.* Chicago: University of Chicago Press, 1981.
Planté, Christine. *La Petite Soeur de Balzac: Essai sur la femme auteur.* Paris: Editions de Seuil, 1989.
Plat, Hélène. *Lucie Delarue-Mardrus: Une Femme de lettres des années folles.* Paris: Editions Grasset et Fasquelle, 1994.
Ploye, Catherine. " 'Questions brûlantes': Rachilde, l'affaire Douglas et les mouvements féministes." *Nineteenth-Century French Studies* 22 (Fall–Winter 1993–94): 195–207.

Pollock, Griselda. *Vision and Difference: Femininity, Feminism, and the Histories of Art.* New York: Routledge, 1988.
Pougy, Liane de. *Idylle Saphique.* 1901. Reprint, Paris: J.-C. Lattès, 1979.
_____. *Mes cahiers bleus.* Paris: Plon, 1977.
_____. *My Blue Notebooks.* Translated by Diana Athill. New York: Harper and Row, 1979.
Prince, Gerald. *Guide du roman de langue française, 1901–1950.* Lanham, MD: University Press of America, 2002.
Quella-Villéger, Alain. *Belles et rebelles: Le Roman vrai des Chasteau-Tinayre.* Bordeaux: Aubéron, 2000.
Rabaut, Jean. *Histoire de féminismes français.* Paris: Stock, 1978.
Rachilde. *La Jongleuse.* 1900. Reprint, Paris: Des femmes, 1978.
_____. *Monsieur Vénus.* 1889. Reprint, Paris: Flammarion, 1977.
_____. *Monsieur Vénus: A Materialist Novel.* Translated by Melanie Hawthorne. New York: MLA, 2004.
_____. *Monsieur Vénus: Roman matérialiste.* Brussels: Brancart, 1884.
_____. "Pourquoi je ne suis pas féministe." In *Leurs raisons,* edited by André Billy. Paris: Les Editions de France, 1928.
Ramazanoglu, Caroline, ed. *Up Against Foucault: Explorations of Some Tensions between Foucault and Feminism.* New York: Routledge, 1993.
Reinvillier, A. *Hygiène pratique des femmes: Guide médical pour toutes les époques de leur vie suivi de quelques considérations sur les maladies des femmes.* Paris: Bureaux du journal *Le Médecin de la maison,* 1854.
Ribbing, Seved. *L'Hygiène sexuelle et ses conséquences morales.* Paris: F. Alcan, 1895.
Richard, Noel. *Le Mouvement décadent: Dandys, esthètes, et quintessants.* Paris: Nizet, 1968.
Richer, Paul. *Etudes cliniques sur la grande hystérie.* Paris: A. Delahaye et E. Lecrosnier, 1885.
Richet, Charles. "Les Démoniaques d'aujourd'hui." *Revue des deux mondes* 37 (January 15, 1880): 340–72.
Ricoeur, Paul. *Temps et récit.* 3 vols. Paris: Seuil, 1985.
Riley, Denise. *"Am I That Name?" Feminism and the Category of "Women" in History.* London: Macmillan, 1988.
Ripa, Yannick. *Women and Madness: The Incarceration of Women in Nineteenth-Century France.* Cambridge: Polity Press, 1990.
Roberts, Mary Louise. *Civilization without Sexes: Reconstructing Gender in Postwar France, 1917–1927.* Chicago: University of Chicago Press, 1994.
_____. *Disruptive Acts: The New Woman in Fin-de-siècle France.* Chicago: University of Chicago Press, 2002.
Rosario, Vernon. *The Erotic Imagination: French Histories of Perversity.* New York: Oxford University Press, 1997.
Roudinesco, Elisabeth. *Histoire de la psychanalyse.* Vol. 1, *1885–1939.* Paris: Seuil, 1984.
Rubin, Gayle. Preface to *Une Femme m'apparut,* by Renée Vivien, translated by Jeannette H. Foster. Tallahassee: Naiad, 1976.
Rzewuski, R. P. Preface to *My Blue Notebooks,* by Liane de Pougy, translated by Diana Athill. New York: Harper and Row, 1979.
Sand, George. *Indiana.* Paris: Folio, 1984.
Sanders, Virginie. *"Vertigineusement, j'allais vers les étoiles . . .": La poésie de Renée Vivien.* Atlanta: Rodopi, 1991.
Sartori, Eva Martin, and Dorothy Wynne Zimmerman. *French Women Writers: A Bio-Bibliographic Sourcebook.* New York: Greenwood, 1991.
Schor, Naomi. *Bad Objects: Essays Popular and Unpopular.* Durham Duke University Press, 1995.

_____. "Female Fetishism: The Case of George Sand." In *The Female Body in Western Culture: Contemporary Perspectives,* edited by Susan Suleiman. Cambridge: Harvard University Press, 1986.

_____. *George Sand and Idealism.* New York: Columbia University Press, 1993.

_____. *Zola's Crowds.* Baltimore: Johns Hopkins University Press, 1978.

Schwartz, Vanessa. "Cinematic Spectatorship before the Apparatus: The Public Taste for Reality in Fin-de-Siècle Paris." In *Viewing Positions: Ways of Seeing Film,* edited by Linda Williams. New Brunswick: Rutgers University Press, 1995.

_____. *Spectacular Realities: Early Mass Culture in Fin-de-Siècle Paris.* Berkeley and Los Angeles: University of California Press, 1998.

Scott, Joan. *Only Paradoxes to Offer: French Feminists and the Rights of Man.* Cambridge: Harvard University Press, 1996.

Scott, Malcolm. *The Struggle for the Soul of the French Novel: French Catholic and Realist Novels, 1850–1970.* Hampshire: Macmillan, 1989.

Sellers, Susan. *Hélène Cixous: Authorship, Autobiography and Love.* Polity Press, 1996.

Sheringham, Michael. *French Autobiography: Devices and Desire, Rousseau to Perec.* Oxford: Clarendon Press, 1993.

Showalter, Elaine. *The Female Malady: Women, Madness, and English Culture.* New York: Pantheon, 1985.

_____. *Hystories: Hysterical Epidemics and Modern Culture.* New York: Columbia University Press, 1997.

_____. *A Literature of Their Own: British Women Novelists from Brontë to Lessing.* Princeton: Princeton University Press, 1977.

_____. *Sexual Anarchy: Gender and Culture at the Fin-de-siècle.* New York: Viking, 1990.

Silverman, Willa. *The Notorious Life of Gyp: Right-Wing Anarchist in Fin-de-Siècle France.* New York: Oxford University Press, 1995.

Slama, Béatrice. "De la 'littérature féminine' à 'l'écrire femme': Différence et institution." *Littérature* 44 (December 1981): 52–71.

Smith-Rosenberg, Carroll. *Disorderly Conduct: Visions of Gender in Victorian America.* New York: Knopf, 1985.

Spackman, Barbara. *Decadent Genealogies.* Ithaca: Cornell University Press, 1989.

_____. "Recycling Baudelaire: The Decadence of Catulle Mendès (1841–1909)." In *The Decadent Reader: Fiction, Fantasy, and Perversion from Fin-de-Siècle France,* edited by Asti Hustvedt. New York: Zone Books, 1998.

Spacks, Patricia Meyers. *The Female Imagination.* New York: Alfred A. Knopf, 1975.

Staël, Germaine Necker, Baronne de. *Corinne ou l'Italie.* 1807. Reprint, Paris: Gallimard, 1985.

Stanton, Domna. *The Female Autograph: Theory and Practice of Autobiography from the Tenth to the Twentieth Century.* Chicago: University of Chicago Press, 1987.

Stockinger, Jacob. "The Test of Love and Nature: Colette and Lesbians." In *Colette, the Woman, the Writer,* edited by Erica Mendelson Eisinger and Mari Ward McCarty, 75–94. University Park: Pennsylvania State University Press, 1981.

Stora-Lamarre, Annie. *L'Enfer de la IIIe République: Censeurs et pornographes 1881–1914.* Paris: Editions Imago, 1990.

Suwala, Halina. *Autour de Zola et du naturalisme.* Paris: Honoré Champion, 1993.

Swain, Gladys. "L'Ame, la femme, le sexe et le corps: Les Métamorphoses de l'hystérie à la fin dudix-neuvième siècle." *Le Débat* 24 (1983): 107–27.

Talman, Francis. *Monsieur Vénus par Francis Talman.* Paris: Fourneau, 1995.

Thérèse of Lisieux, Saint. *Histoire d'une âme.* Translated by John Beevers. New York: Doubleday, 1989.

Thiesse, Anne-Marie. *Le Roman du quotidian: Lecteurs et lectures populaires à la Belle Epoque.* Paris: Le Chemin Vert, 1984.
Thompson, Hannah. *Naturalism Redressed: Identity and Clothing in the Novels of Emile Zola.* Oxford: European Humanities Research Center, 2004.
Thurman, Judith. *Secrets of the Flesh: A Life of Colette.* New York: Knopf, 1999.
Tinayre, Marcelle. *Madeleine au miroir, journal d'une femme.* Paris: Calmann-Lévy, 1912.
_____. *La Maison du péché.* Paris: Calmann-Lévy, 1903.
_____. *La Maison du péché.* 1903. Reprint, Paris: Editions d'art G. Boutitie, 1922.
Tissot, Ernest. *Nouvelles princesses des lettres.* Paris: Fontemoing et Cie, 1911.
Ton, Delfeil de. "Le Rêve de l'écrivaine." *Le Nouvel observateur,* June 22–28, 2000, 112.
Unwin, Timothy, ed. *The Cambridge Companion to the French Novel: From 1800 to the Present.* Cambridge: Cambridge University Press, 1997.
Vallette, Alfred. *Le Roman d'un homme sérieux.* Paris: Mercure de France, 1994.
Vicinius, Martha. "Sexuality and Power: A Review of Current Work in the History of Sexuality." *Feminist Studies* 8, no. 1 (1982): 133–56.
Villers, Syriex de. *Lucie Delarue-Mardrus.* Paris: Editions Sansot, 1923.
Vivien, Renée. *La Dame à la louve.* Paris: Alphonse Lemerre, Editeur, 1904.
_____. *Dans un coin de violettes.* Paris: E. Sansot, 1910.
_____. *Une Femme m'apparut.* 1904. Reprint, Paris: Régine Deforges, 1977.
_____. *Une Femme m'apparut.* Paris: A. Lemerre, 1905.
Waelti-Walters, Jennifer. *Feminist Novelists of the Belle Epoque: Love as a Lifestyle.* Bloomington: Indiana University Press, 1990.
Wajeman, Gérard. *Le Maître et l'hystérique.* Paris: Navarin, 1982.
Walkowitz, Judith. "Dangerous Sexualities." In *A History of Women in the West,* edited by Geneviève Fraisse and Michelle Perrot. Vol. 4, *Emerging Feminism from Revolution to World War,* 369–98. Cambridge: Harvard University Press, Belknap Press, 1993.
Weeks, Jeffrey. *Sexuality and its Discontents: Meanings, Myths, and Modern Sexualities.* Routledge: New York, 1985.
Winnet, Susan. "Coming Unstrung: Women, Men, Narrative, and Principles of Pleasure." *PMLA* 105 (May 1990): 505–18.
Wittig, Monique. *Les Guérillères.* Paris: Editions de Minuit, 1969.
_____. *The Straight Mind and Other Essays.* Boston: Beacon, 1992.
Wolff, Janet. "The Invisible Flâneuse: Women and the Literature of Modernity." In *The Problems of Modernity: Adorno and Benjamin,* edited by Andrew Benjamin, 141–56. London: Routledge, 1989.
Zabé, Docteur. *Manuel des maladies des femmes.* Paris: Léon Vanier, 1884.
Zeldin, Theodore, ed. *Conflicts in French Society. Anticlericalism, Education and Morals in the Nineteenth Century.* London: George Allen and Unwin, 1970.
Zola, Emile. *La Bête humaine.* 1889. Reprint, Paris: Gallimard, 1977.
_____. *Le Docteur Pascal.* 1893. Reprint, Paris: Gallimard, 1993.
_____. *La Faute de l'Abbé Mouret.* 1875. Reprint, Paris: Garnier-Flammarion, 1972.
_____. *La Joie de vivre.* 1884. Reprint, Paris: Garnier-Flammarion, 1974.
_____. *Nana.* 1880. Reprint, Paris: Garnier-Flammarion, 1968.
_____. "Les Romanciers naturalistes" (1881). In *Oeuvres complètes,* 15 vols., edited by Henri Mitterand, 11:24–252. Paris: Cercle du Livre Précieux, 1968.
_____. "Le Roman expérimental" (1880). In *Oeuvres complètes,* 15 vols., edited by Henri Mitterand, 10:1175–401. Paris: Cercle du Livre Précieux, 1968.
_____. *Les Rougon-Macquart.* Edited by Armand Lanoux and Henri Mitterand. 5 vols. Paris: Gallimard, 1960–67.

Index